Broken: The Story of Public Education in America

Jared Hiple

Published by Jared Hiple, 2024.

While every precaution has been taken in the preparation of this book, the publisher assumes no responsibility for errors or omissions, or for damages resulting from the use of the information contained herein.

BROKEN: THE STORY OF PUBLIC EDUCATION IN AMERICA

First edition. June 21, 2024.

Copyright © 2024 Jared Hiple.

ISBN: 979-8224992645

Written by Jared Hiple.

Table of Contents

PREFACE

I open my eyes to stare at the ceiling fan methodically rotating above my head and roll over to glance at the alarm clock, hoping I still have a couple of hours. Drat...it's almost 6:30. Time for another day. I drag myself out of bed to start my Monday through Friday morning routine, the same one I follow nine months out of every year. I work in public education, but I'm not a teacher. I was one for many years, though. I'm not an administrator either. I got lucky and somehow managed to escape the soul-crushing daily grind of a public school classroom while also avoiding the day-to-day perils of working in the realm of school administration. My current job title is Behavior Facilitator, but I'm more of a consultant. I help a wide variety of schools—high schools, middle schools, and elementary schools—with behavioral problems and an endless array of other issues. I work with teachers, students, parents, counselors, and administrators from a wide range of backgrounds.

So why am I so reluctant to start my day? Why am I so pessimistic about the day ahead? Because I've recently been on the outside looking in. I now see many aspects of public education from multiple perspectives, and to put it mildly, things ain't great. It's hard to show up every day at a failing institute I no longer believe in, and to be bluntly honest, I have never truly believed in it since day one.

Despite both of my parents working in the field their entire lives, I never in my wildest dreams thought I would pursue a career in public education. My father was a high school vice principal, and my mother taught high school English, literature, and journalism, which meant she also managed the school newspaper. As a child, I witnessed first-hand how much they seemed to loathe the profession. If someone had approached me in college and told me in a few years, I'd be working as a special education teacher, I would have laughed them out of the room. But sometimes, life has a strange sense of humor.

The fact is I never wanted to be in education. Hell, I still don't want to be in education, but at some point, you just throw in the towel and press on. At this point, I can only strive to be the best catalyst for positive change within the system I can be...plus, a good pension is a hard thing to find these days, right? Fresh out of college, it wasn't easy to find my path. I graduated with a degree in criminal justice but had no idea what to do with it. I bounced around from one menial job to another. I tried unsuccessfully to get into the legal field, which included a quite unpleasant experience working as an investigator for a Dallas lawyer. I was having trouble making ends meet between jobs. A friend suggested substitute teaching and gave me a recommendation. It was easy and good money at the time for basically babysitting a room full of kids. Not a bad gig for a young, struggling college grad. So I continued to substitute on and off for a couple of years until someone convinced me to get a teacher certification over the summer (and, yes, it's that easy). The plan was to teach full-time for a couple of years until I figured out what I wanted to do with my life. It was a good move that meant I was making a lot more money and gave me access to a wide range of teacher benefits. The only problem was figuring out the rest of my life.

I started as a special education teacher in a behavior management program, and I worked there for 16 long years. I also taught in an alternative disciplinary school for 2 years and worked briefly as a behavior specialist in the special education field. At this point, I have worked for multiple school districts in multiple cities for over 20 years. Many times I have ventured down other career paths in hopes of escaping this collapsing institute, but every path has led me to yet another dead end. I even spent several years getting a graduate degree in biology, a subject I love. But no one in that field would hire me because I didn't have any experience. So, back to the classroom, I went.

I've even left education several times to try other professions. I acquired insurance licenses and dipped my toe into the insurance industry over a summer break. It didn't take long for me to figure out it wasn't for me, so back I went into the classroom. A couple of years later, I had an opportunity to work in finance. I obtained all the proper credentials and became a financial representative for a large investment firm. This gig lasted only a couple of months—I loathed the industry. Back to the classroom. Merely chasing money, I discovered, is often not a great idea. A couple of years later, a friend approached me to manage a small business with a chance to start my own franchise. Of course, I jumped on it, but it turned out to be another short-lived failure. Which...is why I'm back...in my current position...back in public education...yet again. None of these endeavors has been an epic failure, but they have all merely led me in a huge circle right back to where I started...public education.

Even this project is yet another fork in the road, another path not yet traveled. I decided to take this path and write this book, not because I expect it to become a best seller but because I care. My goal is to help readers understand what has happened to our public education system, how it has affected our society, and how we, as a nation, can move forward into a brighter future. Understanding the current landscape of the nation's public education system and its history is not only beneficial for those who have children attending these schools daily, but it's also beneficial to the millions of citizens in this country who do not have kids but are still required to fund this system through taxes—sometimes burdensome taxes. Furthermore, the kids attending public schools throughout the country today will soon be the adults determining the course of our nation in only a decade or two. Thus, the quality of our public education system should be of great concern to every citizen in this country.

Millions of incredible people from all walks of life work in public education. Most of them care immensely about the children they serve and what's best for their current and future livelihoods. The problem with public education in the United States is not a people problem. It's a systemic problem. With so much going on in the world, from pandemics to economic issues to foreign wars, most people simply don't have the time or energy to unwrap and comprehend the multitude of problems facing the nation's public education system. The COVID-19 lockdowns recently forced the classroom into homes across the country. Parents finally got a first-hand look at the reality of classrooms, and many of them were none too pleased. School districts were either ill-equipped to address parents' concerns or, in many cases, they just simply refused to answer.

This book will give you an all-encompassing review of the entire U.S. public education system. Our journey begins with a historical introduction that transports you all the way back to our earliest colonial schools. We then move through the tumultuous Revolutionary and Civil War eras to understand their impact on the evolution of the nation's public education system. From there we pass into the fast-paced, progressive, and reformative 20th century years to close our adventure in the heart of the dynamic technological world we presently live in.

The remainder of the book is broken down into four sections. Part 1: The Machine describes the major components of the systems and entities that work in unison to create the powerful beast we call public education. The first two chapters focus solely on teachers, their daily lives, and the detailed aspects of their job. Chapter 3 takes an up close and personal look at the fiscal side of public schooling and explains how schools are funded, who funds them, and where exactly all that money goes. Chapter 4 tackles the bureaucratic design of our public education system by reviewing the massive increases in administrative staff now overrunning school districts and exploring how they have contributed to the continued degradation of the system. The final chapter in this section takes you on a brief tour of teacher unionization and how it has impacted schools across the country, both past and present.

Part 2, Fuel for the Fire, takes a detailed look at the components that not only feed the public education machine but have become integral parts of the system for better or for worse. We begin this section with an odyssey through public school curricula, analyzing what is, is not, and should be taught in schools today. This curriculum discussion leads us to a comprehensive investigation into standardized testing and how it has impacted public schools. We then continue our foray through the fire as we take a detailed look at special education. You will learn what disabilities are included in the special education realm, how schools address these disabilities, and how the overall special education system has impacted students and teachers. We close Part 2 with a thorough examination of the technological beast that has infiltrated our world during the last 2 decades. This new technological landscape has taken over classrooms, and we look closely at how this trend has affected teachers, students, and their schools.

We touch on more controversial topics in Part 3: The Hard Truth. This section opens with a difficult but important examination of the current behavioral issues wrecking classrooms across the nation. I explain how behavior impacts student performance and safety and review possible reasonings behind the current surge in disruptive and violent behaviors in public schools. This opening then leads us to my brave but relevant attempt to address the current firestorm of issues surrounding social-emotional learning and critical race theory. These are major areas of contention, and we'll take a hard look at truth and hyperbole concerning these issues. Then we embark on the touchy yet critical topic of gun violence in schools. We'll investigate theories behind what motivates school shootings, how schools have responded to these horrible tragedies, and what we can do as a nation to stop these events from occurring. Lastly, we break down the role parents must play in the educational process and discuss how public schools can work harder at increasing and improving parent engagement and overall community support.

In the grand finale, Part 4: The Road Ahead, we close out our journey by peering into the future of public education and discussing how we can all do our part to shift course in the right direction. We start with a thorough examination of the COVID-19 lockdowns and their impact on public education. We examine how school closures affected student performance and how school closures shook the mental health and cognitive development of kids across the country. We probe the issue of teacher shortages and how they are currently impacting schools, as well as what future classrooms may look like if school districts cannot find a meaningful way to address these colossal shortages. We then take a hard look at the school choice debate currently raging across the nation. We discuss the types of school choice options as well as the pros and cons of each. We then step into our time machines and travel into the future of education by surveying various predictions about what public schooling will look like in the years and even decades to come. We will attempt to discover new and innovative ways for public schools to shift course and move to a more sustainable and productive model of learning that addresses the current needs of our nation's youth. Lastly, I conclude our journey with a brief summary of our various adventures and a few final thoughts.

At the end of our journey, I hope you have a thorough understanding of how our public education system works and why it is failing all of us. This book is designed to be read either from beginning to end or as a reference regarding certain topics; thus, chapters can be read straight through or independently, depending on your preference. Additionally, if statistics regarding certain topics seem a bit outdated, it's because I chose to primarily use pre-COVID data due to the highly discrepant and disjointed data sets that arose with the onset of the pandemic and its ensuing lockdowns, making *current* data unrealistic.

Public education in the United States is utterly broken and has been highly ineffective for quite some time in producing intelligent, productive young adults who live and work independently in the current world. We must work together as a nation to mend this broken system. This book is not the antidote to the problem, but it can function as a starting block. We must finally acknowledge the massive shortcomings of our current system and begin conversations about how to pick up the pieces and move into a more promising future. Let us all hope this book is merely the dawn of brighter days ahead.

INTRODUCTION: History of Public Education in America

"A diffusion of knowledge is the only guardian of true liberty." ~James Madison

"An educated citizenry is a vital requisite for our survival as a

free people." ~Thomas Jefferson

Democracy is beautiful but fragile, and American democracy at the finale of the American Revolution was extremely delicate. The Founding Fathers believed the success of the newly emboldened republic rested in the competency of its citizens, and the preservation of this newfound republic would require a highly educated population that could understand the social and political issues of the time enabling them to vote both actively and wisely, fulfill civic duties, protect their rights and freedoms, and resist future despots and tyrants. Education was seen as an essential element in providing moral and character-building instruction in order to create virtuous citizens.

Public education in the United States has served a myriad of purposes and roles throughout its history from colonial days into the 21st century. In the early colonial period, public education was a haphazard system which excluded many children based on income, race or ethnicity, geographic location, and gender, among myriad other reasons. This landscape began to change as the West moved through the Enlightenment Era with educational opportunities beginning to expand across the nation. The Progressive Era of the early 20th century brought waves of reforms and progress, finally reaching the milestone of free and equal education for all centuries after the first Europeans set foot on this land.

The nation now finds itself at a turning point. As the 21st century has unfolded the world seems to be moving beyond the current scope of public education, and the system appears to have lost its way as of late with failures around every corner and no real vision for the future. This is not a history book, yet one must have a general understanding of past events to adequately understand current events. Therefore, it is prudent to begin this journey with a brief but hopefully thorough account of the origins of public education in the Unites States and the circumstances and events which have led to the present-day system. Our journey begins in the far corners of present day New England where the first wave of settlers attempted to create a new way of life in a beautiful but sometimes treacherous new world.

Colonial Period

During the early colonial days, children, primarily White children, were educated through an assortment of arrangements including church based schools, charity based schools run by churches or other societies, boarding schools for the wealthy class, tuition based schools created by nomadic schoolmasters, local schools organized by towns and parent groups, "dame schools" run by women in their homes, work apprenticeships with basic instruction in math, reading, and writing, as well as home schooling and private tutoring. With no formal funding system for education, early schools used a combination of property taxes, tuition, charitable contributions, fuel contributions, and sometimes even state support. It was not until the American Revolution that some cities began fully funding schools, but this only occurred in small pockets of the Northeast. Free schooling did not become the norm for the rest of the nation until nearly the 20th century.

The governing body of the Massachusetts Bay Colony created the initial colonial education system consisting of schools designed to teach Puritan values and how to read the Bible. A majority of the teaching was done initially in the home, but several organized Latin schools were established for the wealthy class. In 1635, Boston Latin School, the first public school, was created and soon after in 1639, the Mather School in Dorchester, became the first public school supported by tax dollars. In 1642 the Massachusetts Bay Colony took public education one step further by mandating compulsory attendance for all children within the colony. This new law forced all towns to set up some type of public schooling option. Throughout the 1640s and 1650s, other New England colonies soon followed Massachusetts' lead, and by the turn of the 18th century, common schools were established in most of the New England colonies with students of various ages being taught in a one-teacher classroom. Yet, although a majority of schools were locally funded, they were not always completely free requiring some families to pay tuition or "rate bills."

Despite the fact that education took off and evolved relatively quickly in the northern colonies, the situation in the southern colonies was vastly different. Rates of literacy were much higher in the North because a large portion of the population had been deeply involved in the Protestant Reformation in England which emphasized literacy in order to read scriptures. The literacy rate was much lower in the South where a majority of the population followed the Anglican church which required much less scripture reading. In addition, the South was primarily populated by working class individuals arriving as indentures servants. Finally, the smaller elite planter class who controlled most of the South did not support broad education. They generally arranged for private tutors, sent their children to private schools, or even shipped them back to England for more advanced instruction and training.

The upper South did manage to create some basic schools early in the colonial period around the Chesapeake Bay area, and in other parts of Virginia, some rudimentary schooling for the poor was provided by local parishes. In the deep South in areas such as Georgia and South Carolina, schooling was carried out by a combination of publicly funded projects and private ventures. However, compared to the northern colonies, education in the southern colonies was very much lacking. Many schools were parent organized and nearly all charged some form of tuition. Most rural areas had no schools at all, and if present, they were generally extremely isolated, overcrowded, and severely underfunded. In no region in the South was education compulsory or supported fully by taxes, and this would remain the norm until the later part of the 19th century during the post-Civil War Reconstruction era.

American Revolution to Reconstruction

Public schools continued to expand throughout the northern colonies and even somewhat throughout the southern colonies during the early to mid-1700s, but a major push to fund and expand public schooling throughout the entire colonial realm did not occur until after the American Revolution. Many influential leaders such as Thomas Jefferson and John Adams led this newfound movement to create a more formalized and unified public school system throughout the newly formed republic. By the late 1780s, many northeastern communities had already established a system of publicly funded schools, and from 1785–1789 federal ordinances gave large acreages of land to new states entering the union as long as those states agreed to set aside a portion of that land for public schooling. These land grants help to establish stable communities across the new republic; however, until the turn of the 19th century, many rural areas still had few schools, and there was a complete lack of unity across the newly formed commonwealth.

Publicly funded schools and their adjoining communities continued to grow in the early 1800s, but major changes were on the horizon. In the 1830s the common school movement took off with a Massachusetts legislator named Horace Mann leading the charge. Mann began to push for the creation of universal public schooling throughout the United States, stressing that publicly investing in education would transform all children into moral, literate, productive citizens thus benefiting the entire nation. Mann emphasized the Prussian model of education with common schools advocating a focus on reading, writing, and arithmetic as well as other subjects such as history, grammar, and geography. A strong curriculum of moral instruction was also included in this model with the goal of preparing children to be equipped to obtain good jobs thus strengthening the nation's economy. Mann fought for longer school years, better teacher wages, and more classroom resources. He believed education was the foundation for overcoming poverty, bridging social gaps, as well as creating a more overall equal society.

We must take a brief detour on our historical odyssey and embark on a quick hop across the Atlantic. This new Prussian model of education beginning to spread across the United States had its inception in 18th century Europe. In 1763 Frederick the Great of the Prussian Empire began to expand the existing school system in Prussia (basically present-day Germany), requiring that all boys and girls between the ages of 5–14 be educated through a tax funded compulsory primary education system consisting of eight years of primary schooling. Frederick also began to introduce the concept of state funded secondary schooling. This educational model revolutionized education in the empire by instituting compulsory attendance, advanced training for teachers, curricula for each grade, mandatory kindergarten, and a national standardized testing system. This system continued to evolve, and in 1810 teaching standards were significantly raised by implementing a state teacher certification system. By the 1830s the Prussian model had established systems including:

- -Massive government school funding
- -Professional college-trained teachers

- -A livable salary for teachers
- -Free primary schooling
- -A strong state sponsored curriculum

- -Secular instruction
- -An extended school year
- -Supervision at multiple levels

This model soon spread across not only Europe but eventually to the rest of the world with nations as distant as Japan and the United States adopting its methods and tenets. This new model of education not only led to the first statewide compulsory school attendance law in Massachusetts in 1852, but it also began to revolutionize the way the United States public school system operated throughout the entire country. This educational model is still used in the United States to this very day. Nonetheless, the Prussian model of education has come under some scrutiny especially in recent times for a variety of reasons.

The major critics of this model summarize their complaints by stating this system only creates an obedient dumbed-down work force easily influenced and controlled by the state, to keep elitist systems in place. Some critics point out that this model leads to blind obedience to authority and much of what students are forced to *learn* is boring rote memorization of useless information or facts. This model, some say, leads to massive conformity with the goal of making all children the same thus suppressing individuality and personal freedom. Amassing cumulative records throughout a student's schooling, including their historical standardized test scores, can be seen to be problematic, resulting in children being funneled onto a predetermined track that limits a child's full potential and access to different learning paths. The advantages and disadvantages of this Prussian model of education will be referenced and thoroughly discussed throughout the entirety of this book as well as its impacts on the way we educate our youth.

Throughout the rest of the 19th century, minus a brief setback during the Civil War years, public schools continued to grow throughout the United States. However, schools still lagged in the South compared to the North especially for children of color. This continued to be an issue well into the 20th century. Despite these obstacles, public education continued to grow into the latter part of the 1800s. During the Reconstruction Era the federal

Department of Education was established in 1867, and in the same year the Republicans seized power in the South creating its first system of taxpayer funded public schooling. The Freedmen's Bureau also created nearly 1,000 schools across the South for Black children. For perspective on just how much the surge of public education spread throughout the 1800s...in 1830 around 55% of U.S. children ages 5–14 were enrolled in some type of public school, but by the 1870s that figure had risen to nearly 80%.

Progressive Era and The New Deal

The nation soon moved into the Progressive Era of education lasting from the 1890s to the 1930s, marked by an extensive expansion of the U.S. public school system as well as the successful, and sometimes failed, implementation of various new programs and plans. Historically, many states only offered schooling in the primary grades, but secondary schools soon began to spread during this time. In 1910 high schools began expanding more and more, and by 1940, 50% of all young adults had obtained a high school diploma. Progressives mainly sought out means to remove waste and improve the efficiency of the U.S. school system, including reducing the size of school boards, increasing the power of local superintendents, centralizing purchasing power for school districts, establishing more uniform standards for hiring teachers, revising curricula, as well as improving architectural designs to create a more cohesive school atmosphere. It was also during this time, in the year 1918, that school finally became compulsory for all children in the United States. From this point forward, all parents were required by law to send their children to school or else they would receive, at times, harsh fines.

However, many other newly implemented experimental practices were not so successful. The Gary Plan, adopted by over 200 U.S. cities, pushed for more highly efficient use of school facilities, dividing students into academic classrooms and vocational programs. These vocational programs aided many students by preparing them for skilled jobs after graduating from high school. These programs were moderately successful, but at the onset of the Great Depression the plan became too expensive causing most cities to abandon it. John Dewey was also a major proponent of progressive education and widely pushed for more democracy in schools, moving away from rigorous academics and focusing more on individualism, teaching children to "learn how to live." A small number of institutes briefly experimented with his methods but his ideas never took off due to the overly bureaucratic nature that had begun to take over the majority of school districts in the country. This monstrous bureaucracy has continued to hinder educational reforms to this very day.

As the Great Depression spread into the early 1930s, tax revenues began to fall drastically, and with little assistance from Roosevelt's New Deal and the federal government, the quality of the nation's public school system began to decline. Many budgets had to be significantly reduced, and some teachers even went without pay for an extended period of time. The New Deal did help some poor students and did result in the construction of a handful of new schools; however, this new system was not based on professional standards and left many students' needs unmet. FDR's system relied solely on his inner circle of experts, shutting out all outside advice and influence from those with real educational knowledge and expertise. Due to these and other ineffective policies, historians look at the New Deal era as a major step back for public education in the United States.

During this period, however, some advancements in secondary education began to take off with high schools growing in number and size. From 1910–1940 the number of high schools, as well as high school graduates, began to significantly increase. In 1910 only around nine% of Americans had acquired a high school diploma, but by 1935 that rate had increased to 40% with a further increase to 50% by the end of the decade. So by 1940, fully half of U.S. citizens had obtained a high school diploma. This was a uniquely American situation with no other nation being able to compete. Even in Europe, few children attended school past the age of 14, and most secondary schools in Europe at the time were rarely attended by anyone other than children of the wealthy and elite. U.S. secondary schools generally emphasized instruction in universal skills that were widely applicable to multiple disciplines, resulting in flexible and diverse employment opportunities for high school graduates.

It was also during this time, that many teachers started to organize, and various teaching organizations and unions began to form. For example, the National Education Association (NEA) had an early membership totaling around 8,500, but by the 1930s that number had risen to over 220,000. The American Federation of Teachers (AFT) also grew during this time forming alliances with many local labor unions. These teacher unions and the powers they would come to yield have become a hotly debated issue over the last few decades and will be discussed in a later chapter.

Civil Rights and The Reformation Era

Education and segregation have unfortunately gone hand in hand throughout much of the history of the United States. Although some free Blacks in small pockets of the Northeast managed to become literate, the majority of Blacks received no formal education before the Civil War. In many southern states, it was actually illegal to teach enslaved Africans. However, as early as 1835, the first integrated school was founded in New Hampshire. This new way of schooling faced massive local opposition, and fully integrated schools were not attempted again until the Reconstruction Period after the Civil War. During this time, the Freedman's Bureau set up many schools in the South and attempted to protect free public education for freed Blacks, but aside from than a handful of cities, these schools were still racially segregated. Many Black communities began to fight against these separate and almost always unequal facilities and services. In 1896, their plight made its way to the Supreme Court in the case of Plessy v. Ferguson. The 1896 Supreme Court ruling upheld segregation in public schools, as long as schools for Black children were "separate but equal." Despite this ruling, Black students did not receive close to an equal education for many decades to come.

The New Deal era began to end as the nation moved into the 1940s. The United States along with the rest of the world, was distracted by the rise of fascism in parts of Europe, which eventually led to WWII. The progress of education stagnated during this time as the world was wrecked by a brutal war and the ensuing recovery process. Not until the 1950s did the push for education reform hit the mainstream once again as the Civil Rights movement began to take off lasting nearly 2 decades. In 1954 the Supreme Court returned to the topic of segregated schooling. In the case of Brown vs. Board of Education, the Supreme Court reversed the 1896 Plessy vs. Ferguson decision, declaring unanimously that separate facilities were not only unequal they were unconstitutional. Districts in the South did not completely integrate until the 1970s, but this decision was a huge victory for Black children who had been fighting for equal access to free and public education since the colonial days.

Despite the Supreme Court's decision, full integration of schools in the South was met with ferocious opposition. For example, in 1957 President Eisenhower had to take control of the National Guard in Little Rock, Arkansas to ensure the safe integration of public schools. The process of integration slowly continued throughout the rest of the 1950s and 1960s, creating opportunities for Black students unlike anything seen before. Many, however, would still argue that full integration of schools was not yet complete. Funding for school systems was based on local property taxes. Many claimed this system created a wide disparity of funding depending on local socioeconomics. Many times, poor inner-city areas highly populated by people of color received far less funding than wealthier suburban areas or smaller towns creating a system of pseudo-segregation still debated to this very day.

Various other school reforms began to emerge toward the end of and following the Civil Rights era. In 1965 the Secondary and Elementary Education Act was established, which authorized funds for various resources to support instructional material, educational programs, professional development, and incentive programs to increase parental involvement. In 1975 The Education for All Handicapped Children Act was passed, which required free and appropriate education be available for all students with a disability. This law would be further expanded in the 1980s, and in 1990 the act was retitled the Individuals with Disabilities Act (IDEA) changing the label handicap to disability. This law created a variety of services and opportunities for students affected with a wide range of disabilities.

During the decades following WWII, the public school system also began to move toward addressing the social needs of children, especially those from low socio-economic backgrounds. Many districts began to employ school nurses and provide free or reduced breakfast and lunch to students from low-income families. In the latter decades of the 20th century, these social services began to expand even further creating services such as substance abuse programs, safety and violence prevention and training, before and after school care, and even counseling services. Some school districts turned into virtual community hubs, providing students and their parents with a plethora of assistance programs.

In the latter part of the century as the nation limped into the 1980s, the Regan Era commenced. In 1983, the National Commission on Excellence in Education published *A Nation at Risk*. This report detailed how poorly the country's public education system was functioning compared to peer nations around the world. However, the result was mostly more standards and mundane curricula paired with more standardized testing. It was also during this time that questions over school choice began to take form with various public charter schools beginning to pop up across the nation. This topic of school choice and the impact and effectiveness of charter schools are still hotly debated and are discussed later in detail.

21st Century

As the United States moved into the 21st century, the goal of public education began to shift priorities to focus on establishing a high-quality education for all students. This shift led to a controversial emphasis on creating a national assessment system to adequately measure the quality of education on a nationwide scale. In 2002 President George W. Bush signed the No Child Left Behind bill into law. This system required states to measure progress. Schools that performed well were rewarded with more federal aid; schools that failed to meet the goals and standards set by the federal government were punished. This policy has been nothing short of a disaster. Its pitfalls are discussed throughout our journey in much more detail. No Child Left Behind was an extremely poorly planned and implemented program with unrealistic goals. It was eventually broken apart at the national level by President Barack Obama in 2015, and control of the remaining elements were then handed over to the states.

Throughout the last decade, school districts have attempted to initiate some reforms and various curriculum adjustments to better prepare students for our rapidly changing technological world. Many attempts have been made to increase the rigor and standards in public schools. Programs and techniques have been consistently implemented with a focus on deeper learning, complex problem solving, teamwork, and analytical reasoning. Many schools are experimenting with different learning environments and learning spaces in an attempt to move to a system that can provide more of an active learning experience. However, most of these attempts have resulted in subpar results at best. Additionally, districts have spent hundreds of millions of dollars to keep up to speed with the technological revolution by purchasing large caches of laptops, iPads, smart boards, and other forms of technology in order to enhance the learning process. Some of this technology has aided students in gaining ground in an increasing technological world; however, there is still much debate on the proper implementation of these new devices in the classroom setting as well as the level of their efficacy, value, and safety.

Thus, the direction the nation's public school system will now take remains undetermined. It is plagued with more issues and setbacks than at any time in recent history. This lack of a clear vision for the future has left many parents and students wondering if they are actually receiving the services they have been promised. Additionally, this lack of a clear path forward has left teachers and school administrators fumbling around in the dark for answers as to what their role should be as the nation moves further into the dynamic world of the 21st century. Furthermore, the catastrophic mishandling of the recent COVID-19 pandemic by government officials and educational leaders has done nothing but make matters exponentially worse. We've now found ourselves on the precipice of a much needed educational revolution. As a nation we must decide if we are to continue with the same system that has done nothing but create failure after failure, or is it finally time to shift course and create a new and better system that actually works. Only time will tell.

Since the first European settlers stepped onto this land, the nation has come a long way in creating a national standardized system of public education. However, this system has historically been fraught with many issues that still linger to this very day, and the quality and competence of our nation's public schools seem to be getting worse by the minute. This book will attempt to address the root of these issues, the direct and indirect consequences of these issues, as well as possible ideas on how to solve some of the problems that have plagued our system for far too long. Hopefully, this brief (and not too boring) historical tour has provided a baseline understanding of how the nation's public education system has evolved into its current state. We will reference aspects of this historical timeline throughout our voyage as we venture much deeper into the foundations of the most important aspects of our current education system. So now, let us begin the journey.

Part I: The Machine

Chapter 1: Life of a Teacher

"What are your top three favorite things about being a teacher...? June, July and August." ~Every Teacher

"Those who know, do. Those that understand, teach." ~Aristotle

I roll out of bed, slap the blaring alarm clock, and holy shit... Here I go again. Fortunately, the commute isn't bad. Many teachers live in or near their district making the commute easy, but that will be the least stressful task of the day. Most teachers arrive at school well before the bell rings and the doors open. Some teachers arrive up to an hour or more before their required start time to handle any last-minute needed classroom or lesson preparations, possibly tutor students, or to conduct the myriad morning duties they are required to fulfill even if it means working outside of contract hours. Bus duty, cafeteria duty, hallway monitoring, traffic control, and a cornucopia of other supervisory roles must be addressed throughout the day, and many times it is classroom teachers who are responsible for these roles.

So I've been at work for an hour or more already, and school hasn't even started. The bell rings. The elementary school doors open. And the chaos ensues. The kids rush in, and I make my best effort to put on a smile and greet each one as they enter the classroom. Backpacks, lunch boxes, and jackets begin to fly around the room, eventually making it to their intended destinations while kids hustle about in a strange mix of organized mayhem, and before long, if I'm lucky, 20–30 faces will be staring at me anxiously waiting for the next hint of instruction.

At this point I quickly assess the current situation taking in the mood of the room. Students come to school each day from all nooks and crannies of life, and at that moment a teacher must assess what these 20–30 little humans may have encountered in their topsy-turvy lives over the past 18 hours. Some may have not had a decent meal. Some may have spent the night supervising younger siblings. Some may have experienced a wide range of physical, sexual, or mental abuse. Some may have had the loveliest 18 hours of their young lives and want to tell the whole world all about it. Every one of these young minds brings everything they've experienced through the classroom door. A teacher must read the room and, in a moment, attempt to understand all these shared experiences because they will most likely determine the course of the day.

As I move forward with the morning lessons and the day unfolds, I make an attempt at instruction, but I find myself overwhelmed with seemingly constant distractions. Managing the barrage of behavior problems infecting the classroom seems to devour more and more time, and the class begins to fall further and further behind schedule. The classroom phone rings as I glance over to see 15 unanswered email messages. A random person just walked into the room, and I have no idea what she wants. The roadblocks to actually teaching my students never end...I look up at the clock...it's only 10:00!

It's now time for my students to go to their specials period (music, PE, art, computer). This respite generally functions as a teacher's conference period to work on grading, lesson plans, classroom arrangement, etc. However, on many occasions, even this time is usurped by meetings, conferences, committee duties, and other nonsense the system creates to monopolize time. My 45–60 min *break* flies by, and before long, there's a room full of students awaiting my next move. I manage to accomplish somewhat of a lesson before heading out to lunch. At this point, I ensure my students make it down to the cafeteria so I then race to the hen's den of a teacher's lounge or make my way back to the classroom. By the time I get situated, I may have 15 minutes left to siphon up my food before heading back to pick up a sure-to-be rowdy bunch of kids who just pumped themselves full of either whatever garbage their parents stuffed into their lunchbox, or sometimes even worse...the government procured cafeteria lunch that appears perhaps only slightly more nutritious than prison grub or military rations.

I finally manage to corral my fructose fueled students back to the classroom, and eventually get them settled in for the afternoon. After a couple of lessons, I feel I have accomplished almost nothing because I had to spend a significant amount of time dealing with behavior issues and the countless other distractions that bombard nearly every minute of my instruction, then it's time for recess. This is the one and only time of near unadulterated freedom for every student in the school. It's the only 20–30 minutes of the day kids can truly be kids...run, play, climb, fall, throw, kick...all the things that kids were meant to do. The time is up, I blast my whistle, and the sound echoes, resulting in a Pavlovian rush of little humans stampeding toward the door as they attempt to form what will never be an actual line.

I come back to a classroom full of sweaty, tired children who now reek of a combined aroma of wet socks and the lawnmower man which emanates throughout the small space biting at the back of my nose. Luckily, I have become accustomed to it rather quickly and regain my strength to push through the last 2 hours of the day. The time slowly ticks by, but the end is finally approaching. I wrap up the day and allow the organized chaos of the dismissal process to ensue. Jackets, lunchboxes, and backpacks fly around the room again, but this time thankfully they are all heading out the door. I didn't accomplish what I set out to today, but that seems to be the trend most days. I sit back at my desk. Everyone survived. There were no major catastrophes. Hopefully someone learned something today. I allow myself to try and grasp some sense of success from the day...Oh crap! I'm late for my after-school staff meeting!

It's damn near 5:00, and I'm finally heading out to the parking lot. I toss the plethora of unfinished work in the back seat of my car, open the front door, sit down, and stare at the dashboard. The day that felt like a month is finally over...but is it? I wish I could go to the gym. I haven't worked out in several days, and my waistline is continuing to expand. I haven't seen my best friend in over a month. I'd love to meet up for a couple of drinks and catch up. I snap out of the fantasy world abruptly realizing I have almost 100 papers to grade, Friday's lesson plan to amend, an upcoming appraisal form to complete by the end of the week, special education paperwork that annoying lady keeps bugging me to fill out, and, oh yeah, I still need to go home and tend to the needs of my spouse and kids. I finally manage to push the ignition button and head home in a mental fog that never seems to fully dissipate...just another typical day for the average elementary school teacher.

Hours, Hours, and More Hours

So I only have to work nine months out of the year. That sounds like a pretty good gig...right? A typical teacher works 180–190 days a year, depending on district contract requirements, compared to 250–260 days for the average U.S. worker. Taken at face value, it would seem teachers work significantly less. However, numbers can be quite misleading.

A teacher's contract hours generally require an 8-hour day which includes a 30-minute duty-free lunch and a conference period, generally around 45 minutes, to attend meetings and work on lesson planning or grading. Unfortunately, most teachers don't have enough time in the day to accomplish everything it takes to be an effective educator. Teachers work more than their contract hours, starting early in the morning or late into the evening, or both.

Most teachers spend a significant amount of time logging in additional hours before and after school in their classrooms *and* at home, and many spend countless hours toiling over lesson plans and ungraded papers over the weekend. Moreover, during the summer, many teachers are expected to attend mandatory training ranging from several days to a few weeks, depending on the school district and their area of teaching. Many teachers also use the summer to earn required professional development hours to maintain their certifications. While these professional development courses are generally free of charge, they do require a significant investment of time and some travel. Teachers are neither paid for their time nor reimbursed for expenses.

Don't be mistaken. Having summers and seemingly endless major and minor holidays off sounds awesome. All that valuable time to spend with family and friends, take on a second job, travel, work on personal projects one may be passionate about, volunteer, start a small business, or any multitude of other activities. It is indeed a huge benefit to those working in education, but the assumption that teachers work their 40-hour week for several months and then philander about living a relaxing life of luxury for a fourth of the year is completely inaccurate and often damaging to both professional and corporate reputations.

So, what if someone were to offer you a $ 50,000-a-year job that required you to work 12–16 hours a day? Sounds like a great deal, right? Yeah, I didn't think so. The average school day in the United States is about seven and a half hours, so where did I come up with 12–16 hours? Teachers' work patterns are extremely different from other professions, making it difficult to compare teaching with other types of employment. Teachers are generally required to complete an array of tasks in addition to instruction, such as developing lesson plans, grading papers, serving on various committees, completing professional development hours, engaging in an assortment of supervisory duties, attending meetings and trainings before school, after school, and during the summer, and fulfilling a litany of other tasks depending on individual districts. In addition to all these tasks, teachers are more likely to have multiple jobs than any other profession, and they also generally spend more time doing household activities.

A simple Google search returns a wide variety of studies that claim to have data indicating teachers work about the same or even slightly less than the average worker in the United States. The results of these studies, however, are quite inaccurate. For example, these results show on average, teachers work 42.2 hours per week while nonteachers work an average of 43.2 hours per week. I will explain why this narrative is far from accurate, but we're going to have to do a little math. I know. It's a bit daunting...but stay with me. Additionally, I will use the *lowest, most conservative numbers available* to preclude any claims of inflating the statistics.

As stated earlier, teachers generally work around 180 days a year for eight hours a day, so to make it simple we'll use this figure as our starting block even though most teacher contracts fall between 180–190 days. That sounds like a pretty sweet deal at face value. But wait. Let's do the math. A teacher works for 8 hours a day based on most contracts. When we multiply those 8 hours by 180 days, that gives us 1,440 hours of contracted work per year. Most teacher contracts require a teacher to arrive anywhere from 5–15 minutes before school starts and stay 5–15 minutes after school ends. This is how we come to a total of 8 hours of work per day even though the typical school day is around seven and a half hours. However, teachers who regularly show up to school 5–15 minutes before school starts and leave shortly after dismissal are generally not the most efficient teachers.

Effective teachers arrive up to an hour before school begins to get lessons and their classroom ready, use the copy machine, or to tutor struggling students. Teachers also stay after school for 1–3 three hours for meetings, clubs, sporting events, and to prepare for the next day. Based on data collected from nationwide teacher surveys, teachers spend anywhere from 300–600 hours a year engaging in activities and tasks before and after school. We'll go with the lowest number in the range and set teachers' time spent working before and after school at 300 hours. So at this point, we have a total of 1,740 hours (1,440 + 300).

Well, school is out, and a teacher's day has ended, right? Well, not exactly. The average teacher spends anywhere from 5–10 hours a week grading papers, most of which occurs in the home. Using a typical 36-week school year and the lowest estimate of 5 hours gives us another 180 hours (36 x 5) per year spent grading papers. However, grading papers isn't the only task many teachers complete at home. Quite a bit of lesson planning occurs outside of the school as well. Based on data and surveys, teachers spend an average of 140 hours per year planning lessons at home. This gives us a total of 320 hours (180 + 140) per year (at home) to grade papers and plan lessons outside of contract hours. Where are we now?

Contracted school-day hours	1,440
Before and after contracted hours (at school)	300
Hours grading papers (at home)	180
Hours planning lessons (at home)	140
Sub-total to this point	2,060

But wait. There's more…how are you enjoying your summer? Unbeknownst to most, the majority of teachers do not get the entire summer off. Teachers must complete professional development hours, attend trainings and workshops, and begin school 1–2 weeks before students arrive in the fall. On average, most teachers spend about 100 hours over the summer on various work-related activities. That currently puts us at 2,160 hours (2,060 + 100) at this point, but there's one last addition: communication. Teachers must maintain consistent communication with parents, students, and other school personnel. Much of this communication has to be done outside contract hours. The advancement of technology has made it almost impossible to avoid being bombarded by dings, chimes, vibrations, and buzzes on your tablets and phones 24 hours a day. Furthermore, most school emails are now linked with Gmail, so your cellphone is never completely disconnected from work. This doesn't take up a huge amount of time, so let's use a low estimate of around one hour per week on communication outside of contract hours which we'll round up to 40 hours a year.

Previous sub-total	2,060
Summer hours in trainings and workshops	100
Communication	40
Grand Total	2,200

So what does all of this mean? What we should take away from this painful, but important, math lesson is the fact teachers don't actually work a total of 180 days a year. When we use the actual hours worked, even using the lowest estimated figures, most teachers actually work closer to 275 days a year. (2,200 hours/8-hour day = 275 days). The average full-time worker in the United States works an average of 261 days a year. I'm not insinuating anyone should cry a river for all the overworked and underpaid teachers out there. Other professionals, of course, bring work home as well, and many other professionals also work a large number of hours outside their normal contracted hours. However, the myth that teachers only work 40-hours a week for 9 out of 12 months is exactly that—a myth. Now that we've broken down the hours most teachers are required to work, what about all that time off?

A Profession of Endless Vacations?

Only working for nine months out of the year must be great… summers, major holidays, spring break, and all those other random holidays that only bankers and teachers seem to get off!

Do teachers ever work?

It must be nice to have all that time off, huh?

Oh, another 3-day weekend, what a shocker!

Although you may have heard wisecracks like these let's explore how much time off teachers actually get.

Teachers generally get a week for Thanksgiving, 2 weeks for Christmas, a week for spring break, and around two months for summer break. Teachers are also off on most government holidays like Labor Day, MLK Day, or Memorial Day, and most districts also give teachers 10–12 days of personal or sick leave per year. All teachers don't necessarily function under this type of schedule though. Coaches and teachers who are involved in extracurricular activities must report to work earlier in the summer for practices, camps, and related events. These teachers are usually paid a stipend, but it is generally mere peanuts. Many coaches and other extracurricular teachers wind up making a small fraction of additional compensation for their services. The hourly rate of a stipend means most coaches don't even make minimum wage for the time they put in after or before school hours.

Historically school calendars mirrored agricultural timetables, so kids would be available to help out on home farms. This meant teachers only worked when kids were in school. The historical logic, then, justified paying teachers less than full-time workers. But things have changed! The modern economy and modern school districts require much more from teachers during their *summer vacation*. The antiquated relationship between compensation and summer vacation no longer holds true.

Teachers are now required to undertake a wide range of duties during the summer months including attending meetings, developing school curricula, training or mentoring new teachers, organizing or relocating classrooms, fulfilling professional development obligations, and contacting students and/or families just to name a few. Most of these duties and responsibilities, while expected, are unpaid. Certainly, some teachers opt to teach summer school classes for additional income. And some events, camps, and or even certain trainings provide supplemental income. Nonetheless, most teachers don't earn anywhere near their normal hourly rate teaching summer school or working in other paid summer opportunities. But, it's generally still higher than what a teacher could earn during the summer with alternative part-time or seasonal employment. As a result, many teachers still find this as the best option to supplement their income though.

What about other times of the year teachers get vacation time? Most school districts do not require teachers to attend work-related functions during Thanksgiving, Christmas, or spring break. But many teachers use these vacation times to catch up on grading, lesson plans, professional development hours, or other work-related obligations that can be accomplished at home. And while the hours teachers spend during these times varies greatly, most teachers do work during vacation times throughout the calendar year.

Like any other employee, teachers get sick and need to take personal days throughout the school year. Most school districts provide teachers with at least 10 days of leave per year. That would seem like a pretty nice deal on the surface, but as with most practices and policies in education, superficial information can be very misleading. Most school districts mandate fairly strict—and sometimes downright outrageous—rules and guidelines defining how and when a teacher can use leave days. Here are a few typical examples: days that pre-or succeed a holiday weekend are not allowed, the number of consecutive days is limited. In addition, districts typically black-out large blocks of dates throughout the year when which teachers are not allowed to use personal time. Generally, unless a teacher is sick, supervisory approval is required for all personal days, leaving teachers at the whim of whoever gets to put the stamp of approval on their weekend getaway for their 10-year wedding anniversary. Teachers, like any other employee, get around unreasonable policies by simply calling in sick rather than rolling the dice on getting planned days off approved. Policies like this, and the behaviors they incite, are detrimental to the system because they create unanticipated yet avoidable absences.

Furthermore, even if a teacher obtains permission to take a day or two off, that process comes with several caveats. Teachers are usually required to find their own substitute—a difficult time consuming process particularly in light of the current substitute teacher shortage. To make matters worse, substitutes often cancel at the last-minute causing teachers to either scramble to find a quick replacement, or cancel their own plans. Even when a teacher is lucky enough to lock down a substitute, the teacher still has to create an entire outline and plan for the substitute which consumes quite a bit of extra unpaid time.

Substitute teachers generally aren't experienced enough to present or explain new material, so more often than not students work on review or enrichment—a fancy name for "busy work"—types of assignments. Nonetheless, even after a brief absence, when the teacher returns there is usually a significant amount of work to do...stacks of ungraded papers, incidents that may have occurred in the classroom that have to be addressed, plus the extra time and effort needed to get students back on track and up to schedule. Many teachers also deal with a lot of guilt for leaving their students with a stranger. Certainly, some of this guilt is self-inflicted, but many times it subtly trickles down from the powers that be.

Another major point of contention is maternity leave. Given that approximately 77% of U.S. teachers are female, and their average age is 42 a significant percentage of our teachers is in their prime childbearing years. The United States does not mandate paid parental leave like many other nations, and only a handful of states and a few individual school districts offer paid maternity leave for teachers. Much research has shown that access to paid family leave results in improved health outcomes for children and mothers, more and longer periods of breastfeeding, and lower postpartum depression rates. But the prevailing mindset on maternity leave precludes all but only a couple of options.

Teachers planning to have a baby must either attempt to time their impregnation so that the birth of their child will be as close to summer break as possible giving them at least a couple of months of paid leave, or they must wait until they have accumulated enough personal days to take an extended period of time off. Obviously, neither of these options is ideal. The absence of reasonable maternity leave policies may be a major factor in teacher retention. Many teachers are fortunate enough to have partners who earn sufficient income to support the family, allowing at least some of these teachers the option to resign, temporarily or indefinitely, in order to have adequate time at home with their newborn child. Quite a few of these teachers never return. Even worse, many times, some teachers chose this route even if their significant other does not earn an adequate amount of income, creating financial stresses on a young family.

A teacher schedule can be beneficial for a family as well though, and some teachers do enjoy their routine because it accommodates their lifestyle. Having a work schedule that generally matches the school hours of your children can be very convenient when it comes to child care, and having at least one parent off work when your children are out of school can be a major cost saving perk. Time off does allow many teachers to spend time with their children to supervise them when school is not in session. Parents working in other professional areas would most likely need either the support of a relative or friend to supervise their children when out of school, or they would have to spend copious amounts of money for babysitters, day care, or camps to ensure the safety and well-being of their children.

So what's the verdict? Teachers do get a significant amount of time off throughout the year. This much is true. This can provide a valuable break for teachers and gives them extra time to spend with their family, especially children. Time off is a big motivating factor for teacher morale as well. The week-long vacation dangling off in the distance can be a major carrot for some teachers, pushing them through tough days and making them more effective at their craft. However, the common perception that teachers only work nine months a year is a misperception. Teachers spend a significant amount of their personal time engaged in work related activities for which they are almost never compensated. In addition, taking time off during the school year for personal or health related reasons is very difficult. So the next time someone scoffs at teachers claiming to be overworked, underpaid, and unappreciated, remember that when we do the math and understand the time that actually goes into the profession, the overarching narrative that has so long been attached to the field of teaching may not be so accurate.

Burnout and Morale

Overcrowded classrooms, exceedingly long hours, mind numbing workloads which generally wind up following you home, and meeting the expectations to satisfy the physical and emotional needs of students are just a few examples of the stressors teachers and support staff deal with daily. A recent study by the Hammill Institute on Disabilities surveyed over 100 teachers. Many reported high levels of physical and mental health issues and below average levels of job satisfaction compared to other professions, fueling physical as well as physiological absences from work. In fact, 93% fell into classes characterized by high levels of stress. What exactly is the cause of all this teacher stress?

People tend to thrive in controlled, predictable, and autonomous environments, but these types of environments are not where teachers generally find themselves. Teachers face not only a uniquely challenging job but facets of their job are outside of their control. Don't get me wrong. Teachers do have some control over their own destiny. They have direct control over their physical classroom environment and management as well as some autonomy in creating their lesson plans. However, these facets of the job which teachers control involve long periods of managing emotions and time throughout the day, as well as uncompensated effort after hours at home, straining personal and/or family life.

So what is it, then, that teachers cannot control? The answer? Pretty much everything else. Teachers have no control over the number or personalities of students assigned to their classroom. Physical classrooms are randomly assigned by the school principal. Teachers generally have no say in creating their daily schedule. If a teacher has multiple areas of certification, they may not even have a choice in the subjects or grades they teach. Teachers are frequently shuffled between schools or grade levels based on the district's needs at the time. Sometimes teachers are even forced or strong armed into serving on committees, clubs, or contracted "other duties." Basically, most teachers are subject to the whims of their school principal, program coordinator, or some other supervising entity who seldom has the teacher's or even students' best interests in mind. More and more, teachers face increasing verbal and physical aggression and violence in the classroom. Students from all age groups have become more violent and aggressive toward staff and other students creating an unpredictable and tense work environment. This has led to significant mental and even physical harm to teachers across the entire country.

Teachers also usually have no say in the curriculum they must use in their teaching. So, although teachers may have some control in creating lessons and presenting the material, they almost never have any control in the content that is actually taught in their classroom. What's more, an overwhelming majority of curriculum is based on what is being tested on state assessments. State sanctioned standardized testing is wrecking classrooms, teachers, and students all of whom have been overwhelmed by the stress involved in preparing for, administering, and dealing with standardized testing. Teachers are often even penalized in some states when their students don't reach adequate benchmarks. These, many times, unattainable goals and benchmarks are a major source of teacher stress.

The discussion so far has only touched on a brief list of the most soul crushing stressors a teacher faces. While some of these stressors are similar to those experienced in other lines of work, many are unique to the teaching profession. One of the most unique aspects of teacher stress is the impact it can and does have on those around them and on the overall education system. The stress level and coping abilities of a teacher affect not only the students in their classroom but the entire climate of the school and even the entire school district.

Do we want our children in classrooms where the teacher is stressed out of his or her mind? Or where the teacher cries multiple times a week, sometimes in front of students? Or a teacher who juggles grading papers and creating lesson plans every night while they down copious amounts of bourbon or occasionally puff on the joint or vape pen always within arm's reach to help take off the edge? Or how about a teacher on daily doses of antipsychotics or mood stabilizing pharmaceuticals to maintain enough stability to make it through another day? That's probably just enough bit of reality to cause most parents to immediately start searching for the best private school in the area that won't drive them into bankruptcy. So let's take a closer look at how teacher stress affects us...That's not an editing error. Teacher stress affects ALL of US.

When teachers are stressed, the relationships they have with their students almost always suffer, which leads to more negative behavioral and academic outcomes for students. This stress, in turn, leads to teacher burnout. Burnout can lead to emotional exhaustion, cynicism, and lower levels of self-efficacy. Burnout is generally a more short-term condition, which arises from an excess of demands placed upon a person when that person does not have the adequate resources, abilities, supports, or training to handle those demands. But when burnout is unaddressed and continues to worsen, it can lead to demoralization—the point at which teachers believe they can no longer perform their job. This in turn leads to teacher turnover and absenteeism.

This is not a huge problem when an adequate number of new teachers is coming into the field and adequate numbers of substitute teachers are available to fill in when full-time teachers need a break. The problem is that the trend today is moving in the opposite direction. Young college students are not studying or going into the field of education. There's also currently a massive substitute teacher shortage across the entire country. People seeking short term or part-time employment are moving away from substitute teaching to find higher paying gigs in the private sector. When a teacher is out, and a substitute cannot be acquired, those students can be uprooted and moved into another teacher's classroom for the day. At times, teachers may even miss out on their planning time to cover portions of an absent teacher's classroom. This obviously has a negative impact and creates more stress on the teacher having to take in several more students that day, increasing their already massive workload.

Nationwide surveys have reported that one in four teachers have recently or are currently considering leaving the profession. Thus, 25% of teachers are on the verge of walking away. In addition, half of new teachers quit within the first 5 years. One can see how this is a major problem when we consider the cascading snowball effect that lies in wait in the near future. More teacher turnover and fewer substitute teachers means larger class sizes and more work for teachers, leading to? More stress. The consequence is more teacher turnover, bigger class sizes, and even more stress. This then leads to... I think the point is obvious. It's a vicious degrading cycle. A system in this type of free fall will not last for long. In the short run we will have to dig deeper into the current teacher shortage crisis if we want to minimize the long run future problem. I will discuss this in greater detail, but for now, just know it's a big problem, and one that is going to get a whole lot worse before it has any chance to improve.

How does all this affect students? Let me emphasize—the relationships teachers have with their students always suffers when teachers are overly stressed and burnt out. Various studies have shown that increases in teacher stress lead to more negative behavioral and academic student outcomes. Teachers with high stress and low coping skills have been associated with lower student adaptive behaviors, lower math achievement, and highly disruptive student behaviors. Additionally, emotionally exhausted teachers engage in low levels of positive behavior supports, meaning there tends to be a low inverse ratio of interactions between the teacher and students as well as higher rates of harsh reprimands. This damages the quality of teaching and impairs relationships with students, which results in lower student achievement and a multitude of classroom behavior problems, especially aggressive and/or violent behaviors.

It's not difficult to see how increasing the stress in a classroom environment causes increased tension and aggression from students. Stress can be very contagious, and many times students can sense and even emulate the stress of their teacher. The impact teacher stress and burnout has on students has elicited negative behaviors including criticizing teachers, demonstrating verbal or physical aggression toward other students and/or teachers, damaging or destroying school property, tardiness and absenteeism, and even substance abuse both on or off campus. It has also been shown time and time again that students' academic achievement and yearly gains are directly linked to teacher behavior. Teachers with higher levels of self-efficacy feel more confident in their abilities and thus have a better capacity to manage their classrooms which results in more effective teaching practices and more positive student outcomes.

Teacher morale and burnout can be addressed through a variety of approaches. First, teachers need more supportive services to manage their stress; each school district must decide how best to approach this issue with the resources they have available. This brings us to our next point: resources. Teachers must be provided the resources they need to be successful, and these resources may vary and depend greatly on the district in which they work. Teachers with high levels of stress and low coping skills may need to be screened at various times during the year and given extra support before they reach the tipping point of complete exhaustion and demoralization. With mounting pressures from administrators, parents, and society at large, practices that foster a more nurturing environment should be implemented. Higher rates of positive feedback for teachers, permanent removal of violent and aggressive students from general education classrooms, adequate preparation time and training, social networks to bring teachers together, and more financial incentives for teachers would be a great start.

Today's students are the leaders of tomorrow. We hear catchy phrases like that all the time, but they are true. If we cannot find a way, as a society, to provide teachers with the resources they need to do their jobs in a safe and productive manner, who will educate our children? We saw what a disaster home schooling was during the COVID-19 lockdowns, and even middle-class families can't afford private school anymore. My brother was paying nearly $10,000 a year for my niece to go to a private elementary school. That's only a couple thousand dollars less than I paid for my entire graduate degree about a decade ago. The education and growth of students academically, socially, and behaviorally is in jeopardy if something is not done to alleviate the stress levels of teachers in this country. This is a problem for ALL of US.

Children are the future of our country and the entire world at large. If we fail to adequately prepare them for the world ahead of them by screwing up their little brains with maniac teachers gone wild from stress and lack of proper resources, we will all be affected. Even worse, if we continue to lose teachers without replacing them at the same pace, how will schools be able to function? During the Omicron wave of the COVID-19 pandemic, many schools in north Texas had to shut down for several days. This is not a shocking revelation until you understand why. Districts did not shut down schools due to concerns about spreading the virus. Instead, districts had to shut schools down because when a dozen or more teachers at a given campus called in sick because they had to quarantine for several days, the school could not operate. There were literally not enough adult humans available to safely run the school. So what happens say 5–10 years from now in August when schools don't have enough applicants to adequately staff schools? Yes, this is a problem that should concern ALL of US.

Chapter 2: Salary, Benefits, and Advancement

"Teachers have the hardest and most important jobs; they're building our nation. And we should appreciate them, respect them, and pay them well." ~Jim Hunt

"When we become a really mature, grown-up, wise society, we will put teachers at the center of the community, where they belong. We don't honor them enough, we don't pay them enough." ~Charles Kuralt

If I take the $60 from donating plasma this week and add that to the $40 I made selling off some old clothes at the consignment store, I can pay my electric bill. Nice! Now if I use the extra $400 I made this month working part-time at the American Airlines Arena to cover all my grocery expenses, I can use what remains from my regular paycheck to cover my rent...Awesome! I'll have $350 left over for the rest of my expenses. I think that'll be enough this month. Man, that was close.

This may seem like a comical scenario, but it's not a mere hyperbolic anecdote. This scene plays out in every state across the country every month for some teachers.

Many teachers struggle every month just to make ends meet. The 3 million+ full-time public school teachers in the United States are currently experiencing one of the worst wage stagnations of any profession. Adjusting for inflation, most teachers earn less than they did in 1990. The pay gap between teachers and other professions is at an all-time high, and according to the Economic Policy Institute, teachers currently earn 18.7% less per week than other comparable professions. In some states, teachers make thousands less than they did a decade ago (adjusted for inflation). In Oklahoma, teachers earn $8,000 less per year than they did 10 years ago, and in Arizona, teachers make around $5,000 less annually.

This is too much. With the ineffectiveness of teacher unions and the recent trend of stripping or restructuring teachers' pensions, most teachers no longer earn enough money to survive. especially for teachers who have advanced degrees and decades of experience. Most teachers don't go to college to work in public education for monetary reasons. But when even teachers with advanced degrees and decades of experience struggle financially—it's too much. And when you couple the financial stresses with the increasing loss of control of their classrooms and the overwhelming standardized curricula with unachievable benchmarks—it's just too much. If districts can't figure out a way to properly compensate the individuals who care for and educate our children on a daily basis, there may not be anyone left to do the job.

Salaries

Teachers are generally paid based on a rigidly defined single salary schedule typically based on nothing but years of experience. While this has the obvious effect of virtually erasing discrimination from teacher pay, this seems to be its only benefit. And while most districts do offer some type of stipend or slight increase in pay for a graduate or doctorate degree, they usually adopt a take-it-or-leave-it attitude making salaries a non-negotiable point. Additionally, it is not unusual for districts to reset a teacher's seniority if they change school districts or states. This has the effect of strong-arming teachers into sticking around when there may be greener pastures elsewhere. This practice is great for school districts because of the stability it engenders but it's not so great for the teacher who is stuck in a place they don't want to be.

The single salary schedule system comes with significant disadvantages. This rigidly defined system does not consider teacher expertise, teacher effectiveness, or even market conditions. Thus, a rock star teacher putting in 20 plus extra hours of work a week and whose students crush it academically usually makes the same salary as the yahoo across the hall who shows up to work hung over, right at the bell every day, with half of their students failing. Not a very motivating system, huh? Some positions require specialized knowledge or training, and some positions even require physical interventions that put teachers in constant physical danger. These teachers, although occasionally given a small stipend, are generally paid the same as all others. Many teachers also seek out advanced degrees to acquire better knowledge and expertise in their field. Most of these teachers are rewarded with a pitiful $1,200–$1,500 annual stipend. At that rate it takes over a decade just to make back the money a teacher has invested to get the degree, and on top of that, multiple studies have shown little to no evidence that students even benefit from teachers with advanced degrees.

The range of teacher pay in the United States is extremely vast ranging anywhere from a low of $30,000 to over $60,000 a year. According to the National Education Association, the average teacher salary in 2020–2021 was around $65,000 with an average starting salary at just over $41,000. However, data from the BLS show a median teacher salary during this time of only $51,000. Even worse, the average substitute teacher salary comes in at a measly $29,000. Teaching assistants fair even worse. They are the lowest paid instructional staff in the entire district even though they are vital assets to many classrooms, especially in the special education department. Many teaching assistants make barely $20,000 a year, causing a large portion of them to leave the field permanently. No one can survive in this country on a $20,000 salary. It's just not a reasonable expectation for anyone.

Salary variances are based mainly on two factors: region and urban or rural areas. Teachers in the Northeast and the Western coastal regions of the United States have the highest salaries, with the Midwest and deep south having the lowest. Urban teachers, not surprisingly, earn much more than teachers in rural areas across all states. These salaries generally do track with cost of living, but many times that formula doesn't always add up, especially with recent increases in inflation raging and costs of basic goods and housing soaring.

One of the biggest problems with teacher salaries is the lack of long-term increases when adjusted for inflation. Teachers get a step increase every year, but it's minimal, usually less than $1,000 annually. Every few years, the state or local district may bump up the pay scale a couple of percentage points, but overall, teachers usually never actually get a raise. When adjusted for inflation, the national average teacher salary has only increased by 0.9% in the last 10 years. That's less than a 1% raise in a decade. In addition to inflation, increases in health insurance costs tend to eat away at pay increases. Let's just say a teacher gets an $800 (per year) raise from his or her step increase. But the district health insurance plan goes up $50 a month. That $800 raise is quickly reduced to $200 after the increased cost of insurance.

So how do teachers make ends meet? Well, some don't. That's why many leave the profession for good. The nation is in a teacher crisis. Less than 900 school districts across the country have a starting salary of at least $40,000. That means over 6,000 school districts in the which employ over 800,000 teachers do not meet the $40,000 a year minimum threshold. Teachers in the United States are three times more likely than any other worker to take on a second or even a third job. A recent Pew Research study found that around a third of new teachers obtained non-school jobs over the summer, and around 20% of teachers with 2–4 years of experience had summer jobs. Further, the fact that 17% of teachers with 5–10 years of experience take on additional employment during the summer proves that even experienced higher paid teachers can't make ends meet. Overall, around 20% of teachers work a second job at some point during the school year. These secondary jobs account for almost 10% of their yearly income.

There also seems to be a rare nationwide bipartisan consensus on the issue. In a recent survey, almost 60% of respondents agreed that teachers are underpaid, and a majority of both Democrats and Republicans believe teachers have a right to strike to improve their working conditions. In some states teachers have done just that. In 2016, across the state of West Virginia, 20,000 teachers walked out forcing nearly all of the 680 schools in the state to close. After a 9-day strike, the state agreed to a 5% statewide raise. Teachers in other states such as Oklahoma, Kentucky, California, and Arizona have also recently walked out with mixed results, but state and federal lawmakers have recently begun to change their tune and criticize teachers for striking, feeding on their guilt about failing to serve their students.

Strikes and walk outs will continue as long as lawmakers do not adequately address the issue of underpaid teachers, and in the long run, it will be the students and parents who suffer because of the government's lack of leadership and competence in this matter. The mass exodus of teachers from the profession will continue forcing schools to further increase class sizes, shorten school weeks, and enact more emergency certifications, putting even more inadequately trained and unprepared teachers in the classroom. I myself got into the field of teaching via an emergency certification. I can tell you from personal experience, I was not even close to being adequately prepared for what I had to deal with in my first year, and that lack of readiness to affected me well into my career as an educator.

Is there an answer to solving the impending teacher salary crisis? How can we pay teachers better? Well, the experts have not quite figured that out yet, but there are some alternative pay structures out there. The pay-for-position model incentivizes teachers to work in higher demanding and harder to staff positions such as STEM classes, certain special education positions, as well as teaching positions in low socioeconomic areas. A pay-for-demonstrated-skills model would increase wages for a teacher who possesses a particular important skill set such as a second language or an advanced technological skill set. And in a pay-for-added-responsibilities approach, teachers would receive additional pay for taking on extra responsibilities such as mentoring, peer reviewing, or tutoring. A recent popular and debated incentive system is pay-for-performance. In this model teachers are paid based on their student's gains and learning, which would reflect test scores, grades, and other district created evaluations.

The problem with all these salary structures is that most of them have not been properly tested and the one that has, performance pay, has not yielded very positive results. Some teachers regard pay- for-performance as patronizing, as most teachers are not in the work for the money. If money was their main motivator, they would not have gone into teaching in the first place. It's been shown that incentive pay can actually interfere with intrinsic motivations, and data from the Teacher Incentive Fund has shown that merit pay can produce mistrust and conflict among colleagues. Many times it creates more of a distraction than an incentive. When an aggressive performance pay system was implemented in an experimental trial in Washington DC, the result was that mainly low-performing teachers quit the field. I'm not exactly sure we can count that as a positive result.

Nonetheless, states must figure out new and innovative ways to incentivize teachers. Salaries have simply not risen at anywhere near a reasonable rate over the last couple of decades. Moreover, what's most infuriating about this situation is that there is plenty of money to go around if districts would only choose to spend it more responsibly. Districts could simply stop wasting millions upon millions of dollars on endless amounts of poorly implemented technology, over-hyped and costly security measures, and highly paid but mostly ineffective district administrators. This money could then be spent hiring and incentivizing the most important and effective aspect of the entire educational system. Teachers.

Health Insurance

On top of these salary issues, teacher benefits are beginning to have a similar impact on the system. Complaints about higher health care premiums matched with decreasing coverage and dwindling pension systems have been key issues in the recent spate of teacher protests and walkouts. We've touched on higher insurance premiums, but more recently, teachers have been required to pitch in a higher contribution to their pensions further eating away at any increase in income. Let's first take a look at health care.

Health care and health insurance have become increasingly hot topics, even more so since the COVID-19 pandemic. We seem to be engaged in a never-ending debate over whether health care is a privilege or a right. Regardless, the fact is that 99% of teachers have access to some kind of health insurance or plan. Comparably, only around two-thirds of private sector employees have access to any type of health care. This would seem like a huge benefit for teachers at first, but just because you have something, doesn't necessarily mean it's good.

There are definitely some advantages to teacher insurance benefits. Teachers generally do have a few different health care plans from which to choose, and most school districts do contribute varying amounts on teachers' behalf. Teachers generally are offered dental and vision plans, and from my experience those plans are usually pretty reasonably priced and offer good value. A large array of other benefits is also offered such as disability and cancer insurance, supplemental legal protection, and life insurance. However, these additional benefits are usually only taken advantage of by a small subset of teachers. And give the high premiums, there's not much money left over for many teachers to cover those additional benefits even if they may need them.

Despite the handful of advantages teacher insurance benefits offer, the costs of basic health care have skyrocketed over the last couple of decades. I'll use myself as an example. When I started teaching in 2001, my monthly contribution to my health insurance plan was $0. That's right. I said zero dollars. That's a damn good deal. I certainly thought so at the time. At the start of my second year of teaching, my monthly contribution went up to $30. Okay, that's still a great deal...even though my rate was 30 times higher than the previous year. Then my third year of teaching came around, and my monthly payment rose to $60 doubling from the previous year. By the time I was five to seven years into teaching, I was paying over $200 a month. That is utter madness. Again, it's too much.

Although prices have leveled off a bit as of late, most teachers still have to pay between $250–$300 a month for a decent health care plan with a reasonable deductible. I now opt for the lowest plan with the highest deductible, which still costs me around $200 a month. I only go to the doctor once or twice a year generally, and I don't take any expensive life sustaining pharmaceuticals. For someone who frequents doctors' offices and is on a litany of drugs, however, the plan I'm on probably isn't going to cut it. That person would need to pay significantly more, and if they have a family, their monthly costs are going to be in the high hundreds, if not over $1,000 a month. I have actually met some teachers who only work for their health insurance. When a fourth to even a third of a teacher's take home pay is eaten up by health care premiums, the fact that 99% are offered some type of health insurance seems like a bit of a nonfactor.

In addition to all of these costs, the coverage is generally not even very good or even adequate for some, especially if one opts for the more reasonably priced plan like myself. I played college basketball and still deal with pains and injuries to this very day. Sometimes when a part of my body flares up, there's only one way to determine what's wrong: Imaging. X-rays, MRIs, and CAT scans have become outrageously expensive. I mean, it's just a picture. I had a flare up in my knee a few years ago, and I needed to get an MRI. If I had gone through my insurance, because I had not met my deductible, it would have cost me nearly $1,200. That's $1,200 dollars for a 20-minute shot of a leg joint. You may think that is insane, and you are absolutely correct. However, the most insane part of the story is yet to come...I lied. I told the imaging office I didn't have insurance and I wanted to pay with my credit card. They quoted me $350. So, if I use my insurance plan which I'm already paying a couple hundred dollars a month for, it costs me $1,200 dollars for a 20-minute MRI. If I just walk in the office with a credit card, it costs me $350 dollars. That is utter madness.

Studies and surveys vary when it comes to determining exactly how much of a disadvantage teachers have when it comes to health insurance, but the consensus seems to be that teacher health care costs are at least slightly higher across the board compared to private sector employees. Data from the Bureau of Labor Statistics (BLS) showed that the gap between teacher costs and private sector costs for insurance rose from 12% in 2004 to more than 20% in 2012. Looking at the data from 2004–2012, annual employee costs in 2012 for teachers were $8,559 compared to $6,803 for private sector employees. One might argue these are old and outdated statistics, but things have not significantly improved.

Insurance costs have continued to soar for teachers, and it's beginning to look like more of a top down problem. Local school districts depend on funding from the federal government to cover many of their costs. In the last decade, that stream of revenue has begun to drastically shrink. Federal funding to public schools has dropped by nearly 20% according 2018 data from the NEA. This has resulted in state and local governments spending 14.5% more to cover their portion of employee insurance plans. Like most situations, the burden of these bureaucratic budgetary conundrums falls on teachers. From 2008 to 2018 teacher contributions to insurance plans have increased by more than 25%, and the average annual cost for a basic family plan by 2018 was over $7,000. These increases in insurance costs directly cut into the measly salary increases teachers get each year. The majority of teachers are lucky to get a 1% yearly raise while insurance costs, on the other hand, increase an average of 2.5% a year. One can easily see how this type of system is not sustainable.

So what's the solution to all of this? We could try to convince insurance companies to offer more reasonable premiums and better coverage. I'll wait a bit while the laughter subsides... We could perhaps convince the federal government to spend less on proxy wars and filling big business pocket books, and instead decide to support the foundational systems that are the backbone of this country. Sorry, that was only a bit of sarcasm. We all know the odds of that happening. We could attempt to persuade local or state governments to increase their share of the costs, but if the coffers are bare, that would be a futile effort as well.

Unionization has proven to be one avenue to success. Nationwide unionization is directly correlated with lower insurance costs, but this holds true for teachers as well as private sector employees. In addition, unions come with an entirely new set of issues, that we'll delve into in a later chapter. Unfortunately, there aren't many answers to this situation. The only obvious path to improvement is more efficiency and more options for employees. One step in that direction would be for districts to offer insurance plans from a wider array of companies. Teachers generally only have three to five plans from which to choose, and all of those plans are with the same insurance company. What's more, many states and districts lock in long-term contracts with certain insurance companies in the process becoming beholden to the whims of that company. Perhaps there is a way to offer teachers plans from multiple competing insurance companies. Wait. Does that sound like an actual free market? This would lead to greater variance in costs with lower subsidies, thus lower costs for teachers. More options are almost always better for everyone. Why do I have 150 different cereals from which to choose at the grocery store, and I have three options for my health insurance? Nothing but utter madness.

Pensions

Teachers' salaries have definitely not increased by a reasonable amount compared to other professions. However, teachers get amazing retirement options through their state pensions, so that makes up for all the salary and health care issues, right? Well, not exactly. Currently, around 90% of public school teachers are enrolled in a pension plan. However, some of these plans do not live up to expectations and have become fraught with problems, resulting in serious concerns about their *guaranteed* future. Thus, many states have begun to rewrite their pension formulas, and some teachers are getting the short end of the stick. Let's first take a brief look at the history of pensions in the United States.

There are basically two types of retirement plans offered by employers: defined benefit, or defined contribution plans. With a defined benefit plan, workers know exactly how much they will get in retirement. They will receive a defined dollar amount based on some type of formula, usually involving salary and years of service. In these plans, the organization or employer is generally responsible for managing the plan and contributes a significant amount to the employees' pension fund. In a defined contribution plan, however, the employee makes most of the contributions and controls the investments and management of the retirement plan themselves. There is no way to determine exactly how much money an employee will get with a defined contribution plan, and an employer may or may not match the employee's investment in this type of plan. Defined contribution plans, such as 401Ks, 403bs,

457s, or Thrift Savings Plans, are usually much more vulnerable to volatile market swings. If the employee has little to no investment knowledge, it may be very overwhelming to self-manage a plan like this. So for a variety of reasons, a defined-benefit plan is often the most beneficial type of plan to secure an adequate retirement package, and this is the type of retirement plan nearly all public school teachers are given.

Pensions have been offered in the United States as far back as the Revolutionary War but were designed mostly for veterans. In fact, many early plans were funded by charitable institutions such as church communities. In 1832 the U.S. Bureau of Pensions was established; it was eventually taken over by the Department of the Interior. By the latter part of the 1800s, pensions had begun to expand beyond veterans. In 1857 the city of New York set up a pension system for injured and disabled police officers, and the American Express Company created the first corporate pension program in 1875. By the turn of the century, pension programs began to take off, with railroad companies and banks leading the charge.

As the nation moved into the 20th century, defined-benefit pension plans began to explode. Companies from Standard Oil to AT&T to General Electric began to offer pension plans to their employees. With the spread of labor unions in the 1940s and 1950s, pensions became the norm. By 1950, 25% of private-sector employees had a pension, and by 1960, that number doubled to 50%. However, around this time, some pension programs began to feel the financial strain, and some even began to fail. The government stepped in creating the Employee Retirement Income Security Act (ERISA) and the Pension Benefit Guarantee Corporation to ensure payment of failing pension plans. As the 20th century came to a close, government regulations continued to increase in an effort to protect what seemed to be an epidemic of failing pensions across the country. From 1980 to 2000, private companies began a major shift away from pension plans, instead opting for more defined contribution-type plans such as 401Ks and 403b plans. Today, less than 10% of private sector employees are offered any type of pension package. Thus, defined-benefit pension plans have become one of, and sometimes the only, golden goose of government employment.

What's the problem then? It still sounds like teachers are getting a great deal. However, like many topics in education, once you begin to dig a little deeper, the problems surface. For starters, teacher pension plans make up the largest share of unfunded liabilities, accounting for around half of all pension debt in the United States. Teacher pension plans are also generally funded less than pensions for police or firefighters, and there is an extremely wide variation in the funding of teacher pensions from state to another. What's more, average annual benefits for new retirees vary from as low as $17,000 a year in Idaho to as high as $63,000 a year in the District of Columbia. That's nearly a fourfold difference.

Thus, many teacher pension plans are quite modest, depending on the state in which a teacher lives. In addition to that, there has been a slight decline in states offering teacher pensions. Although around 90% of teachers receive a pension plan today, that figure was closer to 95% only a decade ago. These pension plans also don't necessarily guarantee a pension to all teachers either. States have employed rules called vesting requirements which require teachers to stay in the profession for a minimum number of years before qualifying for a pension.

Most states require teachers to serve at least 5 years before qualifying for a pension, but nearly a third require teachers to serve 10 years before they can qualify. Often, even after qualifying, some teachers opt to cash out their fund for a variety of personal or financial reasons. And, with the extremely high early-career turnover rate in public education, nearly half of all new teachers will never qualify for a pension—at all. Further, pensions are always attached to the state in which a teacher works, so if a teacher moves across state lines for whatever reason, they must start the process all over again in a new state. This results in a situation where geographic mobility cannot really exist in the field. In addition to these issues, not all teachers are covered by Social Security. About 40% of public school teachers concentrated in 15 states pay no money into Social Security, meaning they will not receive any Social Security money or benefits during their retirement and will be solely dependent on their teacher pensions.

Teacher pensions come with a high price tag for the state as well, and they are also extremely backloaded. This means workers earn a very meager retirement for the first 20 years of service and rapidly accrue much more valuable benefits as they approach the end of their careers and move toward retirement age. I'll use myself as an example. Where I work in the state of Texas, my pension is based on the average of my five highest annual salaries. This would almost always mean the last 5 years of employment are the most valuable because one would generally be making the most money at the end of one's career. So I could have an average annual salary of around $60,000 a year for 20 plus years, but if I get a promotion that bumps my salary up to $80,000 a year, and I work at the position for the last 5 years of my career, my entire pension amount would be based solely on those last 5 years.

Teacher pension plans have increasingly become more expensive for states to operate, and returns have continued to go down. Many states invest heavily in Treasury bonds which are generally very secure investments that can produce moderate yields. However, these bond rates have been decimated recently. A 30-year Treasury bond yielded around 7–8% in the 1990s. Today that same 30-year Treasury bond only yields around 2–4%. That's a significant difference in return, and when states fail to reach their investment targets, the additional costs involved most often trickle down to teachers leading to lower take-home pay and a slowdown in teacher hiring, which leads to larger class sizes. Rising pension costs also result in declines in spending on supplies, new facilities, and technology for schools. In the end, it's the students who wind up suffering the most.

Public pension reform is a hot topic these days on many city and state agendas. Policy makers need to think about alternative options to the current model. A more modernized teacher pension system could move away from the current backloaded system which has created a situation where teachers who leave the field early in their career subsidize those who stick through the long haul and make it to retirement age. One suggestion is to move toward what's called a cash-balance-defined-benefit plan. Under this type of plan, the value of a teacher's retirement benefits would be equal their annual contributions in addition to guaranteed earnings paid out in the form of a lifetime annuity, thus allowing teachers to accrue retirement benefits at a smoother rate throughout their careers. This plan would basically let teachers earn their retirement based on a constant percentage of their salary as opposed to a percentage of their final average salary. It has been predicted that this type of plan would be cost-neutral to taxpayers, not cut into the amount of teachers' retirement pay, and allow higher benefits for teachers who leave the field before retirement age or relocate across state lines.

Whether this or another type of system will help improve the situation is unknown. However, something must be done to adapt to the changing world in which we live to ensure the future well-being of teachers and, in turn, ensure the well-being of those young lives who will shape our future.

Advancement and Incentives

The most glaring aspect of career advancement for teachers is the clear lack of career advancement. In the corporate world, military service, and various other types of government employment, there is generally a clear upward mobility path. Even creative fields and freelance gigs allow individuals to move up into higher-stakes positions with greater opportunities. The education sector, however, lacks any clear path for promotion. Teachers remain teachers. The limited advancement opportunities teachers do have tend to come with an insufficient pay raise, an increased bureaucratic mire to navigate, endless [useless] meetings, and many times, involve travel and other expenses as well as time-devouring advanced degrees and research.

Yet, after several years of teaching, many teachers find themselves yearning for more. Some pursue advancement opportunities strictly for higher compensation, and there are several positions that do offer such an opportunity. But those opportunities come with many added responsibilities and a significant increase in work hours. Other teachers may need a change of pace and seek out more challenging responsibilities, while others may just be looking for a bit of personal development to refine their craft. Some teachers may only be looking for a bit more satisfaction from their work and are seeking new roles to contribute to the system in different ways. So let's take a look and travel down a few of the limited paths teachers have available to move up the educational ladder.

One of the most common routes of advancement for teachers is campus administration. Teachers opting for this route would start out as an assistant principal and eventually hope to move up to the position of principal, thus gaining control of an entire school. However, this process requires a graduate degree, certification as an administrator, a minimum number of years teaching in the classroom, and navigating the painful bureaucracy and politics involved in getting a foot in the door. This process is very rigorous, time-consuming, and costly. School administrators do exactly that. They administrate. They must create school policy, handle public relations, push to meet educational goals, deal with increasing discipline problems, and perform all the other administrative duties such as record keeping, hiring, evaluating teachers, and budgeting.

This route can be quite lucrative if one is willing to handle the heat. The average salary range for public school administrators is fairly wide at $72,000–$91,000 a year. Some districts start at a bit less, and some principals can even earn over $100,000 annually depending on their years of service. It's not an easy gig though, and it often takes many years to work up to the point where the money starts to flow. Depending on the district, a starting assistant principal generally gets only about a 20–25% pay raise compared to a teacher. This may seem like a lot, but the number of contract days required to work, and the number of hours needed to fulfil the obligations of the job, significantly increase. Assistant administrators work well into the summer and are required to return to work several weeks before school starts. Furthermore, most school principals don't even get a summer break, unless they use vacation time. There's summer school to deal with, new teachers to be hired, summer trainings to attend or conduct, and a litany of other summertime obligations. They also work many hours before and after school and on weekends. Breaking down their earnings by hour, some administrators find they really aren't making much more than they did as a teacher. These positions are also extremely political in nature in most districts, and when they consider having to traverse the bureaucratic labyrinth in combination with the high stress and workload, most teachers opt out of this path.

Some teachers may seek other paths out of the classroom that aren't as lucrative as the administration route but allow a teacher a bit more freedom and the ability to work with kids in a setting other than the classroom. The majority of school librarians used to be teachers. This path does require a degree or at least some type of training in library science, depending on the school district. School librarians take care of the school library, but they also deal with technology and other informational resources, as well as work with individual classrooms during their weekly library time. At an extremely wide salary range of $36,000–$68,000, librarians generally make about the same as teachers or just slightly more depending on the district, so this is not a path to financial freedom. Librarians do, however, get to work with students in a different environment and don't have to deal with the same stressors as a classroom teacher.

Another path is counseling. With the increased amount of social, mental, and behavioral issues bombarding classrooms recently (much more on this later), schools have begun to hire counselors in droves. Counselors would, of course, need to acquire the appropriate degree and certifications as well as the required intern hours, which is time time-consuming and expensive. Counselors also take on quite a bit of responsibility, such as advising and talking to students about all types of personal issues, handling school behavior and social needs, teaching lessons to classrooms on various social and emotional issues, and a variety of other administrative duties assigned by the school.

There are also multiple types of counselors. Guidance counselors deal with all the duties described above but generally also deal with academic and administrative issues. Many districts are also beginning to hire teams of crisis counselors to deal with the therapeutic side and work with the increasing number of students experiencing trauma and severe emotional issues. There are also counselors who deal solely with academics, helping students graduate and determine their next steps after high school. These can be very rewarding jobs, but they do come with the mental stress of having to take on the problems of an entire campus. These jobs are also not very financially rewarding. The average salary range for a school counselor is $50,000–$63,000 a year, with a median annual salary of $56,000. So counselors mak about the same or slightly more than a teacher. Therefore, this is also not a path to financial freedom but instead, a path to get out of the classroom and help students and teachers in different and unique ways.

Yet another route teachers may take is to become a department head. This path is for teachers who have a strong command of their subject material and exhibit leadership qualities. Teachers in this role usually still teach in the classroom, but they may teach fewer classes in lieu of extra duties. This job comes with many roles such as coaching and mentoring to assessing and managing other teachers. These roles generally do not require any advanced degrees or certifications; however, this position does not come with much of a financial incentive. Department heads usually receive some type of insignificant annual stipend—some are only a few hundred dollars a year. Even higher paying districts generally only offer $1,200–$1,500 for this role. This is still a decent route for teachers to choose if they want to take on a few more responsibilities and create a better reputation for themselves in their district while earning a little more cash. At the end of the day though, they are still a teacher. This is a good stepping stone to perhaps a more advanced position in administration or in a specialist area, but I wouldn't consider it a major career advancement.

Another route for advancement that has become increasingly popular is as a specialist. The field of specialists in education has been a rapidly growing area of opportunity for teachers. There is an extremely wide range of roles specialists can serve in all areas from reading, math, and data analysis to technology, behavior, and other types of curricula. There are even more specified roles that focus on treating students with dyslexia, autism, speech problems, and the myriad of other issues students may face today. Specialists work with individual students, groups, and even teachers and administrators. Many teachers find that these jobs are a great way to get out of the classroom without having to invest a whole lot of time and money into training. Some of these positions do require a graduate degree, but not all of them. These positions also offer some room for significant financial gains. The salary range for specialists is $56,000–488,000 a year, with an average annual salary of $67,000. So teachers can acquire a decent bump in pay, making close to what many assistant principals make with fewer work hours, much less stress, and far fewer bureaucratic hurdles. However, these positions are generally highly sought after, and having connections in the right places definitely helps increase a teacher's chances of nabbing one.

These specialist positions can also be stepping stones to move up into district-level administration, where the lucky ones can finally reach the summit, finding themselves residing in an office located atop the *castle on the hill*. There are a multitude of high-level specialist and administrative positions at the district level that offer a wide range of salaries and require an even wider range of skill sets and experience. Many campus administrators, as well as specialists, qualify for these highly sought-after positions, yet only a select few make it to these elite roles, which many times pay close to or even over $100,000 a year. Although the number of these positions has increased exponentially in the last couple of decades, this is not a path most teachers have an opportunity to take, so I won't delve much into it.

Several of these district-level administrators and specialists do work hard and can make a big difference in many areas of public education. However, many others fit the archetype of the typical government employee who attends Zoom meetings, sends tons of emails, and does various trainings here and there while making copious amounts of money. More bureaucracy nearly always requires more administrators to keep the bureaucratic beast alive, and public schools are currently being eaten alive by this bureaucratic behemoth. The majority of these positions are also highly politicized, and one would need to have good connections and a very good reputation in the district to pursue them. They come with quite a bit of prestige, financial gains, and job security. However, these positions and their unprecedented growth are responsible for many of the financial woes districts currently face due to the massive amount of educational funds that must be siphoned away from school coffers to cover their ballooning salaries. We will discuss this topic in much more detail.

So that's pretty much it. As one can see, the best route for a teacher to achieve monetary gains is most likely the administrator route. However, this path requires extensive training with advanced degrees and certifications which can be very costly and time consuming. Additionally, this path is fraught with endless work hours, stress, and a level of bureaucracy that would make the finest government agent cringe. Therefore, it appears the best overall path of advancement for most teachers may be the specialist route. This offers opportunities for teachers to make some fairly significant financial gains and at the same time allows them to get out of the daily drudge of the classroom and help students and staff in different, and many times, creative ways.

There is, however, one last path to advancement we haven't yet mentioned, and it's one many teachers unfortunately find themselves considering more and more as of late. Leaving the profession. Teachers bring a wide range of skill sets to the private sector that many employers seek. Teachers generally have zero trouble finding work outside of education. I've tried this myself multiple times. I've left teaching to try my hand at insurance, finance, and most recently a failed business venture. They were all busts, but I learned something from each experience and was able to get right back into education which is one advantage of the field. If a teacher does quit, it's very easy to get back into the field given the massive teacher shortages across many states. This brings us to a conundrum that we'll discuss much more thoroughly throughout our journey. Many teachers find the only way to adequately provide for themselves and their families and gain the financial security they're looking for is to leave the profession and move into higher-paying, higher-opportunity positions in the private sector. This obviously adds to the current nationwide teacher shortage, and like almost every other topic we discuss, it's the students who will suffer in the end.

Chapter 3: Money in Education

"The amount of money we spend on education is important, but not nearly as important as how the money is spent." ~Bob Riley

"Education costs money, but then so does ignorance." ~Sir Claus Moser

Money, money, money. The world revolves around it. We all need it. We all want more of it. And schools cannot function without it. With rising taxes, out of control inflation, and the recent debate about school choice, money in education, although always a hot topic, has become an increasingly relevant and fiercely debated issue. In the 2018–2019 school year, spending for public K–12 education in the United States totaled over $750 billion, which comes out to well over $15,000 per student. That's a lot of money… and unfortunately a large percentage of it is not well spent. Public school funding is fraught with many problems. So let's take a deep look into the financial world of education. I know fiscal discussions can become quite confusing and a bit boring, but I promise I will try to make the journey as painless as possible. Let's start with an overview of exactly how public schools are funded.

Public School Funding 101

Funding for public schools comes from three sources: federal, state, and local government. Based on the most recent data from the U.S. Census Bureau, the percentages of funding are:

State	47%
Local	45%
Federal	8%

State funding originates from sales and income taxes while local funding primarily comes from property taxes. The percentage of money that comes from the state and local government can vary slightly depending on the state funding formula, revenue sources, and distribution of funds.

Local school funding revenue is generated from a combination of property taxes, sales tax, and income tax, with property tax accounting for the largest percentage of the pot. But what exactly is property tax? Property tax is basically a tariff paid by the owner of a property which is based on the assessed value assigned to that property by a governing authority. This tax is assessed primarily on residences and businesses but can include vehicles and other forms of property depending on the state. Public or government-owned buildings, as well as religious or charity-based institutes, are generally exempt from property taxes, and certain businesses are given tax abatements. Many cities offer these tax abatements to various companies in order to generate new business and employment opportunities. As a reward, these entities will go untaxed for a specified number of years or even decades, which can cause some obvious problems further down the road.

Property taxes are not a new concept and can be traced back to the 11th-century feudal system when William the Conqueror divided up England after his Norman conquest. Property taxes were also used by the Puritans in Massachusetts to fund public schools as far back as the 1640s. This type of system worked very well in the colonial period and created much equality in schools throughout the colonies for the children who attended (keep in mind this would have only included White children at that time). This began to change in the latter part of the 19th century as more and more immigrants started to pour into the United States, and, in turn, massive inequality in public schooling began to bear its ugly teeth.

In 1980, property taxes made up almost 70% of school funding, but as the United States became more and more urban and industrial, demographics shifted, and regional inequality soon led to school inequality. As the nation moved into the 20th century, states began to provide grants to fill in these funding gaps, and following the end of WWII, the federal government began to take a more active role in funding due to the massive exodus of higher-income, generally White families moving out of cities into the newly fashioned world of suburbia. This mass exodus caused property values in cities to plummet, massively decreasing the funding available for inner-city schools.

Currently, although the numbers vary, state and local governments contribute relatively equal proportions of money to fund public schools. State governments use formulas that are complex, politicized, and too generalized to meet specific district needs. States must forecast how much money a local district will generate based on these formulas. However, if the state's calculations are off, and many times they are, the state may not be able to adequately fill the funding gaps for a particular district.

After the state determines its formula-based budget, each local government body completes and approves its school district's budget. Then, school district governing bodies, sometimes referred to as local education agencies (LEAs), manage [allocate] the state and local funds they receive. School districts create budgets detailing where all the money goes (such as central office, schools, facilities, capital projects, etc.). These local district budgets must be approved by a school board or district council, and LEAs allocate funds accordingly. This can all be a bit confusing, so let's break it down in simpler terms:

1. State and local funds are collected and combined in the treasury.

2. States use combined funds to create and approve the projected state budget.

3. States allocate those funds through local government bodies to each local school district or LEA.

4. Local districts or LEA's divide the money between schools within the district based on their approved budgets.

5. Funds are then used for salaries, supplies, materials, and services.

But where exactly does the federal government fit into all of this? The federal government supports K–12 public education through specified grant programs. These programs include Title 1 grants under the Elementary and Secondary Education Act (ESEA) and Part B grants under the Individuals with Disabilities Act (IDEA). Federal funds accounted for nearly $60 billion of educational funding based on 2019 data. Title 1 grants provide funding to LEAs with high percentages of low-income students; these grants made up the largest grant program involving ESEA at just over $14 billion in 2019. These funds are allocated through formulas based on the number of eligible students as well as various other provisions. Part B grants, which totaled almost $12 billion in 2019, are awarded based on the total population with disabilities between the ages of 3–21 and the percentage of individuals living in poverty.

The federal government also provides a massive allocation of funds for child nutrition. This amount totaled $16.6 billion in 2019 and was used mostly to reimburse the thousands upon thousands of free or reduced-price lunches and breakfasts schools offer throughout the year. Another set of funds, about $4.7 billion in 2019, go directly to particular LEAs for a multitude of programs such as magnet schools, dropout assistance programs, gifted and talented programs, and many others. The federal government also provided over half a billion dollars for vocational programs in 2019 and an additional $10.1 billion on various programs for which reporting units could not provide details.

This basic but reasonably thorough trip through the world of public school finance provided a very rudimentary glimpse into how the process generally works. The rest of the chapter digs deeper into exactly how this process translates into the day to day operation of schools. We'll also delve into the litany of problems associated with the system.

Bonds, Title 1, and Other Financial Hogwash

We've all seen the signs posted around town: "Vote for New Bond Package!" But does anyone really know what that means? From where do these funds originate? Does the government pay for that? It may seem confusing, but the school bond business is not really so complicated once its secrets are revealed. The majority of folks are, no doubt, familiar with the concept of a mortgage. School bonds function fairly similar to a typical home mortgage. Basically, school bonds serve as promissory notes. Bonds are, in a sense, loans paid to companies or institutes by investors. In return, the company or institute pays the investor interest over a specified period of time. When that specified time period ends, the full amount of the initial money invested, or the principal, is returned to the investor. When it comes to school bonds, the school district borrows money to purchase large capital assets or to make renovations and/or repairs that would normally not be covered under their district budget. The district will then pay investors interest over the course of a specified number of years out of future tax revenues. At the end of the bond term, the district will return the initial principal back to the investors, completing the cycle.

School bonds start at the voting booth. The state government grants authority to a board of trustees to sell bonds and conduct bond elections. During the initial phase, a volunteer citizen committee creates the details of the bond package and presents it to the board of trustees for approval. If voters approve the bond, the district can begin selling bonds to investors. Although the term of a school bond can vary, the maximum term limit is 40 years. School bonds are an attractive investment; they almost always have a very high rating because they are most often guaranteed by the government. School bonds are sold for a specific amount of money, usually in the tens of millions. The funds are generally earmarked for certain goods and projects and can, except for rare circumstances, be used only for those specified goods and projects. Bonds have recently been used to purchase large swaths of technology for schools as well as build state-of-the-art athletic, fine arts, and other learning facilities.

This system can sometimes be highly beneficial—all the money stays in the district and is not eligible for state recapture. Bonds can also allow the district to spread out expensive projects without negatively affecting normal district budgets and operations. Bonds can be used to purchase resources and upgrade facilities, which can have a very positive impact on students, improving their learning as well as enriching their overall school experience. School bonds can benefit investors as well. Because of their high ratings, school bonds also yield high returns for investors. They also offer a distinctive advantage to investors because school bonds are exempt from federal taxation and, many times, state taxation as well. This is a great way for investors to avoid the dreaded capital gains tax.

This system is far from perfect, though, and it does come with some major disadvantages. Citizens will most likely pay back the bonds through an increase in property taxes. It is generally a slow increase spread out over time, but it is an increase nonetheless. Investors should be aware, too. Although school bonds come with a high rating, repayment is not a guarantee. If the population of a city drastically decreases or some other situation results in a major decline in property tax revenues, a school district could default on its bonds. This happened in Detroit in 2014 when the city was forced to default on several of its outstanding bonds. When a default happens, investors generally only get back a small portion of their initial investment if anything.

Another problem is waste. I've personally witnessed a massive accumulation of iPads, chrome books, SMART boards, and other such technology. Many of these items never get used, or are used only for a short period of time before they disappear into some storage closet or back shelf. In one of my recent offices, at least $10,000 worth of technology from a previous defunct program remained stacked waist high in closets and on shelves. I've seen state-of-the-art facilities that in my opinion are a bit much. Does a first-grade pod in a school need to resemble a

Google office? Do eighth graders really need a state-of-the-art athletic facility, and do high school footballers need an indoor, as well as an outdoor, practice facility?

So, although school bonds can and do provide valuable resources to schools, a significant portion of the money often seems to be spent in a haphazard manner. Wasted money is a major problem in government as a whole, and it's a big problem in education. Many times, bond packages force school districts to spend money on items and projects that are not *high-need.* For one, bond packages cannot be used to fund staff salaries, which is the biggest overall need, and the largest annual expenditure, for schools across the nation. Thus, if bonds cannot be used to address massive staff shortages which are one of, if not the most, pressing issues public schools face today, then what's the point? Citizens want their hard-earned money to be well spent, and bond packages quite often fall short of that goal. In order for bond packages to have the meaningful impact they were designed to have, rules and regulations must be amended to ensure bond funds are spent effectively.

Many people have also heard the term Title 1 discussed frequently, yet even most educators don't fully understanding exactly what Title I entails. For starters, it is one of the largest and oldest federally funded programs in the United States, dating back to 1965 under ESEA. This program's goal is to close the achievement gap between lower income students and their higher income peers. According to the Department of Education, the official purpose of Title 1 "is to ensure that all children have a fair, equal, and significant opportunity to obtain a high-quality education and reach, at minimum, proficiency on challenging state academic achievement and state academic assessments." This bill has been rewritten and renamed several times, but the core of the original program remains intact.

The program works by providing additional federal funding, via grants, to state and local educational agencies. Federal funds are allocated based on four different formulas, and like most government drivel, they are extremely complicated. The formulas are primarily based on census poverty data as well as the education costs in the state. These four formulas are as follows:

1. Basic Grants

These account for the largest component at around $6.4 billion (2015). This grant allocates money based on the number of low-income students served. A district can qualify if it has at least 10 low-income students and 2% of students live at the poverty level. This can sometimes qualify virtually all schools.

2. Concentration Grants

These account for the smallest component at around $1.3 billion(2015). This grant allocates money based on the concentration of low-income students. A district can qualify if it has at least 15% of students in the low-income bracket or 6,500 children of low income.

3. Targeted Grants

These grants account for around $3.3 billion (2015) and are allocated as a district's poverty rate increases. These grants are targeted to schools that most often have the highest numbers of formula eligible children.

4. Education Finance Incentive Grants

These grants come in at $3.3 billion (2015). These are allocated to provide additional funding at an amount compared to the relative wealth of the state and uses spending among other districts in the state to derive a dollar amount.

Still confused? Good, so am I and everyone else who attempts to understand these formulas. Fully understanding how the U.S. government organizes and distributes money is a task that would challenge even the wisest, most seasoned mathematician. Just know that once a dollar amount is derived from these formulas, the money is then sent to an LEA or school district, who then determines how those funds will be distributed to schools throughout the district, which varies based on the demographics of each school within that district. Schools in which low-income students make up at least 40% of enrollment (the number of students who receive free or reduced lunch), are eligible to operate school-wide programs with their Title 1 funds. Other funds may go to more targeted assistance programs to serve struggling students. But take note of the fact that even private schools within the district are eligible for a piece of the pie if they qualify under federal guidelines.

Title 1 money, however, comes with caveats. When a district receives Title 1 money, it becomes subservient to the U.S. Department of Education. The feds can use this Title 1 money as a carrot, encouraging school districts to keep running in circles. Many districts are at the federal government's mercy and must enact often unwanted reforms to keep that government cheese rolling in. For example, many states are required to accept rigorous assessment systems for students, schools, and teachers or risk getting their funding cut. States are often required to adopt "challenging state academic standards" and even set statewide systems of accountability based on federal whims. So this money, like everything in life, does not come for free. Many districts find themselves beholden to the federal government for these funds. When a system is created that becomes dependent on federal funds to adequately operate, problems begin to multiply.

The main question though is whether Title 1 funding is really that effective? Much of the evidence has shown that, in fact, it is not. A significant portion of the money, as high as over 80% in some schools, is used for teacher development and training. Many teachers find little to no value in these programs and trainings which have proven to be ineffective at increasing student achievement. I myself have sat through countless, useless trainings throughout my career that were a waste of time and money. Many times, districts pay guest speakers thousands of dollars to come conduct a training session over the course of day or two. Sadly, when it's over, the recycle bins just outside the professional development center are filled to overflowing with the speaker's PowerPoint handouts.

Title 1 funds are spent in ways other than instruction and trainings, but these have also not exhibited much success in improving student performance. Some funds are earmarked for after-school and summer programs, technology purchases, and other supplemental services. I have worked in multiple after-school and summer programs, and I can attest they result in minimal improvement in student outcomes. These summer school programs mostly consisted of babysitting struggling students for 3 weeks so we could pass them along to the next grade with the same unresolved academic and behavioral issues they've had since kindergarten. World wars could be funded with all the laptops, Chromebooks, iPads, SMART boards, and other cast aside technological items. And what exactly are supplemental services? Title 1 funds, like a large percentage of funds from bond packages, often find their way into programs and products that are simply a waste of taxpayer money.

In a paper published by the GMU School of Public Policy, researchers looked at data from 1966 to 2013 and found little evidence that Title 1 funding had significantly closed any achievement gaps nationwide. That's almost half a century with next to zero positive results. What about studies that did show mild gains? Those gains were only around .1 standard deviations or less—don't miss the decimal point. That's one-tenth of a standard deviation. Considering the program costs around $15 billion a year, we have to ask, are those modest gains worth the price? Perhaps a larger portion of this money should go to research into factors that actually help disadvantaged students, because the typical mentality of 'let's throw endless amounts of money at the problem' that the U.S. government loves to deploy, once again does not work. A more clearly defined program with metrics for success and better guidance about effective programming would be a move in the right direction. Research, research, research. Money can fix problems, but not if there is no plan in place to direct how that money is spent. We do need money to fix this broken system, but we also need intelligent, informed people spending our hard-earned tax dollars in a highly directed and responsible manner.

On the Precipice: The Future of School Sports

The first official football game took place between Rutgers and Princeton University in 1869, intricately linking education and sports. With baseball already having locked in the pleasant spring and summer weather, football became the fall sport. High school football has now become a legendary institute in the United States, with many school districts bringing thousands of fans to multi-million-dollar stadiums. Over the last century and a half, the United States has created a culture of sports. Around 8 million high school students participate in some type of sport in the United States, and 3 million are girls. However, with ever-decreasing school budgets, some districts are having to look to their athletic departments for cuts.

So, what's the scoop on sports in U.S. schools? Do they provide any benefit to students? Multiple studies have shown that students who participate in sports are much more likely to attend college and earn higher wages than their non-sporting peers. Sports have been shown to increase leadership skills as well as self-esteem in students. Some school districts spend hundreds of thousands to even millions of dollars a year on high school sports alone, while in most other nations, sports don't even occupy a single line on the budget. Unfortunately, the discrepancy in state and district spending is so great across the nation that it's nearly impossible to find a trend other than that the money earmarked for sports is running out. If districts can't find a way to fill in these gaps, the endearing sports culture the United States has created may find itself, not unlike the Cretaceous beasts of the past, facing extinction.

School sports, like seemingly everything else around us, are becoming more and more all about money. We've seen this in professional sports, with players, owners, and investors waging war against each other for a bigger piece of the pie. Some of the money players make now is difficult for the average person to even comprehend, especially when it's being earned for playing with a ball. Moreover, it seems as if the financial aspect of the sports industry has sucked the fun and tradition right out of most of the games we used to love to play as children, and these monetary issues have trickled down to the school level.

School districts are increasingly in the race to compete against other school districts for the most state-of-the-art facilities and the most respectable and successful athletic programs. This type of success can be lucrative for a school district. High school sports can bring in money through ticket sales, concessions, and corporate sponsorships, sometimes earning enough to fund other programs. For example, New Balance paid $500,000 to a school district in Massachusetts recently to refurbish its football stadium. Of course, the New Balance logo will be plastered from endzone to endzone, but that's the deal that schools must now make. Some states, such as New York and California, have even signed broadcasting deals with local or regional networks for hundreds of thousands to millions of dollars. Yep, there are actually people out there who watch high school football at home on their couch.

These strategies won't work for most school districts, though. The naming rights and broadcasting game are only optimal means of generating money for a select few locales in the country—they are not the norm. For the majority of states, the money is going to have to come from elsewhere, and many districts are now turning to parents. Today the average parent already spends $670–$1,000 per year per student on sports outside the school environment. This includes uniforms, coaching costs, registration fees, lessons, etc. In addition, many schools now ask parents to pay fees for uniforms and equipment because of shortfalls in their athletic budgets. However, districts will have to waive these fees for parents who can't afford them, so this is not going to solve the issue.

If there isn't enough money coming in via the state, local, and federal government to support these sports programs, districts must find other ways to fund them. They could, perhaps, trim down and eliminate some of the dozens upon dozens of six-figure-salaried district administrative positions, but let's not hold our breath on that one. Therefore, if they can't garner enough extra revenue from creative ventures and partnerships with local businesses or from the piggy banks of parents, the only other answer is to pull the money from areas such as academics or fine arts or simply shut down athletic programs. This last option, although seeming like an unpopular but easy solution, gets a bit more complicated when one fully comes to understand the fallout.

For one, schools can't just indiscriminately shut down sports programs. Districts must be careful not to violate Title IX, which prohibits discrimination on the basis of sex in educational programs and activities. That includes sports. Districts must ensure they are not creating an unequal situation when it comes to boys' and girls' sports, or lawsuits will abound. One such case happened in Florida in 2009 when a school district decided to reduce the number of games for all sports except football. Even though football is by far the most popular and highest revenue-generating sport, this policy was in conflict with Title IX guidelines. Another hidden issue is school credits. Many districts allow students to get graduation credits for playing a school sport. If those sports are taken away, then students would need to earn those credits another way. That would mean additional resources for additional classroom space with additional teachers at, you guessed it, additional costs to the district.

Is there a way out of this mess? Can we imagine school without sports? I have a bit of a personal investment in this topic. I was involved in sports throughout my school years, and I feel my participation in sports, despite the constant barrage of orthopedic issues I now face as I age, benefited me greatly. The relationships I formed with teammates, and the leadership skills and self-discipline that I acquired are hard to value. I tried pretty much every sport that was offered, and my hard work and skills in basketball allowed me to attain an undergraduate degree for no cost but, of course, several pounds of flesh.

There is real value in young people participating in sports. Of course, it's not all rainbows and lollipops, though. There is a dark side to athletics. The shift in focus to monetary concerns often siphons the fun and tradition out of the experience. Sports can also be dangerous. With increasing concerns about concussions and other orthopedic issues to which young people are being exposed at younger and younger ages, some are asking if it's really worth it. Many times, sports participation comes with a massive increase in mental stress as well. Dealing with injuries and the painful recovery process can be a huge mental burden to bear. In addition, pressure to succeed from parents, coaches, and peers, as well as the constant concern about colleges and scholarships, does nothing but further increase the anxiety, stress, and depression many students already wrestle with today. Several young athletes have even taken their own lives as a result of the mental strain and high expectations that plague young athletes.

As students continue to struggle more and more academically in this country, another more fundamental question is: Should districts even be spending taxpayers' dollars on sports in public schools? The United States has some of the lowest test scores and achievement results in the world, yet we spend the most money per student. That stat should irritate every citizen in this country. Compared to our peers, the *best country in the world* is near or right at the bottom of the list when it comes to education. Some accuse the United States of being obsessed with sports, and there is definitely an argument to make their case. Students in the United States spend twice as much time playing sports as Korean students, according to a study by the *Journal of Advanced Academics*. And in European countries such as Germany and Finland, most kids participate in all their sports outside of school in private leagues and club programs. Most schools in other nations do not spend the funds on staff, management, and transportation needed to glorify sports.

So, how do schools proceed in the current environment? Despite the disadvantages discussed, sports do offer real benefits to students and can add much-needed value to school culture. In addition to the creativity, mental and physical prowess, leadership skills, and self-discipline school sports can instill in students, sports have proven to encourage classroom attendance and participation, especially among students who would have no other motivating factor to attend school. This is a huge carrot for low-income students who so often struggle much more than their higher-income peers. Sometimes, participation in sports is the only reason many kids bother showing up to school at all. Of course, schools should not be held hostage by this fact, but it is definitely something to consider.

Thus, this issue is not so clear-cut. There are advantages and disadvantages of having sports in public schools, but I personally believe the benefits do outweigh the costs. I've worked with students who would have 'fallen through the cracks' or been 'left behind' if it were not for sports. But should taxpayers be forced to subsidize those who want to participate in sports? Should the few be required to support the masses? This is generally the way many things work, but there could be another way to save school sports.

Some cost-cutting measures could at least bandage up a bleeding system in the short term. Coaching salaries vary widely depending on the state, and even region within the state, but many coaches are paid too much. A six-figure head coaching salary does not belong in a public school's budget, no matter how many state championship trophies are in the foyer display case. Limiting the number of conferences and clinics coaches attend would also be a move in the right direction. These events can be quite costly, with travel, food, and lodging expenses always on the rise. Travel is another huge expense. Many teams play in games hours away, and they need a means to get there. Aligning boys' and girls' schedules to save on busing expenses and not scheduling games with teams outside a certain mileage radius would be good moves to reduce costs.

Involving parents more in the fiscal side of sports and seeking donations and partnerships with local businesses and institutes could relieve some of the strain. Another more drastic idea is the complete privatization of school sports, moving in the direction of European nations. Many believe that a market would be created to cater to the ensuing demand. Ideally, private sports leagues would pop up all over the country, which would allow young people from all walks of life the opportunity to participate. Concessions and scholarships could be implemented for low-income students who may not be able to afford the costs of participating in private sports leagues. This could be a long-term solution to this problem, but sometimes the free market lets us down, and there's no guarantee a sense of equality could be maintained if school sports became privatized.

Sports in education is a complex issue. I'll be completely honest. Due to my own participation and success in the realm of school sports, I definitely have a bias for sports. I can acknowledge and understand the other side of the argument, though, and I do believe something must change in the way public school districts fund and conduct sports. Like everything in this world, sports require money, and some districts just don't have it or just don't spend it responsibly. Sports have been linked to schooling for over 150 years in this country, and it would be a shame and a massive failure of the system to sever this link. However, schools must adapt to the ever-changing world around them, and this issue is no different. There is a path to ensure that the opportunity remains for students to succeed in the classroom as well as on the field, court, or arena of their choice, but we all need to work together to find the proper solutions to secure a path forward for young aspiring athletes.

Charter Schools

Discussions concerning the topic of school choice have taken over conversations about public education. Parents are taking a more active role in their children's education, and many parents disagree with the idea that the district they live in determines the school their child must attend. Sure, there are waivers and ways around the rules, but those generally require transfer fees, waiting lists, and the discretion of whatever district employee gets the final say in the matter. Also, when students don't attend the campus assigned to them, they generally forfeit their right to free bus transportation. With property taxes rising to ridiculous levels, many parents wonder more and more if they're getting what they're paying for. In comes the hotly debated topic of school choice, specifically, charter schools.

Charter schools claim to offer a better option. They have much more freedom than public schools and offer a wider range of curricula and many more teaching options. With hundreds of charter schools popping up every year serving over 3 million students, more parents question whether they offer a better deal. Why have these schools become a hot topic of contention? The main reason, as usual, lies in the money. These types of schools are basically privately run institutes, but they receive funding from the public school coffers. This has created a situation in which charter schools, who sometimes even operate as for-profit organizations, take taxpayer dollars away from traditional public schools. In theory, these charter schools are held to higher accountability standards, but decades of research have shown extremely mixed outcomes.

What exactly is a charter school? Charter schools set up a contract or "charter" between the school and a local governing body, usually the school district. A charter school must submit an application stating its mission, curriculum, financial information, resources management, etc. Once the government agency approves the school, a contract, or charter, is established, which lays out the rights, responsibilities, and performance expectations of the school. The newly created charter school agrees to accept greater accountability in exchange for more autonomy compared to public schools. Charter schools get money from a variety of federal, state, and local sources like public schools, but some of that money comes directly from individual public schools. Most districts are funded on a per-student basis, so if a student leaves a public school to enroll in a charter school, the funds move with the student. This can create fairly significant funding gaps for certain public schools that are difficult or impossible to close.

The "market forces" approach to the argument for more school choice versus the government-based model dates back to the Nobel-Prize-winning economist Milton Friedman in the 1960s. The debate continued on into the 1970s when Ray Budde of the University of Massachusetts first introduced the idea of charter schools. Then, with Ronald Reagan at the helm of the Republican Party in the 1980s, the charter school movement took off. This was followed by extremely disparaging reports on public education published in *A Nation at Risk,* which, in turn, fueled the Republican Party's push for privatization. Ray Budde resurrected his charter idea from a decade earlier, and the idea finally stuck. When Albert Shanker, President of the American Federation of Teachers, caught wind of the idea of charter schools, he began to spread the gospel, and people started to listen. In 1991, Minnesota became the first state to pass a charter law. Within a year, Saint Paul's City Academy, which still exists today, was established as the first charter school in the United States. Later in 1992, California passed its first charter law, and by 1993, six more states had followed. In 1994, the Charter School Fund was added to ESEA, and by the following year, federal funds began to flow. Since then, over $4 billion of federal funds have been dispensed to charter schools, and charter schools have been supported by nearly every president since their inception.

Enrollment in charter schools has increased significantly in the last 10–15 years, doubling between 2009–2018 from 1.6 million to 3.3 million. This increased the participation rate in charter schools from 3 to 7% of all students. Charter schools are tuition-free and generally do not require any type of entrance exams or interviews like private schools, but they are still not very easy to get into. Some charter schools, especially high-performing ones, get bombarded with applications, and many are forced to use various types of lottery systems to determine which students will be permitted to enroll. At times, these lottery systems require parents to plan far in advance due to the early application deadlines, and many charter schools favor applicants who meet certain arbitrary criteria.

The rules, guidelines, and performance standards for charter schools are very different from those in the public school realm. Charter schools are not required to follow the established state curriculum and testing schedules. Charter schools are permitted to create their own unique curricula and academic focus, many times tailoring their lessons to certain areas such as the arts, technology, or science. This freedom allows charter schools much more flexibility in the lessons they create and the teaching methods they implement, giving teachers and students more options on how to learn and grow. Both charter and public schools push a high emphasis on testing, although charter schools generally have much more rigorous testing standards as well as a much higher dependence on technology compared to public schools.

Charter schools are afforded much more discretion when it comes to discipline as well. To put it bluntly, most charter schools choose to simply eliminate behavior problems. In direct contradiction to the public school model, charter school students, like those in private schools, can be expelled. This option is not available in public schools, which must accept and keep any student regardless of the problems that student creates in the classroom or how badly that student disrupts the learning or safety of others. Removing these types of students naturally creates a more conducive learning environment. However, this can have an extremely negative impact on public schools. When these rabble-rousers get kicked out of a charter school, they almost always return to the public school. In other words, charter schools dump their behavior problems back into the public schools. One might say this allows charter schools to padg their stats. Removing or at least decreasing the need for behavior management interventions in the classroom obviously leads to better academic results. Or at least it should.

Judging the success of charter schools can be a fairly daunting task. Understanding the goals and how achievement is measured in these schools can be a difficult process, and with charter school students differing so much in the makeup of their school environment, it can be challenging to find reasonable comparison groups. Nonetheless, despite these pitfalls, much research has been conducted in this arena. Although there is considerable variation across different types of schools, in general, students enrolled in charter schools perform about the same as their public school counterparts. Study after study has come to the same conclusion. Overall, there does not seem to be an overwhelming advantage to either type of schooling.

However, there is one noted area of student improvement in charter schools when it comes to race. Compared to public schools, a disproportionate share of charter students is Hispanic (33%) and Black (26%), and these two groups of students have exhibited better performance compared to their Hispanic and Black peers in public schools. This could, however, be a result of demographic differences since nearly 60% of charter schools are located in urban areas where more Hispanic and Black families reside. In comparison, only around 25% of public schools are located in urban areas. Nonetheless, Hispanic and Black students perform at a higher level than the same category of students in public schools. The data vary significantly across states and even local regions, but if you look at the averages, it is apparent that Hispanic and Black students do benefit by attending charter schools.

So is it worth it in the end? Do charter schools support and supplement the education system in a meaningful, positive way? Do the benefits outweigh the costs? When we look at some metrics, the answer would be yes, but when we look to other areas, the answer may be an emphatic no. Of course, improving the performance of Hispanic and Black students is something any educational institute should strive for, but could there be a more cost-effective, universal means to achieve this? If the only way to improve the performance of certain categories of students is to create an entirely separate school system, I'm not sure we can call that a success of the overall system. Therefore, charter schools leave us in a bit of a conundrum. If one conducts an Internet search on charter schools, an overwhelming amount of negative information will show up, but we do know charter schools provide some benefits.

Proponents of charter schools claim they are a much better alternative to public schools, and states that do have a well-managed charter system with competent authorizers can and at times do outperform public schools. Other supporters of the charter system point to the fact that poorly performing, mismanaged charter schools can be shut down, whereas failing public schools can continue to operate for years or even decades with no improvement remedy. Many parents are also frustrated with the rigidity of public schools and embrace the model of flexibility and variety of curricula and learning experiences charter schools offer. Surprisingly, many parents choose charter schools for nonacademic benefits such as location, safety, or sports. Safety is a huge concern in schools, and when charter schools are able to expel troubled students, the odds of violent incidents decrease dramatically. Parents of charter school students report much higher satisfaction in the areas of school discipline (34% v. 17%), student performance expectations (38% v. 25%), and instruction in valuable character traits (38% v. 21%) compared to public school parents.

There is, however, a darker side to charter schools, and despite the above advantages, charter schools come with a litany of problems, from low performance and failing programs to discrimination and outright fraud. The number one criticism of charter schools is that they steal money from public schools, and this is definitely true in states where funding is based on per-pupil enrollment. When a public school student transfers to a charter school, the funds or at least a significant portion of those funds transfer with the student, many times creating huge holes in a school's budget. This decrease in funds can, in turn, have a detrimental trickle-down effect on the students in those public schools.

Fraud has also run rampant in many charter schools across the entire nation. Remember the $4 billion the federal government spent on charter schools in the last few decades? Well , it's estimated that around $1 billion, or 25% of those funds, was lost to fraud and waste. Some charter schools that have yet to open or that closed soon after opening have even been rewarded grants. Between 2004–2014, 306 charter schools in California that received federal funding closed or never opened. Furthermore, over 200 charter schools are shut down each year due to academic shortcomings, financial problems, low enrollment, or bad/corrupt leadership and management. A study by the Network for Public Education found more than a fourth of charter schools that opened from 1999–2017 were shut down after only 5 years, and about half had closed down within 15 years, displacing nearly a million students.

Charter schools have also historically discouraged or denied enrollment to certain types of students with special needs, disabilities, or other problems. Removing these types of students from the performance metrics is another way of padding your stats. It's much easier to run a school when you eliminate students who need extra support. A 2016 report from the ACLU discovered illegal and/or exclusionary practices in over 200 charter schools in California alone. Charter schools can be pretty sneaky when it comes to this tactic by subtly discouraging enrollment by implementing dress code policies, not providing transportation, or even making parents contribute financially to the school. Thus, they can, indirectly and underhandedly, eliminate certain categories of students. Charter schools also suspend students, especially those with disabilities, at a much higher rate than public schools. It is estimated that some charter schools have expelled or temporarily removed over half of their students at some point, whereas the suspension rate at public schools is only 5%.

Charter schools also have an extremely high turnover rate among teachers. They do not offer contracts, tenure, or any union membership. Teachers can be fired anytime without cause—they are also free to leave at any time. Charter schools lose around 25% of their teachers every year, double the rate of public schools. Charter school teachers also generally work longer hours and for less pay compared to public school teachers. Additionally, many charter school teachers are uncertified and untrained compared to public school teachers, which could be a reason for the high turnover rate.

Although only accounting for around 10–15%, some charter schools are run for-profit, which comes with a whole set of new issues. When a school is set up and managed in a way that shows accountability to shareholders rather than to students and parents, the opportunity for shenanigans can and will run rampant. For obvious reasons, the corporate model may not be the best for educating our youth. There is the argument, too, that charter schools are not accountable to anyone, really. They have little to no oversight from the public or to a publicly elected school board but instead are run by small groups of unelected corporate managers who many times can subcontract out management to other private organizations even further reducing oversight. At times, some charter schools don't even have an administrator available to talk to parents about issues with their child. There have also been widespread reports of cheating and manipulating performance outcomes and test results. When charter schools are judged on high-stakes test scores, one can easily see the temptation to make those scores look a bit better than reality, especially when the life of the charter may depend on those results.

Thus, the verdict is difficult. Charter schools definitely can offer several advantages to students compared to public schools. Charter schools do offer parents and students more flexibility and a greater variety of educational options, but this often occurs at the expense of students in public schools. Charter schools have been successful at improving the performance and outcomes for Hispanic and Black students; however, it might be a better idea to find a way to improve the performance and outcomes for these students in the public school setting in which they're already being taught. Looking at the education system as a whole, it appears the downsides outweigh the benefits.

In the final section, we'll dig much deeper into the topic of school choice and the voucher systems that have evolved over the last several decades to support parents who want to seek out other educational options for their children, but lest we forget, this chapter is all about the money. With billions of taxpayer dollars being wasted by charter schools through fraud and resource mismanagement, it would seem that a more cost-effective approach would be to move toward more meaningful reform based on scientific research within the public school system itself. Would it not be a better idea to create a system that offers equal access and opportunity for all children in the public school setting? In other words, wouldn't it be better to deliver on what the country has promised its people? The real problem is poverty, but this isn't a book about socio-economics. If we have to create an entirely separate school system to serve certain demographics of students, that's a failure of the public education system. A better path forward may be to move away from the charter school model and instead use the billions of dollars flying around to fix the system we currently have, or at the very least, police the current charter system a bit more vigilantly.

Waste, Waste, and More Waste

So far, we've delved into several of the monetary and funding aspects of public education. In this section, we'll focus solely on the enormous amount of waste in public schools. We've become quite a wasteful civilization as a whole, but public schools are significant contributors. From food catering to bounce houses and outrageous security measures to grand pianos, some of these ridiculous expenses would outdo even the most mindless spendthrift. As we will soon discover, many districts who constantly carp about not having enough funding could easily remedy their predicament if they simply spent the money they do have more responsibly.

Energy

Let's start with energy—the second-highest expense for most school districts. During the hottest times of the year, teachers and students go to extremes to avoid freezing to death. Kids roam the halls covered up in hoodies like medieval monks, in 95 degree weather. Thermostats do not need to be set at 65 degrees. Sure, there's the argument that the colder environment may keep kids awake, alert, and more attentive, but does that idea justify $6 billion? In fact, some research has demonstrated energy efficiency has improved student performance because students respond positively to proper lighting and temperatures in classrooms. According to the Department of Energy, an average school spends 67 cents per square foot on electricity and 19 cents per square foot on natural gas. With some schools well over 100,000 square feet, annual energy costs can be as high as $150,000 for one school.

Schools can adopt a variety of strategies to reduce energy costs. Simple acts such as incorporating more natural light and turning off lights in rooms that are not in use could put a dent in that sky-high electric bill. Many cost-reducing strategies, especially behavioral changes, come with little to no cost to the district. A school district in Seattle saved $20,000 a year just by turning off vending machine lights. Schools could also retrofit older equipment and incorporate more energy-saving practices. Schools moving in this direction have already reduced energy costs by tens of thousands of dollars. Reducing energy costs can undoubtably aid in filling in funding gaps in public schools. And it's not even a very complicated task...just turn up the thermostat.

Food

We can all agree this country wastes more food than can be imagined...unless you can imagine $161 billion—the USDA's estimate annual value of wasted food in the United States. With the insane number of people living on the streets struggling to eke out a meager existence the amount of food wasted, especially in public schools, sickens me. The World Wildlife Fund estimates that over half a million tons of food are wasted every year in school cafeterias across the nation. An equally troubling aspect of this rampant food waste is the cost. Food that winds up uneaten in the trash, is just like tossing cash in the dumpster. Moreover, "free" and "reduced" lunches and breakfasts are not actually free and reduced. That money comes from somewhere, and that somewhere is taxpayers' pockets.

The federal government spent nearly $15 billion on the national school lunch program in 2020. Although this was a significant decrease from the nearly $19 billion spent in 2019, the decrease was only possible because schools were allowed to use COVID-19 relief funds to supplement meal programs in 2020. In addition, there is a separate school breakfast program. Not as many students take advantage of this program, but the government spent $4.5 billion on this program in 2019 alone. Combining the free breakfast and lunch programs, the federal government spent over $20 billion feeding kids in public schools in 2019. With a large portion of that going into the trashcan, there has to be a better way to fund and/or run these programs.

Reduced and free meal programs do serve a huge proportion of public school students. The numbers vary by state and region, but around 80% of students who eat cafeteria food access these programs to some extent. How is it that 80% of students who eat school cafeteria food qualify for these programs? If a student is at or below 130% of the federal poverty line, that student qualifies for some assistance. If the student falls between 130–185% of the federal poverty line, that student qualifies for a reduced-price lunch and/or breakfast. If the student falls above the 185% federal poverty line, that student qualifies for a free lunch and/or breakfast.

We won't go into reimbursements or the split between the federal government and states and local districts. I've already bored readers enough with this type of fiscal baloney, and these figures can vary greatly across the country. Besides, that's not the point. The point is massive amounts of money are being thrown out the window every day in schools due to food waste.

An even more complicated issue is students who don't qualify for these programs but still can't afford to eat. Schools have to feed students. It's the law. A public school cannot say, "Sorry chap, but I guess you're not eating today if you have no money." What's more, having "hangry" kids running around classrooms all day doesn't produce the best learning environment. Schools must feed these kids. However, there still has to be a transaction. The cafeteria can't just hand the kid a plate. So, the cafeteria rings up the normal price and the kid just keeps accumulating debt. Of course, schools attempt to get reimbursed from parents, but if they can't pay, they can't pay. Schools can't deny enrollment the following year, because a student has outstanding food debt. National school meal debt cost an average of over $260 million a year in 2021, and the average meal debt per child is just over $170 per year. States handle food debt in various ways, but if parents can't repay this debt, and most can't, the school has to eat that debt which affects their overall budget, taking money away from other valuable areas of need.

Kids in school need to be fed. No one can argue that. We all know the importance of having a full stomach with at least somewhat nutritious food, and it doesn't take much mental effort to understand that students function better behaviorally and academically in school when their basic needs are met. There has to be a better way to accomplish this. First, with governments and schools spending more and more on social service type programs, we have to ask ourselves, is this really the job of schools? Funding this program and that program like food services, counseling and social work services, after school programs, as well as a multitude of other specialized services, is causing some schools to go broke. Kids do need a lot of help in today's world, but we can't collapse the entire school system in the process of addressing those needs.

Schools can, however, easily address the issue of food waste. Getting students more involved in the planning process could be one helpful start. Creating meals students would actually enjoy eating, would definitely keep them from throwing away so much food. Schools could also implement occasional food waste audits to take a closer look at how much food is being wasted and how to reduce that waste. If schools don't have the data, they can't act appropriately. Some schools also hand out pre-prepared meals with items many students don't even want. These schools could move to an offer vs. serve model where kids pick from a salad bar type setup only taking what they want or are capable of eating. Schools could also use share tables, defined by the USDA as a table or station where kids can return beverage or food items they don't eat as long as the practice follows health and safety codes. These items could be reused by the school or at least donated to a charitable organization.

Students need at least 20 minutes to sit down and eat. Simply allowing them adequate time to eat all their food rather than rushing them out of the cafeteria and would lead to less waste. Another strategy could be to decrease snack time before lunch. Regardless of the method or methods, public schools have to address the problem of money wasted on food. And much like the energy waste issue, it does not seem like an extremely difficult task.

Facilities

Another interesting area to address is the current condition of school facilities. Despite some claims that school infrastructure is in poor condition, research has actually shown that fewer than one in 20 schools in the United States is in what would be considered "poor" condition with only 3% of all schools and 4% of schools in high-poverty areas being rated as in "poor condition." From my experience, I would have to say many schools are actually a bit too fancy, and schools could definitely implement cost cutting strategies in the construction of some of these facilities. Are multi-million-dollar football stadiums really necessary? Do 6-year-olds need to be educated in a setting that resembles a Silicon Valley startup. I've strolled through many schools expecting to see Mark Zuckerberg or Jack Dorsey pop out from around the next corner. Modern sculptures and lavish architecture are certainly nice to see, but are they really a responsible use of taxpayer money? Even if the facility is built using bond money, it still doesn't need to be wasted on extravagance. News flash: 6-year-olds couldn't care less about modern architectural design.

What's more, U.S. school districts spend close to $3 billion annually on security measures. With locking door mechanisms, face recognition software, increased training and staff, bullet-proof glass, and dozens of other measures, the cost of keeping students "safe" rises every year. The increase in school violence and shootings is usually used to these security measures, but at the end of the day, despite how traumatic and frequent these events may seem, the chance of an event like this happening on school property remains extraordinarily low.

Yes, it's maddening that even one student could die from gun violence in a public school, but with 50 million students attending schools nationwide, the simple fact is that the number of students who die from shootings and other violent incidents in public schools is an extremely low number statistically speaking. We simply must ask the difficult question. Is it reasonable to spend $3 billion to turn schools into makeshift correctional facilities with government agents roaming the halls, and students entering every morning like mindless minions shuffling to their flight in a frustrating and generally useless TSA line? It is school's paramount duty to keep students and staff out of harm's way, and this nation, without a doubt, has the least safe schools of any other peer nation. Nonetheless, schools must use reliable data to make difficult yet logical, reasonable, and responsible fiscal decisions to secure schools. If you're passionate about his topic, that's good. We will dig into this issue very deeply in a later chapter.

Administrative Bloat

The next chapter focuses on administrative bloat and the bureaucratic monster it continues to feed, so I will only touch on a few crucial points here. Yet, the massive increases in the number of administrators, especially district-level administrators, currently infiltrating public schools is smashing the piggy banks of most school districts across the entire country. Administrative positions have increased at an exponentially higher rate than that of students and teachers. This massive increase in the amount of administrative staff and their eternal expanding salaries has created a major financial strain on the budgets of school districts in every state of the union. By merely eliminating some of these positions, school districts could save millions upon millions of dollars which could then be shifted to higher need areas.

COVID-19

Another chapter has also been devoted to COVID-19 and its effect on public schools, but it's imperative to touch on this topic a bit here. Many schools are using COVID relief money to fund projects not related to pandemic recovery. One school district in Wisconsin spent 80% of its $2 million in COVID-19 relief funding to replace natural turf with synthetic in their athletic fields. I'm pretty sure natural grass is not responsible for the spread of COVID-19. Yet another district in Texas spent $4 million in COVID-19 relief funds to expand the construction of a city-owned nature center that won't even be completed until 2024, meaning half the students who were earmarked for those funds will never benefit from them. These scenarios are only a couple of the countless documented abuses of COVID-19 relief money and exhibit further evidence of the waste and mismanagement of resources in public schools.

The Big Picture

The U.S. government currently spends around 4% of the nation's GDP on public-schooling, and those schools employ over 4% of the nation's workforce. Many times, the market economies that sustain these schools mask their inefficiencies. Yet, U.S. per-pupil spending on public education has tripled in the last 50 years and now stands at an all-time high in most states. Per-pupil spending increased from $4,720 in 1966 to $13,847 in 2016 (2018 dollars). The U.S. spends more money per pupil on public schools than any other peer nation. We spend 10% more than the United Kingdom, 28% more than France, and roughly 35% more than the average OECD country. The most damning aspect of these statistics is that this massive amount of money has resulted in little to no correlation with student achievement or a boost in teacher pay. Teacher salaries have actually decreased over time in many regions after adjusting for inflation.

In a rare ceasefire of bad news, there does seem to be a glimmer of hope at least when it comes to equality in funding. Due to increases in federal and state funding, court ordered changes in state funding formulas, and Title 1 spending, the average racial and socioeconomic gap has effectively closed when it comes to per-pupil funding. A 2008 study the Tax Policy Center, the Brookings Institute, and Urban Institute examined changes in per-pupil funding from 1972 to 2002 and found spending differences have mostly disappeared with average per-pupil spending on non-White students greater or equal to spending on White students in 47 out of the 50 states. A more recent study in 2017 by the Urban Institute discovered that "poor students in most states attend school districts that are about as well funded as the district's nonpoor students attend in their state." Although states vary greatly in per-pupil expenditures and some inequality in funding no doubt remains in certain regions of the country, the differences show no statistical significance when adjusted for cost of living. So even though schools are spending copious amounts of money, much of which is being wasted via a variety of means, they have at least spent and wasted it in an equal manner.

This brings us to the final question. Is all this spending worth it? What are the benefits of those billions upon billions of dollars? For those who have been paying attention, the answer should be an emphatic "not much." Time and time again, the research and data have shown that increases in spending generally do not result in improved student performance. For example, Kansas has the 15th highest per-pupil spending at nearly $16,000 per student but ranks 36th in achievement. This is a common trend. School districts have varying expenses based on their region and location with a wide range of cost of living, crime rates, and student demographics. However, the fact remains. These districts are not spending money responsibly. The data do not lie, and countless studies have shown that more money does not result in higher achievement. High-spending school districts consistently perform at the same level or worse on state assessments, college entrance exams, such as the ACT, as well as other metrics compared to low-spending districts.

The nation needs to hold schools and their district administrators accountable. Schools should be required to create a database on expenses and revenues that can be easily accessed by the public. People need to know where their tax dollars are going, and that information shouldn't be so difficult to uncover, especially with the insane property tax rates that are increasing insanely across the board. These data could also be easily reviewed by financial experts who could guide district spending in a more productive manner.

It's quite simple. Cut the waste. We've discussed a multitude of ways to reduce waste and create more efficient spending practices. We can sit around and discuss these strategies all day, but it's time for schools to start implementing them. Most of them are not very complicated. Turn off the lights when you leave a room. Do high schoolers really need a stadium that carries a price tag of $60 million? Perhaps the federal government can stop for a few minutes and look at the data before shooting cash at schools from an air cannon. I'll say it again one more time. More money does not equal better results. The proof is everywhere. School districts, state governments, and the feds must spend taxpayers' hard-earned money in a more responsible manner, and administrators at every level must be held accountable for their actions. An audit in Arizona found that over $25 million had been fraudulently spent or stolen over a 15-year period. A North Carolina superintendent once spent $16,000 in federal funds which included bounce houses and a video game trailer.

It would seem schools are consistently underfunded and constantly pleading for more money. It would also seem this claimed lack of resources is true based on much of the information being blasted out by various media pundits and political outlets. However, when we take a closer look at the data, the money appears to be there. The problem is incompetence, unaccountability, and most of all, waste. We are the wealthiest country in the world. We have plenty of money. We just need to learn how to use it in a more responsible and productive manner.

Chapter 4: Drowning in Bureaucracy

"Bureaucracy is the Art of Making the Possible Impossible"
~Javier Pascual Salcedo
"Bureaucracy is the Death of any Achievement" ~Albert Einstein

By this point it should be fairly evident that the public school system in the United States is vastly underperforming, especially compared to our international peers. However, reform is not possible until we understand how this institute is structured and what lies at its foundations. It may have surprised some, when in the Introduction we discussed the Prussian origins of our education system. What may be even more surprising is that schools still use the foundational principles of a system that was created nearly 200 years ago. Therefore, it is no surprise the masses are howling for reform. Many even say we are past the brink of reform and must eliminate the entire system, thus creating an entirely new model of education.

It's unfortunately becoming harder and harder to deny the inefficiency and incompetence of our entire system of government—this inefficiency and incompetence has undoubtedly percolated throughout our public education system. With recent failures in how the COVID-19 pandemic was handled, increases in economic hardships, the dilapidated infrastructure around every corner, the continued collapse and corruption of our justice, immigration, and health departments, as well as the surprising decline and incompetence of our once greatly feared military, it looks more and more like our government is not up to the tasks it is entrusted to perform. The intense bureaucratic structure contained within our government systems has been touted as the root of much of this chaos and discord we are forced to navigate on a daily basis. What's more, this bureaucracy is part of the foundation of public schooling, and it has expanded to stupefying levels in the last couple of decades. This chapter will take a broad look at this foundation, attempt to navigate through its bureaucratic structure, and discuss how it has impacted the system as a whole as well as those within it.

Prussian Origins

Where the hell is Prussia? Good question. It actually does not exist anymore. Prussia is basically modern-day Germany. It was a historically prominent Germanic state whose origins date back to 1525. Before today's Germany became Germany, the region was a hodgepodge of states comprised of Germanic people. Prussia was one of the most powerful states in the region and eventually unified all the Germanic states, except for Austria, in 1871. It remained a dominant power until its dissolution following the end of WWI.

Now for a bit more time traveling. The earliest seed of government-mandated schooling was planted back in the 16th century by Martin Luther, leader of the Protestant Reformation, who was a strong advocate for compulsory schooling—but not because of education. Luther envisioned a system to inject the beliefs of Lutheranism into Europe's youth in order to convert Catholics, Jews, and other non-believers to his Lutheran cause. John Calvin, a French reformer from the same era, was also an early advocate for state-mandated schooling. His views and tactics were notably influential years later among the Puritans of the New England colonies. However, this idea of compulsory, government-funded schooling was slow to take flight.

To arrive at the inception of our modern-day system, we must travel forward a couple of centuries to 1763, when the basic foundations of the Prussian education system were laid out by Frederick the Great. Frederick was a product of the Enlightenment with a deep sense and promotion of intellectualism, social and cultural evolution, and artistic expression. He envisioned Prussia as a kingdom with military and economic might. His 1763 decree significantly expanded the school system by requiring all boys and girls between the ages of 5–14 to be educated primarily by government-funded schools. Soon after, Prussia became one of the first countries in the world to introduce a system of taxpayer-funded schooling with compulsory attendance.

This system included teaching skills such as reading, writing, music, and religious studies and ingrained a strict ideology of sobriety, discipline, and duty. Mathematics and calculus were eventually added to the curriculum, as well as state-funded and compulsory secondary schooling. At the height of its success, the Prussian system had created specific teacher training with state certification requirements and a modern salary system, compulsory attendance, national testing for all students, age-based grades, letter grades based on performance, professional hierarchies, minimum number of school days, secular instruction, student tracking with permanent records, mandatory kindergarten, a focus on science and technology, and a national curriculum for each grade, all of which were implemented in order to strengthen national identity, respect, and obedience for authority. Sound familiar?

Around the early to mid-1800s, a liberal intellectual wave began to spread across Prussia and into other parts of Europe and the United States. Liberals encouraged the idea that universal education was the main path to a united national consciousness and eliminating inequality and strife. Educators in the United States became fascinated by Germanic educational trends in the early 1800s based on favorable reports of the Prussian model emanating from various sources across the United States and parts of Europe. This leads us to the first and most important American advocate for public education, Horace Mann. Mann was an extremely influential figure of the time with a resume that included stints in the Massachusetts State Legislature and Board of Education, as well as serving in the United States Congress. In 1843, Horace Mann decided to embark on a grand tour of Europe to investigate the inner workings of the national school systems of various European states. During his travels, he became overwhelmingly impressed with and convinced by the policies, structure, and results of the Prussian education model. Upon his return, Mann began a massive lobbying campaign for its adoption.

Mann's efforts soon paid off, and by 1852, his home state of Massachusetts became the first state to go all-in on the Prussian model and instituted the first state-wide compulsory attendance laws. Soon after, New York set up a trial program in 12 schools using the same method. This model soon began to spread like a virus with Rhode Island and Connecticut shortly following suit, and by the end of the 1800s, 34 states had compulsory school laws with over 70% of young people attending a public school. This model began to solidify and morph more into its current form as the nation moved into the 1900s. By 1918, compulsory schooling was established in every state, and within the following decades, the system was expanded to include an increase in the number of days and years students were required to attend school. This was enforced by imposing fines and penalties for truancy, as well as the creation of the federal Department of Education and the eventual adoption of the Every Student Succeeds Act (ESEA). In just over a century, Horace Mann's dream of a nationalized public education system based on the Prussian model was realized.

So what's the problem with this model of education? Sometimes it's hard to see the forest through the trees. First, a model that dates back nearly 300 years probably is not the best model for our 21st-century world, and the format hasn't changed all that much. The Prussian system is nearly identical to the U.S. system still in use today. The threats and opportunities posed in today's world are no comparison to those that characterized the Prussian Empire. The skills, attitudes, and aptitudes needed during the heyday of the Industrial Revolution are not the same now needed to address the ever-changing technological beast in which we currently live. Changes in family structures, employment procedures, and the seemingly constant imbalance of quality vs. quantity have brought the nation to a point where the models of old no longer provide us with the results we want and need. A model of education based on an Industrial Age mindset is not appropriate for the postindustrial globalized society of today.

In the early years of the American government, there was no stockpile of theories or research-based practices on education. There simply was not much knowledge about how to build a functional educational system and how kids learn, but the country needed a system that provided a path to support favorable learning outcomes. The Prussian system provided a convenient, established model that gave the United States an effective, manageable education system. However, we now have a huge reservoir of research, knowledge, theories, and 150 years of experience. Should we still be using a system that traces its ancestry to the Protestant Reformation? In addition, when we look more closely at the actual goals and motivations behind the Prussian system, the situation tends to become, for lack of a better word, downright sinister.

The most outspoken critics of the Prussian model claim it was designed to crush individualism and independent thought while fiercely advocating subservience to the state. The actual goals of the Prussian education system, from a governmental perspective, were to remove education from the hands of the family or church, in turn placing it in the hands of the state. The state's educational goals were:

1. Obedient workers

1. Obedient soldiers
2. Well-subordinated government civil servants
3. Well-subordinated industry clerks
4. Citizens who think alike when it comes to major issues (Conformity)

This totalitarian model is in clear contradiction to the practices and philosophies upon which the United States was built. If this seems like libertarian hyperbole or propaganda, let's take a look at what the Prussian government said about its own system. One of the most prominent Germanic education reformers of the 1800s was a fellow named Johann Gottlieb Fichte. Fichte viewed compulsory schooling as the perfect tool to indoctrinate children. His description of the aim of the Prussian system follows:

Then, in order to define more clearly the new education which, I propose, I should reply that the very recognition of, and reliance upon, free will in the pupil is the first mistake of the old system and the clear confession of its impotence and futility....You must do more than merely talk to him; you must fashion him, and fashion him in such a way that he simply cannot will otherwise than you will him to will.

Education should aim at destroying free will so that after pupils are thus schooled they will be incapable throughout the rest of their lives of thinking or acting otherwise than as their schoolmasters would have wished....When the technique has been perfected, every government that has been in charge of education for more than one generation will be able to control its subjects securely without the need of armies or policemen.

Thomas Alexander of George Peabody College for Teachers wrote in 1919:

We believe however that a careful study of the Prussian school system will convince any unbiased reader that the Prussian citizen cannot be free to do and act for himself; that the Prussian is to a large measure enslaved through the medium of his school that his learning instead of making him his own master forges the chain by which he is held in servitude; that the whole scheme of Prussian elementary education is shaped with the express purpose of making ninety five out of every hundred citizens subservient to the ruling house and to the state.

Does the term *sinister* still seem a bit hyperbolic?

It's time to face the facts. Based on an overwhelming amount of research and data, the apparent objective of this system was to nationalize the youth to fit a particular mold, and some hardcore opponents to our current model would say the United States is still doing just that. Although it's almost impossible to prove, many would claim it seems to be the only logical reason we haven't made a much stronger push toward education reform in this country. During the intense and expansive age of the Industrial Revolution, cogs in the wheel made a bit more sense, but those days of intense factory labor and the drudge of the assembly line have nearly become extinct. We have robots and cheap overseas child labor now. Thus, Americans strive to engage in more meaningful and creative ventures and lines of work.

Remember that in the beginning, schooling in the United States was mostly voluntary and private. I'm not necessarily suggesting we make a dramatic shift back in that direction, but we have definitely created a system with goals, motivations, and outcomes that are far from those upon which this nation was founded. Diversity, individualism, and free thought need to be injected back into our schools. Charter schools and specialty schools such as STEM academies are growing more and more. The current system is being bombarded with challenges such as massive increases in home-schooling, vouchers, school choice, and other reforms and innovations. In addition, more parents who can afford the insanely high costs of private schools are opting for that route. People are evidently not pleased with the nation's current system, and when we look deep into the foundations of that system, it's not too difficult to understand why.

We live in a dynamic environment that sometimes seems to change before our eyes. We must allow our education system to adapt to this dynamic landscape. The ways in which we have organized and operated public schools is not working anymore. Of course, we still need structure in schools, as well as some type of hierarchical system that retains remnants of the old model. However, our schools must not operate like correctional facilities. This may all sound a bit exaggerated, but it is troubling to see kids drudging through the rigid and strict routines of daily school life like little soldiers who have had their free will and independent thought thoroughly siphoned away. Students still pledge allegiance to the United States government with their hand over their hearts every morning before the school day begins. The bureaucracy of old remains strong and dominant in our public schools. Many, if not all, of the government institutes we have in place have, well let's be honest, gone to shit. The education system is no different; we need to finally come to the realization that we're still using the same model used centuries ago to create subservient soldiers and cogs in the industrial machine. That is not the world in which we live, and those are not the values the country claims to represent.

Crushing Bureaucracy

The common theme in public education throughout the last couple of decades has been that of more bureaucracy paired with higher costs and lower performance. Yet, the debate around bureaucracy in schools is not new. It traces back half a century ago. Merriam-Webster defines bureaucracy as "a system of administration marked by officialism, red tape, and proliferation." Britannica says bureaucracy is a "specific form of organization defined by complexity, division of labour, permanence, professional management, hierarchical coordination and control, strict chain of command, and legal authority." It goes on to state: "In its ideal form, bureaucracy is impersonal and rational and based on rules rather than ties of kinship, friendship, or patrimonial or charismatic authority." Does this sound like something that belongs in public schools?

The one common element of bureaucracy is that although it seems to be infused into all of our systems, no one likes it, and surprisingly this disdain even crosses party lines. The political Left was the first to embark on its crusade against public school bureaucracy in the 1970s claiming it was built to perpetrate inequality in schools with a top-down system in which administrators and other policymakers at the top levy their will on teachers, students, and parents at the bottom. By the end of the 1980s, the Reagan era had created a mindset within the country that government was bad and more of a problem than a solution. (Perhaps he was on to something.) This created a shift to the political Right, who launched their own crusade against bureaucracy, insisting it was the principal barrier to effective schooling and arguing for more organizational autonomy. They continued to insist the current bureaucratic structure of schools stifled the imagination, creativity, and free will of both educators and students. So, for once, the Left and Right actually agreed on something, but as usual, they did nothing about it.

Like most things in life, the hated term *bureaucracy* is not an evil concept straight from the gates of hell. Structure in schools is definitely a prerequisite for success, and some aspects of bureaucracy are valuable components in our public schools that serve a purpose; however, this system can be very destructive, and it most often is. Good use of bureaucracy can aid in defining roles of employees as well as providing an equal delegation of responsibilities. Rules and regulations can preserve a sense of professionalism among staff and can promote school policy and goals. If a healthy environment can be established (which is extremely difficult in today's schools), teamwork and cooperation can flourish, and every person involved contributes equally to student success.

That sounds great, right? This bureaucracy stuff sounds pretty awesome. Well, the above description is more like a utopian pipedream than the reality in which we live. There are isolated examples of a good system like this in public schools, but they are extremely rare, and the systems that do operate in this manner are generally the ones who actually have moved away from the core system into a hybrid model. These situations are found mostly in site-based school districts in which individual schools have extreme autonomy in the way they operate. This comes with its own set of problems but is at least a move in the right direction. So when districts decide to use an a la carte form of bureaucracy, it can provide a meaningful lattice to organize a school. But bureaucracy almost always comes as a full-course meal.

At its roots, bureaucracy is in direct contradiction to the liberal values the United States has espoused since its inception. Despite its checkered past, the United States has represented and exuded a strong commitment to individual liberty. However, this individual liberty is a needle in a haystack when it comes to public schools. The Lindberg baby may be found much faster than the discovery of free thought and individualism in today's classrooms. Rules are rules, procedures are procedures, and roles are roles. Rigid organizational frameworks with little room for flexibility, whether it comes to curriculum, rules and discipline, testing, or the simple day to day operations of a school are fundamentally imbedded in the bureaucratic system which guides public schooling. Furthermore, hierarchical structures tend to be overemphasized by administrators, and this leads to unhealthy school environments in which staff morale is crushed, and teamwork and collaboration cease to exist. When the system begins to waiver, leaders move even more in the direction of bureaucracy by further integrating stricter rules and punishments for students as well as teachers. These hostile policies and fear tactics decimate school morale and create an unhealthy and sometimes even toxic environment.

Administrators and policymakers must begin to understand the detrimental essence of extreme bureaucracy. However, this is only a small step in the direction of meaningful change. The intense, stifling element of bureaucracy is completely enmeshed within the foundation and structure of the entire system. Bureaucracy lies at the heart and soul of the Prussian model that we still use. As we've discussed, it's not all about administrators, even though I've experienced some pretty horrible ones. Nonetheless, the administrative leviathan has grown to excess in the last couple of decades, and this dreaded monster has surfaced, bringing with it a tsunami of bureaucratic weapons that may soon capsize our entire education system.

Administrate, Administrate...and then Administrate Some More

There's nothing that pairs better with a fine course of bureaucracy than administration, and school districts across the United States are being infiltrated by hordes of bureaucrats. Tax dollars being spent on district-level, as well as school administration (principals and vice principals), have soared over the past couple of decades, while teacher pay has stagnated. Current estimates show that around half of states now have more noninstructional personnel than teachers, and some of the figures are quite alarming.

There are two types of administrators in public education. District-level administrators deal with issues affecting the entire district or certain district-wide programs. These types of administrators are the highest paid; therefore, they are by far the most detrimental to the overall financial stability of the system. Simply navigate to any local school district website and click the link for district-level departments; endless lists of names and departments will pop up. When I searched the website for my school district, I found 78 different departments. All of those departments need administrating, and I work in a fairly small school district. The second type of administration is campus-level, which includes the principals and vice principals who manage and run the day-to-day operations of individual schools. Each school has one head principal, but the number of vice principals varies depending on the type of school and number of students enrolled. These campus-level administrators work at a specified campus directly with teachers and students. So, when we consider administrative positions, we are generally referring to both of these types unless otherwise specified.

The expansion of public school administrative positions in the United States in the last half-century is utterly mind-blowing. From 1950 to 2014, the growth in public school students was right around 100% compared to a 240% increase in teaching staff. However, during this same time, administrative and nonteaching staff increased at a rate of nearly 700%. Even more concerning are the data we uncover when we delve into the U.S. Bureau of Labor Statistics. In 1999, there were 186,220 people working as "education administrators, kindergarten through secondary," earning an average yearly wage of $66,480. By 2019, there were 271,020 individuals in this same category earning an average yearly wage of $100,340. That is a 45.5% growth in administrative positions and over a 50% increase in salaries. For comparison, elementary teachers (excluding special education teachers) grew at a rate of only 5.4% during that same time period, from 1,357,340 to 1,430,480.

We can look at other sources that actually break down the district-level compared to the campus-level increase in administration to further confirm our suspicions. The Department of Education has also released information comparing the 2000 school year to the 2017 school year, resulting in the following data:

School Year	District Administrative Staff	School Administrative Staff (Principals/VPs)	Teachers
Fall 2000	97,270	141,792	2,941,461
Fall 2017	170,158	189,155	3,169,750
Increase	74.9%	33.4%	7.7%

What's even more alarming when we look at these data is the fact that during that same time frame, student enrollment increased at a rate of only 7.4% from 47.2 million to 50.7 million. Thus, if the student body has increased at a rate of less than 10% percent over the last couple of decades, why has district-level administrative staff increased at a rate of over 10 times that? Increases in teacher hiring mirror increases in student enrollment. How on earth can anyone explain the preposterous increases in administrative positions? This table speaks for itself. Administrators are taking over the public school system in a Mongol-like invasion sweeping across the entire system.

In addition to these distressing data, the dollar amounts siphoned off by this administrative behemoth are just as sickening as their burgeoning numbers. A most startling example is the $233,180 salary the superintendent of Tatum ISD in Texas earns. What is really shocking and extremely irksome is that Tatum ISD has a student enrollment of 1,716 students. I'll pause while you laugh out loud. Then there's Charleston County, South Carolina. In 2013, they had 30 administrators earning over $100,000 a year. In 2019, that number increased to 133. The total cost adjusting for inflation for educating a student from grades K–12 rose from $57,602 per student in 1970 to $164,426 in 2010. That's a 185% increase in cost, and I don't think it's a coincidence this increase in per-student cost has risen in concert with the increased numbers of administrators and their ballooning salaries. This is yet another example of the seemingly undeniable fact that schools do, in fact, have plenty of money. By simply removing many of these administrative positions, schools across the nation could find themselves with plenty of resources to actually address the needs of teachers and students.

I could ramble on and on with example after example of rampant, uncontrolled, and irresponsible spending of tax-payer dollars on administrative salaries, but the following figure sums up everything. When we extrapolate the U.S. Bureau of Labor Statistics data on increases in administrator numbers and their salaries across the entire nation, the result is nearly three $100,000-a-year administrators for every single public school in the country. It would be an extremely ambitious task to argue against the utter lunacy of this situation.

But what have we gained from this colossal expansion of administrative staff throughout the entire scope of our nation? Well, if you've been paying attention, you already know the answer to this question: Jack Squat. Students are still underperforming and failing at unprecedented levels, teachers are fleeing the field en masse, and all levels of government involved in the process have opted to waltz around fiddling while Rome burns.

We might not welcome these high increases in administrative positions and the costs they demand, but we could perhaps live with them if we could, at the very least, find any meaningful results from their escalating numbers. Unfortunately, academic outcomes have not soared. Public school graduation rates peaked around 1970, and test scores have continued to decline year after year. We've already discussed the pathetic performance of our students and will explore this topic in depth throughout our journey. For now, just know that the huge costs involved in the massive influx of administrative positions in public schools have not led to improvements in educational outcomes for students or better supportive working environments for teachers.

Therefore, in addition to the zero improvement in student performance, this enhanced force of administrators has not even improved the environment or workload for teachers, and if anything, the situation has worsened. Campus-based administrators are vital components of the system, and they are much more valuable to schools and the students and teachers they serve compared to district-level administrators. These campus-based administrators work very long hours and can make a huge difference in the success of a school. However, they have become so bogged down with meaningless duties overseeing this committee and that committee as well as attending this meeting and that training, that they have nearly lost the ability to support teachers. Disciplinary issues constantly go unaddressed, administrators increasingly have minimal time to meet with teachers, and students and teachers suffer.

Classroom teachers are consistently required to fill out more and more paperwork related to literally every aspect of their job, in addition to supervising teaching assistants, constantly putting out parental fires, and leading team meetings and curriculum planning. Some teachers have even claimed the amount of time they spend doing paperwork takes up the highest percentage of their time. In some surveys, up to 70% of public school teachers state the amount of paperwork they're required to do prevents them from effectively teaching their students. This pile of paperwork grows even higher for special education teachers dealing daily with legal IEP documents. If schools have so many administrators, why are teachers being forced to complete so many administrative duties? No one, as of now, has answered this question.

What's even worse, many times these campus-based administrators get little to no support from district-level administration. On many occasions, one side may give a completely different answer than the other on even the simplest of issues. Every district in which I have worked has had drastically inadequate communication and cohesion between the two-headed administrative colossus. When so many individuals are involved in the process, situations tend to get very confusing, communication breaks down, and not much gets accomplished. Then the obvious political element is infused into the mix with its boundless circumstances of quid pro quo, and our current disaster ensues... And I haven't even brought in the state and federal government. You see, some researchers look to the amplification of laws and regulations at nearly every level as the motivation behind the massive increase in administration staff. With Bush's No Child Left Behind, Obama's Race to the Top, and a more vigorous enforcement of Title IX, it's no wonder schools have begun to hire people to administrate the ins and outs of these various programs and laws. Yet, the towering administrative staff schools have amassed is still highly ineffective at addressing and understanding the components of all these laws and regulations constantly coming down from above.

In addition to all the federal bureaucracy being hammered down onto the states and their school districts, an additional flow of nonsensical rules, regulations, and testing requirements originate from the states themselves. The typical scenario involves a congregation of government buffoons mandating statute after statute directing the operation of schools from discipline and attendance to testing and curriculum. Many of these law-making government agents have never worked in a school or even been inside a public school since they graduated from high school.

So is the reason this system is utterly broken starting to become clear? Let's recap: the surge of rules, laws, and regulations emanating from the highest level of federal government trickling down to the states. The states then incorporate these federal laws into their own alphabet soup of rules and regulations, which they then dispense to the district-based administrators of each school district. These district-based administrators, in turn, lay out the district guidelines for individual schools based on federal and state rules. Finally, the campus-based administrators ensure those rules and regulations are understood and enforced on their individual campuses.

Federal Gov't—>State Gov't—>District-Based Administration—>Campus-Based Administration

Beautiful isn't it? The perfect bureaucratic system: Complicated, expensive, and incompetent with little to no results.

Fix It or Destroy It?

Public schools are being crushed by decade after decade of incomprehensible, costly, and ineffective legislature and mandates. Instructional minutes, seat time, teacher hours, student/teacher ratios, standardized testing rules, compliance procedures, funding regulations, schedules, graduation requirements, grading policies, special education, and 504 guidelines, and a litany of school board policies have bombarded schools with so much paperwork and boxes to check off, there is hardly any time to actually teach. This system resembles more of a typical bureaucratic, nonfunctioning appendage of the federal government than the professional education system it was intended to be.

The bureaucratic model does not fit our dynamic, complex world, and many would argue it's the principal reason our government systems can't seem to accomplish much of anything these days. The multiple subsystems operating within the educational bureaucracy of schools soon become disconnected from the operations and functions of the larger system. In turn, random unmonitored endeavors begin to arise throughout the entire district, creating organizational chaos, which results in nothing more than sustaining the declining, mediocre system that continues to produce mostly lousy results.

I seem to continue to beat this bureaucratic horse to death, but the point cannot be emphasized enough—this system is not sustainable and has no place in our public schools. In the late 1800s, Max Weber wrote: "Bureaucracy develops the more perfectly, the more it is 'dehumanized,' the more completely it succeeds in eliminating from business love, hatred, and all purely personal, irrational, and emotional elements which escape calculation." The creators of this destructive force are not to blame, though. The abuses of power by monarchs and priests of the Middle Ages led individuals of the Enlightenment to create a system that attempted to remove abuse of power, impulsive decision-making, and human error. A move toward a system like this spawned the seeds of bureaucracy, and the emergence of the Industrial Revolution became the fertilizer that sustained and supported its massive germination.

Bureaucracy is great for the assembly line. Precise, linear, and controlled measures are the perfect analog for producing automobiles, furniture, and computers, but those measures are not so great for producing productive, educated humans. In the age of the Industrial Revolution, perhaps one could argue that an assembly-line mentality in education was a perfect fit for the assembly-line society that existed during that era. The world has advanced far from that time as a civilization, and this model is no longer useful or appropriate. Students are not products to be controlled, measured, and predicted, and schools should not operate on nothing more than a command and control mentality. Weber went on to refer to bureaucracy as "the iron cage of modernity" that "traps individuals based purely on teleological efficiency, rational circulation and control." This model seeks only to "measure, predict, and control."

The accumulation of so many laws and regulations has also morphed many school districts into litigious hotbeds. Public schools are terrified of lawsuits, and many lose hundreds of thousands to even millions of dollars a year to cover some of these legal fees and settlements. Some of these costs are as high as $100 per student in some districts. I'll refrain from reviewing examples of these legal disputes because they're honestly quite boring and usually result in a finale that will only infuriate readers even more with the system we have in place. With so many rules that are difficult to keep track of, it's easy to find yourself in an "Oh shit!" type of situation. Don't put your arm around a child. We might get sued. Was the paperwork in by the deadline? *We might get sued!* Was due process followed throughout the entire investigation? **We might get sued!** People might wonder if they were in a school or an episode of Law and Order SVU. Misbehavior, disrespect, and chaos run rampant, while teachers are forced to remain strong and tolerate widespread disorder. Why? Well, we might get sued. We've allowed the American sue-happy virus to infect our schools, and bureaucracy is patient zero.

The saddest aspect of this system is, strangely enough, also the most optimistic: It doesn't have to be this way. This insanity can be stopped. It certainly won't change overnight, but school districts can take simple steps to move away from the bureaucratic, assembly-line model that is splintering the entire education system and proceed toward a system that supports deep learning, independent thought, and welcoming learning environments. After decades of endless laws, regulations, and mandates, it's still apparent that there is no formula for successful schools. Perhaps allowing teachers and principals to follow their instincts and training to create new and improved ways to reach students will result in productive learning spaces that keep students engaged.

Study after study has shown that good teachers significantly improve the learning of students, but this research has also uncovered something interesting. Great teachers have one thing in common: Nothing. There is no secret ingredient to being an effective teacher except a commitment to the field and an aptness for engaging students. Each teacher has his or her own distinctive technique and style. We cannot allow such rigid and strict foundations to undermine the spontaneity, wit, and creativity teachers need to engage and enrich students' learning and experiences.

Schools must annihilate this bureaucratic beast once and for all and pivot to a model that does not interfere with human interactions the way this Prussian-based model operates. Teachers should be thinking about how to effectively communicate with their students, not what box they have to check off, what rule on the list they have to make sure they're not breaking, or what form they have to fill out that most likely won't even be read by anyone other than the person filling it out. Law and rule are everywhere in public schools. It you don't believe me, go to any district website and download any of the litany of handbooks available from the Employee Handbook to the Student Code-of-Conduct Handbook, and don't forget the Student Services Handbook and the Parent Handbook. There's a handbook for this and a handbook for that. One could pen a Doctor Seuss book about all the handbooks lying around most school districts.

Let's stop demoralizing teachers and students and give them back the respect and independence they deserve. When we treat staff and students like machine tools in a factory, their individualism, passions, and creativity get chiseled down to dust by the rigid, strict protocols and rote drills we have injected into public schools over the past century and with increasing gusto over the last 20 years. The real question is, can we fix this system, or must we destroy the entire mammoth it's become and build anew? There is no one right or wrong way to learn or to teach. Every student and teacher has his or her own unique skill set and personality, and we must allow our system the flexibility to adapt to the ever-evolving needs of our students. We must maintain some type of accountability for success, but we must accomplish this via a healthy school culture, not by rules, regulations, and standardized test scores.

Chapter 5: Teacher Unionization

"The unions are the worst thing that ever happened to education because it's not a meritocracy. It turns into a bureaucracy, which is exactly what has happened. The teachers can't teach and administrators run the place and nobody can be fired. It's terrible." ~Steve Jobs

"I believe that the teachers' unions are doing exactly what they're supposed to be doing. They were designed to be professional organizations that protect the rights and privileges and pay of their members. The problem is that we don't have an organized national interest group with the same heft as the teacher's union that's advocating on behalf of children." ~Michelle Rhee[1]

The thought of unions generally transports one back in time to the post-WWII era when Jimmy Hoffa was king, strikes were rampant, and debates around collective bargaining were frequently heard around the dinner table. As the nation burst into the 21st century, it seemed as if unions, strikes, and the fight for workers' rights had become concepts of a bygone era. There has, however, been a recent surge of interest in improving working conditions in certain areas of factory-based work as well as in certain retail and other service sectors. Groups of employees from Starbucks and Chipotle to Walmart and Amazon have begun to organize in an attempt to gain more favorable working conditions as well as better pay and benefits. Leaders and managers of these companies have, in turn, fought back hard to block any unionization efforts from their employees by discouraging participation, threatening and firing "problematic employees," and even closing down stores that attempt any type of organizing effort.

Although a newfound return to unionization and a renewed push for worker's rights appears to be emerging on the horizon, these concepts never quite disappeared from the field of public education, and they have been major factors in shaping our current school system for the past hundred years. Teachers' unions have historically fought to earn public-sector educators the same rights and privileges as their private-sector peers, but many argue these unions can take their fight a bit too far, resulting in negative outcomes for students.

The union debate has raged since the inception of the first teacher unions in the late 1800s. Proponents of these unions claim they protect teachers from arbitrary and sometimes politically motivated administrative decisions, help increase wages and benefits, and improve intellectual freedom and working standards, as well as provide assurances of tenure, thus affording adequate job security for teachers. Opponents, however, state these teacher unions merely protect and insulate bad teachers, increase district expenditures, impede needed educational reform, and negatively impact student learning, performance, and success.

This chapter delves into the history of teacher unionization and takes a look at the benefits these unions do indeed provide, as well as the many problems and negative outcomes that accompany them. Like many topics in this book, we will discover the answer to the teacher union debate lies somewhere in the seemingly impossible-to-reach middle of the swinging pendulum.

Unions 101

The birth of the modern-day union can be traced all the way back to the 18th century during the rise of the Industrial Revolution. During this time, jobs began to increasingly transition from rural to urban areas, and the daily grind moved from the field to the factory. This new way of earning a living came with a much more hazardous work environment in which laborers found themselves working in close proximity to highly dangerous machinery in extremely hazardous settings. Furthermore, it was not uncommon for industrial workers at the time to work up to 12–14 hours a day, 7 days a week. In addition to these perilous working conditions, workers realized their meager

---

1. https://quotlr.com/author/michelle-rhee

compensation did not quite match that of the owners of these highly lucrative industrial businesses. These workers soon began to band together in an attempt to balance out this uneven distribution of power. Thus, unionization was born.

Unions were created to work directly with employers to increase employee wages and benefits as well as improve conditions on the job, such as those related to safety issues or hours required to work. Employees in a given company generally will vote on whether or not to unionize. If a majority of employees vote yes, then the union and its governing body are created through a democratic process. Workers who want to opt out do have the right to refuse to join the union, but depending on the type of union contract, some employers are required to hire only union workers for certain types of jobs. Unions also require a fee for membership, which generally represents around 1–2% of an employee's annual salary.

Unions work with employers via collective bargaining. Collective bargaining is the process in which the union negotiates terms with a particular employer. The union representatives present a plan of action to the employer stating what adjustments to wages, benefits, or working conditions employees have requested. The two then negotiate and settle on the collective agreements, which are then implemented in the workplace. Unions can negotiate with a single employer or a group of businesses depending on the employees they represent. Once all parties have agreed on a plan, the end result is generally referred to as a Collective Bargaining Agreement or CBA.

Unionization began to seize the reins of the industrial world in the mid-19th century with the emergence of national unions in the United States. In 1866, the National Labor Union was created, and shortly after, the American Federation of Labor was founded. The trend toward unionization surged throughout the remainder of the 1800s and accelerated even more as the United States roared into the 20th century. The Progressive Era of the early 1900s brought the creation of the Department of Labor in 1913 and the Clayton Antitrust Act of 1914, which legalized employees' right to strike and boycott in the private sector. Unions continued to grow during the first half of the 20th century, improving pay and working conditions with the government's passage of mandatory minimum wages and overtime pay. In 1935, the Wagner Act was also passed, which outlawed discriminatory practices against workers who organized and prohibited the formation of a company union.

Unionization took another significant leap in the 1960s when President John F. Kennedy announced an executive order that allowed most federal workers to unionize, with many cities and states following suit. This new public-sector unionization movement soon tied itself closely with other social movements, such as the civil rights movement and the feminist movement (more on this later). Martin Luther King was also a strong union advocate and was actually in Memphis to support a local sanitation worker strike when he was assassinated.

Union membership, especially in the public sector, began to soar in the early 1970s. In 1955, there were around 400,000 members of public sector unions. That number had risen to more than four million by the 1970s. However, this surge in unionization was extremely short-lived and turned out to be the final burst of a dying movement. Several elements throughout the decade began to slowly decimate unions such as increased deregulation in various sectors, industrial restructuring, an unprecedented upsurge of imported foreign goods, as well as the new push for globalization. These and other economic factors, such as oil embargos, currency management issues, high budget deficits, low interest rates, and massive inflation, helped lead to widespread factory closings, which further depleted union membership.

As the United States staggered into the 1980s, unionization would soon encounter its biggest foe to date with the inauguration of President Ronald Reagan and his anti-union administration. By 1985, union membership had dropped by five million members, and the portion of unionized labor had decreased by 25%. By the end of the 1980s, less than 17% of workers were unionized, which was half the rate from the early 1950s. Throughout the rest of the 20th century and into the 21st, union membership continued to decline as globalization and automation became the forces behind the new industrial business model. Union membership in the United States has drastically declined since the Reagan Era and now sits at just under 11%. Furthermore, during this time, many surviving unions drifted away from engaging in collective bargaining and instead shifted to a more politically driven mode of operation, taking up stronger positions in political campaigns and lobbying efforts.

There has, however, been a recent uptick in worker organization in the United States. Companies such as Amazon and Walmart have been fighting unionization in many of their factories, distribution centers, and stores. Retailers and restaurants have also begun to see a rise in worker organization and unionization rhetoric. Many large companies thrived during the COVID-19 pandemic and continue to thrive in the aftermath of its economic wreckage. Employees are standing up and demanding a larger piece of the pie. It's yet to be determined how this new-found organizational movement will evolve, but unionization is once again a hot topic and could play an important role in the economic future of the United States.

Now that we have a rudimentary understanding of what unions are and how they originated, we can take a look at how they have impacted public schools. Although unionization has risen and declined throughout the last couple of centuries, its impacts have been significant in the field of education and still guide legislature surrounding public schools even today. However, to fully understand the impact unionization has had on education, we must time travel a bit more and take a brief look at the history of teacher unions in the United States.

History of Teacher Unions

The evolution of teacher unions has been fraught with many struggles and setbacks but has also resulted in many victories. Although public school teachers encompass the largest segment of the public workforce, historically, teachers have not generally been entitled to the same rights afforded to private sector workers. Since the earliest days of unionization, teachers have battled the same issues: stagnant below-market wages, conditions on the job, and tenure. These issues remain at the forefront even today, and the battles have not stopped raging. But where did this all begin? There is a deep, rich history in the birth of teacher unions in the United States, and the growth of the movement was led mostly by brave women who many times fought not only for improvements on the job but for their way of life.

Although a push for unionization began to emerge during the Industrial Revolution in the late 1700s, the movement did not trickle its way into public education until the mid-1800s. In 1857, the National Teachers Association was founded in Philadelphia. This organization was the forerunner to the National Education Association (NEA), which was created in 1870 and still exists today. This organization was founded to use its influence as a means to professionalize the teaching profession, much like careers in law and medicine. Teachers were fed up with control of schools being left in the hands of politicians, reformers, and other community leaders. They pushed for more standardized entry requirements for the profession, higher wages, and a seat at the discussion table. The NEA, at this time, was led mostly by male education administrators who focused on influencing legislative decisions instead of changes in the classroom; thus, few actual classroom teachers chose to join the NEA in its early days.

As the nation moved into the later stages of the 19th century, the demographics of public educators began to drastically change. The education profession was dominated by White educated men from the colonial period up until the late 1800s. The massive increase in industrialization, immigration, and westward expansion that arose in this period created many more lucrative job opportunities for men. Those who were unable to move into school administration began to exit the field in large numbers. Schools, in turn, began a massive recruitment effort to draw young, educated White women to the profession, and by the turn of the century, they became the dominating force.

Teaching before this time was never really considered a profession but more often functioned as a transient activity performed by men during the farming off-seasons or as a preliminary path into other more advanced careers. As Horace Mann's movement toward publicly funded widespread education emerged in the mid-1800s, many more women began to enter the field. As women moved into teaching positions, men shifted to more supervisory administrative roles. Mann encouraged this trend, claiming that "women's innate gentleness and caring equipped them to be superior teachers in the new public schools." However, some claimed that this push for demographic change was embedded with a bit of malice. This system was accused of being sexist, exploiting women because they could be paid a third less than their male counterparts. Most women lacked other professional opportunities, and many women were also only permitted to teach prior to being married.

Hence, it should be no surprise that it was women who were at the helm of the unionization revolution in education. The turning point in this battle came in Chicago in 1897 with the formation of the Chicago Teachers Federation led by Catherine Goggin and Margaret Haley, who pushed for increases in teachers' salaries and pensions. As the nation coasted into the 20th century, Margaret Haley soon became the face of teacher unionization. She was a highly vocal advocate for teacher reform and improvements in the field. At a 1904 NEA convention, she boldly proclaimed that "in order for students to be free, democratic thinkers, their teachers must be as well." She went on to state that "teachers, therefore, must have better conditions in their classrooms and have their rights respected and their voices heard in the shaping of education policy."

As the following decade approached, the unionization surge in teaching gained more steam. The election of the first female president of the NEA, Ella Flagg Young, was accompanied by a new agency focus on improving classroom conditions. This culminated in 1916 when numerous local teacher organizations merged with the Chicago Teachers Foundation to form the American Federation of Teachers (AFT), which became and remains one of the most dominant forces in public education. From this point forward, the NEA and AFT became the major players in the teacher union game. However, they both followed very different paths and adopted fairly contrasting strategies throughout the 20th century.

The NEA drifted away from the dreaded term union and continued to focus more on cooperating with educational administrative bodies as well as the intense lobbying of national and state governmental legislatures to further professionalize the field of teaching. The AFT, on the other hand, proudly referred to itself as a union and concentrated more on actual changes in the classroom, such as better pay and benefits. The AFT became extremely teacher-focused and enacted a full ban on administrators joining their ranks. The AFT also moved to cooperate with other organized labor groups, but both the AFT and NEA agreed, at least at the time, not to engage in strikes.

Both the AFT and NEA grew in membership during WWI, but many entities were still in direct opposition to unionization, limiting their growth, especially the more radically viewed AFT. Once governments began to fall following the aftermath of the war, hostility toward unions began to swell. The Boston police strike of 1919 further ignited the anti-union sentiment, causing many states to enact laws banning most public sector unions. AFT membership, in turn, plummeted. However, the NEA continued to grow in numbers and influence by sticking to its foundational philosophy of distancing itself from classroom issues and education reform and instead focusing on cozying up to as many local legislators as possible.

While the roaring twenties were accompanied by a further decline in teacher unionization, that trend soon changed as the United States tumbled headfirst into the Great Depression of the 1930s. The crushing economic disasters facing the nation resulted in massive decreases in educational spending, causing incomes of both rural and urban teachers to nosedive. Many teachers even lost their jobs. Both the AFT and NEA stuck to their long-running modes of operation but made little progress throughout the decade. However, unionization received a major boost with the passing of the Wagner Act in 1935, but this law only applied to the private sector, thus excluding public sector employees, such as teachers, from any protection or collective bargaining rights.

As the nation moved into the 1940s, the labor movement took center stage once again after the conclusion of WWII as wartime price controls expired and wages stagnated. Private sector strikes ran rampant, and teacher unionization began to surge once again. AFT membership grew dramatically, and the NEA continued its politically based path, shifting its alignment to the Cold War-era political right. The 1950s finally brought teacher unions the success they had been fighting for when, by 1951, 97% of school districts had adopted non-gender-based pay scales, thus at last closing the pay gap that had existed between male and female teachers for over a century.

From the 1950s to the 1970s, public sector unionization flourished. Private sector collective bargaining had become fairly routine by this point, resulting in a noticeable increase in living standards for union workers. Many Americans at this time began to adopt the view that a worker's ability to join a union was a basic civil right, and the various other civil rights-based movements of the time further influenced and solidified these beliefs. Unionization in the public sector became more accepted by most Americans, and this resulted in the election of many politicians with similar views on the labor movement. In 1959, Wisconsin became the first state to legalize collective bargaining for public sector workers, and shortly after, in 1962, President John F Kennedy issued Executive Order 10988, granting collective bargaining rights to most federal workers. Although these new laws secured wide gains for public sector employees, they varied greatly by state, and public sector workers never quite attained the same rights granted to the private sector by the Wagner Act.

Despite these setbacks, unionization increased tenfold throughout the next 20 years, and strikes were frequent. A large successful teacher strike took place in New York City in 1963, earning teachers collective bargaining rights. These strikes became so successful that AFT reversed its no-strike policy the next year, advancing their cause and creating a massive upsurge in membership. As the tumultuous sixties ended, the decade-long gains made by the AFT did not go unnoticed by the NEA, and they began to adopt the many aspects of unionization from which they had long sought to distance themselves. They began using the loose synonymic phrase, professional negotiations, instead of the dreaded collective bargaining boogeyman they had tried for so long to avoid, and in 1973, the NEA opted to expel and ban all administrators from its organization. The NEA even set about creating a new reputation for advocacy around racial and gender equality and other progressive ideologies historically attached to their AFT adversary.

These 20 or so years could be seen as the golden age of teacher unionization. From 1960 to 1974, teachers were involved in over 1,000 strikes involving over 800,000 teachers, and by the close of the 1970s, 72% of public school teachers were covered by collective bargaining agreements. During this time, the NEA finally designated itself as a union, and the AFT moved its headquarters to Washington, DC to be closer to the action.

History, however, sometimes makes unexpected turns in unpredicted directions. Public school teachers were on the cusp of finally gaining the federally protected collective bargaining rights for which they had long battled, that is, until the U.S. economy collapsed in the 1970s. The reasons were many, but the end result was the worst recession the United States had witnessed since the Great Depression. A good crisis should never go to waste; thus, opponents of teacher unionization used this upheaval to paint a picture of public sector workers as greedy, privileged prima donnas who did nothing but achieve gains at the expense of the general public. This sentiment and newfound public hostility toward striking teachers helped catapult the conservative movement, resulting in the emergence of the new Reaganized kingdom of the eighties.

Strikes would continue to run rampant into the early 1980s, however, in 1981, unionization tactics would forever change when over 10,000 air traffic controllers went on strike. Ronald Reagan, in turn, fired all 10,000 plus air traffic controllers, garnering overwhelming public support for his actions and causing public sector workers to rethink their strategies. This was a major turning point in teacher unionization. From this point forward, strikes became increasingly rare, and unions quickly shifted toward endorsing politicians and engaging in coincidental lobbying efforts. Basically, unions stepped back into the old NEA philosophy. As the 20th century wound down, so did union participation within the private sector, and membership plummeted to less than 10% of the workforce. These trends continued into the 21st century, with teacher unions leveling off somewhat. Membership remained stagnant, and strikes became an endangered species of the past; unions focused primarily on legislative gains.

With terrorism rampant, wars raging, and economic disasters looming throughout the onset of the 21st century, the United States had little time to fret over teacher unionization, even with Bush's passage of the No Child Left Behind Act that upended public education and created long-lasting negative effects still seen today. However, in 2008, when the Great Recession commenced, teachers and other public sector workers became the scapegoats once again with their supposed privileged lifestyles and greater rights and benefits than those of private workers. Wisconsin, which had been the first state to legalize public sector collective bargaining, attempted half a century later to complete the circuit by becoming the first state to abolish that protection. Even liberals who historically had led the charge for unionization began to disappear into the shadows, arguing for school choice and bashing teacher unions and public education in general.

Despite the newly inspired war against unions, teachers and other public sector employees did not back down, and massive protests ensued, which eventually led to the Occupy Wall Street movement in 2011. In 2012, the first teacher strike in 25 years erupted in the city of Chicago. Teachers used the corporate monster narrative and attached themselves to the Occupy movement. This was a successful tactic because these teachers received overwhelming support from their community and the nation at large.

The sentiment around teacher unions and public sector labor issues seemed to level out, leaving the nation somewhere smack dab in the middle of the debate. The last 10 years have seen most unions continue down the path generally followed by the NEA in their early days, with few strikes and most of their resources being allocated to political endorsements and lobbying efforts. However, teachers still feel the heat—now from both sides of the aisle. Traditional union opponents on the right remain strong in their opposition, and their views have not changed much. These same teachers are now besieged by leftwing reformers who have recently begun to attack tenure policies and push for more high-stakes testing.

There has, however, been a recent surge in unionization attempts in the private sector, and this has trickled over into the public sector as well. Several states have dealt with teacher strikes over the last few years, but these strikes have lasted for only a matter of days in most instances. Nonetheless, teachers are shifting back to a defensive stance and have been increasingly forming alliances with community coalitions and labor unions. Teachers seem to be returning to their roots when it comes to unionization. They have and will always have to fight for improvements in the field. For now, we will have to wait and see how the battle proceeds.

Tenure

Tenure is a fairly easy concept to understand. It benefits educators by providing them with the highest level of job security possible. Before the introduction of tenure, teachers could be fired for decreases in enrollment, shifting political ideologies of the school and/or administration, economic issues resulting in a depletion of education funding, or, many times, merely due to the whims of a belligerent school principal. Therefore, in the late 1800s, some states decided after a number of years on the job, generally 2–5, teachers would procure tenure. This protected them from dismissal for specific causes, many of which were not related to performance. By the mid-1900s, 80% of U.S. teachers were tenured.

A majority of states currently offer some type of tenure system for public school educators. Generally, depending on the state, a beginning teacher is on a probationary contract for the first 1–5 years of employment. A unionized teacher in his or her probationary phase still possesses a significant amount of protection, but a probationary teacher can often easily be terminated for a variety of reasons. State laws constantly change, but at the time of this writing, 45 of the 50 states have tenure systems in place. Of these 45 states, only 22 require their districts to consider teacher performance when making tenure decisions, and six states have no policy in place at all.

Understanding the concept of teacher tenure is not complicated. However, teacher tenure has long been an extremely controversial subject. The prevailing question centers on whether the system is detrimental or advantageous to our educational system and student outcomes. For example, proponents of tenure argue it provides protection against being terminated for personal or political reasons and prevents experienced, high-paid teachers from being replaced by less experienced, lower-paid teachers. Opponents claim tenure makes it extremely difficult to remove poorly performing teachers and encourages teacher complacency. With nearly 2.5 million teachers currently under tenure, this perpetual controversy has no end in sight. So, let's take a closer look at some of the individual pros and cons of this system.

Before tenure, political transitions of power were often accompanied by a barrage of firings to either eliminate teachers who might possess opposing views or to make positions available to prop up friends and allies of the new administration. Defenders of teacher tenure cite this as one of the foundational reasons for creating the tenure system in the first place. Many times, female educators were terminated for becoming pregnant, getting married, not following the typical female dress code, or even being spotted out too late in the evening. Historically, teachers were also laid off during economic downturns, and with budget deficits looming over many school districts in the United States, this is not just a fear of the past. Proponents of teacher tenure state that it provides teachers the job security they need to adequately perform their job duties by alleviating worries about economic issues affecting their job status or a younger lower-salaried teacher usurping their position.

Supporters of tenure also argue that teachers are allowed more academic freedom as a result of the system. It affords teachers the latitude to try new and innovative teaching methods and ideas without the fear of retribution. The system also facilitates recruitment by promising would-be teachers a secure, stable profession. With much higher salaries available in other fields, tenure advocates worry that removing or drastically altering this system would severely stymie teacher recruitment efforts. Proponents of teacher tenure also point to the fact that it is school administrators who determine tenure based on their evaluations of a teacher. Ergo, granting tenure to a teacher who performs poorly is solely the fault of poor administrative judgment. They go on to claim that the tenure system has merely become a scapegoat for other school-related problems, such as overcrowding, lack of funds, or bad parenting.

These proponents also argue that teachers would not be able to properly advocate for students or disagree openly with ineffective or pointless school policies, procedures, or rules in the absence of a tenure system. Without the protection tenure offers, teachers would be afraid to stand up for what is right and just. They also maintain tenure protects teachers from students as well. Many times, districts may attempt to immediately fire a teacher based on an accusation from a student, coworker, or supervisor. These accusations often turn out to be false, and the tenure system provides teachers with due process when situations like this arise...and they arise much more often than one would think. With the recent wave of firings across the nation during the massive cancelation movement, it is no surprise workers would want to seek some level of protection from the mob.

Defenders claim the tenure system actually encourages districts to be much more selective when hiring teachers. Since their removal could be difficult, it is argued the tenure system creates a sort of a checks and balances type system in which schools must strive only to hire the best and most qualified teachers while at the same time removing those underperforming teachers before their tenure can be reached. The formal dismissal process created by the tenure system, proponents state, can also protect teachers from premature termination, providing them with adequate time and motivation to improve their skills. Lastly, advocates for teacher tenure contend that, overall, this system produces more effective teachers because they can teach without the fear and anxiety of losing their job and instead focus on providing the best educational outcomes for their students.

Opponents of teacher tenure, however, have their own set of arguments, often siting the massive perception of complacency that results from a complete lack of fear of losing one's job. They claim the tenure system removes any incentives to be a good teacher, resulting in tenured teachers putting in the bare minimum effort when it comes to planning, teaching, and improving their craft. Opponents also point out that because of tenure, it can take schools months and even years to remove an underperforming teacher, causing districts to waste time, energy, and money that could better be used to serve students.

When surveyed, over 80% of school administrators stated they had at least one under-performing tenured teacher on their campus. Removing a tenured teacher can be quite a costly affair. In New York state, it costs over $300,000 to fire a tenured teacher, and the New York Department of Education spends between $15–20 million a year on salaries earmarked for tenured teachers who have been removed from the classroom because they are in the drawn-out termination process. Remember, this process can take years, and these teachers are paid their full salary until the outcome is determined. Because termination proceedings under a tenured system involve unions, courts, the school board, as well as other administrators, many districts simply decide it's just not worth the time, effort, and money to navigate through the labyrinth of procedures, paperwork, and regulations to fire someone.

Tenure adversaries also like to point out that layoff decisions are based on seniority—last hired-first fired. This means circumstances that call for faculty reductions end up retaining poorly performing teachers merely due do the hierarchical tenure model. Tenure systems frequently allow experienced teachers the latitude to choose the classes they teach, leaving the scraps for the less experienced teachers. This creates an unequal distribution of talent and skill sets throughout the school, resulting in a potentially negative impact on students.

Rivals of teacher tenure go on to claim that tenure does not significantly affect recruitment, as supporters claim it does. Further, with the myriad protections already granted by recent state and federal laws as a result of previous court rulings and collective bargaining agreements, opponents of tenure argue that this system is no longer needed. They also point out that due to the stringent requirement of more recent laws such as No Child Left Behind, teachers no longer have any academic freedom anyway, so proponents of tenure are merely shining light on a moot point.

Opponents of teacher tenure have also noted that the 2–5 years required to attain tenure is just not enough time for teachers to adequately show their aptitude or worth. Looking at the chart below, we can see that a majority of states offer tenure after only two to three years of service.

Years to Earn Tenure	Number of States
2 years	4
3 years	28
4 or more years	19

A University of Washington study has recently shown that the first 2–3 years of teaching have no correlation with future teacher performance. In colleges and universities, professors must exhibit proof of at least some significant contributions to their field of study. Public schools have no comparable standard requiring teachers to contribute to the body of knowledge—they simply need to stick around long enough for tenure to kick in. What's more, two different studies in 2009 and 2017 revealed that < 1% of teachers received an unsatisfactory evaluation, underscoring opponents' claim that the bar for obtaining tenure has been set extremely low.

Lastly, adversaries of tenure claim the system has little to no educational value for students and is highly unpopular. In 2017, an EdNext survey of around 4,200 Americans found that nearly 50% oppose tenure compared to 33% who support it. Even among teachers, a mere 61% support tenure, while 31% oppose it. Given the long-term spending commitments and wasted time and resources that accompany the tenure system, opponents argue that it's just not worth it.

So, what's the verdict? Both sides of the debate have conjured up very thought-provoking points. Extant data and research do indicate tenure provides at least some benefits to the public school system, but this system also comes with many flaws. First and foremost, research and data on the topic are inadequate. More research is required to determine the precise effect the tenure system has on student outcomes. Does tenure improve or degrade student performance? Or, perhaps, it has no ramifications whatsoever on the success of students. Either way, it would be a good idea to figure it out.

Teachers do need job protection, but at what cost? School districts must find a reasonable way to provide educators with the job security they need, but they must also identify better ways to remove poorly performing teachers whether or not they have tenure. This seems to be the foundational criticism of this system, and addressing the problem of underperforming and complacent tenured teachers is the first step states could take to address this situation. States should begin to incorporate performance standards into the tenure process. Furthermore, the bar to achieve tenure should be significantly raised so that poor-quality teachers no longer slip through the cracks. States and districts could integrate an amendment to include poor performance as a cause for termination, regardless of tenure. Even something as simple as a three-strike rule—meaning if a tenured teacher receives three unsatisfactory evaluations, they're out—would be a significant improvement. This would, at the very least, reduce complacency and increase teachers' motivation to improve.

Increasing the amount of time it takes to achieve tenure would also be an excellent first step. Two to three years of teaching is not adequate time to demonstrate the required skills to earn tenure. This time frame should be increased to at least five years and perhaps even more. With nearly 50% of new teachers exiting the field within the first 5 years, this would significantly decrease the number of teachers eligible for tenure and create more incentive for teachers who choose to remain in the field and improve their craft.

At the end of the day, students are what matters. If new research indicates tenure does impact student success negatively, then maybe it's time to move past this model. On the other hand, if tenure proves to increase student performance, then maybe we should find a way to accept this controversial practice. Researchers must look deeper into this issue to determine its outcome, but regardless of the results, teacher tenure has and always will be directly linked to unionization—unions are the reason teacher tenure exists at all. Therefore, in order to understand how teacher tenure may affect the public school system, we must dive even deeper into the negative and positive consequences of teacher unions.

The Case for Teacher Unions

Teacher unions have been fighting to improve and reform the field of teaching for over a century, and they have achieved many victories along the way. Despite their opposition, teacher unions have managed to thrive and maintain their existence now well into the 21st century, while many of their counterparts in the private and public sectors have faded into irrelevance or been completely wiped out. Their goals have been simple: to establish a grievance system to protect teachers, to enhance and improve working conditions for teachers, and to increase the safety of teachers.

Most proponents of teacher unions point to the due process protection unions have worked to ensure for teachers. Collective bargaining agreements have stipulated specific guidelines that all parties must follow when any problems with a teacher arise. Unions protect teachers from unfair firing practices that could result from a variety of reasons. This goes beyond the concept of teacher tenure, with unions ensuring this system of due process for any and all teachers within the union, regardless of their years of experience. Administrators and other district officials cannot whimsically terminate a teacher because policies have been put in place by union negotiations to protect them. In addition, unions shield teachers from shifting politics within their district or community. Unions work with, and many times against, legislatorial bodies to fight against changes in laws or regulations surrounding teacher salaries, student testing performance, curriculum changes, or other issues that may negatively impact teachers.

Union membership also safeguards teachers from reprisal when attempting to advocate for students or their peers or when teachers speak out against unfair or problematic educational policies. Teachers are most often the front-line experts since they, not the politicians or the administrators, are in the classroom every day. Teachers are the ones who see what happens with students day in and day out and are most often the best at determining what students may need. Unions provide teachers the protection they require to speak out for what their students need to maximize their opportunity to succeed in the classroom. Often, there is much disagreement over what is necessary for a student; thus, unions allow an arena for worry-free debate in which teachers can speak openly without fear of retaliation.

As discussed in the previous section, tenure only exists due to union efforts. We've already discussed this concept in detail, but tenure builds upon the protections already put in place by union negotiations. Tenure further defines and extends teachers' rights to due process and provides extra job security, which reduces anxiety in a field that is already ripe with angst. Unions still protect teachers during their initial probationary period, but once tenure is attained, that protection expands and becomes more solidified.

Unionization, however, is not free. Union fees represent around 1–2% of one's annual salary but can reach as high as 5% in some districts; however, supporters point to the fact that these fees are generally tax deductible. In addition, the wage gains provided by unionization offset any and all fees or dues. It is estimated that unionized teachers make around 10% more than their non-union peers, thus still earning 5–8% more after deducting union fees. Moreover, most teacher unions provide valuable discounts to restaurants, retail centers, and even health care providers, offering teachers additional means to fatten their eternally diminishing bank accounts.

Advocates of teacher unions also argue that unions create a sense of unification, encouraging people to work together in a peaceful and productive manner. Bringing teachers, administrators, and parents together creates an environment in which meaningful change can occur at a much faster pace. Unions allow teachers to organize and push for relevant revisions to the system, providing teachers the opportunity to positively influence the entire district or even the state. Unionization also grants teachers timely access to resources and other assets that they may use to push for policies to ensure better student outcomes. Union defenders go even further, claiming that the unification provided by unionization typically results in better student performance. When teachers are able to safely advocate for their students, these students may then be afforded access to a better curriculum, less testing, or more adequate learning opportunities.

The correlation between unions and student outcomes has been hotly debated, and more research needs to be implemented to get a better overall picture. Of course, union proponents claim that teacher unionization can be directly correlated with higher student achievement levels. They point to Singapore and Finland as excellent examples of the positive impacts of unionization. Both countries have a 100% unionization rate and not only produce significantly better academic results than the United States but also lead the world in numerous educational categories. Schools in New York and Maryland with extremely high rates of teacher unionization perform much better than schools in states such as Mississippi or Louisiana, which have low rates of unionization. The Washington Post has pointed out that of all the non-unionized states in the United States, only Virginia ranks above the median in education, with an overwhelming majority of the other non-unionized states falling below the bottom 15 states in performance. However, some of these data may be hand-picked to fit a narrative, or there could, perhaps, be other regional and/or demographic differences affecting student performance in addition to or irrespective of unionization.

Much more research must be conducted in the area of teacher unionization if the nation ever hopes to find the true answers. Whether student outcomes are improved, impaired, or unaffected by unionization remains a tough question to answer, and it is one schools must diligently push to discover. It's apparent teacher unions have achieved many great leaps in protecting teachers' rights and providing them with the resources and confidence needed to fight for improvements in an extremely difficult job. However, have these unions gone too far? Have teacher unions done more to enhance and protect their own interests than those of schools and students? We will see there are almost always two sides to every story.

The War Against Teacher Unions

Despite the success teacher unions have achieved throughout the past century, they have encountered many tenacious and outspoken opponents along the way who have consistently emphasized a lengthy list of complaints and accusations against unions. For starters, rivals claim that teacher unions don't quite aid teachers to the extent they claim. There is most often a complete lack of any union presence in the workplace at all. The average school does not have union representatives lurking around every corner. In most schools, the only trace of a union is the sole sign pinned to the workroom bulletin board and one campus union representative who is generally just a highly influential teacher who has been a union member for many years but who has no actual power.

Unions also may altogether fail to provide adequate teacher representation. Union leaders spend little if any, time in actual classrooms; therefore, they may be a bit out of touch when it comes to what teachers really need. If what the union feels is important does not align with what teachers feel is important, then what's the point of a union? Many times, it can take a great deal of work to get unions involved in the particular issue teachers want to fight, thus negating the entire process.

Union adversaries point to one major factor when it comes to teacher unionization: Money. The simple fact is that teacher unions cost schools millions upon millions of dollars a year. It can take years and cost upwards of $200–300 thousand to fire one teacher in some states. That money could be used to pay the salary of four to six full-time certified teachers. Some states spend millions, even 10s of millions every year to pay the salaries of teachers caught in limbo while their case is investigated. And don't forget, districts must also pay for substitute teachers to fill in for these teachers during this investigation process. While the investigation drags on, teachers relax by reading a book, playing Candy Crush, or merely twiddling their thumbs all the while collecting $70k a year. Sounds like a pretty good gig.

Foes of teacher unions also look at the distribution of union fees as a very problematic issue since teacher unions are permitted to spend monetary resources on needs that may not align with educational interests. A large portion of union funds is allocated for lobbying efforts and to provide financial support for certain political candidates. Depending on the state, teachers may have little to no part in deciding where these funds go or who receives them, and those funds may wind up in the coffers of political entities these same teachers may not support. Some states have implemented laws to address this situation, even allowing teachers to deduct a portion of their dues earmarked for these activities. Nonetheless, teachers still find themselves caught in this situation in many states across the country. Some unionized teachers have also been pressured to perform specific duties or actions by their union without compensation. Teacher unions may pester members about showing up for a protest or rally, going door-to-door seeking community support, or having their personal information made publicly available. Unions can, at times, be very dictatorial, and many teachers opt out of them for this very reason.

The overall public school system, however, is not the only suffering party in this unsustainable financial situation. Teacher unions, of course, represent the interests of teachers, and those interests, at times, can even benefit students and administrators. However, at no point are the actual funding parties—taxpayers—represented in any collective bargaining or negotiation process. The United States does require local politicians to protect the interests of taxpayers, but communities have no representative to send on their behalf. If these politicians are inexperienced and lack the skills to deal with unions, they may be hoodwinked into agreeing to costly concessions that may result in increased costs for local taxpayers.

Districts may also find themselves locked into poorly thought-out long-term contracts as a result of bad negotiations on either side of the equation. Both sides must have experienced and effective negotiators in order to achieve effective and meaningful outcomes. For example, bad contracts could result in increased difficulty in removing underperforming teachers or a situation where teachers receive below-market wages due to locked-in salary arrangements in the contract. The majority of these agreements last for 2 years, although some contracts can be enforced for 5 years or more with few, if any, opportunities to renegotiate or amend the agreement. This creates an ongoing struggle between administration and teachers which, once again, results in students being caught in the middle.

As adamantly as pro-union advocates tout the high student performance that results from teacher unionization, opponents seem insistent on the exact opposite outcomes. These opponents claim unions change the entire school dynamics as well as the learning process. Unions can wind up creating a narrow path for teachers to follow, which provides consistency but lacks the flexibility needed to adapt to the ever-changing environment of a public school classroom. Teachers must be versatile, and meaningful change cannot be correlated solely with salary, benefits, and safety. Additionally, unions can have a direct negative impact on students, which can be summed up in one word: Strikes. When teachers strike or merely threaten to go on strike, they're essentially using students as bargaining tools. If a strike actually does occur, there will certainly be no teachers to teach, classrooms will be empty, and all learning will cease. I'm not sure how else you could describe that situation other than a direct negative outcome on students and their taxpaying parents.

At the end of the day, we must wrestle with the question of whether children should be used as pawns in this game, and this is the most ardent opposition to teacher unionization. Unions tend to transform schools into venues of economic opportunity instead of the educational institutes they are intended to be. Perhaps students should not be caught up in this inexhaustible struggle between teachers and administrators, but unfortunately, this is the situation in which we find ourselves. There are obvious pros and cons of teacher unions, but we have to find a place to move forward that not only provides the protection teachers need and deserve but also ensures the best outcomes for students.

Teacher Unions: The Final Cut

Criticism of public education in the United States has shifted from scholarly assemblages to dinner table chatter. One can hardly turn on a talk show, news outlet, or podcast without hearing some talk of education reform or school choice. The finger has been pointed at various culprits, but teacher unions have endured more of the blame than nearly any other group. Unions are consistently characterized as nefarious entities concerned only with their own survival and interests instead of the success and welfare of students. Public outcry has accused teacher unions of inadequately pushing for meaningful change and reform and actually hindering the entire process through bargaining procedures that have more influence on public education than any other entity.

Teacher unions have, in fact, been major drivers in public education policy for nearly a century. Collective bargaining became an extremely important tool used by teacher unions to establish policy and govern the ways in which administrators, teachers, parents, and students interact in the educational process. This "web of rules," as it was termed, influences every aspect of the system and can have direct as well as indirect effects on educational outcomes. Here is just a sample list of categories and items included in some collective bargaining agreements:

1. Rights and duties
2. Participation in governing and policy-making
3. Grievance and disciplinary procedures
4. Working conditions
5. Length of school days, hours, and preparation time
6. Class size limits
7. Professional development requirements
8. Student grading and promotion procedures

9. Instructional policy
10. Teacher evaluation and performance metrics

This is not an exhaustive list yet, it is not difficult to understand how influential teacher unions can be. These bargaining arrangements, although including metrics for performance evaluation, are primarily focused on the "interest" of teachers as opposed to their actual performance and how it affects their students. The collective bargaining process used by teacher unions has had a tremendous impact on the public school system in many unexpected and seldom explored areas.

Several detailed studies have found that teachers covered by collective bargaining agreements earn between 5–12% higher wages than their non-unionized peers. These bargaining agreements have an even larger effect on teacher benefits. Researchers note these wages and benefits result in higher costs for the district, but they may also increase education outcomes by attracting better, more qualified teachers. Investigators have also found that student-teacher ratios are 7–12% lower for unionized teachers. These researchers did, however, find that students in these classrooms are affected in different ways depending on the type of student. Unionized schools rely on less specialized instructional methods, resulting in a 42% decrease in the time students spend with a specialist, which could, and most likely does, have a negative impact on lower-functioning or struggling students as well as higher-functioning students.

It makes sense that increases in pay, as well as improvements in benefits, come with significant increases in costs for school districts, and the limited but detailed studies addressing this have arrived at the same conclusion. Operating costs of a unionized elementary school are up to 15% higher than those of a non-unionized school. The increase in costs for unionized schools at the high school level comes in a bit lower at 8–12%. Unions, without a doubt, have an overwhelming influence on the way public schools allocate resources. Funds shifted to cover increases in teacher pay and benefits must be siphoned from funds generally earmarked for other instructional resources, resulting in, at the very least, indirect negative impacts that will eventually trickle down, affecting student success rates.

The most crucial question, however, is exactly how teacher unionization affects student performance. The evidence and research available on this topic are, unfortunately, sparse and inadequate, but several studies have been conducted on how these unions shape the effectiveness of public schools. The data on whether the increases in wages and benefits of unionization attract better-quality teachers are inconsistent and a bit contradictory. One study found that higher wages do attract a more proficient pool of applicants, but a similar study uncovered the exact opposite, showing no evidence of a correlation between the higher wages and benefits offered by unionization and increased applicant quality.

There is one way to link student performance to unionization: the dreaded test score. Although the studies could be problematic due to lack of controls, research has shown that students attending unionized schools score between 4.5–8% higher on the SAT or ACT and have 4.4% higher graduation rates. Several other studies have shown increases in standardized test scores for students in unionized schools, but the increases were mostly minimal, with only a 1–2% increase. These stats look promising, but one caveat has been noted by researchers studying this phenomenon. These relatively small increases in achievement in unionized schools have only been experienced by average-achieving students. It appears that lower or higher-achieving students, in fact, make out far worse in unionized schools. These studies also revealed that unionized schools have been linked with a 2.3% increase in student dropout rates, and dropout rates have historically been highly correlated with student success.

These results sound a bit contradictory. If unionized schools produce higher standardized test scores as well as higher graduation rates, how do they also produce higher dropout rates? This confusing bit of data makes much more sense when we combine it with the notion that the positive outcomes resulting from unionized schools are found primarily in average-achieving students, while lower and higher-achieving students are left in the dust. If the success of underperforming students is further reduced by teacher unions, higher dropout rates should be expected because they are the students who opt to leave school early. These results also point back to the fact that unionized schools most often follow much more traditional instructional methods and lack the specialized teachers and methods that lower as well as higher-achieving students need to succeed. Lower-functioning students get lost in the shuffle as traditional methods of instruction do not properly address their deficits. Higher functioning students become bored and frustrated with traditional methods that cannot stimulate their minds, causing them to become unmotivated and cynical about the entire system, which also results in lower achievement and higher dropout rates.

Determining exactly if and how teacher unionization affects student performance has no simple answer. From the limited research available, we can, unfortunately, make no all-encompassing generalizations about the effects these unions have on student success. However, extant research does indicate that students in the middle of the achievement spectrum seem to be unharmed by unionization and may, in fact, slightly benefit from it. In addition, though, these studies concluded that teacher unions can have a detrimental effect on those higher and lower-achieving students located on either side of the spectrum. Much more research must be done in this area, but there may already be enough to safely claim that the benefits of teacher unionization may not be worth the increase in costs for districts.

So, what are we to do about teacher unions? It seems even after laying out all the facts, both sides have valid arguments. We can rightfully conclude that unionization does, in fact, lead to increases in teacher wages and benefits, improves working conditions, and reinforces job security, but the effects of unionization on student performance are extremely varied depending on the achievement level of the student.

Regardless of their effects, teacher unions have evolved into powerful behemoths that single-handedly dictate education legislation in many states across the country—and therein lies the problem. The interests of teacher unions have begun to drift out of alignment with those of the public in many places, and the interests of these unions have, without a doubt, strayed far from any concern about student achievement or success. Teacher unions have even begun to lose the support of actual teachers, with up to a 16% drop in approval ratings in some states.

Teacher unions amass large sums of money, and many teachers, as well as taxpayers, wonder where all this union money goes. Based on 2016 data from the Center for Responsive Politics, the AFT and NEA combined have spent more than $56 million on political contributions since 1989. This is nearly as much as Exxon, Chevron, Mobil, Lockheed Martin, and the NRA combined during the same period. With massive amounts of funds allocated for union compensation, overhead, and leadership conferences, as well as many political activities not associated with the union's direct representation, teachers question whether they're actually getting what they're paying for. And although that question may be up for debate among teachers, the overall public school system may want to return to the bargaining table. With increases in funding reaching 15% for some districts, a 1–2 percentage point gain in test scores of a select demographic of the student population probably does not balance out too well at school board budgetary meetings. The ends do not seem to justify the means when it comes to teacher unionization.

Is there any reasonable way for school districts to move forward? Unions have amassed so much power many states have found themselves impotent in this battle. There are several ways to improve this system, though, and schools must begin to push back. Limits should be implemented on the amount of money teacher unions are allowed to allocate to political candidates through campaign contributions or lobbying efforts. States could even put measures in place to allow teachers to vote on exactly how and where part of their dues are to be spent. The interests of unions must also be more aligned with those of the taxpaying public and focus more on the performance of students. Teachers and administrators must learn to work together and collaborate to determine the goals, instructional procedures, and governing of the school. If the relationship between teachers and their administrative bodies could somehow become less combative, the need for unions would be significantly diminished.

Thus, there is no easy answer to addressing the problems of teacher unions. They, no doubt, have helped teachers gain many rights and improvements in the workplace, but these gains have come at great cost. And students have footed the bill. With nearly zero reliable data linking unionization to overall improvements in student performance, it's time to question teacher unions' role in the education process. However, don't expect them to disappear anytime soon and reforming them will be an extremely difficult and lengthy process. But the nation must find a more efficient and productive means to protect teachers while at the same time providing the best environment for students to reach their highest level of achievement.

Part II: Fuel for the Fire

Chapter 6: Curriculum

"I imagine a school system that recognizes learning is natural, that a love of learning is normal, and that real learning is passionate learning. A school curriculum that values questions above answers...creativity above fact regurgitation...individuality above conformity... and excellence above standardized performance... And we must reject all notions of 'reform' that serve up more of the same: more testing, more 'standards', more uniformity, more conformity, more bureaucracy.[1] " ~Tom Peters

"Today, in the age of standardized testing, thinking and acting, reason and judgment have been thrown out the window just as teachers are increasingly being deskilled and forced to act as semi-robotic technicians good for little more than teaching for the test.[2] " ~Henry Giroux

It's becoming increasingly evident that, as a nation, we must ask ourselves: What is the purpose of public education? This may seem like a nonsensical question, but with curricula becoming more and more outdated and standardized testing proving to be a not very accurate gauge of performance, this question is becoming progressively relevant. However, there does not seem to be a consensus about what this purpose might be, or perhaps our public schools have gotten to the point where they have lost sight of their purpose altogether. Academic accomplishments and college placement leading to career prospects would seem to be a reasonable purpose, but what about the ultimate value of what kind of human being that student becomes? From a government perspective, the purpose may be to create an informed citizenry that can develop a socially mobile and productive workforce to advance the nation as a whole. Man, that should be on a poster with Uncle Sam pointing directly at you. Governments would obviously want productive citizens who are informed, engaged, and involved in civil service, government, and elections to drive the economy.

Perhaps though, we should focus more on the future self of the student. Maybe the purpose of public schools could be to produce learners who can thrive in a competitive and professional world by engaging in deep thinking and using meaningful solutions to address real-world problems. Now that's a poster! Whatever the purpose of public education should be, it has recently shifted in the wrong direction. Many parents see public school today as nothing more than free, relatively safe childcare, and others view schooling as a place for entertainment and extracurricular activities. Yet, some see and use public schools as basically another social services outlet. Although much of the current school curriculum has deteriorated into useless rubbish, public school is not daycare, and it is not Chuck E Cheese.

The purpose of public education has undoubtedly evolved over the last couple of centuries despite its most recent stagnation. Through the late 1700s and most of the 1800s, public schools' main focus was to preserve the new and uncertain American democracy and inoculate democratic values and beliefs. As the country began to dive headfirst into the heart of the Industrial Revolution in the late 1800s to early 1900s, the Prussian model began to take flight with the goal of preparing everyone for vocations, resulting in the assembly line style of education we've already discussed. In the latter part of the postwar 1900s, the Cold War with the Soviet Union intensified, and the new economic Communist force, otherwise known as China, stepped onto the world stage. This new geopolitical configuration created a shift to maintaining the competitiveness of the United States with a hyper-focus on how well students performed in schools. From this shift, an increased focus on student outcomes emerged, resulting in a fixation on quantitative data and standardized test scores. Once the nation arrived at the dawn of the 21st century, the purpose deviated again toward a focus on marginalized groups and eliminating poverty. This shift in

---

1. *https://www.azquotes.com/quote/860408?ref=curriculum*

2. *https://www.azquotes.com/quote/728094?ref=standardized-testing*

purpose-focused not only on test scores but on ensuring all student demographics achieved a basic measure of efficiency in all core subjects, which, in theory, would lead to more equal opportunities and outcomes.

So, 20 years later, what's next? The world we live in has changed more in the last 20 years than it has in the last 200. Think back to the early 2000s...no cellphones (at least not widespread use). No Facebook, Instagram, Twitter, online dating, nonstop news, or minute-by-minute updates in the palm of our hand. Zero notifications and messages bombarded us every minute of the day. None of this existed only 2 decades ago. The mere speed at which everyday life proceeds today is exponentially faster. We've gone from waiting minutes for those clicking sounds emanating from our dial-up modem to connect and download a single webpage to instantly connecting to anyone and anyplace across the globe in a matter of seconds or even milliseconds in less than half a generation's time.

A multitude of jobs from 2 decades ago don't even exist today, and many other barely surviving occupations continue their path toward extinction every day. Of course, these changes come with both positive and negative results, but this book is not about that. The question we need to address is how our public education system has evolved to adapt to the environment in which we currently live. Unfortunately, we find that public schools may still be searching for their new purpose, and if they don't discover it soon, we could all find ourselves in quite a predicament.

Common Core Standards

To start our journey through the world of public school curricula, we must have a starting block, and nearly all starting blocks in this country begin with the federal government. Our current curriculum model can be traced back to the Common Core Standards initiative rooted in Bush's No Child Left Behind policy that began in the early part of the 21stcentury. At this time, nonprofit groups (including the Council of Chief State School Officers, the National Governor's Association, and Achieve), took over the crusade for a more unified national curriculum and began writing a set of high-quality standards for mathematics as well as language arts and literacy which became known as the Common Core Standards. These new learning goals were finalized in 2010 and ensured students would graduate with the skills and knowledge required to succeed in college, their career, and life in general anywhere across the United States...or at least that was the plan.

This new system set out to address two glaring issues in the U.S. model. First, the performance of students continued its downward trajectory as the first decade of the new millennium got underway. Our peer nations continued to outpace us in almost every realm. Second, each state had its own individual standards and its own idea of proficiency in the older model, which made between states comparisons of students extremely difficult. This also made it much more problematic for states to collaborate to improve the overall system at a national level.

One of the most interesting aspects of this new plan, besides the lack of government involvement in its actual creation, was the fact that acceptance and implementation by the states were optional. Although the federal government did not write the Common Core Standards, it relentlessly promoted them like Don King on the eve of a fight night. The feds assembled a $4.4 billion stimulus grant to distribute to states that adopted these new standards. They also waived some of the requirements from the No Child Left Behind bill to states who opted for this new path.

Despite the fact that many states regarded Common Core Standards as nothing but more rigid, bureaucratic regulations and rules, siphoning off local control of schools, over 40 states, plus the District of Columbia, and several overseas territories adopted them. (Interestingly, some states have since repealed them.) States that could prove their own standards were proficient at preparing students for college and careers could be exempt from adopting the new standards, and since 2010, only Texas, Alaska, Nebraska, and Virginia have never adopted them. Minnesota has partially adopted them, and Arizona, Oklahoma, Indiana, South Carolina, and Florida have all repealed their previously adopted standards at the time of this writing.

The most mind-numbing aspect of this system is that we haven't even gotten to the actual curriculum yet. Federal law, in fact, prohibits the education department from interfering in curricula that are determined at the state and/or local level. Of course, federal laws such as No Child Left Behind and the Every Student Succeeds Act can unquestionably influence how state and local governments proceed in creating their curricula. You see, there is a distinct difference between standards and curricula. Standards outline what a student in a particular grade should either know or know how to do, whereas the curriculum is the actual content that addresses those standards and how to teach them. For example, a standard may state that a student should be able to compare two stories in the third grade. The curriculum would then determine exactly what stories students would read and the methods used to teach them how to compare the stories.

The Common Core Standards are basically a template schools use to create their own curriculum as well as the standardized tests to assess those standards. And when it comes to creating curricula, like many topics related to public education, methods and procedures vary widely from state to state. Some state governments take a more active role, whether that curriculum is based on the Common Core Standards or other standards created by the state itself. Other states may allow local governments and individual school districts to take the reins of curriculum creation as long as it adheres to whatever standards the state has adopted. More often than not, though, most states function as a hybrid model in which representatives from local and state governments collaborate to create curricula.

So, how have the Common Core Standards stacked up against standards of the past? Well, as usual, the federal government has, like the Galactic Empire, struck back, but their results have been overwhelmingly feeble. Performance is almost always based on standardized testing in this country (we'll look at this troubling topic in greater detail in the next chapter). Let's look at one study that compared testing proficiency for both new and old standards in the states of New York and Kentucky based on 2015 data. This study compared testing proficiency from old standards vs the new Common Core Standards, and the results were fairly disappointing. In both states, students scored at least 60% in both math and reading when tested using the old standards. However, test results in math and reading that used the new Common Core were all at or slightly below 40%, except for reading scores in Kentucky, which were just under 45%. That is a significant decline in performance.

As we can well see, the results are not promising. However, these data are from 2015. Perhaps 5 years is not enough time to yield adequate progress. Yet, today, we're more than a decade beyond the 2010 inception of the Common Core Standards, and there is zero evidence this new model has had any significant positive outcomes for students. For example, according to the National Assessment of Educational Progress, fourth and eighth-grade reading scores have remained stagnant for 10 years, and some scores have declined. Fourth-grade reading proficiency actually decreased from 39% in 2017 to 37% in 2019, and neither one of those percentages is something of which anyone should be proud. Moreover, according to further data reported from the Department of Education's National Assessment of Educational Progress, average testing scores have gone down since the implementation and adoption of the Common Core Standards.

Once again, the data speaks for itself. Also, keep in mind all the data collection from above ended in 2019, so we cannot attribute these decreases in performance to anything related to that little bat virus from Wuhan. Apparently, the Common Core Standards, along with their resulting stronger academic standards, more standardized testing, and the near draconian teacher evaluation systems that accompany them, have done nothing but precipitate regression. These results are simply unacceptable. Public schools need to determine how to pave a better path forward, but thus far, we've only delved into the framework and foundation of the public school curriculum. Journey with me now as we take a closer look at where exactly the public school curriculum originates and how it is implemented in the classroom.

Curriculum Basics

What exactly is curriculum? The most encompassing definition of curriculum I've encountered is: "the totality of student experiences that occur in the educational process." The term often refers specifically to a "planned sequence of instruction, or to a view of the student's experiences in terms of the educator's or school's instructional goals." To put it in the simplest of terms, curriculum is essentially anything a teacher provides for instructional use. Curriculum includes student textbooks, teaching handbooks, manipulatives, PowerPoints, worksheets, online material, software programs, any types of literature or media, videos, and even computer games. The list is virtually endless. Curriculum is the way teachers teach, and it guides nearly every aspect of what occurs in the classroom. Thus, curriculum is not actually what is taught but how it is taught. A good way to delineate between standards and curriculum is this: Standards are WHAT has to be taught, and curriculum is HOW those standards are actually taught.

Okay, all that probably sounds reasonable. But from where does all this magical curriculum originate? Remember, education is no different than any other entity in this world. Just follow the money. There are countless companies across the globe constantly vying for merely a few minutes of any district's ear to hear their sales pitch. Like any other product or service, companies look to make money by marketing their product or service to as many people or entities as possible. A larger customer base generally results in a larger opportunity for profits, and the public school curriculum market is no different. Of course, school districts review multiple bids and most often follow the quality vs. price model when making their decision.

The problem with these curriculum companies is when one creates a product or service that will be marketed to a large swath of consumers, it's almost always going to be accompanied by a lot of useless stuff no one actually needs. Curriculum can be so flooded with resources that many teachers find themselves overloaded and at a loss as to how to proceed with meaningful lessons. Boundless objectives and standards have to be met by the end of the year, and many of these objectives and standards have various checkpoints that must be achieved at specified times throughout the year. These standards and objectives are also linked to the standardized tests that accompany them, and there are multiple practice tests throughout the year to monitor progress. Therefore, teachers must make sure they pace lessons at a rate that matches the testing schedules. They definitely want to make sure they've covered all the material that's going to be on the next round of practice benchmark tests. The results of these practice tests administered throughout the year are used to gauge how a student is progressing with the state standards. This information will then help to guide more individualized instruction for struggling students.

This brings us to another extremely important point. All curriculum is linked to standardized testing. This is a major problem we'll get more into in the next chapter, but understand that nearly every aspect of what is taught in the public school classroom, except for the early primary grades, is directly related to standardized testing. State standards should certainly be in line with testing standards, but whatever standards the state implements, whether Common Core or their own standards, will be directly associated with and assessed based on standardized testing. The basic trajectory is as follows:

State Adopts Standards⇨Tests Created Based on Standards⇨Curriculum Teaches to Standards/Test

The problem is that a bulk of content in public school curricula is not always part of the standards on which students will be tested. This leaves teachers wrestling with the time-consuming process of determining exactly what in the resources they've been given actually aligns with what needs to be taught. Of course, teachers have various resources and collaborate with colleagues to address this problem, but it only increases the difficulty of an already tough job. And, by the way, school districts update their curriculum every few years. A new and updated curriculum always pairs nicely with a barrage of trainings, meetings, and extra hours of figuring out how to implement it effectively. A career teacher could go through half a dozen or more different brands of curriculum in his or her tenure, all of which coincide with a great deal of extra work, headaches, and the need to have a drink...or two...or...well, probably the whole bottle.

Call it perhaps a time crisis, but teachers frequently run out of time and are unable to cover every topic. There just isn't enough time in the day to adequately teach all the standards needed for students to perform at a high level. Way too many resources are embedded in most school curricula, and the pacing schedule that accompanies most curriculum packages does not always match up very well with the testing schedule. This results in a situation where there is simply too much information to cram into one year of learning, and once a teacher gets a little bit behind schedule, it tends to snowball from there. Teachers then find themselves playing catch-up for a large portion of the year, which leads to frustration and stress for the teacher and the students. This can, in turn, create a poorly functioning, nonproductive, and even toxic classroom environment.

Public schools should begin adapting to the modern world in which we currently live. Student demographics, as well as many other aspects of education, have shifted dramatically in the last 20 years, and schools have struggled to handle these transformations in a responsible and productive manner. The curriculum in our public schools is bad, and from the many observations I've done in classrooms, I would have to say it's very bad. It's imperative schools learn how to adapt their curriculum to ensure students acquire the skills and knowledge they will need to become competent and prolific citizens. So, what has occurred in the last couple of decades to cause such a dramatic shift in how kids learn? Let's take a brief look at some of the glaring reasons.

Times Are a Changing

We are currently in the midst of a rapidly evolving world that is transforming faster and faster every decade, while throughout human history, change has been relatively slow and gradual. However, the speed at which the world evolves has exponentially increased throughout human existence. The Paleolithic era lasted for over 2 million years, and the Mesolithic and Neolithic eras spanned nearly 10 millennia. As human civilization moved into the Bronze and Iron Ages, technology and innovation began to accelerate, with these periods only lasting a few thousand years. The Renaissance and Enlightenment ages persisted, at most, only a few centuries each, and the Industrial Revolution seized the world in less than a hundred years. The birth of the World Wide Web and its ensuing avalanche of emerging technologies that have drastically changed the way we live our daily lives only began a couple of decades ago. This new technological revolution in which we find ourselves has provided more processing power, information, and connectedness than the world has ever witnessed.

However, this new beast is proving difficult to tame, and we have had a hell of a time trying to understand and manage it. So far, human civilization has not done a great job of adapting to this new world that seems to have escaped control. We continue to be nothing more than a bunch of Wylie Coyotes chasing our Roadrunner world, only to wind up at the bottom of a chasm in a heap of rising dust. You see, a person living in, say, the year 1900 would have much more in common with someone from 200 BC than they would with someone from today. Our environment has transformed at such a breakneck pace our brains cannot keep up. When our brains are built to function in an environment that has only witnessed gradual changes since the dawn of humankind, it should be no surprise that we humans are so utterly lost and confused in this brand-new, globalized, high-tech world.

This new hyper-accelerated mode in which we now find ourselves has, without a doubt, further exacerbated the seemingly endless list of problems with education in this country as the system attempts to keep pace. We've moved beyond the need to mold young citizens into the assembly line drones of the past, yet it seems as though our education system has not quite figured out how to adequately meet modern needs. Media, culture, art, and most importantly, technology have completely transformed our environment and way of life, not just in the United States but across the globe. These recent transformations have led to policy and demographic changes, mass globalization, and emerging technologies that we don't fully understand. We have rapidly and haphazardly incorporated these aspects into our daily lives without really grasping their long-term effects on us, particularly on our youth.

Many features of our insanely dynamic world must be considered to address the curriculum needs of our students. For starters, the demographics in the United States have shifted dramatically in the last couple of decades, creating rapid and profound alterations to the demographic profile of public schools. Baby boomers are aging, birthrates are changing, and immigration has increased, resulting in dramatic racial and ethnic diversity in public education. It is predicted school-aged children will soon be the most diverse segment of the U.S. population. The percentage of White students in the United States was at 61% in 2000. By the 2022 school year, that number had decreased to 46%. This trend undeniably has increased the ethnic and cultural diversity in public schools. These new students bring with them varying levels of competency, motivation, maturity, and social skills, as well as variations in their culture, beliefs, and socioeconomic backgrounds. This has, in turn, created a massive chasm in differences in the learning styles and needs of today's average student, and many teachers aren't adequately trained or prepared to deal with these changes.

Today's diverse learners are just not a good match for the traditional instructional methods of the past. Schools now labor over how to prepare students to learn, collaborate, and work in these new, diverse environments. Teachers scramble to get adequately trained on how to appropriately address the culturally based needs of their students in the academic and behavioral realm, and schools struggle to create content and curricula that support the diverse needs of the quickly evolving student body. Every student has the right to receive an engaging, high-quality education in this country; thus, public schools must move toward developing a more diverse and inclusive curriculum that prepares ALL students of the 21stcentury to actually live and thrive within it.

Persistent changes in education policy have also had a significant impact on curricula. At the onset of the new millennium, George Bush's No Child Left Behind and the tsunami of standardized testing that rolled in with it created a notable shift in the trajectory of the public school curriculum. Not much later, in 2009, Obama's American Recovery and Reinvestment Act funded "Race to the Top" grants, which doled out incentives to states and districts that established and enforced school reform measures. These reform measures were only able to be met by adjusting the curriculum and methods of instruction to match the goals of the program. Then, a year later, we saw the Common Core Standards. We've already discussed in detail the cascading effects this new plan had on the curriculum and its ensuing disappointing performance results.

That's three shifts in policy in a single decade. Schools have been using the Common Core model for over 10 years now, but it hasn't been effective. So what's next? What new and improved system will the powers that be conjured up? I would bet that whatever plan they evoke will be just as beneficial as the others. At the end of the day, however, with all of these changes in focus and methods from the federal government, which lead to confusing, mind-numbing alterations from the states and their districts, teachers find themselves wondering what on earth they're supposed to do half the time. This clearly does not lead to quality teaching and productive learning environments.

One of the biggest current challenges to public school curricula is emerging technology and its impact on students in and out of the school setting. Today's students have become technophiles. They're constantly on their phones. Most kids play well over 2 hours of video games a day, they're on a cornucopia of social media sites, they spend hours a day scrolling through useless, idiotic TikTok videos, and they can't even keep track of all the streaming services they access daily to watch shows and movies they have no business watching. Some schools have even moved to a "bring your own device" policy when it comes to technology. I don't believe cell phones and other personal electronic devices are appropriate for school, and that includes teachers. I have observed countless times in classrooms where students, as well as teachers, were on their cell phones or other personal devices, and they were not engaged in any type of learning and/or teaching. It's just too tempting for most people. Cell phones and personal devices, if allowed at a school, should be stored in student lockers or teachers' desk drawers. Schools spend way too much money on their own technology. There's already plenty there for everyone.

From my experience, technology is, many times, not the master key to unlocking students' motivation and intellectual abilities. I've observed countless instances in which technology is more of a distraction in the classroom. Sure, teacher-guided lessons and activities using technology can be extremely beneficial to students once the rules of use have been established and students have been trained to properly use the device. However, this is not how the situation usually plays out. Many classrooms have unsupervised and unrestrained use of technology. Half the students are on their phones messaging each other and browsing social media, and the other half are on their laptops or Chromebooks playing Minecraft or watching YouTube videos while the teacher stands at the front of the room actually teaching to maybe five out of his or her 25 students.

Don't mistake me; we do need technology in schools. It's become so ingrained in our everyday lives we essentially cannot live without it. One is almost literally unable to function in today's world without at least a cell phone and a decent Wi-Fi signal. The real conundrum with technology is exactly how to incorporate its applications in a way that unlocks students' interests and potential. One seemingly obvious problem is that some teachers don't understand how to use this technology themselves. Not every teacher is a Gen Z or Millennial tech wiz. So, how are some teachers supposed to incorporate this emerging technology into their teaching when they struggle to operate that technology themselves? Of course, there is training available, but those trainings are usually not very effective at empowering educators and giving them the technological confidence they need in their classrooms.

When technology is poorly taught, used, or monitored in the public school setting, it not only becomes counterproductive but can also be dangerous. Privacy issues are becoming a big concern. Students are not permitted to take photos or videos in the school setting due to privacy and confidentiality issues. Students obviously follow this rule as well as they follow all the others. There are daily incidents of students posting online videos and photographs taken at school, which can create many problematic and sometimes even litigious situations for schools and parents. Students are relentlessly bullied through technology as well. In years past, even the most browbeaten students could at least have a few hours of reprieve once the final bell rang. Now, with constant berating on social media and via other technological means, many students have no escape from their tormentors.

Another issue is cheating. Having access to endless amounts of technology in the classroom clearly leads to many more opportunities and routes to academic dishonesty, especially with the recent addition of ChatGPT. Monitoring student technology use and teaching more responsible ways to wield technology would be a great path forward. These are kids, and they don't yet have the faculties and capabilities to monitor and self-regulate themselves and their behavior the way adults are wired to do.

We've strayed a bit from the curriculum, but it's important to understand the impact of technology in our public schools. We will be discussing technology frequently throughout this book and how it affects certain realms and aspects of the public school system. Technology can help generate inclusive, diverse, and meaningful novel methods to motivate, engage, and enrich the learning experience of all students. Teachers and administrators should embrace this new technology and use it as a tool to create deeper learning experiences to actually prepare students for the crazy world into which we're thrusting them. However, schools must train teachers how to best use the technological means available to them in the classroom and ensure students use technology responsibly to gain knowledge and access relevant information. Furthermore, schools and parents must also be vigilant in monitoring and tracking the type of information students access and the types of activities they engage in online. Although we should strive to instill independence and self-control in young people, they are still immature, undeveloped children, no matter how old they act or want to be.

Thus, the massive demographic shift in schools must be addressed, and schools have to adapt their culture, structure, and, most importantly, their curriculum to match the needs of the diverse student body that now exists. Governments also should begin to use research-based methods to develop meaningful, easily adopted, and engaging standards that are relevant to the real world in which students will find themselves upon graduating. Schools can then take these new standards and create a curriculum for today's students that actually matters to them and prepares them for real-world scenarios. Schools also need to continue to focus on technology and how to incorporate it into the classroom in a way that benefits all parties. Schools have yet to figure out a way to accomplish this. Technology can be an extremely valuable aid to learning, but it can also be a very dangerous tool for students when its use is not properly planned, implemented, and monitored.

There must be an increased investment in teacher training to better prepare teachers for the changing dynamics of the public school system. Today's teachers need to be able to meet the specific demands of the student populations residing in their classrooms every day, and the curriculum and instruction must evolve to more adequately match the skills not only to survive but also to thrive in today's world.

So exactly what is wrong with public school curriculum? Let's take a tour down Curriculum Lane and attempt to uncover what's being taught, what's not being taught, and what should be taught.

What are We Teaching Anyway?

When's the last time anyone did long division? It was probably in grade school. Why do schools spend over a decade teaching a language students have been speaking since birth? Nearly every European I encounter on my travels speaks at least two languages, and many speak three or four. How often does one encounter someone born in the United States from an English-speaking family who speaks any language other than English? When was the last time a teenager knew much of anything about how the scientific method works or could accurately recount important historical events and their significance? We've all seen talk shows made famous by Jay Leno, where the host wanders through various cities, asking random citizens basic questions like, "What's the name of our current Vice President?" We're amazed every time at the blank look and corresponding inane response the host always gets.

Well, when teachers merely teach to a test by cramming formulas and facts into students' brains while ensuring rote memorization via an education model based on "hearing" rather than "doing," the situation described above is the end result. Of course, we will always need the three R's, reading, writing, and arithmetic (that these three subjects are referred to as the "three R's" when in fact, only one of them actually begins with an 'R,' should tell us all we need to know about our current education system). However, can we not teach those subjects and others so that students don't hate them?

Many students love coming to school, but when asked why, the answer rarely has anything to do with a particular class or subject. Most students who enjoy being at school say it's because of recess, PE, lunchtime, extra-curricular activities, or perhaps seeing a teacher they like or friends. Some students, unfortunately, enjoy their time at school because it is a safer or much less chaotic environment than their home or the only place they can get a decent meal. Are schools really that incompetent in finding ways to make the classroom more meaningful and enjoyable for students? I don't believe they are. Humans have achieved such greatness in their short time on this giant space rock, and I believe our powers can be used to fix this problem. However, it won't be easy.

The media, arts, music, culture, and technology of the 21st century have completely reshaped the minds of our youth. I'm not going to bore you or myself with a bunch of brain talk and neuroscience mumbo jumbo, but today's students have lost quite a bit of processing power as well as short-term auditory memory, working memory, and executive function. Perhaps it's the result of hours in front of various screens and the ways in which we're all instantly "connected" today. Maybe it's globalization, pollutants, and contaminants, or exposure to non-age-appropriate visual and auditory input. Or, most likely, it's a litany of variables, some of which could never be guessed in a million years. That is a question for someone else. We're well past the how and the why. It's time to figure out what we're going to do about it.

In the past, schools used to teach math, reading, and writing in a very explicit manner. Today, they teach half a dozen different ways to solve a problem because you never know which way the "test" may want you to solve it. Teachers drudge through one mathematical heap after another, leaving confused students scattered along the path. Decades ago, students would sometimes spend an entire year focusing on only one single step when addressing particular math topics. Today, students are lucky to have even a few days to grasp the entire process in some mathematical arenas. Reading isn't much better. Districts demand primary grade students compare various texts and analyze the motivation of characters in stories or passages they have no interest in reading and, on many occasions, can't even read competently. Based on numerous studies and surveys, it is even estimated that over half of school-aged children in this country cannot read adequately. What's more, they're asking third graders to write two-page essays on boring and unengaging topics the teacher wouldn't even want to read, much less assign to students. But that story or writing prompt was chosen...well, of course, because it's similar to one which may be on...you guessed it. The test!

Schools used to do a lot of things. They used to teach math in a slow and progressive manner so students could remember and apply what they learned later. Schools now stumble through topics in a matter of weeks or even days that would take the average adult months to understand. Students used to read in school, and they used to read frequently. Even when I was in school, we were always reading entire books in class. In many schools today, students are lucky if they have one day per week in the library. Teachers and parents also used to read to students, which helped build a particular set of skills most students now lack: the ability to listen. Schools used to teach extensively about geography, but today, you would be hard-pressed to find so much as a globe in most teachers' classrooms. It's no wonder a majority of the population cannot find their own arses anymore without GPS. Schools used to teach students the importance of the scientific method and how the magical field of science impacts their daily lives. Now, students merely color diagrams, memorize vocabulary words, watch cool YouTube videos, and never get to blow up anything while incinerating their eyebrows.

Students are missing out on great opportunities to grow and learn. They are missing out on the great variety of books that could better shape their minds and their understanding of the people, places, and things that make up the world. They could, in fact, learn grammar on their own. When one reads, one is also studying grammar. Why jam down a dozen worksheets or online modules on punctuation, commas, and capitalization when all that can be figured out just by reading? Seems we could save a lot of trees. Schools also teach vocabulary. Why? Do you know how you cultivate a great vocabulary? By READING!!! Unfortunately, most students today hate reading. Until schools figure out a way to make reading more entertaining and enjoyable for students, their reading skills, as well as their grammar and vocabulary skills, are always going to be subpar. Most importantly, though, reading builds curiosity, which leads to a love of learning and an increased ability to think critically about the universe in which we live.

If schools can't figure out how to successfully teach mathematics and reading to students, we are all doomed. If you've seen Mike Judge's silly but increasingly more relevant movie, *Idiocracy,* you understand the point. Being able to read and understand basic mathematical concepts is an essential skill not only for acquiring gainful employment but also for sustaining one's life. I've previously mentioned the reforms of the Reagan era based on the *A Nation at Risk* report, which was the first real wake-up call about how badly our students were performing compared to our peer nations. We've also frequently touched on aspects of Bush's No Child Left Behind and the Obama-era Common Core Standards. Yet, in spite of all that, compared to other nations, the United States still has one of the highest per-pupil spending rates, accompanied by some of the lowest performance results.

Based on 2019 data (pre-COVID) from the Education Department's National Assessment of Educational Progress, only 21% of 12th graders scored at a proficient level in math, and only 31% scored at a proficient level in reading. Let that sink in. There are around 4 million high school seniors in the United States. This means we're unleashing millions of students into the world where less than a third of them can proficiently read and, shockingly, just over a fifth have any proficiency in math. Yet still, the most stunning figure is that the graduation rate in the United States is nearly 85%. How do more than eight out of 10 high school seniors graduate when only three out of

10 can read effectively and merely two out of 10 possess adequate skills in mathematics? Something has definitely gone horribly wrong, and public schools are most certainly doing a disservice to the children and parents who depend on them. How on earth did we get ourselves into this mess?

The Mess

Don't get me wrong. I'm not some curmudgeonly middle-aged man spellbound by the nostalgia of days past. I don't want to return to the "good ole days" or "make America great again." However, demonizing the past doesn't in any way help to solve our current problems. When we, as Americans, discount and vilify the past, we impede our ability to learn from the mistakes we have made. Accepting our past, no matter how embarrassing, flawed, or brutal it may be, is the first step toward understanding and learning from it. When we finally begin to acknowledge our history, we can then begin to analyze it, understand it, and delineate between its good and bad aspects.

The realm of public education is no different. We must evaluate which teaching methods worked in the past and then integrate those with new research-based methods that more closely match the modern world. To shift this focus, for starters, schools must move away from standardized testing. An educational system based on standards and curricula, which focus solely on teaching information related to a test, is not a good system, and it is utterly failing us. This isn't the way the real world works. It's no wonder young adults who graduate from high school roam around the planet like lost sheep. They have no clue how to live their lives. They're unemployed, unskilled, socially inept, and living in their parents' basements. It is estimated that up to 40% of U.S. parents have an adult child living at home. The birds are literally having to be kicked out of the nest.

This, however, will not be an easy reformation. In fact, a reformation may not be adequate. It may take an educational revolution, an Educational Enlightenment if you will. We may need social and civic movements to ignite and germinate meaningful changes and shifts in ideology, like the desegregation era eruptions in the 1950s, which resulted in a much-needed evolution in the nation's public school system. It was a difficult, painful time for the nation, but we eventually worked it all out, and the end result was a more inclusive and more effective public school system. Be certain, I'm by no means comparing the hard-fought denial of a public education based on race to our current dilemma. I'm only suggesting it's going to take the same vigilance, hard work, and desire to repair our current system as it did over half a century ago.

Many of the basic abilities that used to be the norm for students in public schools appear to have become lost or completely extinct in our current stock. Students struggle with basic comprehension today. They just don't seem to "get" anything anymore. They're not bad at memorization, which is great for standardized tests, but ask them to conceptualize and integrate what they learned into a comprehensive understanding, and the resounding response will be mostly crickets. Independent thought has also become an endangered species in public schools. Of course, much of that is a result of the rigid Prussian model, which we've already beaten over the head enough at this point. Regardless, today's students generally look around the room at their peers for answers or allow their emotions to take control of their vocal cords. Students rarely rely on critical thinking and informed judgment to make decisions or draw conclusions. Modern students, for lack of a better word, are downright lazy. The lightning speed and ease at which our lives unfold today has whittled down any sense of delayed gratification and work ethic, especially in our youth. Furthermore, when the only goal is a grade or a proficient test score, cutting corners can be a much easier, less time-consuming path to success...or at least the public school's version of success.

There's also been a push in favor of increasing classroom group activities. On the surface, the motivation behind this move is justified. Students must learn to collaborate with others, share ideas, and learn to respect differing opinions. However, this utopian vision does not generally unfold the way the "experts" intended. This emergent group approach to learning comes with an extremely mixed bag of results. Many students become free riders in group instructional settings, creating dissension and resentment in the group. The quality of group work, on average, is much less exceptional than individual efforts. What's more, these groups most often devolve into social gatherings in which students rarely discuss or engage in the actual assignment. Well-managed and carefully guided groups can be very beneficial and effective, but this method should supplement instructor-led teaching rather than becoming the norm.

Homework does not benefit students anymore. Many schools, especially in the primary grades, have moved away from homework, and I believe that is a move in the right direction. Students are under enough stress, and there is enough work to be done in the classroom. Kids need time to play, interact with friends and family, and just disconnect from school. Parents are also stressed and overworked to the max in most families. They need to come home and unwind as well. Most parents don't have the time, energy, or often the knowledge to assist kids with their homework, which puts everyone in a bad situation. Some parents haven't seen the type of work their kids have been assigned in decades, and most have long since forgotten all that useless information...they passed their standardized tests long ago. Surely, there are times when projects or certain activities must be completed outside of school, but this should not be the norm.

We won't delve too much into educational theory, but there has to be a hierarchical structure to knowledge and teaching. Our public schools have gotten away from this logical progression of learning, given the accelerated pace at which we teach nowadays—the result of a torrential standardized testing downpour. Many concepts must be presented in a sequential order, which means the curriculum must follow that hierarchical structure. Obviously, a student must first learn to add and subtract, then they move on to multiplication before proceeding to division.

History must be taught chronologically for students to understand how one decision leads to another. One cannot understand Reconstruction without first fully understanding the causes, impacts, and ensuing results of the Civil War. Science instruction must also begin with concrete foundational information before proceeding to more abstract concepts. Shouldn't one learn about atomic theory, what an atom actually is, and its relevance to the world before being asked to label a diagram and explain how the parts of an atom work and function? Reading and grammar are not much better. Shouldn't students read many more books to understand how sentences and paragraphs function as they become familiar with language and how it's used before they start diagramming sentences and worrying about nouns, verbs, commas, and onomatopoeias?

Many times, this hierarchical path gets hijacked by scheduling crunches, most often attached to standardized testing schedules. In addition, students learn and grasp concepts at varying rates. If half of the class has mastered addition and subtraction, that means the other half hasn't. However, the curriculum schedule says it's time to move on. If the second half of the class can't catch up on the basics, they may find themselves completely out of the race, struggling academically for the rest of the year and perhaps the rest of their schooling. This frequently, in turn, leads to behavior problems, resulting in further degradation of that student's learning and maybe even that of the entire class. Of course, 504 special education interventions can be made, but only a handful of students qualify for these. These programs can also become ineffective and even detrimental if not set up and managed properly. We'll take a broad look at these various programs in a later chapter but just know for now, although they help many students, they are not the solution to our problems.

The pace in most schools is simply too fast. No Child Left Behind is a joke. Our curriculum is racing ahead to the next "checkpoint" at such a lightning pace that teachers can't even keep track of who's still on the train. Students can memorize and recall reasonably well, but they can't think. They're so incompetent at distinguishing the difference between memorizing and understanding they've become incapable of even realizing they don't actually know something. Students have simply lost the ability to conceptualize.

Standardized testing must go. It is one of the largest, most destructive forces in our public schools. Students hate testing. Teachers hate testing. Administrators hate testing. Parents hate testing. State and federal governments love testing. This is obviously a very unbalanced scale. Schools have to find a better way to assess the progress of their students. Standardized testing does not work. It has never worked, and it will never work. We'll tackle this monster soon, but understand, we must figure out a way to destroy it and simply get back to the basics.

Back to the Basics

It should be painfully apparent that schools are not adequately preparing our youth for the world that lies ahead. Schools are teaching topics and ideas that are no longer compatible with our current environment. We are going to have to revamp our entire national system by returning to the drawing board when it comes to standards, curricula, and assessment methods in public education. Do students know how to change a flat tire? How about the differences between a credit and a debit card? Do students need to know all the facts, figures, places, people, and vocabulary associated with the Civil War, or is it perhaps more imperative to know the causes, implications, and how we grew as a nation as a result of it?

Let's start with mathematics. I believe this is the subject from which we have moved the farthest in terms of what is relevant in today's world. Schools still spend weeks and months teaching students how to solve problems they can accomplish in seconds on their cell phones. They are taught how to solve problems no adult on our current planet will ever have to solve in their daily life. Even adults who once knew how to solve these problems have long since forgotten those skills because they haven't used them since they were in a public school classroom. Understanding how to calculate long division and multi-digit multiplication problems are not skills students need today. Algebra, calculus, and memorizing formula after formula are useless to the average citizen unless one plans to study advanced mathematics, science, engineering, or technology in the near future. And even in those fields, computer systems and applications perform those complex calculations. How often does one measure the various lengths, weights, areas, or volumes of objects around the house or office? Unless you're a carpenter, a line cook, or a drug dealer, not too often. Do myriads of geometric concepts and formulas flood into your daily life? I didn't think so. Then why do schools spend so much time drilling these concepts into young minds when they don't even know how to pay an electric bill?

Mathematic curricula in public education must take a reality check. For starters, young adults graduating from high school know nothing about personal finance. Being able to budget money and understand the financial workings of the world is one of, if not the most important, math concepts a student can learn. After all, they are going to have to deal with mortgage rates, car loans, APR, compound interest, and direct deposit. What's a credit score? How do loans work? Simple terms and questions like these make young adults' heads spin. Perhaps so many young college-bound students would not be caught up in the vicious student debt cycle if they had simply understood the answers to these questions. How does the bond market compare to the stock market? What is GDP? What is the FED, and how does it affect my life? Most adults don't even understand these concepts. Why? Well, they were never taught them in school.

Students certainly must learn basic calculations before moving into concepts like bond yields and escrow accounts. Of course, schools must ensure students can do basic addition and subtraction and understand multiplication factors and how they relate to division. Students should also understand basic concepts of fractions, percentages, and geometry. However, I believe a rudimentary understating of these topics is adequate. That's all anybody ever uses in their day-to-day lives, and if, by some rare chance, they stumble on a more complicated problem, they have multiple technological devices generally within arm's reach to solve those problems in seconds. Schools also must teach about units of measurement and how to understand the differences between them, but they approach this topic in the wrong way. Instead of memorizing metric and imperial units and converting them from one to the other, shouldn't schools focus on how students need these concepts in their daily lives rather than how they will be assessed on the next round of testing?

Lastly, I want to highlight the importance of probability and statistics. Although these concepts are taught in public schools, we must emphasize these topics more. Probability and statistics are embedded in every aspect of our daily lives. We mentally engage in cost-benefit analyses on a daily, sometimes hourly basis. Every decision we make requires us to gauge the probability of outcomes. Furthermore, statistics are hurled at us by governments, media, and corporate outlets like free t-shirts at a college campus credit card booth, yet few understand how to analyze and connect those statistics. The amount of data and numbers smacking us in the face every day has become dizzying. Public schools have to dramatically increase the amount of time they focus on teaching probability and statistics and how to apply those skills to everyday life. Statistics and probability, as well as topics related to personal finance, should make up the bulk of the math curriculum in schools today.

Math simply must become more relevant. If we have any hope for our children to grow up understanding how to navigate the complicated financial and statistical world, we have to start by teaching them. If we want our children to make intelligent, responsible, and well-thought-out decisions in their everyday lives, we need to give them the skills to understand concepts related to probability and the ability to accurately interpret the salvo of statistical data and numbers constantly bombarding them.

Math is not an easy subject. In fact, it is one of the most challenging subjects for many students. But it doesn't have to be. Schools can ease this struggle by avoiding memorizing formulas, terms, and concepts that bear no use in the real world. Schools must begin to teach meaningful, relevant math concepts students can understand and actually relate to their own lives. When they do this, they may find students more engaged in math and, in turn, more successful at it. This success will then carry over into their adult lives, allowing them to understand the world better and to make more informed decisions that will enhance their lives and livelihoods.

Once again, kids need to read more...a whole lot more. I believe students should spend at least an hour a day just reading. The best way to become more literate and gain the ability to grasp grammatical concepts is not found in lectures, PowerPoint presentations, computer modules, or worksheets. These skills are gained simply by reading. Students need to become good readers and foster a love of reading first and foremost. In fact, the ability to read and an understanding of the importance of good reading skills should be the foundation of all schooling.

Schools have to make reading fun again. I used to loathe teaching reading when I was in the classroom. The various texts and stories embedded in the curriculum were hard for even me to enjoy reading. Schools must embrace a curriculum that gives students the opportunity to choose from a variety of reading topics that they find interesting. The current stories and sample texts schools require students to read would cure insomnia quicker than a double dose of Ambien. Of course, some stories have to be read as a whole so the class can analyze and break down those various texts to help them achieve a good test score, no doubt. However, teachers could have a list of multiple stories before the next unit of lessons and let the students vote on what stories interest them the most. The teacher could then pick, say, the top five stories and focus on those throughout the next unit. This would give students ownership and at the same time, increase their engagement and enjoyment throughout the learning process.

Analyzing and comparing different texts, understanding character motivations, and distinguishing the type of text they're reading and its purpose are all important abilities students need to learn, but if schools cannot find interesting and engaging ways to present these concepts, they will be eternally doomed to fail. Students usually get one day in the library as a class per week. Additionally, when schools conduct book fairs, most students bring money to buy trinkets like pencils, snazzy-looking folders, and toys. They rarely buy any actual books. Schools have to find a way to bring back reading. Teachers need to read to students more, and students need to have more opportunities to read, analyze, and hopefully enjoy texts they like and which motivate interactions. Building a solid reading foundation in young students will enable them to carry that skill into any subject they encounter. Nearly everything we do in our daily life involves some type of reading. It's time to get back to the basics.

When it comes to reading and language arts, schools spend way too much time and effort on grammar instruction. Much of this knowledge can be gained via the simple task of reading. Grammar instruction needs to be only supplemental. Sure, kids need to know the difference between nouns and verbs, when to capitalize, and how to punctuate. But once again, these concepts are embedded within the reading process. One can best understand grammar by reading grammar. Schools should teach grammar *through* reading, not in *addition to* reading, especially with primary-aged students.

Students have also become quite appalling writers. But is that really so shocking that students have lost the ability to assemble a coherent string of thoughts on paper when all they have to do is color bubbles on a scantron sheet, click a box on a computer screen, or label a diagram on standardized tests? Schools should be compelled to move away from objective, regurgitative assessment methods and shift toward more subjective and open-ended forms of judging student performance. Students are not given ample opportunities in the classroom to write, and the colossal push toward more technology only exacerbates the situation. Like anything else, if students don't have opportunities to practice writing, they will never be any good at it.

Public schools need to let students write more and at an earlier age. Who cares if their final product is rubbish? Are not failures the best route to learning? Students should write every day. I used to use daily journaling in my classroom as one route to establish routine writing practices, but there are many other creative and motivating means to entrench the writing process into students' daily activities. Humans improve their performance at tasks by doing them, not by listening to someone talk about doing them.

There are entire books written about reading and writing and how best to teach those subjects. Regardless of the theory or whatever research-based method comes up, practicing the skill is hands down the best way to learn. Without a doubt, this practice should be guided, but is that not why teachers have a job in the first place? There are dozens or even hundreds of ways in which public schools can increase the reading and writing abilities of their students. However, the first step is giving them the time and freedom to actually read and write in the classroom and the opportunity to read and write about topics they find interesting, engaging, and relevant to their lives.

We tend to forget that sometimes kids are merely little humans. They have desires, interests, motivations, and their own little quirks, just like adults. It is imperative that schools not only teach math and reading in a relevant manner but also in an interesting, intriguing, and fascinating way that engages students' minds and manufactures a sense of curiosity and love of learning. School should be fun, not the boring, useless drag most students have found it to be.

Reading and math are the foundations of any education and generally attract the most focus and resources. Many districts only actually test for reading and math proficiency in the early grades. However, there are many other relevant topics and subjects in which students miss adequate opportunities to participate. We've touched briefly on problems with other subjects, such as social studies and science, and there are many other applicable skills students may need in the real world that they never get a chance to encounter in public schools.

Many would imagine social studies is not that important, and it may not be compared to the might and power of math and reading. Nonetheless, schools are drastically missing the mark on several important aspects related to this subject. GPS guides our every movement today, but understanding basic geographical concepts is an important tool to have in one's repertoire. It is quite disgraceful when kids, and even adults, can't even distinguish between the county, state, and city in which they reside. This is basic knowledge everyone should know, and it is information necessary at various points in life.

Students and many adults are also quite clueless when it comes to the arena of civics and how our government actually operates. Teachers spend countless hours in the classroom drilling facts, people, places, and timelines into the minds of students, but rarely do their students fully grasp their implications. Being able to regurgitate information about the American Revolution does not translate into actually understanding its guiding principles and how it altered the course of the world. It is great for a test, though, especially when one merely has to bubble in a letter on a scantron sheet.

We also don't teach the real history of the United States in our public schools. It is definitely a much watered-down version of the past, and some may, in fact, call it propagandist. Regardless of what we call it, our history curriculum strays from too many discussions about the more checkered aspects of our earlier years as a nation. Every empire (Yes, the United States is definitely an empire), is manufactured through both honorable and nefarious means. Schools must teach our students ALL aspects of our history, no matter how embarrassing or disparaging they may be. As a nation, we must celebrate those honorable moments of our past, but we must also acknowledge and discuss the more shameful and sometimes heinous aspects of our history.

Students will only become adults who fully grasp the implications of the timeline of events that have transpired to create the United States of today by being taught the truth. We'll expand our discussion on this topic in a future chapter when I make the brave, ambitious, but probably bad decision to address critical race theory in public schools. Regardless of your thoughts on CRT, however, our schools do a poor job of accurately and honestly teaching the important aspects of our nation's past.

Science has become an utterly lost subject in public schools. Sure, many districts have advanced STEM programs and facilities, but those are designated for a select group of students, serving a minute fraction of the overall student population. Students just don't get many opportunities to actually "do" science anymore in schools. They watch a great deal of YouTube videos. They click through volumes of online lessons with cool graphics and funny cartoonish characters. They memorize vocabulary words and how to accurately label diagrams related to various scientific concepts. The question is: When does the science begin?

Science is doing. Schools have to get back to teaching students the scientific method and allow them to explore the world of science the way it was intended to be explored. Students should spend maybe one day a week focused on understanding scientific concepts via a book, lecture, or online module-type avenue. The rest of the week, students should do nothing but conduct experiments and use the scientific method to enhance their curiosity and understanding of the world. Science is my favorite subject, so I am a bit biased in this regard. However, the various branches of science combine to explain nearly every aspect of our existence.

The scientific method has been used for centuries to uncover practically everything we currently know about the world. It's imperative that students understand these steps of inquiry and discovery. Furthermore, possessing at least a rudimentary comprehension of how the field of science operates has become even more pertinent in our current world. With raging pandemics, emerging climate change issues and energy concerns, and the fact the United States has become one of the unhealthiest developed nations in the world, commanding at least a moderate understanding of science may not only enrich one's life and livelihood, it may very well sustain one's entire existence.

Thus, as we can see, public schools could make several major adjustments in how they teach core subjects. However, there are also many other aspects of adult life for which schools do a very poor job of preparing students. Public schools must also find a way to incorporate more curricula that focus on important everyday aspects of our daily lives as we move forward into the 21st century.

Moving Forward

We've covered the core aspects of public education up to this point. Math, reading, language arts, social studies, and science together make up the bulk of what is taught in schools today, with math and reading overwhelmingly consuming the most time, energy, and resources. But should it be this way? Aren't there other topics and skills young humans need to survive and thrive in our modern landscape?

What about home or automobile maintenance? Unfortunately, it is virtually impossible to function in the United States without a car. Only a handful of cities across the entire scope of this nation offer any semblance of a reliable and consistent public transportation system. Most cities don't even attempt this feat. Many times, it seems as if the majority of U.S. cities were purposefully designed to make it as difficult as possible to go anywhere or get anything done with any sort of ease. Therefore, we must all first have a dependable means of transportation to go to work, buy groceries, visit loved ones, or engage in nearly any activity that does not take place within the confines of our home.

Which brings me to my drawn-out point: Nearly every person in the United States obviously will need a home and, because of the way we've designed our infrastructure, will need a reliable means of transportation. Public schools teach nothing about responsible home or vehicle ownership or how to maintain either one. These are essential abilities that nearly every human in our country needs; however, unless a student is enrolled in some type of tech or home economics class, they will learn nothing about them in public schools. What's worse, these types of classes have nearly become extinct and are sometimes only available to certain groups of students in specific types of programs. Is it any wonder many young adults are unable to live independently and are currently stuck living at home with their parents? Or why more and more teenagers put off getting their driver's license well past their 16th birthday? Based on 2020 data, only 80% of adults in their early 20s had a driver's license, which is 10% lower than that same demographic in 1997.

Schools must also start teaching basic life skills to students. It should be both mind-blowing and infuriating to realize that schools spend years teaching students how to solve problems they will never encounter in their adult lives, yet many of them have no clue how to do laundry, change a tire, cook a decent meal, purchase auto or home insurance, pay a utility bill, or even tell the time on an analog clock. The majority of students also have next to zero survival or emergency management skills. It's a paradoxical 21st-century situation—life has statistically gotten easier and less dangerous, but at the same time, this new world has complicated formerly easy aspects of life and created an endless stream of existential threats...climate change, nuclear war, terrorism, groomers, fascists, emerging viruses with accompanying pandemics, the robot uprising, UFOs, UAPs, China, Russia. Aaaggghhhhhh!!!

The lists of our supposed enemies and the constant foreshadowing of impending doom that lies right around the corner are endless and have infected the minds of everyone, including our kids. Certainly, hyperbolic, corrupt media outlets and tech companies and the endless drivel of misdirection and lies emanating daily from the mouths of government agents have contributed to our current situation. Nonetheless, we must also strive to teach children how to navigate the chaotic minefield of the world in which we currently live. We must teach them to distinguish fabricated from real threats. I'm not suggesting we take our classes outside and practice building fallout shelters, but students should at least be able to identify real-life threats and be prepared to address them.

The physical and mental health of those living in the United States is at an all-time low, and childhood obesity is a full-blown epidemic. According to 2020 CDC data, nearly 15 million children in the United States were considered obese, making up close to 20% of the overall childhood population. What percent of the school day is devoted to teaching anything about the mental and physical benefits of proper dieting, nutrition, exercising, getting adequate sleep, or hygiene? Somewhere close to zero. Schools should spend more time teaching health and proper hygiene and help students learn and rehearse good personal health and hygiene practices.

What about topics and subjects that not only enrich students' lives but allow them to connect to concepts and ideas in a more meaningful way? I'm referring to the fine arts. Schools have made a drastic shift away from any type of fine arts education. Students spend minimal time in school, especially in the primary grades, experiencing the wonders of art, theater, and music. These realms have been relegated to extracurricular settings such as clubs or elective classes at the secondary level. Some states do require a minimum number of hours or years students must receive instruction related to fine arts, but it's only a bare minimum. Schools should provide more time and resources for fine arts education. Schools should also more frequently embed fine arts-related media into the curriculum of other subjects to help increase student engagement and enrich the learning process.

I personally was never much interested in the arts, and I pretty much sucked at most anything related to fine arts. I preferred to be outside on the field or the court. However, I still see the value they represent, and I still enjoy listening to great music, staring awestruck at mind-bending paintings, and watching dazzling performances on the stage and screen. I have an appreciation for the arts even though I have near zero aptitude for them. I learned this appreciation through exposure and education. Schools must incorporate more of the fine arts into their curriculum. They may not change a student's life or create the next Beethoven, but surely, exposure to different arenas of the arts and other cultural modes of expression will enrich students' lives and allow them a separate, unique means to connect and understand the world, which is supposed to be the ultimate goal of education in the first place.

Socializing and networking have become the overwhelming norm in our technological world. The idea of teaching social skills, referred to as social emotional learning (SEL), in public schools has become a hot topic these days. We'll discuss this topic in much more depth in a later chapter, but it's important to realize that teaching social skills can be an extremely valuable resource in public schools and can contribute significantly to student success. SEL is at its foundation and core, nothing more than basic life skills instruction.

This confusion over what SEL means and entails has caused many parents to associate SEL with such topics as critical race theory, gay/lesbian/trans issues, sexual education, or other topics they feel are inappropriate for school settings. Many of these parents are, without a doubt, correct, and their concern is warranted in some situations. Furthermore, the federal government, as usual, has recently meddled in the affairs of public schooling with the CASEL movement and their "Transformative SEL" push, and some public schools are, in fact, attempting to teach and expose children to topics and ideas many parents would find inappropriate or even appalling. However, these schools are underhandedly using SEL as a façade to cover up their trickery and deceit. Social emotional learning has been highjacked by parents shouting at board meetings, legacy media outlets relentlessly hyper-focusing on controversial issues, and big government, as always, creating policy issues and manipulating minds for votes.

This is not SEL...perhaps we could call it social engineering, but that's for a later discussion. SEL teaches students about different emotions and how to recognize them. It teaches students about respect, courage, assertiveness, and ways to solve real-life problems. It teaches how to interact with others, how to get along with others, how to communicate properly in the world, and how to follow directions. Think of the last time you went...well, anywhere. Does it now seem as if half the people you encounter every day have no idea how to engage in any of these skills? Schools have created young adults who possess such a lack of adequate social aptitude many find it difficult to even gain employment, much less sustain it. If one cannot listen, share, collaborate, respect others, follow basic directions, and possess a modicum of manners and good hygiene practices, that individual will not be successful in today's world. Proper SEL instruction teaches students all of these concepts and gives them ample opportunity to practice them in real-life settings.

Of course, one might argue these are skills that should be taught by parents or another such guardian in the home. However, I'm a pragmatist, and this is not happening. No doubt, there are some pretty horrible parents out there, but there is also a large percentage of parents who are doing the best they can. A single mom working multiple jobs while trying to take care of two kids has to eat and sleep at some point. Times are tough for a lot of families. It's been this way for quite some time, and unfortunately, it does not appear to be getting any better.

Finally, regardless of the curriculum, schools should begin to experiment more with individualized instructional models for all students. The one-size-fits-all model we have used decade after decade simply doesn't work anymore. Today's students learn at extremely varying levels, and many get lost in the shuffle. Districts should find ways to tailor their curricula to meet the individual needs of each student. We'll discuss a move like this in later chapters, and I believe this is the long-term future path schools must move toward. However, schools could experiment with different ideas and methods to begin finding ways to unlock each student's individual potential. This can only be achieved via more individualized instruction, not the factory-fueled educational model we have used for far too long. As artificial intelligence and other technological wonders begin to infiltrate schoolhouses, individual learning paths could become the norm, and students could find themselves highly engaged and motivated, embarking on a path of discovery that may actually prepare them for the world that lies ahead of them.

It is imperative public schools get back to the basics. Public education's primary focus has always been and should continue to be focused on cultivating informed, engaging, and productive citizens who possess a high degree of social mobility. This is how a strong nation is built and prosperous communities flourish. Schools must also convey to students the knowledge and skills they will need to be adequately prepared for the real world. Students must not only be equipped to think deeply and solve complicated and relevant problems, they must be armed with the skills to accomplish these tasks in the highly competitive and professional world in which we currently live. Students will need skills to communicate and collaborate effectively, and they will need to possess the ability to think critically and solve problems in practical yet creative ways. Public schools can only pull off this feat by fostering authentic and engaging learning environments where students are provided opportunities to address real-world demands with appropriate and relevant solutions.

Schools should begin this process of reinvention by first updating their content and curricula to more accurately and appropriately match the world in which we live and move toward more individualized instructional methods. Academic achievement and content knowledge are extremely important, but they need to be based on the current world and should evolve and adapt to the world as it changes. This knowledge should then be incorporated into meaningful skills. These skills must also be relevant and useful, and they should prepare students to work, live, and thrive in the world they will soon be entering.

Public schools must also become better at instilling more positive habits and ways of thinking while simultaneously generating and maintaining a strong sense of curiosity about the world. In addition, students need to learn self-discipline and the importance of being able to self-regulate. Schools have to find better means of connecting students to the real world, and this cannot be accomplished between four classroom walls. Public school curricula must incorporate more projects and activities into lessons to draw students into real-life scenarios and allow them to address and tackle issues and situations they will actually face when they exit the schoolhouse.

We'll delve much more throughout our journey into the various methods we as a nation could use to improve our schools and catapult our system to one that actually connects our education to the world in which we now find ourselves; however, public schools essentially have two jobs: Keep kids safe, and prepare them for the world ahead. They're struggling to accomplish the first goal, and they've completely missed the mark on the second. Schools have to move forward with a better template. Like I said, I'm a realist. This is not going to be easy. In fact, it will be extremely difficult. But have humans not gone to the moon, reached the deepest depths of the ocean, and created technological innovations beyond our wildest dreams? If we can accomplish all of this, surely, we can figure out public schooling.

Chapter 7: Standardized Testing

"Standardization of our educational systems [which includes testing] is apt to stamp out individualism and defeat the very ends of education by leveling the product down rather than up." ~Harvey Cushing[1]

"Don't let anyone tell you that standardized tests are not accurate measures. The truth of the matter is they offer a remarkably precise method for gauging the size of the houses near the school where the test was administered." ~Alfie Kohn

Standardized testing in public schools has been a contentious issue for over a century, and the debate has done nothing but further accelerate throughout the 21st century. Standardized testing has been part of the public school experience for nearly 200 years. Filling out bubbles with number two pencils, ferociously scribbling out timed compositions, and filing through dozens of mathematical formulas one's mind just can't seem to recall has become today's norm. Passage of the No Child Left Behind Act (NCLB) in 2002 set the stage for mandatory state-calibrated testing for all 50 states for every student in third to 12th grades. This law also created a highly factious link between states' test scores and the amount of federal funding they would be eligible to receive. Based on a study of the nation's largest urban districts, it is estimated students now take an average of 112 standardized tests from pre-school to high school graduation.

Proponents of standardized testing claim that these tests are a meaningful and unbiased means to accurately gauge the progress of students and determine the quality and effectiveness of teachers. Advocates also state that testing data aid in detecting ways to improve instructional techniques and curricula and help to identify marginalized students in need of remediation. Supporters of standardized testing also claim that scores are a great indicator of college and career success. Opponents, however, assert that these tests offer no meaningful measures of progress and merely depict which students are good test takers. Critics also indicate tests do not come close to accurately predicting future performance in higher education or success on the job. These opponents go on to state that testing is neither a reflective nor effective way to evaluate teachers, and they are adamant in noting the overwhelming inherent biases in most standardized tests.

So, once again, the true story of standardized testing most likely lies somewhere in the middle of the swinging pendulum, but fully comprehending the effects of standardized testing will require a much deeper understanding of the benefits as well as the many pitfalls surrounding this issue. Before we dive into this topic, I'll leave you with one very interesting morsel of data. Below is a list of the world rankings for the United States in the realm of three major content areas before and after the implementation of No Child Left Behind (NCLB) by President George W. Bush and the tsunami of standardized testing that followed.

United States World Rankings Before and After Passing of NCLB (2002)

	2000	2015
Math	18th	40th
Reading	15th	24th
Science	14th	25th

The above data speak for themselves and are, perhaps, one great indicator of why the United States and its public education system exist in their current states. In addition to these less-than-stellar numbers, in 2012, baseline

---

1. https://quotlr.com/author/harvey-cushing

annual spending per student for assessment-related expenses was $27, equaling a total of nearly $670 million per year. What's even more troubling, when administrative costs were added, that number rose to over $100 dollars per student per year. Sure, we can continue to blame this blatantly failing system on factors such as poor-quality teaching, socio-economic issues, outdated bureaucratic models, and lousy government policy, but the blame game cannot even commence until we understand the impact standardized testing has had on this system and those confined within it.

So, let's begin with a brief discussion of what "standardized" testing actually means. It's actually fairly self-explanatory. Standardized tests are simply administered and scored in a standardized measure. These tests are most often automatically scorable, comprised of a litany of multiple choice or true and false questions. Many of these questions generally contain convoluted choices such as "all of the above" or "none of the above." Test questions are "standardized" in the sense that they are created by the state in accordance with that state's pre-determined standards. Therefore, every state's standardized test should accurately align with its statewide academic standards.

Two main types of standardized tests exist in public schools. Each state has mandated state assessments which are directly linked to and aligned with the state standards and ideally, the curriculum attached to those standards. Every student is federally mandated to take these tests every school year from third all the way up to 12th grade. Generally, more than one test is required for each grade level. Math, reading, and writing are nearly always tested to some extent, while science and social studies testing are mixed in as well, depending on grade level.

The other type of standardized tests are those used for college admissions, such as the SAT and ACT. These assessments try to determine if a student possesses the aptitude to succeed at comprehending and successfully completing college-level work. Although waivers are available, these college readiness assessments are not free. SAT tests cost around $60, and ACT tests range anywhere from $63–$88 dollars. Furthermore, many students attempt these tests multiple times in hopes of achieving a higher score, and the fee must be paid every time. The SAT and ACT also require many hours of study outside the classroom, incurring additional fees to obtain first-rate study materials or private tutors.

Thus, standardized testing is a two-headed monster. Students must not only pass to exhibit their comprehension and performance level relating to certain subjects and, at times, to move on to the next grade, but they must also achieve a high enough score to have any chance of getting accepted into a decent college. But how did the nation get to this point? We must travel back in time for another brief history lesson to fully answer that question.

A Brief History of Standardized Testing

Although standardized testing has been a part of U.S. public schools since the mid-1800s, its origins can be traced as far back as seventh-century China, where government job applicants were administered tests based primarily on Confucius's philosophy. Educators in the United States began discussing ideas about formal testing methods in schools as far back as 1838. Several years later, school reformers in the pre-Civil War United States, such as our old pal, Horace Mann, as well as one of his contemporaries by the name of Samuel Gridley Howe, began to introduce standardized testing in Boston public schools as the new Prussian Model took hold. These tests were designed to create a "single standard by which to judge and compare the output of each school" in addition to providing a means of evaluating the quality of teaching. This system was quickly adopted by public schools across the entire nation.

Standardized testing throughout the 19th century was comprised of primarily oral and written responses to an array of questions, but it began to morph into its more modern form as the new millennium approached. In 1905, the French psychologist Alfred Binet launched the first standardized intelligence, or IQ, test, which is still used in its modern form today. A decade later, the first multiple choice test was developed by Kansas School Director Frederick J. Kelly. It was also during the early 1900s that debates concerning unrestrained and excessive testing began to unfold. In 1906, the New York State Department of Education conveyed their concerns to state legislators around the new bombardment of standardized testing:

> *It is a very great and more serious evil to sacrifice systematic instruction and a comprehensive view of the subject for the scrappy and unrelated knowledge gained by students who are persistently drilled in the mere answering of questions issued by the Education Department or other governing bodies.*

It's interesting, yet amazing, how this century-old quote still resonates today. History seems at times to never change as it continues to endlessly repeat itself like a syndicated sitcom.

As the 20th century unfolded, standardized testing began to spread even further with the U.S. military's mandating of intelligence tests in 1917 to all new recruits, which, in turn, further ignited the expansion of testing in public schools. Two decades later, standardized testing was transformed into its modern form when in 1938, IBM unveiled their first computerized test-scoring machine. This new device graded answer sheets by detecting electric currents that flowed through the bubbled-in graphite pencil markings. This cutting-edge technology decreased the cost of testing from around $5 to 50¢ per test.

The nation soon moved into the modern era of testing as the turbulent 1960s arrived. President Johnson's 1965 Elementary and Secondary Education Act (ESEA) became the first federal law to make standardized testing mandatory for all public schools. A deluge of testing soon followed throughout the remainder of the 1960s and 1970s, and when it seemed there could not possibly be more testing, the country found itself washed up on the shores of the Reagan era. The release of *A Nation at Risk* in 1984 showed that the United States was performing at a rate well below that of its peers. This report unleashed a firestorm of rhetoric around reform and higher expectations but only resulted in stricter accountability measures in the form of...more standardized testing.

The Reagan era induced a massive upsurge in testing that carried the nation all the way into the 21st century right past Clinton's failed attempt at creating a reasonable system of school accountability and onto the doorstep of George W. Bush and his No Child Left Behind Act (NCLB). If Reagan was the opening act boy, was Bush the closer. NCLB was the crescendo, the climax of a story over 150 years in the making. NCLB passed with overwhelming bipartisan support (remember those days) from the House and Senate. This new law mandated tests in reading, math, and later science for all students in third through eighth grades and once again in 10th grade. If schools did not show adequate progress, they could lose funding, face sanctions, and even be closed or taken over by the state. Talk about government overreach.

If this law does not seem ridiculous enough, it also added a requirement that 100% of students must be "proficient" in reading and math by 2014. I've been on this planet for quite some time, and I don't think I've ever witnessed 100% of humans do anything proficiently. But wait, there's more...based on data from the Pew Research Center, yearly spending by states on standardized testing increased from $423 million prior to NCLB to $1.1 billion in 2008—a 160% increase in expenses. And to top it all off, we can refer back to the table at the opening of this chapter, displaying the United States' worldwide rankings post-NCLB, to see exactly what these expenditures have allowed the nation to achieve. Don't waste your time, though. The answer is...nothing.

Of course, when the metaphorical bill came due in 2014, student proficiency reached levels not even close to 100%. In fact, since 2009, performance in reading and math has done nothing but stagnate. The levels of proficiency reached by Bush's NCLB deadline are almost too embarrassing even to print. For example, based on 2013 test scores, a mere 26% of 12th graders scored at a proficient level or higher in math, and only 37% scored at or above the proficiency level in reading. This massive government failure led to Obama's Every Student Succeeds Act (ESSA) in 2015. This law, in essence, overturned NCLB, freeing states from its unattainable goals and unreasonable punishments. ESSA moved to eradicate the phrase "adequate yearly progress" from the lexicon, eliminated harsh sanctions such as school closures, and removed the requirements that states must incorporate test scores into teacher evaluations. This law also required states to use other factors besides academic performance in measuring overall student performance.

What ESSA essentially accomplished was to return control of standardized testing back to the states. States were no longer required to jump through federal hoops in an attempt to reach ridiculous goals and follow absurd mandates. This was definitely a move in the right direction. Although the federal government was simply correcting its own previous error, we should give credit where credit is due. Without a doubt, ESSA released much of the burden and impending doom public schools constantly faced from NCLB; however, ESSA in no way created a path to significantly curtail standardized tests. It merely lowered the stakes. Creating a mechanism to collect and evaluate data on student performance is a task every state must still undertake, and standardized testing remains the go-to option. Just because ESSA voided the requirements of NCLB, it did not mean states had to immediately cease and desist implementing and using standardized testing principles. ESSA merely removed the federal government from as much of the process as possible. Many states still cling to aspects of NCLB, and standardized testing has not decreased by any means.

Some states have recently altered the makeup of their tests, however, with many states shifting to online testing as well as incorporating more short answer questions. Additionally, some colleges and universities have begun to move away from putting so much emphasis on SAT and ACT scores to accept applicants. But the major recent bulwark against the swarm of standardized testing has been that little bat virus named COVID-19. With the lockdown and closure of schools across the nation for extended periods of time, testing came to a precipitous halt. Standardized testing was briefly paused, resulting in a much-needed respite for students, teachers, and administrators. However, the COVID-19 craze has cooled off, and standardized testing has returned in force.

Pros of Standardized Testing

Let's shift a bit and look at what the researchers and experts have to say about standardized testing. As much as I personally loathe these tests, if that obvious point has not been drilled in yet, there are benefits to them that must be addressed. Standardized testing does provide a useful tool for schools in some circumstances, and there are even proponents who claim these tests decrease bias and aid marginalized groups.

Advocates for standardized testing claim these tests provide an ideal metric for gauging the quality of the standards and curriculum being taught. They also state these tests provide a standard set of data to compare to other schools in the state and across the nation. Other defenders focus on the objective nature of standardized tests. With all students taking the same test, which is graded by a computer, any subjective aspect of the test is removed. Other modes of performance evaluation that rely on teacher or school-made tests, graded by that school or teacher, can lead to conscious or unconscious biased practices or acts of deception. The objectivity of standardized testing is further emphasized by the fact that all students are assessed by similar or identical questions under nearly identical conditions in roughly the same environment. It has also been noted by testing supporters that states often use psychometricians to assure the fairness of tests by flagging and removing problematic and illegitimate questions.

Proponents of testing also claim it provides an excellent outline for areas of improvement for individual students as well as schools and districts as a whole. Standardized testing, they claim, is a great tool to help revise and improve teaching methods as well as pinpoint exactly where certain students are struggling. Backers claim testing has resulted in increased access to services and specialized instruction for students with disabilities or students whose home language is not English. They also claim that scoring is a reliable, replicable, and empirically documented way to capture student performance and compare it across the country or even the world. Additionally, standardized testing can provide the government with data to determine how to allocate funds and other resources, as well as to which category of students those funds and resources should be focused.

Although I adamantly disagree with this statement, many advocates of standardized testing assert that these tests are a great way to evaluate teachers. They claim they provide a consistent, standardized metric to compare teachers across schools and classrooms and demonstrate an accurate portrayal of how that teacher has helped students understand and master the core standards in the curriculum. Guardians of standardized testing also declare these tests are excellent predictors of college, as well as job success. They claim that learning environments that foster higher test scores are the best environments to produce long-term success in students, resulting in high achievement and prosperity in college and career.

We often hear about standardized testing and its litany of negative effects and impacts on marginalized students; however, some proponents of testing allege exactly the opposite. Defenders of testing declare that these tests are an invaluable tool to hold the public education system accountable to ensure all students have what they need to be successful. They claim that the discrepancies between students of color have only been discovered because of the data obtained through standardized tests. These data can then be used to fund and develop programs to address demographic gaps in learning. These tests have also been used to detect students of color who may qualify for gifted and talented programs and other accelerated learning environments such as STEM programs. Supporters go even further, stating test data are the only reliable, objective, and consistent source of information about the inequalities and disparities in public schools. Abolishing these tests would only make it more difficult, if not impossible, to identify and correct issues of equality in schools.

Some advocates of standardized testing claim these tests actually help students of color or other marginalized groups get into college. There are many instances and much anecdotal evidence insinuating that SAT or ACT scores are many times the only means to gain college acceptance for marginalized students. Many students from wealthy and middle-class backgrounds can afford extra-curricular activities, tutoring services, and other resources that may give those students access to other routes of padding their resumes. Some parents have connections and networks that can bypass testing requirements, and occasionally, parents have even bribed their way into college. So, for many students, test scores are the only weapon they may wield to provide the best path to college admission.

We've highlighted quite a few examples of the benefits many point to in regard to standardized testing. Testing certainly does not paint the whole picture, but that doesn't mean testing is completely useless. Proponents make quite a few stretches in many of their claims, which we'll address in the next section, but they also bring up some valid points. However, despite the few benefits standardized testing can and does provide, upon further investigation, it definitely appears the pros may not outweigh the cons.

Cons of Standardized Testing

Opponents of standardized testing have been far more outspoken. When the data are more closely examined, it's glaringly apparent that students in public schools are not performing well, and the intense implementation and concentration on testing seems to actually have exacerbated the problem. According to data collected and analyzed by the Program for International Student Assessment, despite the increase in testing, the United States has made zero significant improvements since the turn of the century. Our students continue to decline in nearly every academic metric compared to peer nations, yet for some reason, we continue along the same path that has brought us to this dead end. Sure, other nations do use standardized testing, but the United States has built its entire system of standards and curricula around these tests, and based on decades of results and research, it's grossly apparent that this strategy has not yielded many positive outcomes for students. It's as simple as that. Although I strive to be unbiased, I've also been very transparent about my opinion on standardized testing. Let's be clear. I believe standardized testing is overwhelmingly bad, but let's take a detailed look at exactly how this salvo of testing has impacted our schools.

The principal complaint concerning standardized testing is that these tests do not paint an accurate picture of a student's progress or knowledge but merely distinguish which students are good at taking tests. These tests many times fail to demonstrate the ability of students who may learn skills and demonstrate proficiency in alternative ways. Critics go on to state that these tests also provide no worthwhile measure of progress and have not resulted in any meaningful levels of student improvement. They point out the fact that many factors can influence test taking, such as the amount of sleep the night before, level of hunger, home-related stressors, or factors as simple as the current mood of the student. These factors change daily or even hourly, and many times, they seem to impact students at the least convenient times. Another factor is how these tests measure achievement. Standardized testing weighs individual student achievement against arbitrary goals created by the government rather than assessing a student based on that student's actual progress and yearly gains.

Standardized testing can also destroy student confidence. When a single test score is used to judge a student's ability, that student can become very discouraged when that score does not truly represent his or her understanding of that subject. This can cause students to lose focus and motivation and eventually give up. In addition, all these tests are tremendously stressful for students. Kids are literally losing their minds because of testing. I've heard countless stories of students as young as 8 years old having panic attacks and problems sleeping or eating due to testing stress. This stress trickles its way outside of school and percolates into the personal lives of students, further aggravating an already demanding home environment for many of them. This stress builds up over time and, in turn, makes test-taking even more difficult. It creates a destructive cycle in which a student's testing anxiety increases, causing them to perform poorly on the test, which fosters even more test anxiety.

Many students are better prepared for tests or just naturally great test takers. I was, fortunately, one of those students. I was always and still am an excellent test taker. I was skilled at pinpointing and removing bad answer choices, increasing my odds of a correct answer. Knowledge of probability and the design of tests, rather than actual knowledge and comprehension of the material being tested, can be a much more valuable skill when it comes to mastering most standardized tests. I can't even count the times I passed a standardized test with little to no knowledge about the subject. On the flip side, I've seen innumerable numbers of students who were highly knowledgeable about a subject completely bomb a test. So, were the results of that test an accurate representation of that student's knowledge and skill, or is that student merely a horrible test taker?

Opposers to standardized testing have also alleged that these tests do not offer the all-encompassing, nationwide comparison base as their opponents claim. Since each state develops its own test, critics say it is very difficult to make accurate comparisons across state lines. If this is the case, which definitely seems logical, the national statistics would be invalid since they are calculated on data from individual states. These tests also do an extremely poor job of educating, fostering, and uncovering entrepreneurial talents and skills, as well as demonstrating whether students can solve complex, higher-order problems. Standardized tests also do not provide the direct and immediate feedback students need to improve. Once tests are completed, the results generally don't arrive until many weeks or even months later. Furthermore, these tests are most often taken at the very end of the school year, and students and parents generally don't discover the test results until well into the summer months when school is already finished. So, the shortcomings and gaps discovered from those test results cannot even be addressed until months later when school starts up again and that student is already in the next grade. This does not seem like a very good system.

Many states have stopped using standardized test scores to evaluate teachers, a move testing adversaries overwhelmingly support. There seems to always be a discrepancy between what is tested and what is taught. Is a single variable an appropriate means to effectively judge someone's teaching ability? Teachers' salaries and job security should not be determined by one test score. Many teachers are under extreme pressure to "teach to the test," which further increases teacher burnout contributing to the continued mass exodus from the field. The rigorous testing regime has made many teachers scared to try new teaching methods or techniques for fear they may not link well enough with testing standards. This then creates a classroom with diminished student creativity and engagement. When the principal area of focus is to ensure students reach testing benchmarks, students miss out on real learning. Valuable time to actually discover and learn about the world has been taken away from teachers and students due to intense testing schedules and the amount of time it takes to prepare students for the litany of testing they're bombarded with each year.

Opponents of standardized testing also seem to be adamantly certain testing does not predict future success. These tests, they assert, do not evaluate the most important skills, such as creativity, critical thinking, and problem-solving, which are needed to survive and thrive in the real world. Standardized tests merely evaluate a very narrow range of skills and knowledge needed to succeed in college or in a career. Teachers also spend copious amounts of classroom time and energy coaching and training students on how to take these tests. So are these students really knowledgeable about the content, or have they just been trained to perform? Training to perform well on a test does not translate into real-world success. Spending countless hours drilling test-taking strategies into students' brains and spending many more hours drudging through practice tests takes away extremely valuable instructional time during which students could acquire knowledge and skills that will actually prepare them for adulthood.

Many critics of testing point to student grade point averages or GPA as a superior way to predict student success in college and beyond. According to a long-term study in several Chicago public schools, GPA is a five times stronger indicator of college success than standardized testing. Test scores basically take a snapshot of one day, whereas a GPA represents the accumulation of many years of progress and knowledge. Achieving a high GPA requires hard work, self-discipline, time management, consistent attendance, well-developed study habits, class participation, completion of assignments, and high scores on classroom-based assessments. These are the skills needed to succeed in college as well as the workplace.

In direct contradiction to testing supporters, opponents of standardized testing allege that these tests are racist as well as classist, and sexist. They claim these tests use socioeconomic scenarios and variables to which many students have not been exposed because of their backgrounds, thus creating a disadvantage for those students. They assert that many test questions require background knowledge often held more by middle to upper-class or White students. Opponents of testing also note that many marginalized groups or students of color don't have access to testing resources such as preparatory classes, tutoring, or the ability to take the test multiple times as many of their peers. Students of color may also experience more test anxiety than their White peers due to the fear of "confirming to the stereotype of inferiority," thus leading to lower performance and more test anxiety.

Some have even accused the testing industry of purposely creating biases within standardized tests to create a wider range of outcomes. Claims have been made concerning the racial-based origins of testing. As immigration boomed in the United States at the beginning of the 20th century, massive increases in standardized testing seemed to mirror that boom. Testing critics declare that with the huge influx of immigrants enrolling in public schools, the pace and frequency of standardized testing increased in order to prove that White students were superior to their immigrant peers. The use of testing by the military has also been viewed through a racial lens, claiming that testing was used to validate the segregation of soldiers. These tests used by the Army were later adapted to become the SAT, which is still used today. These claims seem hard to grasp, but remember, there was a very different atmosphere in the United States in the early 1900s. It was the age of eugenics when people were still trying to wrap their heads around Darwin's ideas of evolution and many times used his theories to fulfill their own racial narratives. So, although these claims seem far-fetched, they do warrant some thought and closer inspection.

Let's look a bit closer at a case study concerning college admission exams. A new study conducted by Mark Kantrowitz analyzed SAT and ACT scores and found evidence of discrimination against minority, low-income, and female students. His findings are very interesting. In regard to income, Kantrowitz discovered that students residing in households earning $100 thousand or more annually were twice as likely to have combined SAT scores between 1400–1600 compared to students in households earning less than $50,000 a year. When he looked at racial disparities, Kantrowitz found that White students were three times more likely to have combined SAT scores between 1400–1600 compared to Black or Hispanic students. His data also revealed that male students have a 42% higher chance than female students of obtaining combined SAT scores between 1400–1600, which could be a result of males frequently scoring much higher than females on the math portion of tests. Basically, this research showed a direct positive correlation between family income and test scores.

Despite these results, Kantrowitz stated they are more of a "statistical artifact" than intentional discrimination due to the normal distribution that follows the bell curve. He went on to explain,

When the location of the Bell Curve is shifted due to changes in the average test scores, small differences in test scores at the mean can be magnified at the highest and lowest test scores. This leads to big differences in the percentage of students with high test scores when test-takers are aggregated by income, race, and gender.

Further,

Because of long-standing differences in scores among demographic groups, expecting incoming students to post extremely high test results guarantees that enrollments at selective institutions will be skewed toward children from white, Asian and affluent families. This process ends up excluding many academically talented young people from historically disenfranchised groups.

This research looked at statistical concepts that may be difficult to fully comprehend, but the main takeaway is that, although there was no intentional bias, there is research-based evidence out there supporting the allegation that standardized testing can be inherently biased toward certain groups. The ultimate conclusion from this study, as well as numerous others, reinforces the idea that standardized tests, including college admission exams like the SAT and ACT, are very weak predictors of college or career success, and more valuable metrics such as GPA should play a higher stake when evaluating student progress and performance.

An Alternative Approach

Although we have seen instances in which standardized testing has provided beneficial results, overwhelmingly, the evidence indicates that a pivot away from testing is the most appropriate path forward for public schools. Assessments can be a useful tool for schools when they improve student performance and teaching quality, but assessments become detrimental when they compel teachers to "teach to the test" and are used as the principal determining factor to judge student progress. Standardized testing data should serve as merely one perspective on a student's abilities and progress and should be combined with other metrics to paint a truly accurate picture of a student's aptitude.

At the end of the day, it's a hard sell to claim standardized testing is worth the time, energy, money, and stress teachers, administrators, students, and parents have to deal with consistently. Not all tests are bad, and schools do need classroom assessments. However, tests should be short, quick, and timely, and they should be administered so that teachers can provide frequent and immediate feedback to help students improve. This technique, known as retrieval practice, allows students to review previous information to boost and augment the learning process. Retrieval practice is a much more efficient way to ensure students retain information as opposed to memorizing material and regurgitating facts. Retrieval practice methods reduce anxiety and the threat of stereotyping students. In other words, tests should be a short, non-threatening, low-stakes game. Further, the overarching objective of tests should be to provide students with an opportunity to improve. The current system of high-stakes testing accomplishes none of these objectives and are worth even less than the paper on which they are printed.

The format and design of classroom assessments can also be a critical component of the testing process. Multiple choice tests are easy to create and even easier to grade; however, these tests, if not created properly, can offer too many vague and imprecise answer choices like "all of the above" or "none of the above." Tests must be well-constructed with clear and unambiguous answers in order to reduce student confusion and guessing. If students can't understand the format of the test, then it is obviously not a good metric of performance. Students need time to take the test as well, and putting them on a timer only further increases test anxiety. Tests that provide fewer, more complex questions that allow students the opportunity to think deeply and truly exhibit their knowledge on the subject are simply a better metric of learning and progress.

There has also been a recent trend of displaying student test scores on classroom walls. I believe this is a bad idea, and research on this topic has my back. Studies have found that displaying test scores in the classroom can actually have a reverse of the intended effect, harming student motivation and resulting in lower test scores and inadequate progress. In fact, displaying test results has led to infighting because students focus on comparing scores instead of working to improve them. Further, the self-confidence of students with lower scores declined even further, leading to more test anxiety and poorer performance. Instead of displaying test results, research has shown the most effective impact on improving test scores is teacher feedback and the opportunity to revise and correct errors.

We can, therefore, conclude that well-developed and properly implemented assessments do hold some significant value for schools; however, these assessments should only comprise a small portion of the overall snapshot of student proficiency. Public schools should begin incorporating a greater variety of assessment tools in their performance metrics. As previously discussed, GPA is an excellent measure of student progress and knowledge. Obtaining a high GPA requires years of implementing successful habits, routines, and practices that can be translated into success in college and career.

Student portfolios , which contain various work samples, assignments, research papers, and projects related to different subjects, must begin to be included as a performance assessment as well as public exhibitions and long-term capstone projects that focus on solving problems within the community. What's more, schools, as well as universities, may want to look into the expanded use of oral examinations and student interviews. On countless occasions, I have worked with students who seem to be completely lost when reviewing their written work, but after talking with them for merely a few minutes, it's apparent that they are actually quite knowledgeable about the topic. Many students lack basic abilities in written expression but can verbally articulate a comprehensive understanding of the subject material. Of course, these students need to improve their writing skills, but should we judge them only on their performance through assessment techniques in which they would not pass even if they had adequate knowledge of the material being tested? There has to be a better way.

It seems overwhelmingly evident that public schools must find a way to improve the way in which they assess student performance. The standardized testing regime must come to an end. Schools can and probably should continue to use these tests to some extent, but their frequency, level of importance, and time needed to prepare and administer them must be significantly curtailed. In addition, public schools and universities must begin to use a wider variety of assessment tools and metrics when judging student performance, progress, and future prospects.

I'll conclude this chapter with this thought. Humans are not "standardized." Every individual has a diverse set of characteristics and a unique personal history. People are not "standardized"; therefore, one might reasonably claim there is no place in this world for "standardized" tests.

Chapter 8: Special Education

"Everybody is a genius. But if you judge a fish by its ability to climb a tree, it will live its whole life believing that it is stupid." ~Albert Einstein

"In special education, there's too much emphasis placed on the deficit and not enough on the strength." ~Temple Grandin

Despite the fact that federal laws mandating states to include special education programs to address the academic deficits of students with disabilities have only recently been implemented, these students have existed in every age and society. This specialized branch of education can be traced as far back as the late 18th century to Jean-Marc-Gaspard Itard's work with "the wild boy of Aveyron." The discovery of this nine-year-old feral child allowed Itard to describe and document many of the boy's strange behaviors, which were consistent with many descriptions of children with mental retardation and various behavioral disorders. Further progress in this field was accomplished in the late 19th century by Ann Sullivan Macy, the "Miracle Worker," who discovered unique and productive techniques to address certain disabilities through her groundbreaking work and success with Helen Keller, who was blind, deaf, and mute.

In the past, extremely deviant behavior was fairly easy to recognize and was generally interpreted as mental retardation or schizophrenia. However, milder and less noticeable disabilities most often went unaddressed. It was not until the widespread implementation of compulsory schooling that professionals began to notice these less severe disabilities. As literacy began to become the primary goal for all children, specific disabilities related to tasks and settings began to emerge, and teachers took notice. Following decades of research and reform, the need for specialized services and teachers for certain subsets of students became apparent. Thus, the concept of special education was born.

Ideally, this new service would provide custom-made instruction with specialized teachers to meet the needs of individual students who may have learning, language, cognitive, behavior, physical, emotional, or sensory disabilities. It would ensure these students had equal access to the same education as their non-disabled peers. Realistically, this system has evolved from a hodgepodge system of delinquency prevention programs serving thousands of students to the nation's universal behemoth of a program currently serving over seven million students. Like all educational reforms, the implementation and acceptance of special education in public schools has been fraught with many uphill legal battles and contentious public debates across the country. It's taken over a century for schools to create an environment in which all students, regardless of their disability, can have the same opportunities as their counterparts. But many of these opportunities come at a cost, and the debate concerning special education and the laws that dictate its existence is far from over.

A Brief History of Special Education

Students with disabilities have historically been excluded from the educational environment in the United States, and that remained the universal philosophy until the turn of the 20th century. In the 1700s and 1800s, individuals—including children—who did not fit societal norms were most often locked up in jails or asylums under less than ideal conditions. Professionals at the time believed that these individuals should be housed and treated in rural residential facilities to ensure public safety. Special schools did exist during this time, but they were few and far between and most often enrolled only the deaf, blind, or students affected by mental retardation. The first special education school, The American Asylum for the Education and Instruction of the Deaf and

Dumb, arose in 1817 in Hartford, Connecticut, and by the mid-1800s, many asylums began implementing special education programs.

Views began to change slowly as the 19th century unfolded, with reformers such as Dorothea Dix arguing for more government assistance for programs to address behavioral issues that were the result of inadequate environmental conditions and other socioeconomic factors. Facilities began to focus more on specific disabilities such as mental retardation, sensory impairments such as deafness or blindness, behavior disorders, and those labeled "insane" or "mad." Children judged aggressive and/or delinquent were soon being sent to reform schools and other such institutes to address and remedy such deficits. State governments began setting up social welfare programs, such as foster homes, and also established a juvenile court system. During the second half of the 1800s, several states even began to set up special education classes in their public school systems in major cities, serving immigrant students with language barriers, as well as students with mental retardation and behavior disorders.

As the 19th century concluded, the study of children and child-related issues became much more prominent as the Reformation Era began. However, the philosophy of exclusion when it came to disabled children in public schools remained the norm. In 1893, the Massachusetts Supreme Court upheld the expulsion of a student due to academic deficits, and this mindset endured well into the 20th century. Almost three decades later, the Wisconsin Supreme Court agreed with a school's expulsion of a student with cerebral palsy because he "produced a depressing and nauseating effect upon the teachers and school children." Thus, even far into the "advanced" mindset of the 20th century, it was the consensus that students with disabilities did not possess the same rights as their abled peers, and the best practice was to relegate these students to the margins of society.

With compulsory attendance being fully implemented across the nation in 1918 and the rising tide of concern for the horrible conditions of most mental institutions, many school districts began creating special programs and classrooms to meet the needs of disabled students; however, this was done on their own accord and not required by federal law. Throughout the first half of the 20th century, most disabled students still found themselves shut out of the public school system, with many remaining in institutions or at home.

The number of special education programs and other supportive services significantly expanded after WWII. Counseling services and guidance clinics began sprouting up across most urban centers, and by the 1950s, special education classes could be found in nearly every major city in the United States. The movement for a more inclusive form of education that incorporated special needs students received a major boost with the Supreme Court case of Brown v. Board of Education. In this case, it was determined that segregating students based on their race was unconstitutional and violated the concept of equal educational opportunity for all. This decision, in turn, inspired a movement and lawsuits to fight for expanding this equal education right to students with disabilities.

By the mid-1960s, public schools still were not required to provide services for special education students, but many were incentivized to begin the process of creating ways to serve these students when the federal government passed the Elementary and Secondary Education Act in 1965. This earmarked federal funding to aid schools in addressing the deficits of students with disabilities. Despite this and other attempts to increase the opportunities for disabled students to participate in public education, by 1970, only one in five children with disabilities was being educated in a public school, and many states still retained and enforced laws excluding these students from public schooling. However, this would all change drastically in 1975 with the passage of the Education for All Handicapped Children Act (EAHCA), which later became the Individuals with Disabilities Education Act, most commonly known as IDEA.

This new law became and remains the foundation of special education in the United States. After the passage of this law, education for students with disabilities became a legal right, with Congress stating that all children would "have the right to education, and to establish a process by which State and local education agencies may be held accountable for providing educational services for all handicapped children." This law also assured due process for these students and their parents and required that all school districts create an individualized education plan (IEP) for each student with a disability, which would become the legal document guiding that student's education and the services provided. The law also mandated that schools provide education for students with disabilities in the least restrictive environment possible.

This landmark decision set the stage for the mass infusion of special education into public schools. In 1982, the U.S. Supreme Court further extended the rights granted through this law by defining the "degree" of educational opportunity states must provide for students with disabilities. The court stated that each student's unique needs must be met, and states must create programs to address these needs. The number of special education students continued to boom throughout the decade. From 1976 to 1990, the number of special education students increased by 23%. Amendments were added to IDEA, which mandated services for three to five-year-olds, provided additional funding to states, and added more disability categories; however, there were not yet any reliable means of accountability for these programs.

This would soon change in 1997 with the passage of additional amendments to IDEA, which directed schools to provide only special education programs that were meaningful and measurable. These new amendments established the requirement of measurable written annual goals as well as the mandatory reporting of progress on those goals to parents. These amendments also mandated assessments be conducted on students, increased parent involvement in the creation of the student's IEP, as well as several other additions.

The U.S. government changed the game in 2004 when the No Child Left Behind Act (NCLB) created a new requirement for increased special education student participation in statewide assessments. This new law also required all teachers to be "highly qualified" in all subjects taught, including special education teachers who already possessed a special education certification. This sounded like a great idea, but some special education teachers teach a bit of every subject, which created certification nightmares for school districts, causing them to lose many much-needed special education teachers. This new law also created an additional burden on schools, as many of these students were not even being instructed on a level equivalent to the level at which they were tested. I know. It makes zero sense, but that's what happens when government goes awry. It was also at this time the response to intervention or RTI, model came about—a new system to identify struggling students and address their deficits before the learning or behavior gap grew too large, thus preventing them from needing special education services. We'll discuss RTI a bit more soon.

Special education continued on the path laid out by NCLB until 2015 when the Obama administration's Every Student Succeeds Act removed the strict certification requirements established by NCLB and basically gave more flexibility to the states as well as more authority to decide their own assessment standards. This is the standard schools still live by today. The number of special education students has varied over recent years, but there has been a newfound surge in referrals and placements due to the losses inflicted upon students by the COVID-19 shutdowns. We'll discuss the impacts of the COVID-19 lockdowns on schools in more detail in a later chapter, but the loss of learning that took place during that time has severely impacted our nation's youth. As more and more students move into the special education setting, schools will need many more skillful teachers and other resources to address their needs. However, these teachers are becoming harder and harder to find, and many districts are discovering it quite troublesome to find the resources they need, even more so in the time in which they need those resources. Schools will have to find a way to adequately prepare these students for the real world, which will many times be even more difficult for them to succeed due to their disabilities.

Basic Fundamentals of Special Education

Special education comprises a litany of programs that use specialized instruction to address the needs of students with mental, emotional, physical, and behavioral disabilities. Currently, over seven million students are educated in one of the many special education programs across the United States. comprising over 14% of students ages 3–21 in public schools. These percentages vary greatly by state, with each state determining its own eligibility criteria. For example, Hawaii and Texas have around 11% of their students categorized as special education, whereas in New York, special education students make up more than 20% of the overall student population. Around two-thirds of special education students are male, and over a third with a specific learning disability.

Several key principles guide the realm of special education based on various aspects of IDEA. All students with disabilities must receive a free and appropriate public education, which means all students have access to the general education curriculum at no cost to parents. All identification and evaluation procedures must be nondiscriminatory in nature, including using nonbiased methods and multiple approaches. All evaluations must be conducted in the student's native language, and no placement can be made based on a single evaluation method. All students must have an individual education plan or IEP, which becomes the foundation of their education and describes in detail the services to be provided to the student. The IEP includes descriptions of the student's levels of performance and how disabilities affect that performance. Learning goals and objectives, the specific educational setting, any accommodations, and all other related services are also outlined in detail in the IEP, which becomes the legal document that guides every aspect of a special education student's day.

Special education students must be educated in the least restrictive environment possible, meaning that students with disabilities should be educated with their age-related peers to the greatest extent possible. If this is determined not to be possible, an appropriate alternative setting must be provided. Parents must be active participants in this process unless they decide to waive their rights, thus letting the school decide the outcome for their child. Parents must also be invited to all meetings concerning their child with disabilities, and they must be given every opportunity to participate in the decision-making process. Lastly, all special education students must be provided with due process safeguards such as parental consent, confidentiality, and a hearing process when disagreements occur between the parent and the school.

Currently, IDEA has defined thirteen categories of recognized disabilities that qualify a student for special education services. We could spend weeks describing and discussing these disabilities, but let's take a brief look at them to get a better sense of the range of students who may be found in special education programs. We'll discuss them alphabetically.

Autism: Historically diagnosed in limited circumstances, its prevalence in students has exploded in the last 20 years, with cases rising from 1 in 10,000 individuals to 1 in 100, and some experts believe rates are currently as high as 1 in 36. Students on the autism spectrum may exhibit a huge range of deficits, from being completely nonverbal and/or overtly aggressive to the mild-mannered savant named Sheldon Cooper from The *Big Bang Theory*. There is a myriad of services available for students with autism, depending on the severity of their behaviors and deficits.

Deafness: This disability is fairly self-explanatory, and schools have been providing specialized services for deaf students in varying degrees since the 1800s.

Deaf-Blindness: The loss of hearing and vision related to this disability is so debilitating that intense and highly specialized environments, as well as teachers, are needed for these students. Programs that address only vision or hearing deficits are inadequate to address their needs.

Emotional Disturbance: Diagnoses under this category include a variety of emotional and behavioral factors. Students must exhibit one or several conditions, such as inappropriate feelings or behavior, a prevalent mood of unhappiness or depression, the inability to establish or maintain appropriate relationships, or a propensity to develop physical symptoms or extreme fear of school or personal issues. These students can become verbally as well as physically aggressive with adults and their peers. As a result, these students are often required to remain in a self-contained classroom until they are ready to be integrated back into the general education setting.

Hearing Impairment: This diagnosis is designated for students who are not considered deaf but still possess some level of hearing impairment that adversely affects their learning.

Intellectual Disabilities: These types of disabilities are found in students who have significant deficits in their general intellectual functioning as well as in their adaptive behavior. These students have historically been identified as individuals with mental retardation; however, President Obama signed federal legislature in 2010 officially changing the label from mental retardation to intellectual disability due to the stigma surrounding the word "retard" or "retarded." Schools have been creating specialized services to some extent for these students since pre-Civil War times.

Multiple Disabilities: This category includes students who have more than one of the listed disabilities, thus compounding the student's deficits, creating the need for even more intensive interventions. This category includes any combination of disabilities, except the previously discussed Deaf-Blindness.

Orthopedic Disability: Students in this category possess orthopedic issues resulting from congenital deformities, diseases, accidents, or other causes of impairment that adversely affect their educational outcomes. These students generally work with district occupational therapists as well as other special education personnel to assist them in their daily activities and learning.

Other Health Impairment: This is a somewhat catch-all category and can result from a virtual cornucopia of health-related issues that negatively affect a student's education, from asthma to diabetes, sickle cell anemia, or Tourette syndrome, to name just a few. This is also a very important category because it is the special education label attached to students with severe ADD (attention deficit disorder) or ADHD (attention deficit hyperactivity disorder). Either condition does not automatically qualify a student for special education. However, with a proper medical diagnosis and recommendations from medical professionals, students affected by ADD or ADHD can obtain acceptance in the special education realm under the other health impairment umbrella.

Specific Learning Disability: Students falling under this category comprise the highest percentage of diagnoses, affecting over a third of all special education students. Students in this category have basic biological processing deficits in understanding verbal or written language to the extent that it severely affects their ability to complete basic school-related tasks such as reading, writing, doing math calculations, or understanding directions. These students are generally much higher functioning than those categorized under the intellectually disabled diagnosis, and most of the time, an untrained individual may not even notice their deficits. These students make up the bulk of special education, but many times, their deficiencies are easier to address and improve than most other disabilities.

Speech Impairments: This type of disability affects a fairly broad range of students. Speech pathologists work with these students to improve their stutter, lisp, or other speech and/or voice impairments.

Traumatic brain injury: This diagnosis is reserved for students who have suffered an unfortunate accident resulting in significant damage to all or portions of their brain, which significantly impacts their learning. This category covers only injuries to the brain caused by external physical factors; it does not include congenital brain injuries, degenerative issues, or those caused by birth defects.

Visual Impairment Including Blindness: Students with any vision impairment that significantly hinders learning could fall under this category. Students with partial or complete blindness, even if corrected, can qualify for special education services under this category; districts have been serving these types of students for many years.

Now that we have a basic sense of what types of students may find themselves in a special education program let's take a closer look at how the process of becoming a special education student unfolds. The first step, of course, is detecting a student's disability. This is an obvious first step if a student is blind or rolls into school in a wheelchair, but high-functioning autistic students and those with specific learning disabilities may not be so easily identified. Once there is enough evidence to suspect a student may have a disability affecting his or her learning, teachers or other school personnel may submit a special education referral for that student to be evaluated. Parents can also request a special education evaluation of their child at any time. This parental request must be in writing, and except for extremely rare circumstances, the school district is required to comply with their request.

We must take a bit of a short detour here because when a student is struggling in class, a special education referral is not the only option, even if that student's performance is being affected by a recognized disability. There is a system in place called RTI or response to intervention. There are many detailed dynamics to this system, but basically it is an approach to identify students as early as possible who are struggling academically or behaviorally. By identifying these students and addressing their deficits sooner, special education services may not even be needed. Specialists can provide research-based interventions for these students, many times filling in their learning or behavior gaps before they regress to the point of needing more intensive and specialized services.

In addition to the special education path or RTI, there is still yet another route to travel for struggling students. In 1973, section 504 was included in the Rehabilitation Act, which provides an outlet to address the deficits of students who may not yet qualify for special education or may never qualify at all. There is a much broader range of eligibilities for 504 compared to special education due to the fact that the law does not designate which disabilities should be included in 504. Generally, 504 includes students with a chronic illness or disorder or other disabilities that might not fall under or be addressed appropriately through special education. Many students with ADD or ADHD who cannot qualify for special education under the other health impairment category are supported through 504. These 504 students are always educated in the general education setting, but accommodations are implemented to assist them academically or behaviorally to address their deficits and help them succeed.

If these other available options are not appropriate or do not work for a particular student, the path then leads back to special education. Once a special education referral has been submitted by a school, parental consent must be obtained. On the date a parent signs the consent form and returns it to the school, the clock begins, and the district has 45 school days to evaluate the student. When the evaluation has been completed, the school has an additional 30 calendar days to hold an ARD (admission, review, and dismissal) meeting. The ARD is one of, if not the most important, aspects of special education. It is the meeting in which a student's IEP is created and approved, becoming the official legal document governing every aspect of the student's education.

Every ARD requires certain individuals to be in attendance. This includes a special education teacher, a general education teacher, an administrator, a diagnostician (person qualified to interpret evaluations), and the parent, although parents may waive their right to attend the ARD and allow the school to decide the outcome if they so choose. In addition, once a student reaches a certain age, generally middle school, that student must also be invited to attend the ARD. All relevant information, including evaluation results, proposed goals and accommodation, transition issues (school to post-school), and assessment requirements, are discussed and decided in the ARD meeting. When all this information is formulated into the IEP, the final step is to determine the appropriate placement or educational setting as well as any related services.

A special education student may be placed in several different settings. In a "mainstream" setting, the student is educated entirely in the general education setting but with multiple accommodations and/or modifications in place. The services are implemented by a general education teacher, with support and consultation provided by a special education teacher. There is also an "inclusion" setting, which is very similar to the mainstream setting; however, with inclusion, there is a special education teacher or paraprofessional present in the general education classroom for a specified amount of time, which is listed in the student's IEP. The special education teacher works directly with the special education student in the general education classroom and supports the general education teacher in that class as well.

In the above-described placements, the student remains in the general education setting. In a "resource" instructional setting, however, the student is removed from the general education classroom for a specified amount of time (stated in the IEP) and receives instruction in an alternative special education setting. These classes most often focus primarily on math, reading, and/or writing, and students in this setting are generally two or more years behind their non-disabled peers. There are also what's called "self-contained" classrooms in which a student has such significant developmental or behavioral disabilities that they receive the entirety of their education in a special education setting. This includes many life skills classes as well as behavior intervention classes with severely disabled students. Students in these settings do, however, often have the opportunity to participate in the general education setting and are also sometimes permitted to attend certain electives like PE or music as they improve their skills.

Some students possess such a scope of disabilities that they cannot be educated in the school setting at all; these students are placed in a "homebound" setting in which all educational services are provided in the student's home. In addition, also several special education programs are available for very young children ages 3–5 who have certain developmental or physiological issues. This is by no means an exhaustive and detailed list, seeing that special education is a complicated and time-consuming process to fully grasp. Nonetheless, these are the most frequently used settings in which one will find special education students. Keeping the student in general education as much as possible is the goal of school districts and also the law, so the majority of special education students fall under the mainstream or inclusion category, which has resulted in some cascading effects which we will discuss later in this chapter.

Once placement has been determined, the ARD committee must also decide what, if any, related services a student may need. These related services fall under a wide range of areas and could include speech therapy, counseling, transportation to and from school, or various types or occupational or physical therapy. If the ARD committee agrees on all items created and discussed in the meeting, all members sign the required forms, and the IEP becomes a legal document guiding nearly every aspect of the student's education. Once the student has been accepted or "ARDed" into special education, the school is required to schedule an annual ARD to reconvene and discuss the student's progress as well as make any needed adjustments to the IEP. In addition to the yearly meeting requirement, an ARD must be scheduled if any major changes are to be made to the IEP during the school year, and special education students are required to be re-evaluated every 3 years to determine any changes in their eligibility. Also, if a school or parent decides a student is no longer in need of special education, an ARD meeting must be scheduled to dismiss that student from the program. Parents also have the right to decline special education services at any time.

If you've made it through this section without your brain exploding, well done. Special education is one of the most complicated areas in all of public schooling. There are more laws, rules, and regulations, as well as controversy and turmoil surrounding this arena of education than nearly any other. Special education and the students served within its programs have created endless public debates about how to best serve these students as well as their impact on other students around them. With the trend of "pushing" as many students as possible into the general education setting through increasing inclusion practices, the boundary between what separates general education from special education is becoming increasingly blurred, and the foundational concept of "individualized instruction" seems to be slowly vanishing for students with disabilities.

Times have certainly changed since the implementation of IDEA, but the need to address the deficits of struggling students remains constant. Students in special education are going to be affected differently by the dynamics of the ever-changing world around them as civilization moves well into the 21st century, and although many of the same issues from half a century ago remain relevant, there is a litany of contemporary factors that students, teachers, and parents must deal with today. Let's take a quick look at the current trends in special education.

Current Trends in Special Education

From funding and placement issues to COVID-19 and endless legal jargon, special education continues to remain a relevant topic.. Students with disabilities have gained unimaginable rights to the services they need to obtain the equal educational access they have been promised, but many problems still remain within this system. More and more students are falling behind, especially after the recent massive loss of learning during the COVID-19 lockdowns, which resulted in schools in many states being closed for well over a year. Parents and teachers also know well enough what a disaster the virtual learning fiasco was for schools across the entire nation. All students—special education and general education—suffered tremendous academic, developmental, and social setbacks during that time. Deficits among large swaths of students have begun to pop up like invading gophers, and districts are beginning to lose this eternal game of whack-a-mole.

In the past decade, the special education student population has grown from 6.4 million students, comprising 13% of all students, to nearly 7.2 million students making up 14.5% of the overall student population. Black students make up the largest percentage of special education students at nearly 17%, with multiracial students coming in second at 15%. The racial disparity in special education has always been a topic of concern, and debates have raged with both sides pointing to relevant evidence to support their case. Federal law does mandate states to review and monitor any overidentification of certain students, but several studies have actually found in many situations that minority students are actually being under-identified.

Recent research indicates both sides may be correct; in some contexts, students of color are under-identified, and in others, they are over-identified. Numbers may also vary based on the population dynamics of a particular school as well as regional demographic differences. Having 17% of Black students in special education in a school in which Black students make up 80% of the student body would not seem to be an issue; however, if, in that same school, Black students made up only 30% of the student body, we may have a situation on our hands. It appears, as is the case with many of the issues discussed in this book that the truth lies somewhere in the middle. Nonetheless, more research should be conducted in this area.

In addition to racial disparities in student demographic makeup, a similar problem arises when we look at the demographics of special education teachers. Regardless of opinion on the matter, research has shown that most students perform better when instructed by a teacher of their own race. When around 75% of special education teachers are White but less than 20% of special education students are categorized as White, you can see the obvious conundrum. Recruiting a more diversified special education staff is an easy answer but a difficult solution. The special education teacher shortage is even more alarming than the general education realm. Districts have become so desperate for teachers that it's gotten to the point where if someone has a pulse and can pass a background check, they're hired. However, this does not work well in most special education programs because they are...well...special. These specialized programs need specialized teachers to properly address the multitude of disabilities that may affect special education students.

This brings us directly to our next problem. The pool of teachers qualified to work with special education students continues to shrink each and every year. From 2006 to 2016, the number of special education teachers decreased by 17%, and as of 2022, 48 states have reported significant staff shortages in special education. The number of individuals who are willing to work in this field continues to decline for a variety of reasons. For starters, there is an overall teacher shortage in most states, so the applicant pool has already been whittled down to a fraction of what it was 20 years ago. Some states have even begun to shut down many of their teacher certification programs due to lack of enrollment.

With special education being the most difficult field to work in, it's not hard to understand why many up and coming teachers opt for another path. Special education also has the highest turnover rate among teaching positions in most states, because it is one of the most stressful teaching jobs available. Many special education teachers find themselves exiting the field within a couple of years, moving into other areas of education or leaving the field of teaching altogether.

Teacher pay has also continued to stagnate across the board. Many special education teachers are required to take on added responsibilities or extra training, as well as deal with the extra personal and mental strains and injury risks that accompany many special education positions. If anything, special education teachers should be paid more than general education teachers due to these and other factors. However, that is rarely the case. Districts must learn to spend their money more responsibly and set aside funds to increase the pay of teachers who opt to work in these less-than-ideal teaching environments. It's quite simple. Intrinsic motivation is just not enough at this stage in the game. If there is no added incentive to work in these arduous areas of education, then there will be no one left to teach in them.

The lack of support most special education teachers receive from administrators, general education teachers, parents, and other district personnel is yet another factor deterring many would be educators from moving into this field of teaching. When special education teachers struggle, it can seem impossible at times to acquire adequate assistance from anyone, not even teaching assistants. Why is that? Well, most likely, they don't have one. If the special education teacher shortage is a crisis, then the teaching assistant shortage is a downright catastrophe of epic proportions. Many special education programs are funded and designed to have one or more paraprofessional teaching assistants to aid in providing the needed services to special education students. These positions are nearly impossible to fill, due to extremely low pay matched with a not so appealing job. This puts an even higher workload on an already overworked position.

What's more, in addition to massive shortages in special education teachers and the paraprofessionals who support them, evaluation personnel are also beginning to leave the field at alarming numbers. These individuals are essential as they are the gatekeepers. They are the ones who must determine whether a student qualifies for special education or not, and the recent shortage of these evaluators has created a major backlog of students waiting on deck to be evaluated. This obviously creates many problems in the classroom for everyone involved, especially when deadlines throughout the evaluation process must be met.

The inadequacy of special education teachers and the essential staff who support them also results in an important compounding effect. Student-teacher ratios have spiraled out of control across the entire nation. The appropriate ratio depends on the type of special education program with more severely disabled students requiring a lower student-teacher ratio, but these ratios should always be lower in special education than those in the general education setting. Unfortunately, the situation has deteriorated to the point where this is no longer a reality. Based on recent statistics, the average general education student-teacher ratio is 16:1, whereas the average special education ratio sits at 17:1. I'm fairly uncertain how this situation would qualify as "individualized" instruction, or even "specialized" for that matter.

If this scenario doesn't already sound bad enough, special education teachers must maneuver daily through the plethora of laws, rules, timelines, endless paperwork, and regulations they are required to follow in addition to their daily stress and workload. It's no wonder many teachers are running as far away from any job related to special education as possible. There are volumes of information on the litany of different rules and regulations surrounding the special education realm. Even seasoned teachers have difficulty at times navigating this bureaucratic labyrinth, and if a teacher by chance forgets to follow one of these countless statutes, that teacher will get thrown under the short bus faster than they can contact the nearest union rep. Sure, these laws were put in place to protect the rights of students and parents, but when they become so excessive and seem to function only to make matters more tedious, it's time to redress some of these laws.

Funding issues in special education have also become a common grievance for states across the nation. We've delved deeply into the finances of public schools, so we already know the money is there. It's the irresponsible and wasteful spending habits of school districts that are the problem. That being said, the federal government never lived up to its IDEA promises. The federal government laid out a goal of supplementing up to 40% of the extra cost for funding special education programs in all states. As of 2018, they have only reached 15%, well below the pledged amount. This becomes even more infuriating when we see the billions upon billions of taxpayer dollars being siphoned up by proxy wars, corporate bailouts, and campaign expenses. Government lies and broken promises are as ubiquitous as they come, but this one was a doozy. Now states are being forced to pull funds from other needed areas to close these funding gaps the federal government has yet to fill.

We will not get too much into special education funding, not only because it is an extremely mind-numbing topic, but also because it is actually impossible. As unfathomable as it may seem, the most recent attempt to account for the overall cost of special education in the United States was conducted over 20 years ago in 1999–2000 making these data virtually useless. At the time of that study, states were spending around 90% more to educate students with disabilities. There are no current reliable data to determine these amounts today which is completely unacceptable. A majority of states require zero reporting of special education expenditures, and the states that do require some type of accountability do not even require the submission of detailed financial data. With absolutely no accountability across the entire scope of the system, this financial circus will continue until the big top collapses.

The most concerning aspect of this situation, is that all these problems, and many more, were prevalent even before the COVID-19 debacle in which endless ill-thought policies resulted in immeasurable damage to students across the entire country. Students were locked out of schools and the educational opportunities promised to them. The United States will feel the reverberations from this incompetent decision for years or perhaps even decades. Bad government has possibly destroyed an entire generation.

During this time, those students already incorporated into the special education system were not provided access to the services needed to maintain even a baseline level of competency. Many of these students fell even further behind their non-disabled peers while schools continued to shut their doors. What's more, struggling students on the cusp of needing special education services are now definitely in need of such services due to the academic as well as social losses inflicted upon them by the COVID-19 regime. If this is not concerning enough, what will be the fate of the toddlers and preschool-aged children who had no access to school services or even daycare facilities? The simple answer is that developmental delays for incoming students are now the norm rather than the exception. This is not nuclear physics. For example, if everyone's face is covered, how are young developing children supposed to learn how to speak and relate facial expressions and body language to what is being said, much less interact appropriately with adults and their peers? There is and will continue to be a tsunami of special education referrals to address the deficits of young children affected by the COVID-19 lockdowns. When young children are isolated, masked, and stuck in front of a screen for hours on end every day, what other outcome would be expected?

This situation does sound quite bleak, and frankly there is not much optimism in the current state of affairs in special education. However, it is not merely these specialized settings in which problems continue to run rampant. The toxic emanations from this dilapidated system have seeped into general education classrooms—when special education classrooms overflow with students, where do they go? Well there's only one place—back to the general education classroom.

Nearly two-thirds of special education students spend at least 80% of their day in the general education setting, and a whopping 95% spent at least a portion of their day in general education classes. To get a grasp on how troubling these statistics are, in 1989 only around 32% of special education students spent most of their time in the regular education environment. This may sound like progress. Allowing students with disabilities to interact as much as possible with their non-disabled peers is a noble philosophy. However, when that philosophy becomes a reality, and these students are unprepared to be inserted into general education classrooms and little to no regard is considered for how their presence affects the other 20–30 students in that classroom, this practice should be seen as quite problematic.

This is a very controversial and touchy topic, and I will most definitely offend some with my position on this matter. That being said, I am not an armchair quarterback shouting from the periphery. I've worked directly in special education for 16 years and have been involved to some aspect with special education for over two decades. It's time to sit down and engage in the hard discussions we've been avoiding for so long. I've seen first-hand how these philosophies and practices play out in the real world, and the story rarely concludes with a happy ending. We must ask the difficult questions. At what point do we begin to take the macro-effects of special education into account? Is it worth it in the long run to focus on increasing the success and performance of one student at the expense of two dozen others?

I've seen countless classrooms become wrecked by special education students who are pushed into general education classes via the tidal wave of recent inclusion practices, and this is especially the case when it comes to students with behavioral and/or emotional disorders. Schools want students with disabilities to have as many opportunities as possible to participate with their general education peers, but schools have to start using more common-sense practices when making these decisions. Strict and nonsensical laws must be vetoed or amended, and new legal guidelines should be created which take all students into account.

Even students with academic related disabilities can slow down the pace of instruction which negatively affects the rest of the students in the classroom dragging down their progress and decreasing their chance of future success. When a teacher gets behind, many times, that teacher stays behind. With the fast-paced speed of today's curriculum, getting too far behind is a death sentence for most teachers because they will never catch up. Special education students with more severe disabilities can also have a negative impact on the classroom. If that student has disruptive tics, shouts out, or has some other distractive manifestation of their disability this can be a huge classroom interruption causing students and teachers to lose focus, get off task, or become irritable and frustrated. This may seem a bit nitpickish, but when daily distractions begin to compound the long-term effects on other students in the classroom can result in overall lower performance.

I've dedicated an entire future chapter to behavior, because it's become one of the most important topics in public education today. Quite frankly, kids are out of control. We'll dig deeper into this issue soon, but it's extremely relevant in the special education realm. More and more students come to school with a multitude of behavioral and emotional issues. These students are often left in the classroom for months on end to "collect the relevant data" needed to test them for special education services, and once they are admitted into special education, they are frequently pushed back into the general education setting, often before they are ready. These types of students not only create constant distractions and disrupt the entire classroom environment, they can also be quite dangerous due to their proclivity for aggression.

I've worked with these types of students for my entire career. They are often intelligent, thoughtful, and extremely enjoyable kids to be around. However, many of them have severe mental deficits and have experienced extreme trauma which can result in behaviors that can present extreme safety hazards for themselves as well as teachers and students. These students have frequent verbal and physical outbursts in the classroom, which can not only disrupt learning, it can also cause physical and especially emotional trauma to other students around them. Schools must keep these students in self-contained classrooms until they are completely confident that they are ready to move into the general education setting, and if a student shows up out of the blue exhibiting these behaviors, this student should be placed in an alternative setting and be immediately evaluated. This is the only option to ensure a safe and productive learning environment for ALL students.

Additionally, there has been a massive increase in the number of students showing up to classrooms with varying degrees of previously undiagnosed autism. Some of these students are nonverbal, aggressive, and can be a significant safety concern to themselves as well as others. Whether this alarming increase is the result of certain vaccines, increases in pharmaceuticals and plastics in our food sources and water supplies, an unknow genetic component, or the result of some previously unheard of phenomenon, it's about time someone figured it out. As a nation, we need to begin to look more deeply into this troubling trend. There has to be a variable or a combination of variables that are causing these young kids to be afflicted with this condition that can often be extremely debilitating.

Unfortunately, there is no quick fix to this problem. With special education teachers becoming endangered species, there's just no one left to supervise and teach many of these students. Special education classes are being discontinued, and in many districts, there's nowhere left to put these struggling students except to ease them back into the general education classrooms. The compounding factor attached to this situation is that once those students are placed back into the general education setting, there's not enough special education staff available to support the general education teacher in that classroom. The situation has become a giant syndicated shitshow that no one wants to watch, but every time the channel is changed, it's the same show.

The Murky Future of Special Education

We can definitely leave the shades at home because the future of special education in the United States does not look very bright. In many states, less than 20% of special education students achieve their annual goals. I hate to sound so pessimistic, but it's time to face reality. Our special education population is achieving progress at a slug-like pace while their teachers continue to be burdened with ever-increasing caseloads and ever-decreasing resources. Improving special education is going to be an extremely arduous task, but schools must be ambitious in this venture.

Staff

The first step to improvement must focus on the teachers servicing these students. If schools can't find enough teachers to work with special education students, then special education will cease to exist. Special education teachers have the highest turnover rates in education, and schools must begin by improving the work environment for these teachers. In some states, more than 20% of special education teachers quit during the course of a single year. It is absolutely imperative that districts address these shortages. Additionally, schools need to find ways to incentivize teachers to move into special education with higher salaries or supplemental pay, tuition reimbursement programs, scheduling priorities, and more autonomy in their daily routines.

The endless amount of paperwork and other bureaucratic nonsense should also be chiseled down to only the bare essentials. When I taught in special education, nearly half of my day revolved around paperwork and documentation. Of course, special education teachers need to collect some type of quantitative data to measure progress on goals, but these teachers should not be drowning in data, charts, and checklists. Students need to be engaged, and it's the job of teachers to create and maintain that engagement. All the time teachers spend on data collection and analysis, filling out all the proper forms, and checking off all the right boxes, most often does little but take much-needed time away from their students.

Special education teachers need time to build relationships with their students. Through positive relationship building, teachers can better connect with students, improving their performance and creating more engagement. This relationship-building is even more vital for students with disabilities. If special education teachers are afforded more time to spend teaching their students and addressing their deficits, perhaps these students will actually achieve some type of meaningful progress instead of the current widespread stagnation running rampant throughout the nation.

It can be difficult given the overwhelming staff shortages, but schools need to put special education teachers in positions that play to their strengths. Many of these teachers are shifted all over the school district and bombarded with many responsibilities because having a special education certification allows one to teach any and all special education arenas in most states. However, not all teachers are efficient in all arenas. Those who excel in teaching should be given direct instructional positions and opportunities to coach general education teachers, while those who have backgrounds in behavior management should likewise be placed in self-contained behavior units. Districts could even create case manager positions to focus on all the staggering paperwork. Some teachers are excellent data collectors, goal writers, and IEP creators, so why not assign a teacher to deal exclusively with those aspects of the program? This sounds quite logical, but pragmatism can rarely be found in public education.

Paraprofessionals, sometimes referred to as teaching assistants, are imperative to the proper functioning of any special education program, and there is an even more massive shortage of them. If schools want to increase interest in these positions, districts have to start paying these assistants more than peanuts. These assistants can barely make ends meet on their current salaries. I've worked with several paraprofessionals throughout my career, and they were essential components to the success of the programs in which I worked. They help monitor students, collect data, provide services to students, as well as assist teachers with other tasks such as running copies, creating learning tools for the classroom, and, at times, supervising students when the teacher is called out of the class to deal with student issues or to attend one of the seemingly endless lists of scheduled meetings.

General education teachers also play a significant role in this matter. The effectiveness of these teachers is directly correlated with higher performance in students. Research shows that when special education students are placed in the general education setting, they have more successful outcomes when paired with high-performing teachers. Therefore, when placing special education students in general education classrooms, districts should place these students in classrooms with the most seasoned, experienced, and effective teachers. Rookie and greenhorn teachers should not be besieged with hordes of special education students, but unfortunately, this is a common occurrence.

With the emerging practice of pushing special education students into general education classrooms or requiring these students to remain in general education classrooms for an extended period of time before being evaluated, general education teachers have to be given the proper training on how to deal with these students. If students with disabilities are thrown haphazardly into these settings, general education teachers will be forced to become much more "specialized" in order to deliver the "special" education these students so desperately need.

Behavior and Mental Health

Schools must shift more focus to behavioral issues and social deficits as the nation moves into the new roaring twenties of the 21st century. More and more students present with behavior and emotional problems on a scale never seen before in public schools. The current state of the world is ripe with discord from economic crises, raging wars, climate disasters, to the continued daily struggles of those still trying to pick up the pieces after the COVID-19 debacle. With the stress and existential angst most adults face today, it's no wonder their kids feel the aftershocks. Students deal with quite a bit of trauma these days, and most are not equipped for it. Therefore, alternative discipline approaches may need to be considered for many of today's students.

The truth is, young people today are extremely fragile, much more fragile than children of the past. Suicide rates in teens have soared, and "killing oneself" has become sort of a go-to for many students these days. It gets the attention kids desire, and although most of them just pantomime what they've seen around them, many deal with serious mental issues. To address these issues, increased counseling, restorative practices, and more positive interventions will need to be considered, as well as more varied cultural-based responses due to the increased diversity in schools today.

The problem of resources, however, arises once again. In order to address the increase in mental health issues facing districts, schools need an army of counselors, social workers, and other interventionists. However, job seekers have little interest in these jobs, and even if they did, districts most likely do not have the funds allocated properly to adequately pay them. Psychologists, counselors, behavioral specialists, and other such professionals are already exiting the field of education en masse to seek out more lucrative opportunities in the private sector. Therefore, schools may need to shift resources by partnering with outside agencies and nonprofit organizations to assist them in addressing the mental health needs of their student bodies. There are many organizations such as counseling agencies, graduate programs, hospitals, and other nonprofit groups available for these partnerships and with the improvement in technologies surrounding teletherapy services and online counseling, these partnerships could find fairly easy ways to connect with students. We'll go much deeper into the topic of behavior and mental health in a later chapter, but schools must begin to find new ways to address these deficits in students as early and often as possible.

Funding

Speaking of money, educating students with disabilities in an expensive endeavor, and the costs are only going to continue to rise. It is essential that districts begin to maximize their resources and spend tax-payers' money in a more responsible manner. States must become accountable to the public with new guidelines being implemented to better track exactly how much money states are spending on special education and where exactly that money is going. It's utterly ridiculous, and the public should be more concerned that there is zero accountability in this realm. The federal government should also live up to its promises for once and provide states with the supplemental funds they committed to 50 years ago. If our federal government can afford to send tens of billions of dollars to corrupt countries in order to rage proxy wars and then shower even more cash down on massive corporate bailouts, the least they can do is provide states the resources they've been promised to create a better life and future for students with disabilities.

Technology

Technology and its widespread implementation into special education programs will be imperative for the future success of the students they serve. However, the application of this technology must be simple and provide a user-friendly mode of operation for teachers and their students. Sadly, many states have not adopted adequate technological innovations to assist special education teachers with their endless stacks of paperwork. Data collection, although overwhelming at times, is essential to measure student progress. When data are consistently gathered, analyzed, and reported, the most frequent result is higher student performance and success. There are multitudes of technological systems available for districts to provide to special education teachers to make data collection and analysis easier, less time-consuming, and more efficient. If schools are not using these types of systems, they should. These improvements can provide teachers the extra time needed to focus on their students.

New and emerging technologies can also be used by special education teachers to enhance classroom instruction and foster more individualized learning opportunities. With technological advances, special education students may finally be able to access the "specialized" instruction they so desperately need. Teachers will be able to personalize student learning to levels never experienced by creating individualized learning modules based on students' specific likes and needs. Increasing improvements in virtual and augmented reality, as well as new advancements in artificial intelligence, will be able to create unimaginable learning opportunities for students with disabilities. Even now, artificial intelligence is being used to aid in the early detection of disabilities, and virtual reality applications are already designing virtual worlds, allowing students with autism to practice navigating through real-world environments and challenges. With the colossal teacher shortage looming, these virtual worlds may be the only place left for students with disabilities to receive the services and resources they need.

Kids love technology, and we can reasonably say many of them are addicted to it. They enjoy working online, and online spaces are where they interact most with their peers. Students today are "digital natives," born directly into the technologically advanced world in which we live. They have been immersed in technology since fetus. Districts should take advantage of these facts and use technology to their advantage. Technological resources should by no means replace in-person learning, but they should be incorporated as invaluable supplemental tools. Technology can even help improve the mental health of students allowing some special education students the option of receiving their services online instead of dealing with the stigma of being pulled from their class for therapy or other services. In addition, technology could even allow students to receive services in the privacy of their own homes, completely removing any associated stigma. We are all moving into a world in which technology will be infused into nearly every aspect of our lives, so schools will need to prepare students with disabilities to take on this new, technologically dynamic world.

Parents

Schools must seek out ways to increase parent involvement in the special education process. Over thirty years of research has concluded the same results: When parents take responsibility and are highly involved in the decision-making process, student success rates exponentially increase, and this is even more imperative with special education students. I can't even count how many ARDs I've attended throughout my career in which the parent or parents opted not to attend. That is sad and pathetic. The power of parental involvement should not be understated, and districts need to find new and improved ways of connecting with parents. Increasing community involvement and providing more opportunities for parents to be included in school-related functions would be a move in the right direction. We'll look closer at parents and their role in schools in a later chapter, but parents and schools must find better means of cooperating and mend the tattered and contentious relationships that have begun to brew as of late.

Students

It's time for school districts to cease all the nonsense and focus on students. Getting students with disabilities engaged in the learning process is only the first step. Schools have to end their practice of making the diagnoses and categorization of students their focal point and instead, actually focus on the individual student and what that student needs to succeed. Districts get so caught up in ensuring that they fit a particular student in the right box, they miss the entire point of their endeavor: To provide "specialized" and "individualized" instruction. Many disabilities come with an extremely wide range of capabilities and demands, and a student's learning should match those capabilities and demands, not some pre-categorized lexicon created by some academic in an oversized armchair with his legs a little too tightly crossed.

If school districts hope to lessen the strain special education programs are currently putting on their bottom line, they will need to adopt a much more student-centered approach long before special education even comes into play. This starts with early student literacy. Today way too many kids lack adequate reading skills. There are many factors behind this trend from poor school curriculum and the infusion of distractive technology into their daily lives to lack of books and reading opportunities in the home. Today's young children are just not prepared for school. Whether this is due to poor parenting, excessive screen time, or merely something in the water is up for debate. Nonetheless, this fact remains: Young children today are atrocious readers. Functional literacy skills are the most vital skills needed to navigate the world. Schools have to discover new ways to not only increase student literacy at an early age but they must also find ways to inspire students to acquire the foregone love for reading that seems to have vanished from our culture.

With up to half of special education referrals being related to reading deficits, public schools across the nation could significantly reduce the need for these programs by addressing an issue as simple as reading fluency. The even more alarming fact is that if these reading deficiencies are not identified and addressed by the third grade, that student will continue to struggle throughout the remainder of his or her schooling. In addition, once that student reaches the upper primary grades where reading becomes an integral skill in subjects such as math, science, and social studies, he or she will be destined to fail. These students with reading deficits then wind up having behavior problems and are extremely less likely to attend college or even graduate from high school.

It's a travesty that schools cannot figure out a means to address the most basic skill required to function as a human in today's world. The fact that recent research has determined that up to half of public school students lack the appropriate skills to adequately read should infuriate anyone and everyone privy to that information. Parents have to expose their children to books at an early age, and schools must spend more time building reading skills and fluency in the early grades. It's not really that complicated... Put a book in a kid's hand, and the rest will follow.

It's time to focus on outcomes. Our special education system in this country, not unlike the system as a whole, is utterly failing to meet the needs of students with disabilities. Schools don't need more laws and rules or any other sort of government meddling. That's what's created this mess in the first place. School districts have historically attempted to add more staff, more coteaching, and more hours of support for these students, but these strategies have only resulted in more expenditures and lackluster results. Costs have skyrocketed while achievement levels have remained at a standstill. Schools will have to start focusing on results and addressing individual student needs if they are to have any hope in successfully addressing and improving the deficits of students with disabilities.

This situation seems bleak, and I do understand it's difficult to accept and deal with the pessimistic outlook that results from this and many other topics surrounding public education. However, this is the reality in which we live. If things were going peachy in schools today, there would be no need for a book like this. There's no quick and easy fix. We've touched on some various ways and means by which to possibly improve this system. Nonetheless, it is going to be a difficult endeavor to mend our current model of special education in the Unites States, and we may in fact need a complete overhaul. What other situation or place would anyone find themselves, in which less than a 20% success rate is considered acceptable?

Chapter 9: The Role of Technology in Education

"Technology is just a tool. In terms of getting the kids working together and motivating them, the teacher is the most important." ~Bill Gates

"In education, technology can be a life-changer, a game changer, for kids who are both in school and out of school... It can bridge the quality gaps."

~Queen Rania of Jordan

Over the past two decades our world has been completely permeated by a torrent of technological devices with computers and cellphones becoming objects of necessity instead of the nonessential, luxury items they were once viewed. People's homes have become like portals to fantasy lands with appliances and other inanimate "smart" devices speaking to them as if they had just been transported to the cartoonish set of Beauty and the Beast. Over the past 50 years, technology has shifted from a detached novelty to being seamlessly infused into our everyday lives. Most jobs today, especially those in high demand, require at least a rudimentary working knowledge of how to maneuver through today's technological world, and schools have begun over the past couple of decades to incorporate these emerging technologies into classrooms across the nation.

Technology has further driven globalization as well as transformed every aspect of our daily lives, and today's students have become natural technophiles being born directly into the midst of the recent technological revolution. However, the consequences of our drastically shifting environment have not yet been fully realized. As technology has become infused into every classroom and home in the country, the effects of these changes are beginning to manifest. Of course, there are many benefits to technology in education, from streamlining curriculum creation, grading, assessment, and instruction to increases in student engagement, collaboration, inclusion, and overall access to knowledge. There are, nonetheless, many negative aspects of technology that must also be addressed including mental and physical health issues, increased distractibility, and social isolation. There are also many safety issues involving children using the Internet. Although it can be a vital tool, the web can be an extremely dangerous place, and many children are consistently engaging in unfettered access to highly inappropriate, and at times alarming, information and media.

The educational technology industry has boomed during the last couple of decades and is projected to grow to nearly a $350 billion a year market by 2025. With the growing advances in artificial intelligence, virtual spaces, and augmented reality, classrooms of the not so distant future could be unrecognizable. Public schools will continue to pump millions upon millions of dollars into the funding of these new and emerging technological tools, but they should ensure these are productive moves that will actually improve student outcomes. This blitzkrieg of a technological revolution has taken over the entire world in less than two decades, and the world is still attempting to fully understand how to interact with these new devices in a healthy and productive way. Children possess brains and bodies that are not fully developed, so the effects of this technology on them will always be amplified. Therefore, parents and schools should take cautious measures as they incorporate more and more of this technology into their lives. We will discover through our journey in this chapter that educational technology no doubt provides significant advantages to schools and students in myriad ways; however, there are many negative aspects surrounding this technology that could be of grave concern. But before we dig too deeply into another controversial topic, let's first take a brief look at what brought us to this juncture.

Annals of Educational Technology and Innovation

Educational technology refers simply to any technological resource used in an educational setting. This may include computers, televisions, Smartboards, iPads, and any other electronic hardware or software. Emerging technology appears to be altering the learning environment like we've never seen, but technology and education, in fact, have a long history of evolving in unison. As far back as the 1680s, technology began to seep its way into the classroom with the invention of the magic lantern, which used light from oil lamps and candles to project detailed anatomical images. This device was actually the ancient predecessor of the modern slide projector. Around the turn of the 19th century, the most basic classroom tools—the modern pencil and chalkboard—were incorporated into schools across the land. These might not seem like earth-shattering innovations, but at the time, they revolutionized classrooms. Before these inventions, students were forced to write with chalk or charcoal on pieces of slate or wood.

Educational innovation stagnated throughout the 1800s, with the only significant development being the invention of the ballpoint pen. However, as the nation moved into the 1900s, alternative forms of electronic media began to crop up in school districts across the country in the form of school museums, which were the forerunners of the district-wide media centers common in school districts today. These organizations managed instructional media for schools by collecting and distributing slides, charts, photos, exhibits, or films from local museums to loan to teachers for classroom instructional purposes. By 1910, more than 1,000 silent films had been approved for use by public schools. Thomas Edison even stated at the time, "Books will soon be obsolete in schools...Our school system will be completely changed in the next ten years." Overstating the future impact of emerging technologies is apparently not a new phenomenon.

Chicago public schools established their own visual education department in 1917, and by 1931, over 30 states had created some type of administrative organization to take charge of films and other school-related media. Despite these early efforts to infuse new technology into the classroom, the revolutionary change Edison predicted did not reach the heights he imagined. Lacking the skills to use these new technologies, the increased cost and upkeep associated with them, and the amount of time needed to find the most appropriate film, most teachers opted for other educational resources.

Although film became the first popular form of educational media, during the 1920s, radio became the new technological frontier. The Department of Commerce began to license educational radio stations, and some schools even began broadcasting in classes. This trend picked up a bit of steam throughout the '20s and '30s, but by the 1940s, its impact and use began to wane. Even resolving issues like poor reception and the high cost of equipment could not overcome the lack of fit between radio broadcasts and school curricula. Ultimately, radio instruction was abandoned when television burst onto the scene. This device soon found its way into nearly every home in the country, refashioning the nation's consumption of information and the evolution of the entertainment industry...it didn't take long before televisions found their way into classrooms.

In the post-WWII Cold War era, educational technology took flight. Throughout WWII, the U.S. government needed to quickly and efficiently train new military recruits and new industrial workers to meet the demands of their war machine. The government spent over $1 billion on training films and purchased over 50,000 projectors for training rooms across the country. The experience and results gained from this media venture, in turn, fueled the expansion of these practices into schools. In the two decades after WWII, 242 television stations were set aside for educational purposes, and the Ford Foundation invested over $170 million into this new-found media.

It was the intense competition with the Soviet Union during this time that significantly impacted the incorporation of technology into classrooms across the United States. The Soviet Union's space program advanced at a whirlwind pace, and while Americans sat by on their sofas watching the launch of Sputnik, the United States' space program sputtered on, leaving much to be desired. This lack of progress caused the government to shift its attention to higher-quality education in math and science and fully embracing technology in public education. This led to the Vocational Education Act in 1963, which provided federal funding for technology in schools.

As the nation moved into the latter part of the 20th century, this enthusiasm began to wane. Like many technologies, schools found it difficult to meet the costs of purchasing and maintaining needed equipment, and it was nearly impossible to get instructional programs broadcasted when teachers needed them. This all changed with the invention of the VHS tape in the late 1970s, which allowed teachers to show media in the classroom anytime without the need for broadcasting. This allowed teachers to more easily incorporate films into their lessons. Access to these videos was, however, limited; they could be quite costly to rent, and copyright issues frequently added a complicated wrinkle. Television and VHS continued to be used throughout the 20th century, but with the rise of the computer in the 1980s, the game would soon change, setting schools on a technological odyssey.

The first efforts to create computerized instructional applications can be traced as far back as the 1950s and 1960s, but those endeavors would not impact schools for several decades. When the microcomputer appeared on the scene in 1980, schools finally began to take notice, and by 1983, 40% of elementary schools and 75% of secondary schools were incorporating computers into their daily learning. Even though most schools had limited numbers of computers and limited access to them early on, this was the seed that would soon cultivate technology being infused into every realm of public education. The 1990s brought the World Wide Web into classrooms, connecting students to people, places, and ideas like never before. By the turn of the 21st century, public schools had, on average, one computer for every five students, and 97% of schools had acquired Internet access.

As the country moved through the first part of the new millennium, technology only became cheaper, more convenient, and easier to access, slowly seeping into nearly every aspect of our daily lives and routines. This is no different in public schools. With the advent of widely available and easy-to-use devices such as cell phones, tablets, and Chromebooks, their embodiment by school districts should not be surprising. These devices allowed instant, seamless communication and access to almost any information one could possibly conjure. Nearly half of all school districts in the United States today possess the resources to provide some type of computing device to nearly every enrolled student, and 99% of schools not only have Internet but high-speed Internet. Of course, large numbers of rural areas lack access to these advancements, but rural areas have always been behind the curve when it comes to technological advances due to their isolation and lack of resources.

Only time will tell how this situation will evolve. The COVID-19 lockdowns were a great litmus test that showed just how unprepared public schools are to fully embrace the current technological storm. Let's be realistic. Virtual learning was a monstrous disaster in most areas of the country. Public schools are not ready to fully embrace modern technology in the classroom for reasons we will discuss. However, this revolution is not easing off the gas pedal, and schools are falling behind. With the world already beginning to shift to virtual spaces, augmented reality, and the infusion of artificial intelligence (AI) into everyday processes and procedures, public schools have a bit of catching up to do. Furthermore, if used properly, these future technologies, may not only augment student learning, they may also be the only hope for rescuing a sinking ship.

Educational Technology Today

Today's technology has allowed students to conduct research and inquire into an endless range of topics, enabling them to construct new knowledge and access learning resources at unprecedented levels. Technology has also further integrated and simplified various aspects of the everyday duties of teachers and administrators. Almost all data are now entered and analyzed electronically, and although this shift comes with significant increases in security risks, it has streamlined mundane and time-consuming tasks, making it easy to access and share information. Nearly all communication is done electronically via emails, text messages, or other online media outlets. Assessments have been moved into the technological realm, with many states opting for a complete online model for state testing and other assessments. Classroom instruction has been enhanced with Smartboards, laptops, and iPads, and some schools even allow students to use their own personal devices, including cellphones, for learning activities in class. Of course, students often use them for other purposes, sometimes nefarious in nature, but we'll get to that a bit later. Keeping up with the never-ending innovations and trends associated with this technological transformation seems to be half the battle, so let's take a look at the current landscape of educational technology in public schools today.

The demand for virtual learning, which encompasses both online learning and e-learning, has increased dramatically, and the COVID-19 lockdowns only intensified this demand. E-learning is a bit different from online learning because it creates a learning environment completely removed from the classroom setting, delivering educational services through phones, laptops, and other computing devices. Online learning, on the other hand, can occur in the classroom or at home and refers only to the act of receiving instruction online via an Internet connection. Therefore, online learning functions more as a blended model, incorporating live classroom instruction supplemented by online tools. These teaching methods use videos, podcasts, and animations to enhance the overall learning experience. Video-assisted learning is yet another way to reach students outside the classroom. This technology is similar to e-learning, but instead of real-time classes, students can view lectures and other recorded lessons whenever they want. These new methods provide much promise, with current research suggesting that video presentations are highly effective at increasing student learning and performance. In addition, with teacher shortages and overflowing classrooms around every corner, virtual learning may be the best route to ease pressure on teachers...still hanging on by a thread.

Big data has become a big issue in public schools. Schools must keep endless records of students' credentials and performance results as well as staff-related data, and the new and innovative blockchain technology could help ease some of this burden. Blockchain technology could make record keeping much easier and eliminate many time-consuming processes, as well as reduce fraud while increasing schools' cyber security. This technology would make schools less vulnerable to ransomware attacks and other forms of hacking. Blockchain technologies could also reduce plagiarism and other types of cheating, especially when combined with AI.

AI, although not widespread, has begun to infiltrate several classrooms as well. This emerging science has actually advanced to the point where programs can grade papers for teachers, giving them more time to focus on curriculum and teaching. AI programs may also be required to fill in the teacher shortage gaps by providing personalized electronic tutoring services to students and even instructing small groups of students on simpler concepts. AI is even being considered to aid in improving the quality of teaching by using learning analytics to help educators measure progress, identify student deficits, and even predict future growth and performance. These programs could provide valuable insight to teachers and administrators allowing them to better understand and address the needs of their students while also gathering data on what motivates them, providing schools with more tools to increase student engagement. These systems could be even more beneficial for use with students with disabilities.

There has been, however, some recent troubling news surrounding AI in the realm of education. The release of ChatGPT has created a firestorm of contentious debate about the role of AI in the classroom and the world at large. ChatGPT is an open-source program run by AI that can generate entire conversations as well as text-based stories, research papers, or news reports by compiling and organizing massive amounts of information via the web in a matter of seconds. This program can spit out a complete script, dialogue, or research paper based on the information one inputs to the application. The work produced by ChatGPT can many times be undistinguishable from work created by an actual human. This new technology has very troubling implications, perhaps leading us to a future in which we may find ourselves unsure of what's real and what's generated by the "man in the machine." This new technology also has widespread implications in the field of education, resulting in scenarios where it will be extremely difficult to determine if students' work is actually their original work.

Video games and the gaming world burst onto the scene in the 1980s, and their expansion into our everyday realm has continued to surge. Educators are constantly searching for ways to make learning more fun and engaging, and the gamification that these new technologies provide teachers a multitude of ways to achieve this goal. Gamification simply refers to the act of incorporating game-like activities into learning to increase student engagement and motivation. This practice enables students to gain valuable information and insight while feeling like they're merely playing a game. Gaming has proven to be highly effective at not only increasing engagement and providing more fun and exciting avenues to learning, but research has discovered that gaming can aid in cognitive development. Furthermore, gamification has been shown to create more positive learning environments as well as increase student collaboration. Of course, students cannot simply game all day long in class; however, gamification can be a great supplemental learning tool to improve the overall learning environment for all types of students.

Social media is wrought with numerous problems, but this highly controversial virtual space has actually managed to find its way into the learning process. Students and parents spend so much time on social media it can function at the very least, as an easy communication tool. Districts and teachers frequently use social media to communicate information to parents, students, or the community as a whole. This is a quick and convenient means to reach a large number of individuals in an extremely short amount of time. Students have also begun to use social media sites or apps to communicate with their peers to share study materials, join group discussions about assignments or projects, and create animated learning videos that, at times, even go viral. So, despite overwhelming legitimate concerns about children on social media, there are indeed at least a few positive trends in this realm.

Although these devices are only beginning to find their way into classrooms, virtual reality and augmented reality could soon take over schools near you. These new technologies provide the ability to create interactive and immersive classrooms like never imagined. These systems would create an entire virtual world for students to explore, capturing their senses and allowing for complete immersion. With virtual reality, students can be transported to any place or time they could conceptualize, creating nearly any virtual environment possible; augmented reality allows students to remain in the real world with added digital elements to enhance their experience. Schools should move with caution and fully research the benefits and side effects of this technology in the classroom, but when combined with AI, virtual and augmented reality could provide yet another outlet to address the worsening teacher shortage, increase student engagement and performance, and further individualize and finetune the learning resources available for students with disabilities.

Cloud technology has also improved the functioning and distribution of the educational process in many school districts. With cloud technology, schools are able to store information in an easily accessible location where students and parents can download programs and files to any device from school or from home. This eliminates the time-consuming processes of consistently updating computers and manually sending out materials to students and/or parents. The cloud also provides more opportunities for collaboration, allowing students and teachers to access resources anytime, anywhere. Furthermore, the cloud and many other technologies we've discussed encourage more asynchronous learning, giving students more flexibility and freedom, essentially taking control of their own learning. Students are now empowered to seize a hands-on role in the learning process, creating self-discipline and time-management skills that will be of great benefit in their adult lives. These technologies also increase exposure to STEM-related topics as well as student creativity.

Thus, it is quite apparent technology has taken over our public schools. All the devices and media that have been injected into our everyday lives have infiltrated the hallways and classrooms of nearly every school in the country. But this technological revolution is still a relatively new phenomenon, and its effects on children are not yet fully understood. It does appear this new tech and its incorporation into daily learning could provide some very promising outcomes for everyone involved in the education process. However, several concerning issues have already surfaced as we ride atop this technological wave, and if we do not take some of these concerns seriously, we may find ourselves face first in the sand.

Educational Technology: The Good, The Bad, and The Ugly

The primary goal of incorporating technology into public schools is to enhance student learning and success. Therefore, we must ask ourselves if this technological infusion is efficient and effective, and the answer is far from certain. Enough detailed and long-term studies have not been conducted to discover and understand the effects these devices have on our youth. Results of recent research have run across the entire spectrum. Proponents point to the engagement and collaborative improvements technology can provide students, as well as the unimaginable access students have to an endless range of knowledge.

However, research by educational technologist Richard Clark, concluded that "media do not influence learning under any conditions..." He went on to state that technology media are "mere vehicles that deliver instruction but do not influence student achievement any more than the truck that delivers our groceries causes changes in our nutrition." Clark believes that the positive results attained via technology are mostly due to varying instructional strategies. Others claim technology is nothing more than a neutral party with nothing inherently good or bad behind the curtain other than the person in the driver's seat. Well-developed and properly implemented technology could provide incredible benefits for students, while poorly designed or improperly implemented technology would most likely not advance learning and could even be detrimental.

The answer to this controversial issue is not unlike most: It lies somewhere in the middle. While technology, no doubt, offers many benefits to students and educators, it does come with many downfalls, which gung-ho advocates have, at times, attempted to sweep under the rug when no one is looking. Let's proceed by lifting the rug and taking a look at the real consequences of educational technology.

The Good

Technology provides easy access to a wide variety of information and creates more fun and engaging opportunities for students. The Internet allows the exploration of new subject material and provides avenues to deeply understand many difficult topics through access to articles, message boards, and videos. Technology has boosted student collaboration and increased student communication and problem-solving abilities—important skills in college or the workplace. The World Wide Web never sleeps, providing students with unlimited 24-hour access to a litany of educational resources that can spark curiosity and increase inquisitiveness. At the end of the day, if nothing else, technology has definitely expanded access to educational resources to levels not seen since the invention of the printing press.

Let's face it. Technology is exciting, and kids love to use it. Many students today used many of these devices before they could even walk, and most of them are much savvier at operating these technological devices than their parents or teachers. These devices increase student engagement and harness their attention, which is a seemingly impossible task most days. Students can also involve themselves in more authentic learning experiences through today's technology, which exposes them to real-life problems better preparing them for the coming world. The technology students use in schools may very well be the same technology they use in college or their career; thus, infusing more technology into classrooms could better prepare students to take on the challenges that await them after graduating from high school. Technology can also encourage more spontaneous learning over which students have much more control. Students who want to learn more about a topic can research it online, most often with a device located right in their pocket.

Another great aspect of technology is that it's always there. It never goes home, and it never closes its doors for business. In addition, there is so much information out there one could not even get through half of it in several lifetimes. This information comes in many formats, making it much easier to match a particular media to a unique need or preference. There are articles, stories, videos, diagrams, pictures, maps, and blogs, just to name a few, and most of these can be accessed on a variety of devices. Technology also allows for up-to-date information, while revisions to textbooks and other hard-copy materials take months or years.

Educational technology has also greatly expanded opportunities for communication and collaboration among students. Though a barrage of research has pointed to the isolating nature of our current technological devices, opponents to this philosophy claim technology in education yields more integration than isolation. Students can simply use handheld devices to create digital and graphic media, classroom polls, collaborative projects, virtual simulations, or engage in live vlogging or other communication media. Classrooms have historically been isolated spaces with little to no interaction between other classes; however, technology has enabled students to collaborate with other students on their campus or even across the entire school district. The ease of communication provided by today's devices allows students to reach out to their peers and teachers nearly anywhere. Students are able to share their thoughts and ideas across multiple forms of media today, providing greater opportunities to work together to solve problems. Students can upload homework and other assignments, turning in work to their teacher from their living room couch. In addition, students may be able to email or message teachers outside of school for assistance with concepts and assignments they are not quite able to fully grasp. This speed of information provides the opportunity for direct and real-time communication, as well as providing teachers with email and certain apps.

Money plays a huge factor in every aspect of our lives, and this matters even more so in the realm of technology. These devices are not cheap—most costing at least several hundred dollars if not over a grand. Nonetheless, some tech advocates point to the thousands of dollars educational technology may actually save school districts. Textbooks and annual photocopying fees can be extremely expensive. In 2018, U.S. public schools spent $42.76 billion on textbooks, and in 2021, schools spent upwards up $1.5 billion on paper and other photo-copying expenses. In addition to the positive effects on the environment due to massive decreases in paper usage, technology can reduce these hidden costs for school districts, allowing those funds to be used in a more productive manner. Hundreds of online textbooks can be accessed with the click of a button, and these digital resources are also, many times, free or require only a nominal fee. Technology has further reduced overhead by computerizing report cards and allowing parents to check grades online at any time, thus, districts not only save on paper costs but postage and time.

We've discussed the multiple benefits of educational technology on students, but this technological infusion has also aided teachers in many ways. Some teachers are beginning to find their roles shifting from the primary source of learning to "guides on the side"—they are becoming passive participants pushing students to take on a more active role by using technology to collect the relevant information needed. The Internet has made it much easier for teachers to collaborate and communicate across distances as well, and teachers are able to access an endless amount of material and resources on any and every subject imaginable. Technology has enabled teachers to not only improve their instructional methods but also to create new and improved ways of personalizing learning.

Technology has also made the teaching process more efficient with nearly every aspect of the job now computerized. Attendance, grades, and behavior referrals can be inputted online and made instantly available, and email, as well as other apps like ClassDojo, have made communicating with parents a breeze. If a student misses class or must be absent for an extended period of time, teachers can simple upload their work to their class website or send out a link to the student or parent ensuring students can easily make up any missed assignments. At the end of the day, technology saves teachers valuable time, allowing them to focus more on what matters—their students.

Thus, it's apparent that there are many benefits educational technology can provide for every party involved in the educational process. It has improved the lives of students, teachers, administrators, and parents by making most mundane procedures less time consuming and allowing for more productive outcomes. However, if something seems too good to be true, it most often is. We will soon discover, despite the overwhelming apparent advantages associated with the widespread adoption of technology in public schools, there are many concerns and potential negative outcomes that must also be addressed.

The Bad

Technology is being incorporated into various school settings at mind-numbing speeds, and some wonder if schools are moving a bit too fast. Despite the research pointing to the seemingly immense benefits associated with technology, there are quite a few concerning issues that accompany these benefits. This situation has evolved into the archetypal double-edged sword, with one side championing the advantages of educational technology while the other side clamors about the impending apocalyptic ending this technological revolution will bring. So, let's take a look at these complaints and the legitimacy of them.

Although technology has the ability to create widespread student engagement, it can very often become an overwhelming distraction. I cannot tell you how many times I've sat in the back of a classroom observing a teacher's class when only about half the students actually had the appropriate material up on their computer screens. Instead, most were watching YouTube videos, playing Minecraft, engaging in online chats, or reading about topics not even closely related to what was being studied. Furthermore, with many schools allowing students to bring cellphones into the classroom, this situation has gotten out of control in many districts. More often than not, educational technology appears to be creating more off-task behavior, and teachers are forced to take time away from instruction to address computer usage issues. Computers also make it much easier to hide off-task behaviors from teachers. Screens are not in full view, and students can close out of apps and webpages or minimize them quickly, tricking teachers into thinking they are doing what they're supposed to be doing.

In addition to the distractibility of technology, students are many times able to access inappropriate or unreliable information. Sure, schools have security measures such as website blockers, firewalls, and other Internet filters. However, these safety measures don't always work properly, and tech savvy students have found ways around these protections. Violence, sex, drugs, and whatever other lewd and lascivious topic one can conjure up can be accessed with a simple click today, and of course, not everything found online is true. The fake news craze, as of late, has at least taught us this much. Teachers and administrators must vigilantly and actively monitor and police student technology use nearly every minute of the day. There are many new and useful tools to aid in this endeavor, and teachers can even access software that allows them to see what webpage every one of their students is viewing in real-time. But this takes away from valuable instructional time, and if school staff must become daily tech auditors, I'm not sure educational technology may be saving schools as much time as the champions tout.

Additionally, Big Brother may be lurking in the shadows of your very home. Schools have, in fact, installed fairly intense security measures into many of their devices, and when students take these devices home, those security features do not magically cease operating. Districts can track the location of these devices and possess the capabilities of monitoring what students do on their computers even off campus. This may seem like a good practice, but some districts have the capabilities of accessing the microphones and cameras of their devices leading to some questionable privacy issues. There are also various software applications that track every word typed into any district-related device or communication system, which flags words deemed problematic like "gun" or "suicide," sending an instant warning notification to the appropriate staff member. We definitely want safety measures in place to protect our children, but some may feel this peeking behind the curtain of students' personal lives is a bit too much. Plus, many parents have no idea these features even exist, and quite often, many of the flagged words are misinterpreted or just innocent banter that winds up being escalated into much ado about nothing.

Technology has also spawned new and exciting avenues for academic dishonesty. It's quite simple to search online for other's work and magically make it your own. Students can share answers on homework or even copy and paste each other's responses. Students are frequently caught texting answers during tests or flat-out looking up the answers on Google during examinations. There are many tools out there to combat plagiarism and other forms of cheating, but many times they are not adequate. Moreover, with the recent addition of the previously discussed ChatGPT application into the technological landscape, the playing field has shifted greatly, with students now able to use artificial intelligence to generate a complete and coherent essay or research paper with a mere click of a button.

Some research has also shown that technology use can actually decrease creativity and increase isolation. This is the exact opposite result educational technology proponents consistently laud. Many technology-based activities are pre-made, reducing the need for students to problem solve or use any sort of imaginative skills. As a society, we must face the fact that online communication simply cannot live up to the experience of actual face-to-face interactions. If students become too accustomed to only communicating via technology, they may not be prepared to effectively communicate when they are forced into a real-life conversation. This may not be a problem if we're all going to plug ourselves into the metaverse and live a Wall-e like existence, but perhaps we should better prepare students for actual conversations just in case Zuckerberg is wrong.

Although technology seems to provide endless opportunities for connecting and collaborating, staring alone into the abyss of a blue screen can be quite an isolating experience. Even with programs like Zoom and Facetime, participants are still not actually present with another human. So whether technology connects or disconnects us as a species is still up for debate. The fact remains that many kids are extremely lonely today, so we must ask ourselves if these online connections really fulfill the social and emotional needs that come with real-life interactions. I believe the obvious answer is no.

We've previously pointed to the cost-saving aspects technology can provide school districts however, technology is expensive. Many schools have used bond packages to fund large technology purchases, but the money must still come from somewhere. Districts also often buy more technology than they need or acquire program-specific technology that quickly becomes outdated or unnecessary. Much of the technology schools procure winds up stacked 6 feet high in storage rooms or closets collecting dust and rodent excrement. I had an office one time in which I discovered countless laptops, iPads, robots, drones, and various other devices that had to be worth upwards of $10 thousand. I reported this to the proper channels and was informed it was from a defunct program and someone was supposed to come pick it up. That technology remained in that office the entire year, and who knows where it wound up. I can almost guarantee not in the hands of a student. So with the high cost of educational technology and the enormous amount of waste that accompanies it, fully integrating technology into classrooms may not actually be the cost-reducing savior as promised.

Technology appears to be an excellent time saving tool for teachers as well as administrators, and this is true in many aspects. However, learning this new technology, especially for someone who has not grown up with it, can be an extremely difficult and time-consuming task. Even once mastered, technology takes time. Teachers must go through extensive set up procedures, and technology also comes with hours of technological training teachers must complete, usually on their own time. Monitoring student technology use has also begun to consume large swaths of time for educators having to constantly police what exactly students are doing behind the mask of that computer screen. Moreover, many older teachers just can't grasp this new wave of technology, and they soon find themselves overwhelmed, confused, and frustrated. Once again, technophiles' promise of the immense time saving aspects educational technology provides, may, in fact, be somewhat empty. Thus, the proposed time technology saves may actually be eaten up by the time consumed throughout the process putting schools and teachers in a break-even situation.

There are also increasing equality issues in the technological realm. The simple fact is that not all students have equal access to technology, and with it being more and more ingrained in every aspect of our lives, this creates a chasm between the tech haves and the tech have nots. Of course, students from lower socio-economic backgrounds will not have the capabilities of acquiring the latest and greatest technological gadgets, but what's worse, many of these students do not have access to decent Wi-Fi, or at times any Internet connection at all. Therefore, even if schools are able to loan out devices to students, it would be a fruitless endeavor if these students cannot access the web. This lack of technological resources results in groups of individuals who may already be at a disadvantage, becoming even further behind on assignments and other learning activities.

Educational achievement has historically aligned with family income levels more than any other factor since the beginning of time. With income levels being directly linked to the level of technology in the home, the move to push for more technological learning will no doubt leave large groups of students in the dark. Up to 70% of homework assignments today must be completed online, yet over five million students have zero access to computers or the Internet at home. In addition, almost 20% of teenage students reported that they had been unable to complete homework assignments due to the lack of the technological resources needed.

When students across the nation were forced to attend classes on computers from their homes during the COVID-19 debacle, the scope of this issue finally came into full view. During the lockdowns, 60% of students from lower socio-economic backgrounds received below-quality virtual learning, and of those students, 40% received no virtual instruction at all. For students from average or above average incomes these figures were reported at 40% and 10% respectively. Furthermore, while average income students lost around 6.8 months of learning during COVID-19 closures, lower income students lost nearly double the amount at 12.4 months. This trend crosses racial lines as well with Black students losing on average 10.3 months and Hispanic students losing around 9.2 months of learning during the lockdowns. Students in rural areas also have much more difficulty accessing technological devices as well as the Internet connections needed to adequately compete with their urban counterparts.

The bottom line is schools have to figure out a way to get the needed technology into students' hands, but they must also ensure students have a means of connecting to the web in the first place. This is partly an income issue but also an issue of government failure. If there is not adequate service available where one lives, then it doesn't matter how many fancy devices one might possess. They become like cars with no gas: mere occupiers of space. Creating equality in any situation can become a highly burdensome task, but schools, as well as other government officials, must figure out a way to address this issue surrounding technology. If public schools are going to base their systems of learning around emerging technology, they must find ways to include all parties, unless their ultimate goal is to even further widen the already abysmal gap that exists between certain groups of students.

Finally, educational technology must be meaningful. Schools can't just put a student in front of a screen while they sit back and let the magic unfold. Not all educational software and online programs live up to their hype, and some are outright garbage. Researchers have been torn over the conflicting results of their studies with large amounts of data pointing one direction while other results send them scurrying in the opposite path. The fact is, we just don't know if this massive influx of technology is good or bad for our kids. One route takes us down a yellow brick road of increased student engagement and performance, yet the other seems to lead us to more problems and despair. But before we come to a consensus, there is one more road we must venture down... and this road may not be very easy on the eyes.

The Ugly

Thus far, it appears we may be locked in a stalemate. There are obvious benefits to educational technology, but there also seems to be just as many troubling concerns. Most of the positive outcomes we've discussed appear to cancel each other out when matched against their converse, creating somewhat of a technological yin and yang. However, when we look deeper into some of the newly discovered mental and physical effects of technology on young people, the results are considerably troubling. With mental health issues, as well as increases in bullying, sleep disturbances, and problems with addiction skyrocketing in our youth, the negative consequences of technology may be deleterious to much more than educational outcomes.

the minds of all those in the hallway as they gawk with a sneering grin smeared across their faces. In addition, the Internet is generally permanent; therefore, these horrible or embarrassing posts or messages live on in infamy.

Some tough minded or more insensitive types may say "just get over it." Suck it up, and move on with life. That's good advice from the periphery, but when a child is 11 years old with a cascading disco-tech of hormones rushing through his or her body, that is easier said than done. The fact is young people across our country are being emotionally wrecked by online predation. Here is the list of the effects experienced by cyber bullying: isolation, depression, anxiety, low self-esteem, sleep disturbances, decreased academic performance and school absences, lack of interest in hobbies and interests, withdrawal from family and friends, as well as increased use of drugs and alcohol. This eventually can deteriorate into self-harming behaviors including suicide. Cyber bullied students are twice as likely to harm themselves or attempt suicide as compared to their non-bullied peers. Countless numbers of students have taken their own lives as a result of the mental effects of cyber bullying.

Thus, when looking at the negative physiological as well as psychological effects that many times result from using the technological devices that have infiltrated classrooms across the nation, the pros do not seem to outweigh the cons in many regards. The physical and mental health of today's youth are in serious decline, and research has shown that the overuse of technology has been a significant factor in this concerning trend. So what are schools to do? It seems technology, like any tool, can be beneficial or detrimental. It all depends on who's behind the wheel.
The Final Ruling

We've touched on some very important issues surrounding technology in public schools, but at the end of the day, it all boils down to one verdict: Oversight. We police and monitor nearly every aspect of children's lives these days. We see danger lurking around every corner. Every stranger equates to potential perilous danger. Long gone are the days in which children roamed freely on their bikes and skateboards through the streets or cruised the corridors of local malls and food courts. We've hovered over every aspect of our kids' lives and kept them locked up and GPS-tagged. Yet, for some reason, we've granted them unbridled access to the most powerful devices ever created, which they can easily slip into their back jeans pocket. What a silly bunch of primates we have become.

The bottom line is that young people's bodies and minds are not affected in the same ways as those of adults. We protect our children against every other imagined danger in the world, so why would we not be more concerned about how these devices affect them? Technology has obviously had significant negative impacts on adult populations across the world. Just look at the state of things around us. Thus, if we know how this technology can affect fully developed adult brains, how are we not more concerned over how it's affecting the formative and still developing plastic minds of our children?

Let's do a quick crash course review session. Here is a list of the effects excessive technology can have on the more sensitive brains of young people: low attention and academic performance, delays in language development and social/emotional skills, decreases in physical activity leading to obesity and other physical health effects, sleep disturbances, increased aggression, mental issues such as anxiety and depression, and increased addictive behaviors.

Don't get me wrong. We should not embark on a war against technology. Wars on [fill in the blank] seem to be all the rage, but there is no need for yet another. Plus, when has the U.S.'s war on anything resulted in much more than wasted resources, pain and suffering, and catastrophic results? How did the war on drugs work out? What about that war on terror? Our war on COVID-19 went great, right? So, let's not grab our bayonets and storm the Bastille. Technology is as neutral as Switzerland claims to be. This new technology has presented the same dual-use problem that nuclear science created nearly a century ago. Nuclear science can be used to produce immense amounts of energy powering entire cities, yet it can also be used to annihilate entire cities in the blink of an eye. It is us who have infused evil into tech. Technology is merely a ship...we are its captains. Technology is like a lightsaber, which can glow blue or red, depending on who wields the sword. Algorithms drive technology, but humans write the algorithms. We are all behind the wheel of this runaway train.

There are indeed tremendous advantages to incorporating technology into the classroom, and students can benefit greatly from its use. However, all adult parties involved must be vigilant in monitoring and intervening when its use is deemed inappropriate. The problem today is that no one is monitoring because all interested parties seem to have better things to do. Most often, the overseers are engrossed in their own technology. Mom and Dad gaze at their cellphones while Johnny and Suzy sit idly by swiping on their iPads. That's the first step. Parents, teachers, and other interested parties are first going to have to put down their own devices and snap themselves back into reality before they are capable of seeing and, in turn, addressing the problems their own children and students are facing.

The long-term potential of innovations like virtual reality, augmented reality, and artificial intelligence...properly used...can greatly benefit schools and address teacher shortages in the not-too-distant future. In fact, I believe the future and health of public education may depend on these and other technological devices and innovations. These devices could help engage students and individualize instruction in ways never imagined. These new technologies could even function as life-saving devices, helping to keep the educational ship afloat. Technology is extremely important in the educational process, and schools have to continue to push for more technological advancements in the classroom. However, these devices must be used properly and productively, and there must be reasonable procedures in place to appropriately monitor and guide students throughout this process.

Unless the earth gets bombarded by a massive solar flare, technology is here to stay. We are going to have to discover a means to live with this technology while simultaneously prospering from it. We have thus far failed in this endeavor. Schools should continue to incorporate educational technology into the classroom, but they must adapt their methods by achieving this goal in a more productive and responsible manner that provides a safe and meaningful learning environment while also using fiscal resources more efficiently. Additionally, parents must be more attentive to what exactly their children are doing behind the screen. If we cannot all work together to enhance the great benefits technology can offer while suppressing its harmful aspects, our youth of today may be in for an extremely bumpy road ahead.

Part III: The Hard Truth

Chapter 10: Behavior and Safety in Schools

"Half of teachers leave the profession within their first four years, and kids with behavior challenges and their parents are cited as one of the major reasons"

~Ross W. Greene

"Research has shown time and time again that infants who receive high-quality child care and early education programs do better in school, have more developed social skills, and display fewer behavior problems" ~Judy Biggert

A pencil flies across the room and hits the teacher in the head, while in the classroom next door, an unruly student tells the teacher to "fuck off." Just down the hall a teacher shouts in frustration after several futile attempts to quiet her class. Further down the hallway, a 5-year-old chokes another 5-year-old while the teacher stands nearby, trying to figure out why the expensive technology recently installed in their classroom is once again on the fritz. Just around the corner in the next hallway, a young boy sprints out of a classroom screaming while a teaching assistant chases him down the corridor. That's just a brief tour of a local public school near you.

Kids today are literally out of control, and classrooms across the nation are in daily turmoil. This unhealthy environment has not only begun to affect the academic performance of students but also has significantly contributed to the mental and physical health issues currently on the rise in public schools today. Based on newly surveyed data, at the conclusion of the 2020–2021 school year, one in four teachers considered leaving the profession, mainly due to behavioral issues in the classroom. Teachers are no longer tolerating the daily disrespect and the increased risk to their safety, and many are retiring early or simply walking right out the door, never to return. I've seen more teachers walk off the job in the last couple of years than at any time in my career.

More and more children arrive at school from troubled and chaotic homes, and they bring that trouble and chaos with them. Furthermore, the older these children get, the more havoc they tend to wreak. These students arrive on campus with aggression, defiance, and disruption literally written on their t-shirts. Their behavior has completely destroyed the learning environment wasting teaching time and disrupting the learning of dozens of other students. These students can also be extreme safety risks and often not only verbally attack their peers and teachers, but they also have begun to physically assault any and all around them at an alarming rate. Toothless, bleeding children and hospitalized teachers have become commonplace news at which we now just shrug our shoulders.

Nearly 20% of teachers reported losing at least two to three hours of instruction per week, with some losing over four hours as a result of disruptive behavior, and this figure is even higher in urban areas. What's worse, the situation has only escalated beyond belief after the COVID-19 fiasco. Some students were out of school for nearly two years in some districts, and they have returned to school in rare form. Many experienced massive amounts of trauma during this time, but some were just permitted to basically do whatever they wanted to do for up to two years. It's not hard to understand why returning to the rigorous daily grind of public school after having a dozen back-to-back summer breaks has been problematic. The reality is before COVID-19, behavior in schools was already atrocious; however, the mismanagement of the pandemic donkey-kicked the situation right off the cliff.

It hasn't always been this way, though. Addressing behavioral issues in public schools is not a novel issue. Schools have dealt with student behavior since the days of Plato and Aristotle. Trends have shifted, though, and the percentage of students exhibiting these behavioral issues is at an all-time high. But what happened? How did we get to this point? The ways in which schools deal with discipline have evolved over the centuries, so let's first take a brief journey to discover exactly how we've reached our current conundrum.

Behavior: An Origin Story

From the first schoolhouse erected in the New England colonies well into the 19th century, corporal punishment was the norm. This type of punishment was even used to address academic shortfalls and errors. Teachers would strike students with birch switches and rulers when they didn't pay attention, follow the rules, or neglect their work. Surprisingly this practice is still legally permitted in 19 states, although few, if any, schools still implement this method due to the extensive liability issues associated with physically disciplining students.

As the mid-1800s brought Horace Mann and his progressive movement into education, discipline policies and procedures began to change. European models, promoted by individuals such as Phillipp Emanuel von Fellenberg, began pushing to discontinue using corporal punishment for academic errors. He went on to suggest that encouragement and positive reinforcement were better methods to address academic issues, which is still the practice in use today.

Behavior issues began to escalate a bit more at the start of the 20th century. When schooling was deemed compulsory in 1918, the part the teacher played on this stage began to shift to a more parental role, forcing the teacher to become a disciplinarian due to the influx of massive numbers of students who had never seen the inside of a school before. This, in turn, led to principals being hired to function as the new disciplinarian, thereby taking some of the burden off teachers. This fresh system attempted to avoid identifying teachers as the discipline source but it also created a new hierarchy that still exists to this day.

During the first decades of the 20th century, the U.S. legal system began to delineate distinctions in the way juvenile and adult offenders were handled. Ideologies shifted to a more rehabilitative model of discipline for young people as opposed to a punishment-based design. As the nation approached the mid-1900s, Maslow introduced his hierarchy of needs pyramid. Maslow's model emphasizes that people, especially children, are motivated to achieve certain needs. If teachers do not create a safe learning environment that meets these needs, then behavior problems will flourish. He went on to underscore the importance of proper classroom management practices and incorporating these practices into everyday curriculum and learning. This basic model of student needs still guides many district policies and procedures today.

As the United States moved into the latter half of the 1900s, corporal punishment began to fade away, and schools moved toward non-physical means of discipline. In the 1970s and 1980s, "time out" began to infiltrate schools, replacing the corporal punishment model. Teachers would send students to isolated corners of the room or perhaps out in the hallway within the teacher's field of view. This technique became somewhat of a double-edged sword. Although using time out can prevent aggressive and disruptive behaviors, ensuring the rights and safety of all students in the classroom, this practice comes with side effects. Students in time out are removed from the lesson, decreasing their learning; they can face humiliation from their peers, and the technique can actually positively reinforce students who want to get out of class.

With the onset of the 1990s, school misbehavior began to escalate to unprecedented levels. Violence and aggression infected schools in every state across the country. Schools and classrooms began to morph into hotbeds of felonious activity, and in turn, felons began to roam the halls and corridors of schools everywhere. More and more weapons appeared in classrooms, and school shootings increased in frequency. There are many hypotheses as to why this trend came about. Some point to drastic changes in the family unit associated with rising divorce rates, which resulted in single parenting becoming the norm instead of the exception. Some argue it was a result of the celebration of violence from Hollywood to video games, while others claim the rise of drug use in young people was the culprit. Yet still, perhaps it was the onslaught of new technology finding its way into classrooms and homes, providing access to tools and information children had never been able to access so easily at any time in history. Most likely, though, it was a combination of all these and other factors.

This massive wave of violence, disrespect, and chaos led to implementing zero-tolerance policies. Schools were permitted to use much harsher punishments for offenses that fell under the category of zero tolerance, and with the passing of the Gun-Free School Act in 1994, schools could expel students who brought a gun to school. These policies are still used today (although they are not often enforced) and have evolved to include any type of weapon, drugs or alcohol, excessive fighting, and threats or harm to a teacher. In addition, although the practice of placing police officers (aka resource officers) in schools began in 1985, their numbers increased significantly, and the fuzz began roaming the halls of schoolhouses in extraordinary numbers.

However, none of these tactics seemed to have much impact on students, and as the nation stumbled its way into the next millennium, the situation only worsened. In the 2000s, the age of the referral was born. Teachers could write a discipline referral detailing an incident in which a student was involved. The student would then be "referred" to an administrator or counselor to deal with the behavior. The goal was to assist students so they could later return to class. This procedure continues and is still in practice in many districts today. Most schools and districts have written codes of conduct, so administrators can match the referred behavior to the recommended consequence, and Bam! Problem solved...or not so much. Referrals did little to improve student behavior, but they did remove the student from the classroom, providing the rest of the class needed reprieve.

However, referrals often resulted in suspensions, which led to many of the same issues that stemmed from using time out. Many students now began to see suspensions merely as extra vacation days. That is until many schools began to use a new system termed "on-campus suspension" or "in-school suspension." This practice is fairly self-explanatory. It requires students to serve their suspension on campus in an isolated classroom with a special teacher. This method is two-pronged. It keeps students in school where they can still receive instruction and not make mischief in the community unsupervised throughout the school day. The practice also allows schools to maintain the daily per-pupil funding flow coming from the government. Each school receives government funding based on daily attendance, so whenever a student is absent or suspended, that money gets deducted. Thus, even though the students were "suspended," they can still technically be coded as being present in school.

This practice is still used today and has come with some positive results. However, it's become nearly impossible to find people willing to do the job. When teachers in regular classrooms are running out the door screaming, there aren't exactly hordes of job seekers knocking on that same door to deal with the worst students in the school all day long. Plus, many schools are so overcrowded they are running out of space to conduct on-campus suspension. Many times, these kids wind up just hanging out in the office all day, which is not beneficial for anyone.

That brings us to the present day. Schools still use many of the techniques discussed, like referrals, zero tolerance, and suspensions, and although corporal punishment has all but disappeared, there is a current push to re-introduce it as a last-ditch effort to improve the chaos. I'm not so sure that's a move in the right direction, but schools and teachers have become that desperate. There has been a strong push for preventive discipline, which aims to start the process sooner by implementing early expectations and rules and sticking with them. Schools have moved to identify and address behavior problems early before they escalate to uncontrollable levels. But this process is not easy, and there is no template on how to accomplish this goal which has made it a bit less impactful.

Positive reinforcement is all the rage today, and it can provide very meaningful behavioral changes in students, but it is being overused. For proper discipline that changes behavior, an equal balance of carrots and sticks must be the norm. In many schools today, fields of carrots can be seen, but not a damn stick can be found anywhere. What's worse, recent laws have restricted schools from suspending and removing young children in the primary grades. This may seem like a reasonable tactic, but some of these young kids are little terrors, destroying classrooms and assaulting their peers and teachers on a daily basis. This is not a rarity—it *is* the norm. Of course, we can't really blame a 5-year-old, but who do we blame, and what do we do with this student when they injure others and destroy the learning environment? Well, I can tell you. Most schools put them right back into the classroom, to further harm others and continue to wreck the learning of everyone. This system must change, and it must change fast.

The most striking fact of all is that while many schools continually push for individualized instruction, they have done next to nothing to individualize discipline. Current research shows that administrators, teachers, and parents must work together to determine what strategy works best for each student. The one-size-fits-all discipline model does not work in public schools, and I would venture a guess it seldom works anywhere. Discipline has come a long way in the United States, but the current systems and strategies do not work. Bad behavior has infected every corner of public schools across the entire nation. But why are these students so out of control, and why are these behaviors increasing in frequency and intensity? Like nearly always, we'll discover it's a combination of multiple factors.

Behavior in Today's Schools

We've frequently discussed the dismal academic progress students achieve, yet students struggle as much, if not more, on a social level. Students today simply lack the basic levels of social aptitude and self-control that were once considered the norm. Many of these youngsters are merely attempting to assert their freedom and independence, but lying, stealing, fighting, eloping, tardiness, and disruption have infiltrated classrooms to the point where some of these students have achieved their goal: They are now the ones in charge, and all the adults around them are at their mercy. Excuses of old, such as peer pressure, fitting in, and the enticement of popularity and attention, just don't encompass the root of these problems anymore. There is something else going on out there.

Today's children simply lack the skills kids used to possess. It's not a complicated issue. Kids today generally have poor attitudes due to anxiety and low self-esteem, and many of them have created smoke screens or façades to disguise their social and emotional deficits. Students have learned to cloak their social shortcomings by distracting the world with their outrageous behavior. Kids today are failing to build positive coping skills or meaningful relationships. Children are losing their sense of personal boundaries and have somehow acquired an extreme misunderstanding of basic expectations and consequences.

Some aspects of the deterioration of behavior in students today are a direct result of the world in which we live and the environment that has evolved around our youth. There is a great deal of stress in the world, and adults are experiencing high levels of trauma. In addition, schools were struggling immensely with these and many other issues even before the COVID-19 disaster struck. The government's mishandling of the pandemic has done nothing but further exacerbate these issues. Take a look at how adults have behaved over the last several years...fighting at gas stations and grocery stores, shouting obscenities like a sailor, and having weekly nervous breakdowns. In their defense, things have not been great in this country or the world for that matter, but kids are watching. When all the adults around them model nothing but disrespect, aggression, and zero coping skills, it's not too far of a stretch to imagine children will pick up on their lead. When a parent storms into the front office ranting and raving while cussing out the attendance clerk, why are we surprised when children treat their teachers similarly?

These behaviors affect not only the architects of the chaos but also those around them. Behavior problems in the classroom distract other students as well as the teacher. They reduce student participation and lower the motivation of both the students and the teacher. These behaviors can even influence fairness in grading, not to mention the safety of students. In the end, all this turmoil in the classroom only leads to more subpar academic performance. Schools have struggled for decades to improve the educational outcomes of students across the entire country, but this escalation in misbehavior has knocked them even further off any correctible course.

But what is causing this alarming trend? Why do more and more students fail to achieve even the most basic levels of self-control and social competence? We live in a new dynamic world that has created many changes in our environment and ways of life in the last couple of decades, and perhaps our brains have not quite caught up. Therefore, there are a multitude of factors we must first address to obtain a better understanding of what has caused this current predicament.

Parenting

Discipline begins in the home. It's as simple as that. Public schools aren't even involved in the process until four to five years into a child's life. In the majority of cases, environmental causes are the primary factors associated with the drastic increases in problematic behavior, and this factor starts and ends in the student's home. Family life can be chaotic, unpredictable, and even hostile. When family members interact with each other in aggressive, negative, and controlling ways with coercive tactics such as intimidation, threats, yelling, and, at times, actual physical force, children incorporate these methods into their daily lives at school. These methods of coercion then manifest themselves in the classroom as whining, shouting, tantrums, disobeying, and hitting. What's more, if these students never experience or practice cooperating behavior skills such as sharing and negotiating, they will be unable to build friendships or even a modicum of social acceptance among their peers in school.

Parents need to teach their kids basic social skills, set rules and limits, and model self-control from day one. Thus, the converse of the above-described chaotic and coercive home environment can be just as detrimental. This situation occurs in many homes where children actually have too much leeway and get away with too much at home. This practice then translates directly into the classroom. Kids show up to school on the first day with terrible manners, inappropriate social skills, and completely self-centered attitudes. When kids govern the home by dictating what gets served for dinner, determining when it's time for bed, and deciding how much time they get to play video games, they will be highly unsuccessful in school

Furthermore, unaddressed, these early onset behaviors will soon escalate in intensity and frequency as the student ages and moves into the middle to upper grades. Thus, whining, shouting, and occasional tantrums evolve into lying, stealing, bullying, and fighting in middle school, and once that student hits adolescence, bullying and fighting soon escalate to robbery, assault, burglary, and vandalism. That cute, little "Trouble Maker" t-shirt-wearing, adorable monster of days long past is now a resident felon. If parents can't figure out a way to seize the reins on their out-of-control children, schools will be left with little option but to shrug their shoulders.

Although uncaring and overprotective parenting can both significantly contribute to behavioral issues, inconsistent parenting is even more of a contributing factor. Parents must consistently model appropriate behavior and teach those behaviors to their children. When a student has regular behavior problems in school, the first step should not be to point a giant finger at the schoolhouse. The first step should be to check yourself and your parenting. I'm not suggesting being a parent is an easy task. In fact, it is one of the most difficult endeavors. But you did the crime; now you must serve your time. Having a child is a huge commitment, and we as a nation need to better understand how important and difficult the job of parenting is and think more deeply about the decision to bring a life into this topsy-turvy world.

Trauma

The troubling fact is that more and more young students arrive at schools with significant levels of trauma, and most districts are not equipped to handle it. Today's students deal with more stress and anxiety than students of the past while at the same time possessing more limited coping skills to deal with these setbacks. Behaviors seen once a week in the past now have to be dealt with daily, and much of this can be attributed to trauma. Trauma can present itself from many obvious points of origin, such as deaths in the family, physical or mental abuse in the home, or the destruction of home life due to some type of natural or manmade disaster. However, trauma can also result from much more mundane origins, such as a car accident, frequent arguments in the home, bullying, or perhaps even a worldwide pandemic.

Understanding and learning how to cope with life's curve balls is part of the growing process for children, but sometimes, due to a lack of experience and the required skills, they get stuck and become unable to move past and properly process impacting events in their lives. Children can become overwhelmed by the negative feelings associated with troubling events in their lives, which can significantly affect their physical, mental, social, and emotional development. Many times, if unaddressed, this trauma can even develop into full-blown PTSD.

Students experiencing trauma tend to blow up and freak out over the smallest of setbacks, and they tend to turn ordinary drama into an all-out war. There are emotional breakdowns lurking around every corner with these students. Most don't have the ability to properly address and deal with the thoughts and emotions racing through their heads; therefore, they act out. Their horrible behavior is their way of communicating something is wrong. The problem is that most schools do not have the staff to properly address the issues these students face, and if these students are not able to receive the help they need, serious mental health issues could arise, as well as increases in anxiety and depression that can, unfortunately, lead to self-harm or suicide. Some school districts have moved to increase the number of counselors, social workers, and behavioral specialists to focus on these problems, but they definitely have a long road ahead and will need the cooperation and support of parents to aid in the process of healing these students.

Technology

We've devoted an entire chapter to technology, but it has become an inescapable aspect of our daily lives. The massive adoption of this technology by children as young as toddlers has, without a doubt, significantly contributed to many of the behavioral issues schools currently face, especially when it comes to attention. Recent data have shown that some kids in the United States spend up to 90 hours a week on some type of technological device. This enormous increase in screen time has resulted in increases in anxiety and depression, as well as deficits in social skills and communication. It often appears as if phones and iPads are raising America's youth, and although they could probably do a better job than some parents, these devices were not intended to be the parental agents they have become. Using screens as babysitters may seem like a great idea. It's easy and cost-effective, and kids love them. But the long-term costs of this practice are much more detrimental than parents realize.

It's not only researchers who have pointed to the damaging effects of excess screen time. Many teachers report similar findings, with nearly 90% of surveyed teachers stating they have observed a direct correlation between increases in learning difficulty and increases in screen time. In another survey, 80% of teachers reported that more screen time in their classrooms has resulted in more behavior issues, and over a third of teachers rated the problem as "dire," stating that behavior has become significantly worse due to increases in screen time. Furthermore, the COVID-19 pandemic has even worsened this issue; between 2019–2021, screen time among 8 to 18-year-olds increased by 17%, and these findings do not even take the excessive use of virtual learning into consideration.

We must acknowledge the fact that excessive amounts of screen time have had a tremendous impact on the behavior of our youth. Cell phones have given young children and teenagers unfettered access to information and media they quite frankly have no business consuming, and what's worse, no one seems to give a hot damn about it. When students view acts of violence, drug use, sexual deviance, and who knows what else at the click of a button, are we to wonder why these kids mimic those same behaviors?

My friend, who is a PE teacher, told me his kindergarten classes came into the gym several years ago asking if they could play *Squid Games*. If you're not familiar with the show, look it up. It's probably not a healthy viewing experience for the most seasoned adults, and yet not one or two, but nearly an entire class of 5-year-olds had apparently seen it. Recently, while I was doing a classroom observation, a kindergartener asked me if I liked *Stranger Things*. Of course I do. While a fantastic show, I'm not sure it's the best media experience for a 5-year-old girl. This, of course, points the finger back at the parents who allow this to happen in the first place, but at the heart of the issue is technology.

We all need to work better to discover new ways for kids to entertain themselves and stop using devices as babysitters. What happened to playing outside, board games, sports, hobbies, and real family time? Excessive technology use involving hours upon hours of screen time is not only wrecking the mental and physical health of our youth, it's turning them into selfish, greedy, intolerable monsters with zero attention spans, which catapults us to our next topic of conversation.

Attention...Or the Incredible Lack Thereof

Student engagement is one of the most important factors that affect learning and progress, and the simple fact is that many of today's kids have lost the ability to focus on anything for more than a few minutes. Teachers now deal with classrooms full of squirrels that have no idea where they've hidden their nuts. Technology and endless screen time have been major contributing factors to this problem. However, this is not a book about neurology and brain science, so we will not delve too deeply into the details behind this phenomenon. Just know this. Screens keep our minds highly engaged and hyper-focused, and the various algorithms and computer codes found within these devices are extremely well-designed to hijack the chemical mechanisms of our brains. These devices literally rewire the way we think and behave. This has, in turn, affected our ability to think and focus properly, and this effect is even more detrimental to children whose brains are still developing.

Although screen time is a significant factor in this widespread attention deficit epidemic, there are many other compounding issues that have become relevant players in this game. Some students are just naturally easily distractible, and colorful displays and interactive arrays of resources found within most classrooms can overload some kids, thus pulling them away from their intended focus. Then, 20–30 more students are tossed into the mix, and it results in serious mental overload. Even having classroom windows can create a huge distraction with kids gazing outside, daydreaming, or just zoning out. Many students find themselves highly unengaged due to boring and irrelevant curricula. What and how schools teach kids have not evolved with the times, and much of the curriculum and lessons can be mind-numbingly tedious. Teachers should ensure they create learning environments that not only reduce visual and auditory distractions, but they also must find creative ways to make mundane material easier and more enjoyable to consume. This is not always an easy task.

Kids also deal with more personal issues than most youngsters in the past. Trauma and other distressing incidents can cause students to become hyper-focused on certain issues such as bullying, family problems, or health issues that distract their focus. The increases in anxiety and depression we've frequently discussed can have major impacts on students' ability to focus. These are some of the most difficult situations to deal with because, many times, a student's personal issues may be outside the school's jurisdiction. Teachers and other staff must tread cautiously and carefully when dealing with personal issues so as not to cross the line into litigious territory. The best approach is to keep parents informed of the concerns and work to address the needs that are capable of being addressed in the school setting.

Some students have legitimate disabilities that affect their ability to concentrate and focus on the task at hand. Many of these students are eventually diagnosed with ADD or ADHD, and others may be diagnosed with more severe disabilities, which most often results in a special education placement where those deficits can be better addressed. There are some disquieting trends when it comes to this arena, though, with more and more kids, overwhelmingly males, being diagnosed with attention disorders. Quite frankly, many of these students are misdiagnosed, and it's a tragedy. All a parent needs to do is find a doctor willing to check off a box, send in the script, and now you have the walking dead in your very home.

This nation is medicating young boys at startling rates, turning them into mindless zombies. Parents should make certain medicating their child is the right move. It nearly always seems like an easy fix, and it may very well be. But do the benefits outweigh the costs? Many of these medications children are given today have some troubling known side effects, not to mention the litany of unknown side effects lurking around the corner further down the road.

Schools have to find a way to pull back the reins on student attention and slow down this stampede. I find myself struggling at times with my own attention due to the new environment we've created for ourselves as we charge into the future. I find myself unable to get through a show at times without checking my phone, and I've worn the rewind button raw on my remote from constantly having to backtrack due to simply zoning out. I can't remember how many times I've read a page in a book and realized I had no idea what I just read because my mind wandered off to some unimportant nonsense. If we as adults wrestle with focus and concentration, how on earth do our kids have a chance? We must all strive to do better in this regard. It will not be easy, but it starts by simply putting down our phones, turning off all the noise, and actually living life.

To Sleep or Not to Sleep

The importance of getting adequate sleep cannot be overstated. There is uncontestable and universal evidence confirming that lack of sleep results in significant behavioral issues, especially in children. Kids don't sleep enough today, and they suffer physically as well as mentally from this lack of rest. Students who do not get enough sleep will undoubtedly perform poorly at school, and their behavior will decline. Even in adults, lack of sleep has significant effects on memory and focus. Most kids should get a minimum of 8 hours of sleep a night, and most need upwards of 9 to 10 hours to properly function.

Kids are dealing with stress, unhealthy home environments, or other factors that may affect their ability to sleep. However, we've recently discussed one major factor contributing to this decline in sleep time: Screens. When kids stare at screens all evening long, it stimulates their brains and scrambles their circadian rhythms. Unfortunately, this is a problem over which schools have zero control. Parents are the administrators of sleep. Thus, parents must create a more consistent sleep routine, which includes limiting the use of technological devices in the evening and ensuring kids go to bed at a reasonable hour. We'll talk more about sleep issues in a later chapter, but simply by ensuring a child gets adequate sleep, parents set them up for many more opportunities for success.

The Epic COVID Failure

To put it bluntly the government response to COVID-19 has perhaps ruined an entire generation. Schools will spend years, if not decades, trying to fully recover from the damage inflicted by poorly thought-out and politically charged decisions by incompetent and corrupt government leaders. The academic and learning deficits resulting from school shutdowns are so extensive it's pretty much immeasurable. These shutdowns, however, not only affected the academic progress of students they also significantly impacted the social and behavioral development of kids across the country, especially those very young children in their early developmental stages.

Even before the lockdowns, schools struggled to adequately address the increases in violent and disruptive behaviors in classrooms across every corner of the nation. For many students, school is their only reprieve from the trauma and conflict they experience daily at home. Homelife for a significant portion of the nation's student population is not a healthy and safe environment. Whether it's food insecurity, arguing relatives, or varying levels of verbal or physical abuse and neglect, schools have become a safe place for many of today's youth. It can be the only place they get two square meals a day (I know this is a stretch, but even government food is better than what many of these kids put in their bodies at home. And many have no food at all). School may also be the only place some kids can go where they are surrounded by adults and peers they can trust to not harm them mentally or physically.

When the government shut down schools for days, months, and years in some states, many children were forced into situations where they only experienced more trauma, more abuse, and more damage. Moreover, schools may also be the only place where many of these kids get any exercise at all. It's mind-blowing how many overweight children are rolling around the halls of schools everywhere. Childhood obesity is at a record high, and it is an utterly disgusting tragedy. At least at school, kids get 20–30 minutes of recess to run around, and they have PE class several days a week. At home, most of these kids are kicked back on the sofa, watching this screen or that screen while stuffing their faces with crap. Kids need to exercise, not only for their physical health but also for their mental well-being.

This is not even the worst of it. With the closure of daycare facilities, summer camps, parks, malls, playgrounds, water parks, beaches, and dozens of other places where kids learn to socialize, many young children have lost the opportunity to learn how to be a human. Kindergarteners show up on the first day of school with the social skills of a 2-year-old. They don't know how to share, how to problem solve, or how to engage in basic communication. These young children have zero coping skills, and they cry, yell, fall on the floor in tantrums, and often hit and kick their peers as well as adults. Why? Well, because they've had zero time to learn and practice these skills. How are kids supposed to learn how to be social when they've been given no opportunities to be in social settings during the most important developmental years of their lives?

Don't worry, there is plenty of data to support this trend, with over 80% of public schools reporting significant increases in behavioral issues since the COVID-19 closures. Disruptive behavior in classrooms has increased by 56%, with out-of-classroom disruptions also increasing by 49%. Disrespect toward teachers has increased by 48%, and the inappropriate use of technological devices has risen by 42%. Wow. Can you believe that when kids are forced to stare at screens all day long, they become even more addicted to these devices? There's also been a 72% increase in student absences. Students have become more violent, and their fuses have greatly shortened. Kids are yelling, cussing, and fighting more than ever.

There is no quick or easy solution to this crisis. We are all just going to have to do our best to work through this situation. Let's face it. These kids are angry, and they have a right to be. Schools fun-policed these kids to death, taking away sports, their homecoming, graduation, and prom, access to their friends, and shut down every outlet for social exploration and amusement (other than the device in their hand, of course). Should we wonder now why they're so pissed off?

The Cornucopia

So far, we've touched on some of the major causes of the recent increases in student behavioral issues in public schools. However, there are enough other factors impacting this trend to fill a horn of plenty. For one, teachers can actually be the problem. Sometimes, those irate parents are, in fact, correct. Most teachers are at least sufficient enough to create a somewhat productive and safe learning environment, but there is a small percentage of teachers who are quite horrible at their job. This should come as no surprise because every industry and institute has some percentage of their workforce that does not live up to expectations. Teachers make mistakes just like everyone else. Sometimes, they inflict too harsh punishments or humiliate students, which can further increase behavioral issues. When teachers design classroom settings where good behavior management techniques are not implemented and students feel unsafe and unengaged, a slew of behavior problems ensue.

Socioeconomic factors can also play a major role in student behavior. All research points to the fact that students from lower socioeconomic backgrounds perform at a lower rate academically, as well as socially and behaviorally, compared to their higher socioeconomic peers. Low socioeconomic areas deal with higher crime rates, more domestic violence, more food insecurity, and lower health outcomes, which simply results in a much harder life for children living in these types of environments. Abuse, trauma, and neglect can be everyday hazards of life for many students navigating these troubling and unhealthy environments; therefore, it should be no surprise when students exhibit violent, disruptive, or other antisocial behaviors. Schools need to provide these students with the best resources and the most support they can in the school setting while also teaching them more socially appropriate and productive means of navigating their world.

Cultural and generational issues can also greatly influence student behaviors. Certain students may arrive at school from foreign countries or other regions of the United States that may have different social norms and ways of interacting with each other. For example, time is relative in more than the Einsteinian sense. Many countries are very punctual, while others may have more relaxed expectations about schedules and showing up at designated times. Body language can also be drastically different as one moves around the globe. Direct eye contact is generally an accepted and expected practice in the United States and other Western nations, but in some parts of Latin America, Asia, and Africa, it can be considered disrespectful or even a threat.

Teachers and administrators must consider the cultural factors that influence behavioral issues in the classroom. This should not be a difficult task to accomplish—talk to the parents or simply do a Google search on cultural norms from whatever region that particular student originates. In addition to cultural issues, schools must also consider the generational issues affecting today's youth. The Baby Boomers of decades ago are vastly different from today's generation. Kids growing up in the 21st century and those who grew up in even the 1980s and 1990s are worlds apart in the way they behave and view the world. If our educational models are geared toward the learning styles and attitudes of previous generations, then the newer generation of kids will have problems fitting into this system. Thus, schools must not only ensure they are aware of cultural differences in behavior but also the generational differences that may exist with certain student groups.

Surprisingly, behavior problems can also sometimes originate from highly intelligent, gifted, and talented students. If a student has a 125 IQ and they're sitting around a bunch of young troglodytes while the teacher rambles on about the colors of the rainbow, it's actually not surprising that they may act out in class. These types of students are simply bored out of their minds most of the time, but they are rare doubloons who only occasionally pop up out of the masses. Nonetheless, schools must consider when a student is being highly disruptive or even aggressive in class; it could merely be a case of extreme boredom, and the simple fix is to give these kids more challenging content and material to consume.

We as a nation must also figure out what in the world is wrong with young males today. As a behavior specialist in the public school system, well over 90% of the students I deal with are males. They are becoming more disruptive, more aggressive, and much more violent. Furthermore, the academic performance of males has continued to decline in nearly every subject. Young males are not working, they're not going to college, they're not joining the military, they're not dating, and more and more, they're disappearing into their mom's basements to become the Unabombers of the future. There are a variety of factors we could point our fingers toward.

With 80% of single parents being mothers, there are simply few to no men in many of these young boy's lives, and modern male role models are an endangered species as of late. Schools are also not the most ideal settings for young, active, energetic males. Young boys are genetically wired to play, run, and explore the world, which can be a bit of a problem inside the four walls of a classroom. Yet still, perhaps the recent cultural shift to demonize males and any type of masculine behavior has sent these young boys in a whirlwind of confusion, creating uncertainties on how to behave as a male in today's society. Maybe it's the influence of media, video games, and the Internet. Whatever the reason, its path to discovery is well above my pay grade. All I know is that if we don't figure out some type of course correction to get young males back on a meaningful and productive path, our society and our nation is going to be fraught with issues beyond our imagination. If you want to see what a country with millions of unemployed, broke men with no meaningful relationships looks like, take a glance at most of the Middle East and Africa and the most dangerous parts of Latin America.

Lastly, most young people these days simply don't face any real consequences for their actions, and they know it. They rarely get any consequences at home, assuming their parents even know what they are doing or where they are. Or perhaps even worse, their parents helicopter over them, treating them like priceless heirlooms, allowing them to do whatever they want, receiving parental pardon after parental pardon for even the most egregious behaviors. What's worse, schools are no different. They have been kneecapped by overreaching laws, overreacting parents, and the latest and greatest catchy, but almost always ineffective, new discipline models. States have removed the ability for schools to suspend many types of students, especially in the elementary grades, and on-campus suspension is no longer an option for most schools due to the lack of staff available to service those programs. There's lunch detention, but that is usually not much of a deterring consequence, and once again, someone is needed to supervise those students. Some schools attempt to implement after-school detention or Saturday school. However, these options require staff to stay beyond contract hours, and they must be paid extra wages for their overtime. Additionally, parents must agree to these options because they are the ones who must provide the transportation.

School districts across the nation are struggling to find any meaningful consequences for students. Corporal punishment is a philosophy of bygone eras, and the resources no longer exist in many districts to conduct on campus suspensions and detentions. Implementing new "buzzword" discipline models has only had limited success, and many times, the costs of implementing these programs far outweigh the rewards. The bottom line is students need consequences. When a teacher sends a student out of the classroom for disruptive or aggressive behavior, and an administrator sends that student right back into that same classroom, what does that tell not only the disruptive student but also the other students sitting in that class? It tells them that the adults are no longer in charge. Schools must find a way to rediscover meaningful discipline.

MISSING: School Discipline...Please Call This Number if Found

Unfortunately, our society has many economic, cultural, and social issues that spill over into schools while the overarching feds and courts have whittled the power of schools down to a sprig, making it nearly impossible for districts to create any type of safe and civilized school environment. Schools used to be able to remove violent and disruptive students from the learning environment, but today, this practice is increasingly difficult. Instead of fixing the problem, schools mainly just whine about the lack of staff, funding, space, and too many rules and regulations. While these are true, the problem remains unaddressed. Little felons roam the halls, terrifying some students with their presence while intriguing others with their rebellious lifestyle...and the number of these unruly, antisocial students is increasing at alarming rates.

Upwards of 20% of students in some schools manifest some form of antisocial behavior, yet merely 1% of these students are offered any type of special education services. If school districts cannot figure out a way to address and reverse this antisocial revolution in the classroom, schools may begin to resemble scenes from *Lord of the Flies*. Since the passage of the IDEA of 1975, the federal government has increasingly been involved in removing disciplinary options from schools, ever restricting and diminishing any control public school officials might have once had. Students constantly fight and cuss out teachers. These out-of-control students not only disrupt classroom learning, they frequently become serious safety risks to their teachers and peers. What exactly are we teaching our youth when we allow them the freedom to do things in school that would land them in jail as adults?

What's worse, all these laws and regulations have done nothing but create a huge job market for up and coming attorneys. States have created a litigious landscape within public schools. Lawyers, who generally have zero knowledge about education and have not even stepped foot inside of a school since their high school graduation, have become active participants in the educational process riding sidecar as officials and administrators craft policies, procedures, and regulations. From zero tolerance to sexual harassment, the legal system has now become fully integrated into the public school system, and when has a move such as this ever benefitted any organization? From day one, schools must now speak to parents, teachers, and students in quasi-therapeutic legal jargon instead of the simple common-sense language all parties can understand.

Elementary schools have become nothing more than glorified daycare centers in most districts, and middle schools now function as a chaotic interlude where students learn to embrace the "adolescent society" filled with consumerism, violence, sex, drugs, and whatever else these kids can incorporate from their handheld device into the real world, before entering high school. It's time for schools to take back the power they once possessed and return some semblance of productivity and order back into the system. It will be a tough and bumpy road, but at this point, there is no other option but for schools to find a way to reclaim the discipline they have long since lost.

Reclaiming Discipline

Public schools must regain control of their students and implement procedures and policies to create more productive and safer learning environments. This process begins with one simple step: early intervention. Schools need to identify these future troublemakers at the earliest possible point, and this is not too difficult a task. The students who engage in coercive antisocial behaviors such as whining, hitting, and stealing in pre-school should be immediately targeted as students in need of remediation. Chances are these behaviors will not just work themselves out over time. Frequent excessive noncompliance or aggression in school or at home in very young children is the number one indicator of future behavioral issues, and this extremely logical statement should shock and awe no one.

Early intervention is the most critical aspect to behavior modification and improvement. If a child does not learn how to appropriately interact socially with those around him or her by the age of 8, that child will most likely continue to struggle with behavior problems their entire life. Without early intervention, around half of these struggling students will retain their antisocial behavior into adulthood, resulting in incarceration, hospitalization, or even early death. The rest of them will fare no better and will continue to suffer from adjustment issues such as high rates of unemployment, marital issues, and various legal problems.

What's more, traditional punishments have not only been ineffective with these students, they have, at times, further escalated power struggles and conflict. Punishment is reactive, whereas discipline is proactive in nature. Don't mistake me; schools still need punishments. Sticks are as important as carrots, but the sticks must be meaningful. Instead, schools should promote guidance, communication, and respect while embracing more natural and logical consequences. These consequences can be punitive in nature, but they must also be meaningful and fair.

For starters, some students simply need to be removed from the classroom. There is no place in a public school classroom for a consistently disruptive student who frequently puts the safety of those around them at risk. Everyone has a bad day now and again, but if this type of behavior becomes a commonplace occurrence, that student needs to be removed from the classroom regardless of their disability until they are capable of behaving appropriately in the general setting. Sure, opponents of this view will site overwhelming evidence that suspensions and other student removals create a vicious cycle in which students miss critical instructional time causing them to get further behind, and these kids get into more trouble outside of school winding up in juvenile facilities with criminal records and lifelong stigmas that cannot be erased. Others will cite the huge discrepancies concerning racial and gender disparities in suspensions and other types of student removal practices.

Without a doubt, these concerns are valid; however, what is the alternative? Would we rather keep inserting these students back into the classroom allowing them to wreak further havoc on the masses? Schools can create alternate career paths for these students if they just sit down and actually think instead of [over]reacting. This may not be a very popular opinion, but are we to destroy the educational opportunities and risk the safety of 20–30 children to slightly decrease or delay the inevitable outcome of one unruly student? I don't believe this is a very good cost-benefit analysis.

Despite overwhelming evidence to the contrary, there are actually some very intelligent and creative individuals in the field of public education. It's time for these individuals to come out of the closet and speak up. This train has been derailed for far too long, and it's time to put it back on the tracks. This process starts with finding a place to put these most disruptive and violent students once they are removed from the classroom. Only a small percentage will qualify for special education services, so this system is not adequate to address the needs of these students. Schools have no other choice but to create alternative settings into which consistently disruptive or violent students can be placed on a short-term or long-term basis, depending on the severity of their behavior.

This will be the first and most critical step to reform school discipline. The reign of students seizing control of classrooms throughout the country must come to an end. Do we as a nation allow these behaviors in any other setting? At work? In institutes of higher education? In other public or private spaces? No. Even on the streets these behaviors are not permitted. So why do we permit them in a public school classroom? Schools act as if they only have two choices: (a) allow a disruptive student to continue destroying the classroom environment, or (b) toss them to the wolves on the streets. Schools can easily shift funds, using any or all of the money saving tips discussed in Chapter 3 to create both short- and long-term alternative settings for students who cannot function in the normal school setting. These students could be placed in these alternative settings where they could learn and practice the appropriate skills needed to be successful, and when they have proven such, they could return to their school of origin.

Of course, there will always be a small percentage of students who just don't get it or refuse the help they need. Unfortunately, these students will need to remain in the alternative setting indefinitely, and schools will need to work with local law enforcement and other social services outlets to formulate the best course forward for those few who blatantly buck any and every attempt to help them. I'll dose you with a real quick bit of reality—some kids must and will be left behind. The more important question is, are we going to allow them to take the entire ship down with them?

Once the most violent and disruptive students have been removed, then schools can begin to incorporate other proactive and meaningful practices and procedures. For starters, schools can become more academically effective. Academic success is almost always directly correlated with good behavior. If schools can improve the success rate of students in their academic subjects by creating more individualized and meaningful curricula the self-esteem of these students, as well as their motivation and engagement, will all improve. This will, in turn, naturally decrease disruptive behaviors. Success also breeds happiness and other positive emotions, which generally reduces feelings of aggression and anger. By simply increasing the overall academic success rate of students, decreases in inappropriate behavior will instinctively follow.

Teachers should also ensure their classroom is orderly and well managed. Direct links have been found between levels of aggression and the orderliness of a classroom. A longitudinal study discovered that the odds of aggressive behavior in boys assigned to more orderly classrooms were 3:1; however, when placed into a less orderly classroom, those odds increased to a whopping 59:1. Classroom management is huge; even the arrangement of furniture and wall decorations can have a significant impact on student behavior. Schools should immediately move away from useless and bureaucratic trainings and instead spend more time training teachers how to create the safeest and most orderly environments for learning. This practice will significantly reduce disruptive and aggressive behaviors.

Schoolwide behavior codes must clearly define appropriate behaviors. This behavior code should consist of five to seven agreed upon rules, and students and parents should be included in creating the code. Including students and parents in the process creates ownership, community, and enhances buy-in. However, in order for a code to be effective, schools must allow students time to practice following these rules, the rules must be consistently enforced with meaningful consequences, and students must be provided incentives for adhering to these rules.

We've devoted the entire next chapter to this controversial topic, but social skills training needs to be a daily part of school life. Many of these kids act the way they do simply because they do not have the required skills to comply with many of today's school norms. If schools do not allow these students to learn and practice these skills, they will never improve upon them. The dreaded SEL acronym should not elicit fear, because it is not about sexual identity, LBGTQ issues, or CRT. SEL, or social and emotional learning, when done properly by teachers without some type of political or cultural agenda, teaches valuable skills such as anger management, problem solving, self-control, proper communication, and empathy to struggling students. What's more, most teachers are not radical maniacs attempting to indoctrinate children. There's always a boogeyman out there somewhere. From Satanic cults to pedophiles and sex traffickers to razor blades in Halloween candy, danger lurks everywhere. But does it...really? Most of these overhyped hobgoblins are nothing more than that: meaningless hype. The fact is all students benefit from social skills instruction, especially those on the margins who are the most apt to engage in disruptive and aggressive behaviors.

Today's students need attention and praise...and lots of it. Extensive praise is even more beneficial for antisocial and problematic students, and it has been proven to be one of the most effective motivating tools for improving behavior. Praise should be immediate and frequent, and teachers must be sure to describe the actual skill or behavior they are praising. Researchers and "experts" have thrown around a wide array of positive to negative ratios, but teachers should at the very least attempt to say three positives for every one negative. Students not only need praise but also acknowledgment. I can't remember how many times I've merely given a kid a thumbs up and a smile, or a passing "what's up buddy?" in the hallway. These kids immediately light up filled with shock and disbelief that an adult actually noticed their existence. A majority of kids just want to be seen and heard, so the simple act of showing them their value by looking them in the eye and talking to them like the little humans they are, can sometimes do wonders.

Schools have to incentivize students. The intrinsic desire to be a good person and do well in life is just not enough anymore. Kids don't care about grades, and they don't care about what their parents or teachers think. They do care about tasty food, toys, computer time, or many other types of incentives that can be used as hares in the race to the finish line. Teachers can use a multitude of incentive techniques from earning free time for completing tasks or complying with instructions throughout the day to simply placing an animal cracker on a student's desk when he or she earns a point for not being a jerk for 30 minutes. Teachers can implement group, individual, and even whole-class incentives. Individual incentives, of course, work well for one particular student, but group incentives get peers involved by pressuring those unruly students to simmer down, otherwise they miss out on their opportunity to be incentivized. It's really quite simple. Schools need a balance of sticks and carrots.

Kids today still need time out. Many times, allowing students to be removed from a stressful or volatile situation for a few minutes allows them to regain their composure and return to class anew. Time out or "cool down time" can even be used inside a classroom if there is adequate space to corner off an appropriate area. Some kids can even be given the opportunity to take their own time out, which fosters self-awareness as well as independence. A student could simply ask permission to go cool down for a bit, and the teacher could direct that student to the appropriate place. In-class time out would be more appropriate for lower grades. As for older students, the office or a designated cool down room would be more beneficial.

Lastly, schools must be more creative when it comes to disciplining students today. The techniques of the past are no longer effective for most students. Schools should not be afraid to be innovative when it comes to addressing behavioral needs. Throw everything at the wall, and see what sticks. If some new technique is an utter failure, that's okay. Now we know not to try that anymore, and it's on to the next big idea. Eventually over time, new ideas will find success, and that success will grow.

Let's start implementing common sense, rational, and meaningful consequences. There are some promising emerging philosophies, like restorative justice, conscious discipline, and positive behavior interventions and support (PBIS), which use many of the techniques described in this chapter, but at the end of the day, schools must create logical consequences. If a raging student destroys a classroom, what would be the logical consequence? Well, making that student clean up the entire mess they made would be a great start. If a student wants to throw food or trash at lunch, what on earth should we do? How about that student has to pick up trash and clean the cafeteria for a couple days? If a student refuses to work and wastes an hour of valuable class time, why not have that student make up that time after school or on the weekend? You see, real and effective discipline is not that difficult. Schools merely need to find the courage to finally stand up to this revolt and take back the control they lost a long time ago.

Chapter 11: Social Emotional Learning (SEL)

"Emotional intelligence is a way of recognizing, understanding, and choosing how we think, feel, and act. It shapes our interactions with others and our understanding of ourselves. It defines how and what we learn; it allows us to set priorities; it determines the majority of our daily actions. Research suggests it is responsible for as much as 80 percent of the "success" in our lives." ~J. Freedman

Social emotional learning (SEL) has become one of the hottest topics of contention in public schools today, and although we've touched on this topic briefly in previous chapters, I believe it has become relevant enough to warrant a chapter of its own. Academic scholars have collided in debate, protesters have run rampant through the streets, and parents at raucous school board meetings have filibustered and shouted themselves right into the arms of law enforcement—all over SEL. A virtual warzone has been manufactured around these far from peaceful and productive conversations. Is all this much ado about nothing, or is the looming horde of the SEL revolution coming for us all? The answer, we will find, once again, most likely lies somewhere in the middle.

One could say I have somewhat of a deep connection to this topic of concern since I have been involved in teaching and creating SEL-related curricula for over 20 years. I have seen the skills acquired from proper SEL instruction transform young lives and aid struggling students to better cope with their lives and even move beyond their daily struggles. On the other hand, I have seen the power and influence some educators have over the developing minds of their students, and injecting students with questionable ideologies and beliefs can and does happen. That is why it is vital to truly understand what SEL is and what it is not. Numerous government agencies, schools, and individual rogue teachers have hijacked SEL and infected it with personal ideologies, agendas, and politics. This is not SEL. This is social engineering, and it has to stop.

An entire book could be devoted to SEL alone, but at its foundation, SEL is really not as complicated or controversial as our maddening world would want us to believe. Although SEL has created a recent firestorm in public education, it's not a new concept by any means. Like most Western ideas, SEL's pedigree can be traced all the way back to ancient Greece. In *The Republic,* Plato proposed a "holistic curriculum that requires a balance of training in physical education, the arts, math, science, character, and moral judgment." Plato went on to state, "By maintaining a sound system of education and upbringing, you produce citizens of good character."

Statistician, portfolio manager, and CEO Ray Gallo stated in his recent book: "While the inherited assets and liabilities of a country are very important, history has shown that the way people are with themselves and others is the most important determinant." He went on to describe positive behaviors in individuals, such as holding themselves to "high standards of behavior," being "self-disciplined," and "whether they are civil with others." These qualities, combined with flexibility and resilience, create productive citizens who are best able to maximize their opportunities. Gallo concludes by stating, "Character, common sense, creativity, and consideration in most people make for a productive society."

Character development and sound moral decision-making have always been part of the growing and learning process of becoming an adult. Religion and the church were the instructing force and model behind most of this "education" throughout much of the Western world's history. Historically, parents and other immediate family were also great drivers in moral and character education throughout a child's life, although many of the tenets they ascribed to were directly regurgitated from some theological doctrine or axiom. Even in the colonial period and early republic, schools spent significant time focusing on religious-based character and moral development in the hope students would grow up to become productive, law-abiding citizens. However, in the mid-1800s, the move to separate church and state took center stage, and slowly, religion was whittled away from various government entities, including schools. By 1962, the Supreme Court had banned prayer and worship in public schools, creating the final severance between the two.

Don't mistake my point. I'm definitely not advocating for the return of religion to public schools, but instead, I'm acknowledging the importance the spiritual realm and its moral framework played in day-to-day life until a century or two ago. With any type of religious instruction or practice removed from the public school setting, there was no longer a template from which to teach character and moral development. It didn't take long, however, for new modes of filling this fresh niche to take flight.

In the late 1960s, the Comer School Development Program launched a long-term social development project in Connecticut focusing on two low-income, low-achieving schools. By the early 1980s, those schools had significantly decreased behavior problems and truancy, and their performance standards surpassed national averages. This program ignited a surge of interest in this new field of social learning, and various programs and grants began to proliferate throughout the nation. A foundation was soon established for outlining principles for social learning as: "identifying and labeling feelings, expressing feelings, assessing the intensity of feelings, managing feelings, delaying gratification, controlling impulses, and reducing stress."

Finally, in 1994, the term social emotional learning was solidified when various groups and individuals, such as teachers, researchers, and child advocates, joined forces to form the Collaborative to Advance Social and Emotional Learning or CASEL. Many books and publications soon followed as the emotional intelligence revolution unfolded throughout the remainder of the decade and into the new millennium. In 2001, the board altered its moniker slightly to Collaborative for Academic, Social, and Emotional Learning with their stated mission: "to establish social and emotional learning as an essential part of education."

In the past 20 years, the implementation of SEL has exploded throughout public schools. At first, it was used most frequently in certain programs, especially special education classes to address significant deficits in behavior, social, and basic life skills. These classes were generally referred to as "Life Skills" or "Social Skills" classes, and that's exactly what they were. I used to teach a class like this daily for many years. We would discuss different emotions and how to recognize and deal with those emotions in yourself as well as others. We talked about how to follow directions, make requests appropriately, solve problems, apologize, get along with peers, and develop organizational skills and proper life skills such as health and hygiene. We would role-play and run through various real-life scenarios to practice applying these skills in simulated situations.

At its nucleus, SEL is nothing more than a "methodology that helps students of all ages to better comprehend their emotions, to feel emotions fully, and demonstrate emotional empathy for others." These behaviors, in turn, help students "make positive, responsible decisions, create frameworks for achieving their goals, and build positive relationships with others." SEL instruction should focus on self-awareness, self-management, social aptitude, relationship skills, and responsible decision-making. No one can argue that these are not skills we all must possess to function and thrive in the real world.

SEL instruction can also be implemented through a variety of methods. Many SEL topics can be interlaced into the everyday curriculum in any subject, or teachers can set aside a specified portion of the day or week to solely address SEL topics. Proper SEL instruction has increased social aptitude and self-awareness, developed positive behaviors in and out of school, and improved academic performance. Some schools have seen over a 10% increase in attendance and overall grades for students participating in some type of SEL program. These students have shown an increased aptitude for managing stress and emotions, solving problems in and out of school, and avoiding negative peer pressure situations.

Learning these positive behavior practices extends beyond the classroom and testing station. The majority of jobs require employees to understand others, problem solve, work as a team, and manage their time and emotions. SEL instruction conducted in an appropriate and honest way does nothing but create highly adaptable, strong-minded, respectful students who are remarkably prepared for the real world. I've personally witnessed students who could barely function in a 45-minute class period become college-bound successes with part-time jobs. It wasn't because of the knowledge they gained about possessive pronouns, the Pythagorean theorem, or the War of 1812. It was the direct result of proper SEL instruction and implementation.

This is what SEL is supposed to be at its core. SEL is basically a tool to create better humans. It would be an extremely difficult task to argue that the above-discussed skills are not vitally important nearly every day of one's life. Schools began to notice how this type of instruction transformed some of their most difficult students into moderately successful individuals. Some struggling students managed to work their way completely out of a special education program, and some even began to outperform their general education peers. As behaviors in public schools started to spiral out of control in the early 2000s, schools began to hunt for a means to incorporate this type of instruction on a more widespread scale to the masses. Let the SEL revolution commence. Since then, the idea of SEL instruction has morphed and evolved into something far removed from its original core and purpose. Government agencies, activists, legacy media, and NGOs have seized the reins of this movement and slowly whittled it down and corrupted it like the maleficent sculptors they nearly always reveal themselves to be.

Since the passage of the 2015 Every Student Succeeds Act (ESSA), which allowed public schools to use nonacademic measures for accountability, the surge of SEL instruction has catapulted in the last several years. From 2016 to 2020, the number of states adopting SEL standards rose from 8 to 30 states and one U.S. territory, encompassing over 67,000 schools serving more than 35 million students. In 2019 alone, there were over 200 pieces of legislature introduced which referenced SEL. District spending nationwide on SEL increased by around 45% from November 2019 to April 2020, and up to a third of school districts have plans in place to spend undisclosed amounts of COVID-19 relief money on SEL education and resources.

As a finishing touch to the bastardization of a once productive and meaningful idea, in 2020, CASEL made the ill-thought-out and dangerous decision to update their definition of SEL as well as their five core competencies to focus not only on social and emotional issues but to include "identity development, education equity, and adults and students working together to build learning environments that were more inclusive and reflective of the communities they serve." This new model was coined transformative SEL.

Unfortunately, the SEL game has recently taken a treacherous turn down the wrong road. If we as a nation cannot figure out a way to stop and head in the opposite direction, we'll all be sitting in the backseat while Thelma and Louise drive us off the cliff to another Wylie Coyote-like climax as the roadrunner kicks up his heels, laughs, and speeds away. This new transformative SEL is not social and emotional learning. It is, in fact, social engineering at its finest and most perilous level. Identity politics and discussions of student equity and inclusion have zero place in SEL instruction. The most troubling fact is currently, all 50 states have adopted some type of SEL standards for pre-K students, and a number of these states will most definitely attempt to incorporate some of the new tenets espoused by CASEL's new transformative SEL movement into their curriculum. However, most four to five-year-olds are still wetting their pants, trying to understand how yellow and blue make green, and figuring out where the hell they even are most of the time. So, do we really think they're ready to debate trans and gay issues and discuss socioeconomic dynamics about race and gender? Leave that for CNN and Bill Maher.

So what are we to do? SEL education has been a proven means to create significant improvements in behavior and social aptitude for a large number of struggling students. These behavioral and social gains have also correlated with an increase in attendance and in turn, academic performance. Thus, there is quite a bit of evidence that SEL instruction can be extremely beneficial if used correctly. However, insidious agents have seized the reins of SEL instruction and incorporated many issues under the SEL umbrella, which relate to sexual identity, sexual orientation, critical race theory, and other socioeconomic-related ideologies. Many outraged parents have claimed schools are trying to turn their children gay or trans or instill them with troublesome racial ideologies in the name of SEL instruction. Unfortunately, a number of these parents are correct, and some schools in certain regions of the country are, no doubt, engaging in these types of acts. But we must understand that this IS NOT SEL. This is SOCIAL ENGINEERING. We all must learn to differentiate between the two.

The primary issue with SEL instruction is nothing more than semantics. SEL is not easy to define, and districts and government agencies have done an abhorrent job addressing this issue. SEL has also been highjacked by these various entities and used as a ruse to disguise teaching sex education, critical race theory, identity politics, and other topics with which parents should be rightly concerned and outraged. These tactics are not necessarily widespread and certainly not found in every school district in the country. Furthermore, certain states or regions will vary in their degree of chicanery depending on their political makeup, so this situation may not devolve into the apocalyptic vision many hyperbolic agents have made it out to be. However, schools are, without a doubt, proceeding down the wrong path.

Confusion about what SEL actually is, in addition to the complicated jargon surrounding it, have left many parents unsure how they even feel about the issue. One poll by Fordham University found that nearly half of parents surveyed agreed schools should focus on academics and leave SEL needs to be addressed in the home. This number increased even further when more conservative parents were surveyed with almost two-thirds of Republican parents stating SEL did not belong in public schools. Yet, in a separate survey, a majority of parents agreed with the statement: "learning life skills and social skills at school is just as important as academics." Obviously, parents are utterly befuddled by the concept of SEL in schools, and districts have done a pretty shoddy job of acknowledging this confusion and providing more clarity to parents.

In a perfect world, I'd adamantly agree 100% with those surveyed conservatives. SEL instruction has historically resided in the home, and I believe that is the best place for it. However, we live in far from a perfect world. The reality today is that most parents just don't have the time at home to address these SEL issues. What's more, many parents I've dealt with are wrestling with their own social or emotional issues. Nearly 25% of all children live in a single-parent home, and of those living in dual-parent homes, almost 60% live in a home where both parents are employed. Parents are unable to spend the same amount of time with their children as others have in the past. With bills to pay, dinners to cook, soccer games to attend, and home maintenance around every corner, where do parents fit in the allotted SEL instruction time?

Unfortunately, a lot of parents do an extremely horrible job at being parents. Don't get me wrong. Most parents do the best they can, even when they sometimes come up short. They love their children and want them to succeed. However, no license is needed to spawn a human, and unfortunately, there is a significant percentage of parents out there who should not be parents. Of course, there's physical and mental abuse that occurs much more often than one would imagine. Heinous individuals engaging in those types of acts should be dealt with by the law in the harshest way. Recently, though, the most colossal enemy I've discovered is apathy. Many parents today just don't care. Either they are too caught up and overwhelmed by their own lives and personal drama, or they don't want to be a parent in the first place. Creating a human is one of the easiest tasks one can accomplish. Nearly anyone with properly functioning anatomical components can do it. Yet, rearing and developing a productive and prosperous human is a task only accomplished through love, effort, sacrifice, and hard work—and lots of each one.

If parents want to take back the reins and move SEL instruction exclusively into the home, they're going to have to do a better job at it. When a child cusses out teachers and physically assaults other students in addition to accomplishing next to nothing academically, can a parent say with a straight face that the home is the best place to teach these skills? Sure, there are some wacky, downright dangerous teachers out there, and some schools are definitely attempting to indoctrinate students with their own ideologies. But fighting at school board meetings, protesting in the streets, and hurling insults back and forth has apparently solved nothing thus far.

Moving forward, it is imperative that we push to eliminate any and all discussions of race, identity, sex, politics, or other socio-economic issues from SEL instruction. Leave these discussions to dinner table conversations and university classrooms. There is no place for personal ideologies in public schools, especially when dealing with very young elementary-age students whose minds are as malleable as silly putty. In addition, parents, teachers, and administrators have to work together and break free from the toxic and unproductive relationships that have developed among them. Parents should not view the school as the enemy and vice versa. Adults must stop acting like children.

Schools need to be more transparent with what exactly they teach under their "SEL umbrella." Schools should provide parents with written, outlined, and easy-to-understand guidelines explaining in detail what students will be taught during their SEL instruction. Parents should also be given a chance to discuss this SEL curriculum in an open forum without concern of repercussions, and policies and procedures should be in place to amend or adjust this curriculum if needed. Parents must also be afforded the option to opt out of any SEL instruction that does not align with their personal beliefs. Real and valid SEL instruction should not actually have too much content that would offend or trouble many parents anyway. So, if SEL content is discovered that seems controversial or inappropriate, it's most likely not actually SEL but something else.

More rigorous scientific research must also be conducted concerning SEL and its benefits to students. Although schools currently have quite a bit of data on SEL, much of that data is anecdotal. Districts will need more longitudinal studies tracking exactly how levels of student performance, behaviorally and academically, are affected by proper SEL instruction. I could recount stories all day with a plethora of examples demonstrating the successes I've witnessed first-hand throughout my 20-plus years in education as a result of SEL instruction. But I'm just some dude writing a book. What do I know? We need real research and real data to show what works and what does not work. I have seen what does work, and that is real and honest SEL instruction. We are now seeing what does not work, and its name is transformative SEL...aka—social engineering.

It is imperative that schools move away from this top-down government-infused approach to teaching children to be socially and emotionally adept. We have discussed many skills throughout this section that are vital components to becoming a productive and prosperous adult, and we have to teach these skills to students. If this goal cannot be fully accomplished in the home, then we as a nation must figure out a reasonable path to teaching these skills in the public school setting. This should be a community-based approach, however, not a Big Brother mandate. Moreover, parents and school personnel must decide to be the adults and stop acting like the children they are trying to protect and serve. It's only through an honest and dynamic partnership between public schools and parents that they will be able to ensure our youth possess the needed social and emotional skills to navigate the chaotic world into which they are being thrust.

Chapter 12: Critical Race Theory (CRT)

"Prejudice is a burden that confuses the past, threatens the future,

*and renders the present inaccessible." ~*Maya Angelou

*"I refuse to accept the view that mankind is so tragically bound to the starless midnight of racism and war that the bright daybreak of peace and brotherhood can never become a reality... I believe that unarmed truth and unconditional love will have the final word." ~*Dr. Martin Luther King Jr.

In September 2020, Donald Trump issued an executive order that eliminated any "divisive" diversity training from federal contracts affecting over 300 different trainings. In 2021, Fox News mentioned the phrase "critical race theory," also known as CRT, over 1,300 times in a 4-month period. CRT has rapidly become the new boogeyman lurking under the bed and hiding inside closets at night across the land. But is this boogeyman real, or another overhyped behemoth? We saw that the SEL monster, although extremely dangerous in some aspects, is not quite the coming apocalypse some agents would have you believe. Like the SEL upheaval, CRT is more complicated and nuanced than the narratives government agencies, media pundits, and activist groups like to spin.

Like SEL, we touched on CRT previously, but also like SEL, CRT is an important and relevant enough topic to warrant a brief chapter of its own. Race is and always will be an extremely delicate subject, especially when being discussed and analyzed by an extremely White male such as myself. I debated whether to even approach this topic, but it has become such a relevant and controversial issue in our nation this book would not be complete if I did not at least touch on the matter. Like many topics in this book, one could write an entire series of books on race in the United States. I'll attempt this feat in a mere few pages. My goal is to lay out a brief history of CRT, what many say it is and is not, and discuss how it has impacted public schools. I will endeavor to create an unbiased account in which I highlight valid points from both ends of the CRT continuum. Let us now bravely but carefully tread into this perilous territory.

The United States is becoming more and more diverse every day. Based on current population trends, the Brookings Institute estimates that by 2045, Whites will make up only 49.7% of the overall population, thus becoming the minority. At the same time, according to the FBI, hate crimes have risen nearly 10% since 2009. When these trends are combined with the ever-increasing number of negative interactions that have been occurring between law enforcement and people of color, especially Black males, many times leading to heinous acts, including unwarranted deaths, it's no wonder discussions of race and CRT have catapulted to the mainstage. But what exactly is CRT, and how did it all begin? We will find there are many parallels between CRT and our discussion on SEL.

In 2021, the *Encyclopedia Britannica* defined CRT as:

An intellectual and social movement and loosely organized framework of legal analysis based premise that race is not a natural, biologically grounded feature of physically distinct subgroups of human beings but a socially constructed (culturally invented) category that is used to oppress and exploit people of colour.

The idea that race is not "biologically grounded and natural" but rather a social construct, is the foundational principle of CRT. Another central tenet of CRT is the claim that racism is ingrained in the legal, economic, and social systems created within the United States. CRT claims racism is not only codified in U.S. law but encapsulated within its structures, institutions, and public policies. Additionally, the concept of "intersectionality" was later enveloped under the CRT umbrella, which seeks to extend these concerns beyond the bounds of race by including categories such as class, gender, disability, and sexual orientation in the CRT lexicon, creating a hierarchy of oppression.

More recently, the 1619 Project created by the *New York Times* in 2019 implored us to alter our view of the United States to that of a nation whose foundation and history are based solely on slavery and racism claiming the dominant reason for declaring independence from Great Britain was to "protect the institution of slavery." This is a direct quote from the *New York Times* website:

> On August of 1619, a ship appeared on this horizon, near Point Comfort, a coastal port in the English colony of Virginia. It carried more than 20 enslaved Africans, who were sold to the colonists. No aspect of the country that would be formed here has been untouched by the years of slavery that followed. On the 400th anniversary of this fateful moment, it is finally time to tell our story truthfully.

The page goes on to state:

> The 1619 Project is an ongoing initiative from The New York Times Magazine that began in August 2019, the 400th anniversary of the beginning of American slavery. It aims to reframe the country's history by placing the consequences of slavery and the contributions of Black Americans at the very center of our national narrative.

There's so much to analyze in those two quotes, but the most troubling two words to take away from them are "national narrative." I'm personally not a fan of forced narratives, especially ones encompassing a national level.

Critical race theory traces its roots back to the post-Civil Rights era and the early writings and teachings of Harvard law professor Derrick Albert Bell Jr. in the 1970s and 1980s. Bell developed new courses and curricula that viewed U.S. law through a racial lens. He eventually resigned from his post at Harvard in 1980 because of what he viewed as discriminatory practices by the university. In turn, a slew of supporters rose up in support of Bell, claiming the university lacked racial diversity in its curricula, faculty, and student body. One fiery young student, Kimberly Crenshaw, organized a student-led initiative in an attempt to infuse more diversity into Harvard, thus leading the charge and igniting the CRT movement to unprecedented levels.

This movement began to take off throughout the 1980s, and by the emergence of the 1990s, with over 300 articles and books already published, the term critical race theory had solidified its key concepts and features. As the nation moved into the 2000s, universities and colleges began offering courses and studies in various topics related to CRT, continuing the spread of the movement. However, events throughout the last decade have brought about much contention between different races and, in turn, a huge resurgence of the CRT movement. Perhaps it is the nation's current deluge of immigrants, our hyper-focus on the many negative interactions between law enforcement and people of color, the media's over-sensationalism, or maybe the unending barrage of identity politics exposed to large swaths of citizens on a daily basis...whatever the cause, racial tensions are at their highest since the Civil Rights era, and CRT has become one of the hottest topics today.

Despite the current upsurge and popularity of the CRT movement, critics of its founding principles and ideologies are not difficult to find. Many opponents of CRT have been involved in shouting matches, fist fights, and property destruction, which have even led to multiple arrests. CRT adversaries have taken offense by some of the more outspoken advocates who have claimed that all White individuals are inherently racist and privileged while all non-White individuals are disadvantaged and relegated to a lower caste. Other critics claim proponents of

CRT rarely, if ever, produce any measurable data, testable hypotheses, or other evidence supporting their assertions, relying instead on "storytelling" and anecdotal accounts to justify their claims.

Other rivals of CRT point to the overwhelming success of other minority groups, such as Asian and Jewish Americans, objecting that if there was so much systematic racism in the United States, why do certain "marginalized" groups outperform even their White peers? Countless critics have even moved to ban all reference to or discussion of CRT in schools and the workplace, insisting it is anti-American, disparages White people, and can be used as a tool to indoctrinate children. Parents have also expressed concern that CRT negatively affects the way history is taught in schools by demonizing the founding fathers and other influential figures in U.S. history. The opposition states CRT is rewriting U.S. history and infecting White individuals with unfounded and unsubstantiated guilt.

Yet, proponents of CRT still press forward regardless of the heat in the kitchen, especially when it comes to public schools. Multiple districts have begun to incorporate CRT teaching into some of their lessons across all subjects in sometimes extremely subtle ways, like utilizing racial-type scenarios in mathematical word problems or incorporating texts about race in reading or English classes. CRT proponents assert that public schools are, in fact, "whitewashing" U.S. history by de-emphasizing the importance of the role race and slavery played in creating the success of the nation and by skipping over or just touching on many of the embarrassing and abhorrent acts employed throughout the course of our nation's history. CRT topics have even found their way into SEL lessons...we've already beaten the SEL horse to death, so we know CRT has no business in the SEL realm.

Advocates of CRT have, in fact, made several direct allegations against the institute of public education regarding race. They claim that much of the public school curricula omit the lived experiences and historical significance of U.S. citizens of color, instead concentrating on the "White narrative" of U.S. history. They also state that the instructional process in and of itself is inclined to treat minority students as "in need of remediation." CRT proponents attest that school discipline policies and procedures are inherently racist and unjustifiably impact students of color compared to White students, citing examples such as dress code policies, especially those related to prohibited hairstyles. Disparities in school funding have also been highlighted, pointing to the underfunding of low socio-economic neighborhoods predominantly populated by students of color. Finally, CRT defenders point out the idea that segregation still exists due to certain district and attendance boundary lines being, many times, drawn out in a seemingly arbitrary fashion, creating large racial disparities in certain school populations.

Let's now address some of the claims CRT proponents have made, as well as those shouted from the mountaintops by its harshest critics. I have stated my opinion more than once concerning the way public schools teach U.S. history, and CRT advocates are correct to a large extent. However, stating that the entire foundation and creation of this country is based on the institute of slavery is incorrect, dangerous, and actually pretty ridiculous. Of course, slavery was a major player throughout most of the nation's history, but slavery is also embedded in the history of every single empire that has ever existed on this planet. Slave labor still exists to this very day in many parts of the world. Additionally, the kid over in China manufacturing the latest iPhone and the young teenager digging for cobalt in the Congo to charge the latest electric vehicle make less than $5 a day, and some, not even $1 a day. I'm not sure what you would call this situation other than slavery, but this is not a book on the effects of globalization.

Public schools many times do, in fact, lean toward a "White narrative" of U.S. history. For centuries, Western nations, including the United States, have used a sort of "political mythology" to reinforce the incorrect idea that the Americas were sparsely populated by "savages scattered across virgin lands" when, in fact, these native people were highly sophisticated groups found in many parts of the Americas in extremely large numbers with advanced societies and systems of government. The European-based racial ethnocentric view of the histories of pre-Columbian America, as well as the continent of Africa, is reflected in many scholarly writings from the past and present, with many "settler groups" playing the victim role, viewing imperial government oppressors as a justification for these brave seekers of freedom and justice who were only fighting to obtain their God-given right to independence in a vast and empty land they "discovered." There are even Western ethnocentric misconceptions of geography—or cartographic distortions. For example, on most world maps, the size of the African continent is depicted in a dramatically minimized form, misrepresenting its actual size. Mercator maps tend to exaggerate the size of North America and Europe compared to Africa. Take a look a most maps, and you will see Africa appearing as nearly one and a half times smaller than North America when, in reality, it contains than 2 million square miles more than the North American continent. Thus, for centuries, the real history of much of the pre-Columbian Americas as well as the African continent, was not only lost or destroyed, it has been flat-out manipulated to paint a more favorable and guilt-free narrative of the past.

Schools must expose children to the history we all want to embrace, as well as the history we all want to forget. Schools should teach more about the individual struggles and important impact African slaves made to the growing and expanding U.S. empire. Schools must also teach and explain the heinous and despicable ways in which these slaves were treated, and they must be more honest about the history surrounding the government-sanctioned genocide of millions of Native Americans who lived in this country for millennia before Europeans arrived at their shores. Although Africans comprised the overwhelming bulk of the nation's slave population, which created a significant impact on the economic growth of the young nation, we sometimes forget the plight of those who originally inhabited this great land we call the United States. History lessons in public schools not only need to highlight the struggles and contributions of African slaves but honestly teach and explain the actual way in which our manifest destiny was realized. Its realization was only finalized by the destruction and decimation of an entire civilization that existed for thousands of years. Therefore, the notion that our immense nation was founded as a result of the mass genocide of millions of Native Americans and that our empirical expansion via extensive economic growth was only thoroughly accomplished through an intense system of African slave labor is nothing more than the truth.

You may notice I've referred to the United States as an empire several times. If you wonder why I would describe the United States in this manner...it's merely because no one has taught you about U.S. empirical expansion. Public schools do an amazing job at sweeping any conversations about the true story behind our nation's expansion discreetly under the rug. But strangely enough even maps in textbooks at the turn of the 20th century frequently showed the true extent of U.S. hegemony. By the early 1900s, the United States had wrestled control over all of the continental U.S., Hawaii, Guam, Wake Island, American Samoa, the Philippines, Alaska, Cuba, and Puerto Rico, as well as a multitude of uninhabited islands throughout the Pacific and Caribbean. At the time, it was estimated that around 8 million people inhabited these various territories, which equated to more than 10% of the U.S. mainland population. What's more, there were only around 8.8 million African Americans in the United States at that time, just to give you a point of reference for just how many people were, for lack of a better word...colonized by the United States. And if you want to get a real wake-up call as to how the U.S. government acquired and operated in some of these territories, do a bit of research into the Philippine-American War. It will definitely serve as a real eye-opener.

Some of these territories have since gained independence or have been admitted to the union as states. Yet, the United States has continued to acquire various regions throughout the world. At present, the United States controls 16 territories: U.S. Virgin Islands, Guam, Puerto Rico, Northern Mariana Islands, American Samoa, Baker Island, Howland Island, Jarvis Island, Johnston Atoll, Kingman Reef, Wake Island, Midway Islands, Navassa Islands, Serranilla Bank, Bajo Nuevo Bank, and Palmyra Atoll which consist of over 3.5 million inhabitants. The most damning aspect of this situation is the fact that none of the citizens in these U.S. territories ever acquire the same rights and freedoms guaranteed to U.S. citizens in the Constitution. It is quite apparent from historical records that racial motivations were one of the biggest driving forces behind these decisions. For one heinous example, the Speaker of the House at the time was quoted with what one might consider a very blunt explanation of the U.S. policy toward its...well, let's just throw out this territory nonsense and call them what they are: Colonies. This government leader summed up the situation by stating, "I s'posed we had *niggers* enough in this country without buyin' more of em.'" I think that's enough evidence to exhibit the overall sentiment about how the U.S. government viewed its colonial citizens.

If this isn't evidence enough that the United States is definitely an empire, do a basic search of the numbers and locations of U.S. bases throughout the world. Actually, I'll save you some time. The United States currently has 750 military bases in 80 countries and colonies globally. These bases are considered sovereign U.S. territory, meaning they function as independently controlled U.S.-governed land scattered within dozens of sovereign nations across the entire globe. The United States currently has more military bases in more foreign lands than any nation or empire has ever had in the recorded history of the known world. Do you still have any question about whether the United States is an empire?

However, our history includes inspirational, courageous individuals who helped shape our nation into one of the greatest empires ever to exist. I don't mean "great" as in an awesome place with zero stains on its robes, but instead "great" as in important and widespread. The American cultural machine has spread throughout the entire globe and soon even into outer space. For good or bad, no one can escape that truth. The founding fathers, like the rest of us, all had an array of skeletons in their closets. They nearly all owned slaves to some extent; many murdered Native Americans with an ostensible zest for blood, and Ben Franklin was a straight-up freak. These were all, however, men of their time, and we cannot fairly judge them based on modern standards of morality and ethics. We should not gloss over or minimize their flaws and weaknesses, but we should also not forget or downplay their successes and the many positive results of their existence. This starts by teaching history in an honest way.

It's extremely difficult to force empathy. Empathy and understanding are best acquired through experience and exposure, leading to understanding. If schools begin to teach ALL of our nation's history and not the hand-picked, propagandized versions of it, we could, in time, see a natural ease of racial tensions, and diversity and inclusion might have the opportunity to begin to self-germinate in classrooms.

CRT supporters have also accused public schools of racially discriminating against students of color academically as well as behaviorally. This accusation has some validity, but I believe it's more complicated than one would imagine while somehow simultaneously seeming surprisingly simple. Public schools constantly delineate students by race. They even have numerical codes for various student races and ethnicities. This is where the problem resides.

Why does a student's race even matter? Schools break down standardized test scores by race, grades by race, athletics and fine arts participation by race, attendance by race, percentages of students in certain programs by race...the list goes on and on. How does this information actually aid in guiding instructional decisions? Do students really need a magical number that follows them around for 12+ years to ensure we all know their race? Are schools going to separate students by race? Isn't that just a return to segregation? Schools need to focus on preparing students for the real world and keeping them safe while doing so. They should stop focusing so much on concepts such as race and start focusing on students and their educational outcomes.

I do not believe the instructional process is inherently racist, and I have not personally witnessed students of color being treated as students "in need of remediation" in any of the school districts in which I have worked. If anything, I have witnessed the opposite, where many students of color have been motivated and encouraged to move into gifted and talented programs and extracurricular activities. If a student needs remediation, that student should receive remediation regardless of race. At times, the number of minority students in remedial programs does climb above the expected natural rate, but to claim this is racism is short-sighted.

For example, the rightful claim is frequently made that many students of color come from low socioeconomic backgrounds where they are not afforded the same resources and opportunities compared to their higher socio-economic peers. This is a fundamental concept of CRT. These students are also generally forced to attend schools that might not live up to the same standards as schools in other areas of the city—not forgetting that those district boundaries are sometimes drawn based on racial motivations. This is indeed another valid argument by CRT proponents. However, if these statements asserted by CRT advocates were true, and I believe in many circumstances they are, would there not be a large percentage of students from these neighborhoods who often need some type of remediation?

Although one could say I reject the notion that instructional processes in public education are fundamentally racist and move to treat only students of color as "in need of remediation," I can agree that at times, the disciplinary process in public schools can, in fact, be quite racist. Certain hairstyles, typically worn by Black individuals, as well as certain types of clothing, have been banned from schools. Night clubs engage in these types of shenanigans all the time, and schools are no different. Whether school districts intentionally ban clothing and hairstyles because students of color tend to wear them is hard to prove, but it definitely looks suspicious. I've also witnessed too many students of color receive harsher punishments than their White peers. Once again, though, racism is hard to prove. Did the individual who doled out the punishment perhaps just not like that student? Was it personal...or was it racism?

I don't want to stray too far from CRT's relevance in public education because that is what this book is about. But there are parallels between discipline in public schools and the justice system itself. There is, without a doubt, at least a morsel of institutional racism in many segments of our society. The drug war is a perfect example. Quick history and chemistry lesson...cocaine and crack are pharmaceutically identical drugs. Cocaine is acquired in powder form and snorted, swallowed, or injected. Crack is acquired in a solid rocklike form and is smoked. Historically, cocaine has been a more upscale, relatively expensive party drug, while crack has been a cheap, fast-acting street drug. Cocaine has been used primarily by White individuals; crack has been used primarily by individuals of color. Possession of **500 grams** of cocaine carries a 5-year sentence. Possession of **five grams** of crack carries the same 5-year sentence. Explain that one to me. Good luck.

Countless numbers of young men of color are currently staring at the inside of a jail cell for nonviolent drug offenses or ridiculous laws and regulations such as three-strikes laws. Sure, one might say the three-strikes law is only for violent felonies, but we all know that is not how it usually plays out. The problem I'm mainly concerned about from an educational standpoint is the fact that many times, these unjustified "criminals" have kids. Raising a child or multiple children in a single-parent home is not an easy task, and these are the children who generally struggle the most in school. These kids "in need of remediation" are sometimes in that state, not because of public schools but because of other systems that continue to embrace, at the very least, remnants of institutionalized racism.

So, that covers a few of the major claims made against public schools when it comes to race. Hopefully, I made some valid points and did not offend too many of my readers. My goal was to ease some of the hype and confusion around CRT. Proponents of CRT do have several valid points that are hard to argue against. On the other hand, critics of the movement have stated some very legitimate claims as well. CRT is another example of the ever-present swinging pendulum that swivels from one extreme to the other when the truth nearly always resides somewhere in the middle. But wait. We haven't quite yet answered the essential question. Is CRT the impending Armageddon so many would have us believe? Are the racist beasts from the Upside-Down world coming for us all? Or, perhaps, like the coming SEL cataclysm, is all this CRT rhetoric much ado about nothing?

The problem seems to be that when one actually searches for examples of CRT in public schools, like the search for the Holy Grail or the Fountain of Youth, the explorers seem to almost always come up empty-handed. The fact is CRT just doesn't exist in public schools the way many pundits would lead us to believe. Most teachers respond with a dumbfounded look when they're questioned about CRT in their schools, and I personally have not witnessed any type of CRT in any school in which I've worked. Granted, I've only worked for public schools in the state of Texas, so my experience is definitely regionally biased.

Nonetheless, countless data have shown that a majority of teachers are not required or even pressured to implement CRT into their instruction. When the Association of American Educators surveyed over 1,100 teachers, 96% stated they were not required to teach any topic related to CRT, and nearly 78% claimed that the "current rhetoric around the issue was interfering with a productive and necessary discussion regarding race in America." Yet another survey found similar results when only 11% of teachers surveyed stated they were required to teach any CRT-related material, and over 60% of those surveyed declared that the media was hyper-focusing on this issue, creating unwarranted contention and concern.

So sure, there are anecdotal accounts of certain districts throughout the country that have attempted to implement some type of CRT-related training or curriculum into the mix. A simple Google search would lead you to a salvo of articles about how CRT is infecting the masses. However, these are mostly hyperbolic and hyper-focused outliers. There is actually little to no widespread evidence of CRT being taught in public schools. Nefarious agents on both sides of the CRT spectrum are playing us all as pawns in their little deceitful game. Furthermore, an interesting point many forget is that the "T" in CRT stands for "theory," meaning it is merely one particular idea about a very complicated and controversial topic.

CRT is not the truth serum the rebel-rousing hordes would push us to believe, but at the same time, it also is not some ridiculous trope that has no valid arguments or significance in our world. We all have the option to accept or reject this theory, just like any other. Let us also remember CRT is a graduate level theory synthesized and formulated by Harvard-educated scholars. Perhaps it is not necessarily an appropriate theory to be analyzed and discussed by a group of 8-year-olds.

Public schools do want to educate and support all children regardless of race. Whether they do a bang-up job or not, I believe their intentions are most often virtuous. Schools can become part of the solution and not continue the same problems that have plagued this country for so long. Public schools must move away from race and begin to move toward culture. Culture, not race, is what defines and drives people. Of course, many times, race and culture are inexplicably linked, but they are not equal partners. Many parts of the world have individuals who share identical racial features yet engage in strikingly different cultural practices and norms.

Schools must learn to respect cultures and their ways of life. Exceptions should be made for hairstyles and dress code issues that conflict with cultural norms. Learning styles should be altered and tweaked at times to meet the varying cultural needs of the diverse range of students in today's classrooms. Cultural appreciation days should be frequent, allowing students to share their personal experiences and showcase their cultures. That is how we teach students to respect others' differences and learn to engage in meaningful interactions with people from all walks of life. I can promise you delineating students by race and shoving graduate-level theories down their throats is not the way to move forward.

Schools can either be the racial tension catalyst or the antidote—they can contribute to higher tensions and anxieties or they can return us to some state of reason and cooperation. Public schools can embrace diversity and create inclusive settings in which students from all races and ethnicities collaborate in a productive learning environment. It's really quite simple: We desperately need all the government agencies, advocacy groups, NGOs, media pundits, "experts," and the litany of other nefarious agents and individuals who constantly pour more fuel on the fire to simply shut up and stop hyperbolizing and micro focusing on outlier events that fit their narrative. CRT is not the looming colossus heading for a city near you, but it is also not lacking valid points and arguments we as a nation all must consider. The truth, more often than not, lies somewhere near the center, and it's time we all began to move in that direction for the sake of ourselves, our children, and the legacy of our nation.

Chapter 13: Gun Violence in Schools

"This strife among ourselves wastes our energy and destroys our unity. My message to those of you involved in this battle of brother against brother is this: Take your guns, your knives...And throw them into the sea!"
~Nelson Mandela

"A man with a gun is a citizen. A man without a gun is a subject." ~Allen West

I must first begin this sure-to-be controversial chapter with a couple of caveats. First, it is surprisingly extremely difficult to find accurate and reliable data on this topic. The figures and data are all over the place and conflict with each other around every turn, but I have tried to provide the best information possible. I was occasionally forced to take an average number for much of the data due to its incredibly discrepant nature. Secondly, I've tried to be as honest and transparent with my beliefs as possible throughout this book to prevent any covert biases. Therefore, I must admit that I do support gun rights in the United States. I'm in no way a raging gun proponent with a limitless cache of weapons hidden behind my house in an underground bunker, but I find myself much more attached to the Allen West quote above than to the sentiments of Nelson Mandela. That being said, there is, without a doubt, an extremely alarming increase in gun violence in schools. Guns have found their way into classrooms across the nation, and as a society, we are not quite sure how to address this situation.

This trend should come as no surprise, because we are a unique nation in this world. Citizens in the United States are afforded rights and freedoms that many other nations could never even dream of acquiring and don't understand at times, but often, these liberties we sometimes take for granted come with a cost. A large portion of Americans believe gun ownership is a right for a variety of reasons; however, to also believe that this right to gun ownership should come with no limitations or safeguards is, well, quite reckless. Somehow and in some way, guns are finding themselves in the hands of young people across the entire country, and this is a dangerous trend. Unarguably, access to firearms by minors should not be as easy as it appears. We must come together to figure out a way to maintain our natural right to protect ourselves while simultaneously ensuring the safety of our youth. Of course, this won't be easy.

Whether gang-related, revenge-motivated, inspired by violent media, or simply the result of unaddressed mental illness, kids today increasingly use violent means to resolve conflicts and settle disputes. This trend, however, should also not be incredibly shocking. Adults today have increasingly begun to employ more violent tactics to resolve conflicts, and what kids see today in movies, shows, and video games is nothing but violent means of conflict resolution. Just try to count how many films out there have the word "revenge" or "vengeance" in their titles. Get back to me when you come up with the answer. It's going to take you a while. In addition, the mental health crisis in our country is overwhelmingly affecting our youth, and no one who has the power to do anything about it seems to care.

Today's youth have simply lost their ability to cope with the most minor setbacks in life, and they possess little to no problem-solving skills. With an estimated 400 million guns in circulation in the United States, young people are merely opting for the quick and easy solution they've witnessed so many times before on their hand-held devices and, unfortunately, sometimes in their homes and neighborhoods. From 1970 to 2021, there were nearly 2,000 recorded shooting incidents on school properties across the nation, resulting in 637 deaths. This is an exploding crisis of epidemic proportions... or is it?

While these facts seem alarming and frankly quite disturbing, active school shooter events in this country are extremely rare. Of course, the death of any child is an utter tragedy. But let's do a bit of quick math: 637 deaths in 51 years (1970–2021) comes out to 12.5 deaths per year out of a current student population of around 50 million.

Yes, the rate of deaths has increased over time, but we frequently hear stats about guns being the leading cause of death among children. Although that statement could be somewhat correct depending on the data set, statistics can easily be manipulated and misleading. The problem with this claim is that the data vary greatly depending on the age range of children in question, and many of these death statistics consider "overall" gun violence in their research, which counts gang-related shootings, suicides, as well as incidents related to domestic violence. However, for this discussion, we're only referring to SCHOOL shootings that happen on SCHOOL property, and we may soon discover that the media hype and scare tactics employed by the overwrought, panicked maniacs shouting into their bullhorns could be doing more harm than good.

The What

The most overwhelming and troubling issue surrounding school shootings is the sheer lack of reliable data. It has been more difficult to find meaningful and accurate data for this chapter than any other in this entire book. Take just one example: Searching for school shooting deaths in 2020, one source listed 27 deaths while another listed only three. Some of these data are way off, and this problem is quite appalling. If school shootings are such an impending doom for our society, why is it so difficult to find any reliable data on the topic? Unfortunately, I've also begun to notice that the more left-leaning the source of data, the more disquieting the statistics become, and of course, the more right-leaning sources seem to do nothing but minimize the situation. This is an infuriating state of affairs because if this nation is going to fix this problem, we're all going to have to be honest and realistic and work together.

The fact, however, remains that these incidents are increasing and have dramatically increased in the last several years. Once again, though, this increase should not be incredibly surprising. All violent crime has increased in the United States over the past few years. In 2020, there was a whopping 30% increase in homicides and 75% of those involved a firearm. What's even more disturbing is that 40% of those murders were committed by individuals between the ages of 20–29. Violence has become increasingly embedded in our way of life, and young people are deciding to use these violent means to resolve conflicts with continued frequency.

Remarkably, though, despite popular belief, school shootings are not a completely new phenomenon. The first reported school shooting can be traced as far back as the Pontiac Rebellion of 1764, when four Native Americans entered a schoolhouse in Pennsylvania, shooting and killing all but two children. From 1900–1970, over 120 deaths resulted from school-related shootings. Of course, this is a far smaller number than the 637 deaths the nation has experienced in the last 50 years, but nonetheless, shootings have occurred in schools since the birth of our nation. We are a gun culture, and guns have been a part of the American way of life since the American way of life began.

Why, then, is it so difficult to find reliable information on such an important issue? Well, the problems begin at the most basic level: How do we actually define a "school shooting"? We must first determine if the shooting actually happened on school property, but what if an incident happened on school property and then spilled over into an area not defined as school property? Is that a school shooting? What about a suicide committed on school property? What about shootings on a bus en route to school or at the bus stop? Does there have to be a victim? Statistics vary greatly depending on how a particular organization or institute answers these and many other questions.

The Center for Homeland Defense and Security (CHDS), which many claim is an excellent source of data, defines a school shooting as any event in which "a gun is brandished, is fired, or a bullet hits school property for any reason, regardless of the number of victims (including zero), time, day of week, or reason." So apparently, if a stray bullet from a nearby 21-gun salute comes down on the rooftop of a local schoolhouse on a Saturday afternoon, that's earmarked as a "school shooting." Call me crazy, but this definition is utterly ridiculous, although you would expect nothing less from a government agency. The Gun Violence Archive (GVA) defines a school shooting as "An incident that occurs on school property when students, faculty, and/or staff are on the premises. Intent during those times is not restricted to specific types of shootings. Incidents that take place on or near school property when no students or faculty/staff are present are NOT considered 'school shootings.'" This definition is strikingly different from the CHDS definition.

We could run through dozens of examples like this, but I'm trying to keep this book under 300 pages. Therefore, with the horribly unreliable data sets available, there is no way to determine the exact number of school shootings, much less deaths, resulting from them. However, enough data are available to show that there has been a significant increase in these events as of late. The following data are from the CHDS, and although these numbers are most likely inflated due to the organization's loose definition of a school shooting, they seem to possess the most detailed statistics available. The year 2021 gave us the greatest number of incidents on record at around 250 school shootings, with the second-highest year occurring in 2019, with around 120 shootings. The year 2018 provided us with the most yearly deaths on record, with over 50 shooting-related deaths, but nearly half those deaths were the result of one incident, the Parkland shooting in Florida.

Thus, despite the overwhelming difficulty in actually finding good and reliable statistics about school shootings, there is enough sparse evidence out there to conclude that these events are increasing and continue to increase every day. We could spend day after day and week after week combing through the incoherent and disjointed data surrounding this disturbing trend, but it would be a futile effort. Until the U.S. government and other organizations come to an agreement on what exactly should be considered a school shooting and how to create meaningful sets of data addressing this issue, the nation must continue to stumble forward in the dark. There are, however, some aspects surrounding these tragic events we do understand quite a bit about: The perpetrators.

The Who

Despite the lack of valid statistics concerning how often school shootings actually occur, we have a good deal of information about the engineers behind these tragic events. The psychological gurus, most likely still sitting with their legs a bit too tightly crossed, continue to claim there is no consistent profile of a school shooter. They emphasize that profiling can result in wrongful accusations that stigmatize students while sometimes excluding those students who may not show outward signs of violence yet could still be a danger to others. This is nothing more than psycho-babble nonsense. It's time for these "experts" to uncross their legs and wake up to reality.

A whopping 95% of school shooters are male, and over 60% are White. These individuals generally feel like marginalized outcasts living on the periphery. More than half of school shooters report a long history of rejection, and many are the victims of relentless bullying. These individuals feel rejected, isolated, and insignificant, and a notable proportion of them have a long history of deep psychological issues such as depression, suicidal tendencies, and an endless list of psychotic disorders for which they often take copious amounts of psychotropic drugs. Often, a significant traumatic event precedes a shooting, and a majority of these individuals possess an unhealthy fascination with guns and violence. They write disturbing passages in their journals, blogs, and social media accounts while constantly exposing themselves to violent images via the endless supply of devices and Internet connections surrounding them.

School shootings are also generally not spontaneous, impulsive acts. Over 90% of school shooters spent days, weeks, or even months planning their attack. The Columbine High shooters began planning their attack more than a year in advance. In addition, nearly all school shooters posted or shared troubling and even threatening images and messages on various social media outlets leading up to their attacks. This is the most troubling fact of all. Many of these shootings could have been prevented. In over 75% of school shootings, concerns were raised about these troubled individuals, yet most often, nothing was done to address those concerns.

So there's no profile of a school shooter? It's not the varsity quarterback shooting up the school. I haven't heard of many valedictorian school shooters as of late. How often does the news report a female brandishing a sidearm on campus? Of course, schools must be careful placing students in any type of box, and they don't want to falsely accuse anyone. But to say there is no true profile of a school shooter is pure and utter nonsense. Let's remove our heads from the sand and focus on the facts. This is a serious problem in our schools, and it's having a considerable effect on our nation. I'm sorry, but we have neither the time nor the patience for the *feelings police*.

The Why

Students struggle today in nearly every aspect of their lives. It seems as if we've made many facets of our lives much simpler, but somehow, we've also managed to make the simple things of the past that much harder. Kids today have fewer coping skills, fewer problem-solving skills, and fewer conflict resolution skills, and they constantly feel isolated and alone. Growing up in the 70s and 80s was no picnic, but kids during those times at least possessed the skills to deal with the world around them for the most part. Times have changed, and these skills are no longer the norm today. Whether due to emerging technology, cultural shifts, degrading school systems, or chaotic homes, kids today are extremely different than kids from decades ago.

Children today have short fuses. It does not take much to make them explode, and these little mushroom clouds are blowing up everywhere. Their isolation and loneliness grow into depression, which further escalates into anxiety and paranoia. This, in turn, leads to anger, resentment, aggression, and eventually violence. Voilà! We now have a young Anakin Skywalker on our hands with little hope of ever escaping the grip of the dark side.

These kids experience trauma at incredibly high rates, and they are not equipped to deal with it. Many hardcore individualists would claim these kids just need to toughen up and be strong. Most of them have already tried that and utterly failed. You see, trauma is not necessarily the result of severe mental or physical abuse but can present itself like Chinese water torture. Days and days of bullying and harassment by peers can be like drops of water falling from the sky and tapping the forehead. This is, at first, a mere annoyance but, over time, can drill a hole through the skull. U.S. Department of Education data show that over 75% of school shooters experience consistent bullying or harassment, which pushes them even further into isolation where they nest up alone, consumed within the violent world of video games, movies, and whatever else they can search on the Net.

When we combine these new dynamics with access to 400 million guns, problems will no doubt arise, and arisen they have. Regardless of anyone's stance on the 2nd Amendment or gun control, we must admit that kids today have way too easy access to firearms. Nearly three-fourths of school shooters acquired their gun from the home of a parent or other close relative. In a 2017 survey, up to 16% of high school students said they had brought a gun to school at least once in the past month. This is not controversial. It's a simple game of numbers. More guns obviously result in more access. To claim that widespread access to firearms does not increase the chance of one being brought to school is ridiculous, and anyone who states otherwise most likely has a distinct agenda up their sleeve.

Thus, it's not so difficult to understand why this troubling trend has only increased as the nation moves further into the 21st century. We have been presented with a fairly basic equation:

Unaddressed mental anguish + Easy access to firearms = Increases in shootings

Where do kids spend most of their day, and where does a significant portion of their inner turmoil originate? At school. These kids have adopted a new dangerous model of coping—Eliminate all perceived threats, real or imagined. Once perceived threats have been eliminated, these shooters then come to the realization that they themselves are the real threat. Between 85–90% of school shooters end their violent rampage by taking their own lives. But this realization is too late. The damage is done, and the violent circle has been completed, while the survivors and those attached to them are merely left to pick up the pieces.

So what are we to do? Shall we repeal the 2nd Amendment and quickly confiscate the 400 million guns scattered across the land? Only a utopian idealist drinking too much of their own Kool-Aid would ever consider that as a feasible option. Go ahead and move to your commune and plant some squash while we grown-ups brainstorm a real solution. Perhaps we should lock up any and all children who present a danger to themselves or others. But there aren't enough facilities in the world to house these masses. We could take mental health more seriously in this country and push for more resources and outlets to help these individuals in need. But that takes money, time, and competent leaders...all of which we seem to currently lack. I can, however, tell you what's not working—Our current model.

The Makeshift Police State

Government organizations generally tend to either overreact or underreact when faced with a dilemma. In this case, public schools and the agencies that support them have chosen to turn a blind eye to the deteriorating mental health of the nation's youth while pumping all their resources into transforming schools into little Guantanamo Bays scattered across the nation. Schools have been locked down like the Iron Mountain Vault. Police and security guards roam the halls like the Night Watch. Lockdown drills interrupt classes and terrify students. High schoolers line up outside school entrances, waiting to pass through security checkpoints like frustrated passengers watching half-asleep, incompetent TSA agents rummage through their undergarments. This is what many schools have become as the overreaction expands.

Countless schools have increasingly begun to resemble detention centers or even the prisons to which some hyperbolic agents have compared them. Every door is a locked door, and surveillance cameras cover every nook and cranny. Drill after drill and imagined danger lurk around every corner. For example, a new 2023 law in the state of Texas mandates every school to have at least one armed guard on campus at all times. What? Talk about an overreaction. Plus, where is all the money going to come from to pay these armed agents who will probably do nothing more than further increase the tension and anxiety already thoroughly permeating most schools. When schools create an environment like this for our kids to live in for 7–8 hours a day, 9 months out of the year, how can we wonder why they're all so on edge? Perhaps we are the ones pushing them to the cliff's rim. Many of these "safeguards" have only further escalated tension and increased the stress, unwarranted anxiety, and fear these kids already face every day.

Public schools in the United States currently spend over $3 billion a year on security measures. That's nearly half a billion more than they spend on books. I've already devoted an entire chapter to the amazing and creative ways schools have discovered to waste money, so I won't spend too much time reiterating that point here. But this further emphasizes the point that public schools do, in fact, have plenty of money. They simply need to figure out how to spend it more productively and responsibly. I can attest from personal experience that useless, overhyped, overpriced, and mostly ineffective security measures are not the best use of tax-payer money. Perhaps some of those funds would be put to better use by acquiring more resources to address the increasing mental health issues ravaging our children. However, that would be a rational and sensical move.

Public schools must also ask themselves if the cost of assumed prevention is worth the price students pay for it. The verdict is not quite in on the effectiveness of lockdown drills, metal detectors, and police and security officers roaming the hallways, but the current results do not look very promising. However, we do have substantial evidence pointing to the increased anxiety and fear these measures have inflicted on students. This is obviously not great since their baseline levels of anxiety and fear are already quite elevated. In addition, these constant drills become habitual, and many schools begin to resemble the little boy who cried wolf...or Chicken Little constantly carping on about the impending collapse of the sky. Other students who are not terrorized by this new security regime view many of these measures as a joke and fail to recognize the seriousness of the threat. Furthermore, a large percentage of school shooters are actual students. Do schools necessarily want to show them their entire hand? Some school shooters have been successful due to the fact they learned so much about the school's security and response measures by participating in them.

Let's also not forget the valuable instructional time lost during these security drills and training procedures. Additionally, many of these security measures are actually unsafe and quite illogical. One particular school district (where I worked) has begun to screw the windows shut in every room to "keep intruders from entering into the building through windows." I'll pause for the laughter to cease...even more ridiculous was their half-sarcastic response when asked *what do we do if there is a fire and we cannot get out of the room. The answer: "Well, I guess you'll have to throw a chair through the window...."* This is the type of logic guiding decisions in public schools today.

Of course, schools need security measures, and security-related drills are definitely appropriate to some extent. However, many schools take these measures a bit too far. Students are constantly bombarded with lockdown drills, training videos, and the endless oversight of law enforcement and security. Cameras literally cover nearly every square inch of the property. Schools have created a scenario where half the kids are terrified of the fully armed boogeyman smashing through their classroom door at any minute, and the other half are giggling and rolling around the floor while shooting each other with their finger guns during lockdown drills. There must be a middle ground. There has to be a means to relate the seriousness of this issue to students while simultaneously not freaking them all out.

The Unpopular Truth

The simple and generally unpopular truth is that active school shooter events in the United States are extremely rare. Schools have built in many natural layers of security and protection to keep schools safe, and some would say they've gone too far. The data-collecting procedures for school shootings in this country are absolutely atrocious. The fact that one can search all day long for statistics on school shootings and come to a different conclusion every time is sickening. How are we supposed to understand and address this issue when there are little to no reliable data out there? When the government and other agencies and organizations consider stray bullets randomly hitting schools and suicides as "school shootings," they achieve nothing but instilling further mass confusion, fear, and frustration around this issue. There simply is no standard definition of a "school shooting," and we must answer that question before we can even begin to address the problem.

We've also, unfortunately, turned this situation into a political issue, and we've seen how well that recently worked out for the nation during the COVID-19 disaster. We've found ourselves in a situation where one set of fearmongers wants to tally up everything and anything possible to jack up the number of school shootings as high as imaginable while the other side shrugs their shoulders idly, pretending nothing is happening. The narrative whiplashes between one side demanding the government seize all firearms while the other wants teachers walking around schools with sidearm holsters like they're roaming the dusty streets of the O.K. Corral. Both of these entities have lost their damn minds.

The "trusted" mainstream media has also done nothing but further exacerbate the entire state of affairs. Whenever a school is placed on lockdown, a firestorm of tweets and breaking news leads to a barrage of retweets and reposts. A brief situation in southern California turns into "shocking updates" in New York, and before long, the local baker in Berlin is discussing gun control issues in the United States. The media has warped our minds on many issues by hyper-focusing on what boosts ratings—and school shootings are a ratings bonanza. These nefarious agents have become nothing more than merchants of death, violence, chaos, and discord. They are literally selling the dead bodies of children for advertising revenue, and it should utterly disgust each and every one of us. The media draws so much of our attention to these isolated events that it often tricks us into thinking problems are a whole lot bigger than they actually are, and the media does this with EVERY single topic on which they report. It's their formula, and as long as people keep tuning in, these malignant tumors will continue to grow and thrive.

The media has misled us in regard to mass shootings in general. School shootings fall under the mass shooting category, so let's do a quick fact-check. Mass shootings, or what the average person would consider a mass shooting, do not happen as frequently in the United States as some would have us believe. Statistics, you see, can be very misleading when they are handpicked and categorized to fit a particular narrative. Many of these "mass shootings" are no more than miscategorized domestic or gang-related violence that has spilled onto the streets and sometimes onto school property. The Violence Gun Archive database found that in some years, up to two-thirds of "mass shootings" were gang-related or involved disputes between different groups of people who were often drunk and/or high. What's more, mass shootings are not even close to a leading cause of death in this country. Every year since 1981, even suicides have outpaced homicide rates, usually by a significant margin. Assault rifles are not the problem either. According to the FBI, from 2015–2020, rifles were only used in 3% of all homicides.

The United States, despite commonly held belief, is also not the only country in which these events occur. The five deadliest shootings in the world did not even take place in the United States, nor did eight of the 10 deadliest. The United States comprises around 4.6% of the world's population yet only accounts for around 1.43% of mass shooters. At the time of this writing, the United States ranks...wait for it... 83rd in the world in murders per capita. Bottom line: We live in a pretty safe country. Additionally, gun control issues may not be the end all and be all some endorse. Ninety-four percent of mass shootings have occurred in places where guns are already banned, and California, which currently has the strongest gun laws in the country, also holds claim to just under 20% of all mass shootings, leading the nation by a long shot in this regard...Pun intended.

What's worse, little miniature news outlets have invaded our pockets and purses en masse. Every time one picks up a phone, there's another notification of some tragedy that's coming our way. We can't get away from the chaos. And if things couldn't get worse, just wait. There's more. The widespread constant exposure to these tragic events has produced what seems like an unhealthy fascination with shootings and shooters, and this intense media coverage has, without a doubt, manufactured endless copycats. Even with the highly questionable data available, this has proven to be true and has become known as the "Columbine Effect." Before the 1999 Columbine shootings, which became a media circus for months on end, there had been around 50 mass murders in the previous 22 years. There have been close to 120 in the 22 years since. Furthermore, nearly two-thirds of all mass shootings in the United States have occurred after the Columbine incident. When researchers analyzed the 12 mass shootings that followed the Columbine massacre, eight of the 12 shooters stated they were inspired by the Columbine incident. Call it a coincidence? Perhaps, but a more logical conclusion is that the media may, in fact, be breeding mass murderers.

It's time for us all to shut out and shut down these odious outlets once and for all, and the only means of accomplishing this long overdue feat is to simply stop tuning in. Without support, these media mongrels would be forced to adapt their current business model or disappear. Let's hope and pray for the latter.

Any death of a child is a horrible misfortune, but there are way more imminent dangers to our youth today than school shootings. Over 100 students are killed every year accidentally while walking or riding their bikes to school. Fentanyl-laced drugs and mental health problems are a far more overwhelming detriment to kids today. Nearly 1,200 kids died of drug overdoses in 2021 alone, and almost 20% of high schoolers have seriously considered suicide based on recent surveys. Every year, around 5,000 kids take their own lives, and over half of those involve no firearm whatsoever. In fact, students are actually statistically safer in any school setting than in their own homes. The government continues to make the claim that firearms are the leading cause of death among children today, but as we've seen, statistics around gun violence are extremely unreliable and very easy to manipulate to fit a particular narrative. In actuality, in most parts of the country, the number one cause of death for children in the United States is accidents, and over half of all accidents involving children occur in their homes. Between falls, poisonings, drownings, fires, choking, and the litany of other means of destruction, guns may not warrant the first-place prize of worries for most parents, but somehow, this real but hyperbolized threat has catapulted to the top of the list.

Please don't overreact and conclude my spin on this topic is to insinuate I don't believe gun violence in schools is a serious matter. There are, no doubt, way too many guns in this country, and children have way too easy access to them. Parents across the country have faced devastating losses and pain from these incidences, and I would never want to minimize that suffering. However, inflating statistics and lying about the facts never gets us anywhere. School shootings happen in this country, and the fact that they occur at all is very concerning and extremely tragic. That being said, there is a high probability that children are completely safe at school, and the chances of them being involved in a school shooting are significantly low. Even when looking at highly inflated statistics, there are generally well under 100 deaths a year from school shootings. These incidents have increased as of late, so let's be extremely liberal with our scenario and say 100 kids die a year. This is well above the average, but we'll look at a worst-case scenario. With around 50 million kids enrolled in public schools across the nation, an individual student would have a .0002% chance of dying from a school shooting, even if upwards of 100 students died per year.

There may be various boogeymen out there preying on children, but chances are school shooters are not one of them. There is most likely an endless list of more pressing dangers lurking in a child's own home than around the hallways and corridors of public schools. We have to stop freaking out our kids and ourselves over these tragedies. We need to come together, cease the fearmongering, and look at the facts if we ever hope to end this problem.

The Future Response

Despite the many failures public schools and government officials have made in regard to school shootings, there are a few possible solutions that could be implemented to decelerate this alarming and tragic trend. For starters, I cannot emphasize enough the need for better data collection procedures, and this begins with the simple step of creating a universal definition of what constitutes a school shooting. This should not be an extremely taxing first step, but for some reason, so far, we don't have one. School shootings must also be better categorized and delineated by the actual events that led up to the shooting. Shootings involving gang-related issues, drug deals gone bad, suicides, or domestic issues that have spilled over onto school campuses are not the same situation as a lone gunman who walks onto campus and indiscriminately murders countless random, innocent victims. These incidents are most often all lumped together into the "school shooting" category when, in fact, they are totally different situations.

Schools, as well as government entities, must also address the dramatic increase in mental health issues across the nation, especially in our youth. There seems to be a perpetual stockpile of deeply disturbed young males who want nothing more than to inflict horrible pain and suffering on the world, and it's about time we tried a bit harder not only to understand why but also to find solutions to this dangerous trend. Part of it is a result of our forever-expanding grievance culture where everyone is to blame, and obsessions with getting even and settling scores have infected our very way of life. Our mainstream media has further cultivated this obsession, offering virtual immortality to these disturbed and violent individuals, providing them with even greater paths to infamy. Their manifestos and images are smeared across the front pages, social media, and cable news outlets. This madness must stop, and we as citizens must refuse to participate in this charade any longer.

These individuals, mostly males, suffer from varying levels of mental illness. Anyone who is willing to take the lives of large swaths of innocent victims due to some perceived real or imagined slight is not mentally stable. I believe we can all agree on that. Many of these mental illnesses do not simply arise from nowhere in adulthood but present obvious signs early on in childhood. Schools must do a better job of identifying and addressing these mental health issues at a much earlier stage. Students need access to more counselors, and schools and parents need to encourage students to get the help they need by normalizing mental health issues. There is only, on average, one counselor per 450 students in schools across the United States, and with massive increases in violence and mental illness, that is simply not enough staff to address these increasing needs. Additionally, by modeling good self-care and merely acknowledging personal struggles, others can be encouraged to reach out for the help they need.

Schools need to also begin implementing better and more effective bullying prevention programs. Students who consistently harass and threaten students must receive harsher punishments, and if this behavior continues, these students should be referred to law enforcement for further legal consequences. An overwhelming majority of school shooters experienced high levels of bullying by their peers for weeks, months, or even years leading up to the day they finally snapped. By simply doing a better job of preventing these vulnerable students from being relentlessly tormented, schools could at least avert a handful of these disasters.

Schools, law enforcement, government agencies, and even students and parents have to do a better job of paying attention to, identifying, and reporting concerning behaviors. Many school shooters post threatening videos and journal entries, and even leak information about their plans well before the shooting. Some even brag about their plan leading up to the incident, enlist other students for help, and warn certain classmates to stay home on the day of the planned attack. Despite these blatant warning signs, parents, students, and educators often downplay or flat-out ignore the red flags. After nearly every school shooting, most individuals who knew the shooter are far from shocked by the shooter's actions. He was a "troubled individual." "I always knew something was off with that fella." "He had a long history of mental illness and posted very disturbing images online."

These are the responses we hear way too often, yet no one chooses to do anything about it or speak up until it is too late. When it comes to school shootings, snitches do not get stitches. Snitches save lives. In addition, why do we allow the government to consistently rifle through our personal data at their whim, relentlessly stomping on our Fourth Amendment rights, when they cannot even identify these dangerous individuals who post violent and disturbing images and other related media on a daily basis? If the government has the time and resources to censor Twitter accounts and social media posts while simultaneously injecting colossal amounts of propaganda onto these same sites, surely, they can allocate some of these technological resources to target and apprehend these odious individuals before they commit acts of mass violence.

Lastly, we all must do a better job of protecting our children by adopting a more responsible approach to gun ownership. Firearms should always be stored in a safe and secure manner. However, if there is ever a chance of a child entering a home, the owner must take even more safety measures. More than 70% of school shooters acquired their gun from a relative. We have to make guns less accessible for our youth. With 400 million guns in current circulation, widespread gun control measures are a Utopian nonstarter. Sure, we should continue performing background checks and find ways to keep truly mentally ill individuals from accessing them, but gun control starts in the home by ensuring children have zero access to firearms.

School shootings have taken center stage today in a wide array of forums. Many want to overhype and sensationalize these events due to political motivations or profit margins, yet others want to turn their heads and pretend nothing is wrong in fear Big Brother may come knocking one day to seize their cache. As always, the truth seems to lie somewhere in the middle. Fearmongering and other dishonest tactics have further accelerated our "freak out" culture, presenting these horrible tragedies as everyday common occurrences, which they are not. However, these events do happen, and when they do, they result in horrible, often preventable, tragedies in which countless innocent victims lose their lives while the survivors must deal with the aftermath. We all must first step back, take a deep breath, and calm down. We must remove the hyperbolic rants, the political propaganda, and the profit-motivated goals from this discussion and come together in an honest and productive conversation if we hope to ever solve this problem.

Chapter 14: The Role of Parents in Education

"A child educated only at school is an uneducated child" ~George Santayana

*"*No school can work well for children if parents and teachers do not act in partnership on behalf of the children's best interests[1]*"* ~Dorothy H. Cohen

"The problem with public school is not overcrowding in the classroom. The problem is not teacher unions. The problem is not underfunding or lack of computer equipment. The problem is your damn kids." ~P. J. O'Rourke

Parents are responsible for every detail of a young person's life, and this is by no means an easy task. Creating a human being requires accepting one of the most important and difficult responsibilities one could undertake. Whether planned and prayed for or an unexpected gift or burden, becoming a parent transforms one's place in the universe. The responsibilities of being a parent are endless, and the first few years are generally ripe with sleep deprivation, drained bank accounts, and endless birthday parties that serve only as an excuse to get drunk with other parents. When it finally comes time for little Johnny to hop on the school bus and disappear for 8 hours a day, 5 days a week, a synchronized sigh of relief immediately ensues. At last, the time has come to pass the torch of responsibility on to someone else. But if parents think their role in education ends at the bus stop, they are incredibly mistaken.

It's quite simple: PARENT INVOLVEMENT IS THE KEY TO STUDENT SUCCESS! Increased parent involvement in the education process has proven to not only increase student attendance and behavior but also to have positive effects on performance. Regardless of race or socioeconomic status, students whose parents are involved in their education consistently have higher rates of attendance, fewer behavioral problems, better attitudes toward school, higher levels of social and adaptive skills, and higher grades and test scores. If parents show interest in education and emphasize its importance, their children will naturally fall in step with their ideologies. At the end of the day, almost all kids are nothing but little miniature versions of their creators.

Yet, despite the importance of the role parents must play on the educational stage, many schools have struggled to define that role or even create the means by which to measure parental engagement. As of late, relationships between schools and parents have increasingly deteriorated and have even become highly unproductive and downright toxic in some parts of the country, and this trend is very troubling. Parents are being arrested at school board meetings and banned from campuses only to fight back by sieging schools with battalions of lawyers and salvos of lawsuits. A recent teacher survey found that 20% of teachers and nearly 25% of administrators identified parents as a significant cause of stress in their jobs.

But how did we get here? Of course, COVID-19 was the last straw for many, and without a doubt, it immediately thrust parents into the educational process like no time in the recent history of public schooling. And if parents were concerned before, the mishandling of the pandemic and the near comical failures of virtual learning did not ease their concerns. Parents are mad, and they're worried about whether their kids are getting the education they have been promised. Unfortunately, their worries about this system are definitely warranted.

COVID-19 and the ill-thought-out policies resulting from it did not create this issue—but they did shine a giant spotlight on it. The situation was not good leading up to this disaster, and parent/school relations were fractured and dysfunctional before any of the madness even began. Schools have to do a better job of getting parents involved in the process and showing them the respect they deserve, but parents also need to do better. Kids show

---

1. https://www.azquotes.com/quote/1142196?ref=parents-and-teachers

up to school unprepared and with the bare minimal skills required to function in a school setting. Some kids show up with zero social skills, and parents expect the school to undertake the entire responsibility of turning these little feral beings into functioning humans. Thus, both sides are equally responsible for this ongoing predicament.

Schools and the government do not bear all the responsibility for this mess. Parents have a vital role in the educational process, and many have simply clocked out. I will move to hold parents more accountable for their behavior throughout much of this chapter and offended, some will be. Nonetheless, I have strived to be as honest and real throughout this journey, and this chapter should be no different.

A Very Brief History...I Promise

Throughout most of history, a child's education has been seen by parents, as well as society, as the sole responsibility of the parents. Parents have long been the lone inoculators of moral values, discipline, work ethic, and basic life skills for children across not only the United States but the world at large. Historically, basic education has nearly always been carried out privately within the family unit with secondary education acquired via trade apprenticeships, which were also arranged and many times funded by the parents. Even during the colonial period, elementary education was strictly controlled by parents. They oversaw school governance, decided on curricula, hand-picked teachers, and provided the framework for religious teaching. Of course, school was not generally free during this era, except for several organized charity schools, and parents were most often required to pay fees for the education of their children. Yet, parents had seized control of the entire educational process leading all the way up to the Revolutionary War. However, once public schools became the norm, that control began to whittle away, and today, many parents are attempting to take back that control of days long past.

The emergence of public education actually began to take hold in Massachusetts as early as the mid-1600s. Local colonial leaders realized parents were not teaching their children to read, so a law was created to fund hiring a local teacher to instruct children on reading. However, this trend did not fully take off until well over 100 years later after the American's surprise victory against their British oppressors. Leading figures such as George Washington and Thomas Jefferson eloquently argued for the creation of a public school system to instill certain basic skills in the citizenry in hopes of improving the functionality of the newly established democracy. These values and ideologies continued into the mid-19th century when our favorite public school champion, Horace Mann, exploded onto the scene with his progressive education movement, and by 1860, nearly every state had developed some type of public education system.

Regardless of this novel idea, participation in the newly created education system was by no means universal. An overwhelming percentage of parents opted to keep their kids at home to help with planting and harvesting crops, and those children who were not tilling the fields were sent to work in factories, mills, and mines to earn supplemental family income by taking full advantage of the perks offered by the second wave of the Industrial Revolution. However, with massive increases in immigration to the United States at the turn of the 20th century, this child labor trend proved to be quite unsustainable because it gutted the market with cheap labor, and working men, in turn, began to protest and unionize in droves. This situation led to enormous political pressure, resulting in federally mandated child labor laws, which unfortunately only resulted in bands of delinquent children ravaging the streets, wreaking havoc throughout urban areas across the entire country.

This chaotic situation came to an abrupt halt in 1918, with every state officially mandating compulsory attendance across the entire nation. These laws made it illegal for parents to keep a child out of school without expressed permission from school authorities, and those who refused to comply were dealt harsh fines. These laws were the first step in removing parents from the educational process and led to further increases in the amount of time children spent in school away from their homes and the care of their parents and families.

As the nation moved into the middle of the 20th century, population numbers began to boom, and increases in urbanization, as well as the adoption of scientific management techniques, led to the massive bureaucratization of the American public school system. This new move to bureaucracy was intended to instill more equality and professionalism into the system, but as we learned way back in Chapter Four, intentions many times do not lead to expected outcomes. This new system resulted in mostly moving the reins even further out of reach of parents. Superintendents began to seize control from districts once run by lay parent boards, and school boards evolved into powerful figureheads who became nothing more than puppets to their superintendent puppet master. So, while some could argue that bureaucratizing and professionalizing the education system produced some positive results at the time, there is no doubt this shift dramatically reduced parental influence in public schools.

As the latter half of the 20th century approached, parents finally began to fight back. Parent/teacher associations or PTAs began to form, which worked to push the "community" back into public schools, as well as aid other parents in need. Before long, parents from all walks of life were attending monthly PTA meetings to express their concerns and collaborate. Parents, in turn, became more aware of their rights and more vocal in their demands. They began to move their battles into the courtroom, recruiting lawyers and advocates to help lead the charge. This resulted in victories across the nation in major cases such as *Brown vs. Board of Education, Serrano vs. Priest, Lau vs. Nichols*, and many more. Laws such as the Elementary and Secondary Education Act of 1965 and IDEA even further extended parental rights.

Throughout the next few decades, parents continued to fight for meaningful change and better access to quality education, and they were quite successful. Parents once again began to become a vital part of the school environment, and the community became more synchronized with local schools. Parents were welcomed and frequently visited classrooms and cafeterias, serving as teaching assistants and volunteering on campuses in countless ways. However, this scene was short-lived, and as the new millennium came crashing down upon the nation, parents began to once again disappear from the scene. PTA membership declined significantly, desks remained empty during open house events, and parents became consistent no-shows for important meetings concerning their children. All of a sudden, parents were missing in action. But why?

For starters, George W Bush's No Child Left Behind Act in 2001 created massive contention between parents and schools that still persists today. School shootings and campus-wide violence also began to significantly increase during this time, which led to colossal and widespread security measures that many times put parents who were merely attempting to visit their children in very uncomfortable situations. Going to have lunch with your child at school became akin to passing through U.S. Customs at a border checkpoint, and many parents, not surprisingly, decided it just wasn't worth the hassle. Many of today's parents also simply do not have the time, and lack of time is, in fact, the number one stated reason for parents' decreased participation and interest in school. Life in today's society is go, go, go, and don't stop to smell anything. In the fast-paced, high-octane world of the 21st century, who has time for public schools?

We have to reverse this new troubling trend. While some parents do have serious time management issues on their hands, perhaps many others may merely need to prioritize and reorient exactly how they spend their time. For many parents, there still seems to be plenty of time for tweeting, bingeing, and living their best lives. Some parents may want to take a step back and reevaluate whether not having enough time is actually the real reason for their lack of involvement as opposed to not properly managing the time they have in a responsible manner. Parental involvement in the educational process has, time and time again, been shown to improve every aspect of a child's learning experience, which will better prepare children for the crazy world in which they will soon find themselves. The involvement of parents in public schools is the key to their success, and it's about time schools, as well as parents, come to this realization.

Roles, Rights, and Barriers
Roles

When a child walks through the doors of the local schoolhouse, a parent's role does not cease to exist but becomes even more important. Parental involvement in the educational process is the most vital aspect of the entire system, and their recent lack of interest has certainly contributed to its downfall. Successful parent involvement requires active and ongoing participation in the education of their child. This can be demonstrated in a variety of ways from helping with homework and reading with children to attending school functions, volunteering at schools, or simply discussing school and school-related events in the home. The national PTA association has stated, "The most accurate predictors of student achievement in school are not family income or social status, but the extent to which the family becomes involved in the child's education at school."

Research concerning parental involvement in public education has led to many of the following conclusions. First and foremost, academic achievement, as well as classroom behavior, is significantly higher and better for students whose parents are highly involved in their education. This involvement increases positive attitudes toward school, motivation, self-esteem, and attendance. In addition, not only does increased parental involvement aid in student performance but it also has been proven to increase teacher morale. Obviously, teachers who have well-mannered, motivated, and well-behaved students are going to be more excited, or at least less dreadful, about coming to work every day; therefore, parental involvement can actually increase teacher performance, which, of course, leads to better student outcomes.

Parental involvement also benefits parents themselves. Mothers and fathers can gain the satisfaction of contributing to their child's learning and acquire more knowledge about the school curriculum enabling them to better support their children academically in the home. Parents who spend more time with their kids also achieve better levels of communication within their family unit, and some parents can even be inspired to further their own education due to extended time spent involving themselves in the educational process of their children.

Becoming involved in the education of a child can actually be quite an easy process that does not consume much time at all. Of course, being present at school whenever possible shows children that a parent cares enough to make that effort, but merely showing interest in a child's schoolwork or exhibiting a positive attitude about school can go a long way. Young children are still forming their thoughts and opinions about school, so parents can greatly influence a child's attitude toward the school setting. When parents show they care about what their kids are learning, this attitude becomes contagious and reinforces the importance of education.

There are also many other strategies parents can adopt to improve the educational experience for their children. Parents must be role models for their children by showing them how important learning is by reading, exploring nature, cooking together, or practicing reading and counting exercises at home. Paying attention to what a child likes and dislikes can lead them to explore and enrich their interests. Discovering how a child learns can also be a huge asset for their success. Whether a child is a visual, auditory, or tactile learner is very important knowledge to possess, and once discovered, parents can practice and reinforce what has been learned at school via the most appropriate learning style for their child.

Parents must also spend time connecting their child's learning to everyday life and the real world. This task can be easily accomplished by simply discussing the weather and world events, using math when cooking or at the supermarket, exploring how common electronic devices work, and emphasizing the importance of being a strong reader. However, parents must be careful not to overwork children and give them the free time they need. School and learning can be a stressful process. With school events, sporting events, trombone lessons, and dozens of pressing family engagements, sometimes kids just need a little downtime to let loose like the rest of us. Lastly, parents should turn off the TV and substitute hours of screen time with books, toys, hobbies, or time with friends and family.

Rights

Despite the fact that the founding fathers of our country adopted a hands-off approach to public education, leaving this responsibility solely to the states, over the past couple of centuries, the Supreme Court has added a litany of constitutional rights to parents and children. Many parents today are completely left in the dark, having no idea what these rights are or that they even exist. Schools and government entities do not exactly broadcast these rights, so it is the parent's duty to ensure they understand their rights and fight for them when needed.

First and foremost, all children have a right to a free public education. Some schools can require certain fees for overdue or damaged books, school lunches, and participation in certain school activities, so it is imperative that parents investigate the local rules and guidelines regarding these additional expenses. This right is extended to immigrant children as well. Immigration status is of no relevance to any public school—schools must enroll any student who lives within their attendance zone regardless of the student's immigration status. It is unlawful for a school to even ask for any type of immigration documents or proof of citizenship. Schools also may not discriminate against any student for any reason, whether race, gender, socioeconomic status, sexual orientation, or disability. Any student with a disability also has the right to receive the individualized instruction they need administered by specially trained personnel at no extra cost.

Parents, as well as students, have the right to learn English and receive translation services in school. If a child is not fluent in English, parents have the right to request the child's lessons and assignments be translated into their home language. Most schools also have bilingual programs in which these students can be enrolled to assist them in transitioning to English-speaking classrooms. Students also have the right to be safe in school, and this has become a recent issue in many schools across the nation. Classrooms have increasingly become unsafe environments for students for a plethora of reasons discussed extensively throughout the entirety of this book. If parents feel their child is being put in unsafe situations at school, they should speak up and demand action. Powerful district administrators rarely listen to teachers or even campus administrators, but irate parents banging on the door threatening to lawyer up and head down to the local news station generally get their undivided attention.

Children even have the right to freedom of speech and religion, although these rights can be limited at times if the practicing of this free speech is an extreme distraction or safety concern. A child has the right to pray in school, wear whatever hairstyle they want, and wear the clothes they choose (some schools do have dress codes, though), as long as they are not blatantly inappropriate. Parents also have the right to information and participation, which means parents can inspect student records and grades, have them explained, request amendments, or have these records transferred to another school. The Every Student Succeeds Act (ESSA) further extended these rights, guaranteeing parents the right to teacher conferences and reasonable access to staff as well as opportunities to volunteer and observe their child's classes. All parents also have the right to participate in any school activities, such as the PTA and various other parent councils and committees, and if parents feel they have been slighted, they have the right to appeal any school decision to the local school board.

Parents also have several more rights that some may find a bit surprising. All students have the right to learn about evolution, which is now included in the Common Core standards. Parents possess the right to opt out of sex education instruction for their child, and they even have the right to opt out of standardized testing as a result of ESSA. Parents can also choose to opt out of the entire public education process, with homeschooling now legal in all 50 states.

Parents have the right to privacy and cannot be required to fill out or complete government demographic surveys about personal data or information. The process can be extremely difficult due to tenure rules and unions, but parents also have the right to remove poor-performing teachers. Lastly, all students have the right to participate in school-sponsored sports regardless of disability or gender. The current issues with transgender athletes have added a new dynamic to this arena, so parents must be sure to check with state and local laws regarding this particular situation.

This was not an exhaustive list, but highlighted most of the important rights afforded to parents across the nation. Some of these rights are quite obvious, while others may be quite surprising. Nonetheless, it is extremely important for parents to know and understand their rights. Every parent must research the state and local guidelines in which they reside because these rules and guidelines may vary a bit across state lines. Only by fully understanding these rights can parents ensure their child receives the quality education they deserve.

Barriers

Despite the many roles parents must play and the rights that have been afforded to them over the past half-century, many barriers to their participation in the educational process still persist, and this disconnect between schools and parents continues to grow. For starters, many parents simply believe their participation is no longer needed, especially when their child moves up to the secondary level, but parent involvement can make a huge difference at every level. Increased parental involvement in the middle and high school years can result in not only increased academic performance and positive behavior but also can decrease dropout rates as well as lead to increased interest in attending college and other postsecondary paths.

Many parents also feel they lack the knowledge about school policies or curricula to help their children in school. However, even without extensive knowledge, through simple encouragement and support, parents can still participate in the education of their children. Parents still must exert the effort to investigate local laws and school procedures, and schools must also improve their communication with parents and better ensure they understand how the school operates. More recently, there has also been an increase in power struggles over cultural and political issues between parents and schools. Lately, political and cultural warfare has infected nearly every institute in our country, and public schools have not been immune to this societal scourge. This new wave of unrest has turned many parents against public schools, and in some instances, parental involvement has not been healthy or productive, devolving into shouting matches at parent meetings, restraining orders, and even arrests.

Many times, a disconnection can grow between schools and parents simply due to language and cultural barriers, especially for immigrant parents. Parents not fluent in English are often wary about being involved in the school due to their inability to communicate effectively or even fear of deportation. A large percentage of parents also did not have a very positive experience with their own schooling and may still hold on to many negative opinions about the education system. These negative feelings toward school can be a significant barrier to parent participation. Also, as sad as it may seem, some parents reported safety concerns as a significant barrier to school involvement with many urban schools located in sometimes not-so-welcoming parts of town.

Lastly, the number one stated reason for lack of parent involvement in schools is time. Today's fast-paced, wham bam, thank you ma'am way of life has left parents with seemingly little time for education. Not surprisingly, lack of time was also reported by school staff as the number one reason for not actively seeking out and finding new ways to increase parent involvement and support. When surveyed, nearly 90% of schools cited time constraints as the number one perceived barrier to parent involvement.

The 21st century has ushered in a much more breakneck pace of existence, but parents and schools have to find the time to invest in working together to improve the learning experience of all students. People constantly complain about time, yet their "phone time" has also significantly increased, as well as their "Netflix and chill" time or their "let's have a glass of wine" time. Everyone needs downtime and the ability to check out, but perhaps this time crisis is a bit self-inflicted. If parents and school staff could do a better job of managing and prioritizing their time, they may find there is plenty left over to focus more effort on improving the education of our youth.

Despite all these barriers and the deteriorating relations between public schools and parents, there are many steps parents can take to alleviate these problems by taking an early, proactive approach to preparing their children for what lies ahead, but this process begins well before the first day of school.

Parenting for Success

Preparing a child for the first day of school does not begin days or weeks before the doors open but must start the moment a parent returns home from the delivery room. The first four to five years of a child's life is the most critical time of a child's development, and parents are the primary drivers of this stage in their child's early physical, mental, and social growth. Parents are literally everything to a child's growth and development during the first few years of life. Based on the results of countless research, parents' own physical and mental health is more strongly associated with the health of their children than any other factor. Regardless of age, race, socioeconomic status, or any other demographic factor, parent health is the best predictor of the health of their children. Children with healthy parents are nearly four times as likely to also have high levels of physical and mental health when compared to those children with unhealthy parents. So, let's take a look at some of the ways in which parents can better prepare their children for a successful future.

Nutrition

There are several factors that may contribute to healthy growth and development, but a nutrient-rich diet is one of, if not the most important aspects of a child's physical and mental health. Children's diets today are riddled with inefficient nutrients and contain excess amounts of sugar, fat, and sodium. They devour chips, candy, sodas, fast food, and every processed glob of mess within arm's reach. Furthermore, a poor diet does not only affect a child's physical health but can cause behavior problems, sleep disorders, lack of concentration, and a litany of other emotional and developmental issues. What's worse, an overwhelming majority of research shows that many kids don't just grow out of these habits. A child's diet plays a vital role in his or her future well-being because eating habits established in childhood generally continue into adult life. Kids don't grow up and mature out of their "fat phase." Instead, they continue their quest for ultimate satiation well into adulthood.

Diet and nutrition fall completely under the purview of parents. Of course, some kids eat school lunches and even breakfasts, but parents control what food is in the refrigerator and the pantry at home. Parents decide whether to cruise through the drive-through or stop to dine at a local restaurant. They are the ultimate decision-makers in this arena, and they simply must do a better job.

Many of the foods children consume on a daily basis produce significant negative impacts on their performance at school. Consuming high levels of saturated fat impairs learning and memory, yet they are usually the most widely available and affordable foods on the menu. Additionally, when children consume high levels of sugar and glucose, it results in a crash, causing energy levels to drop. This trend has resulted in over a third of children in the United States now being considered obese, yet most of them are considerably malnourished due to the lack of adequate essential vitamins, minerals, and nutrients in their diets. These inefficient diets have resulted in widespread problems with children's health, academic performance, and psychological well-being.

Malnutrition can, over time, lead to long-term neural issues in the brain, which impair a child's ability to learn, their reactions to stress, their emotional intelligence, and result in a cornucopia of other medical complications. Researchers have discovered that poor diet and malnutrition lead to developmental delays in social aptitude, language, and fine motor skills, as well as vision. A deficient diet can also severely impact a child's attitude and behavior in a wide variety of settings. Furthermore, poor dietary habits can also eventually lead to serious medical conditions for children, such as Type 2 diabetes, obesity, heart problems, and weakened immune response.

Unfortunately, the federal government has recently begun to poke it's always intrusive little nose into this situation by promoting pharmaceutical options to reduce childhood obesity, recommending kids now receive injections from their pediatrician to combat weight problems. This is dangerous and utterly ridiculous Orwellian nonsense. We do not need Big Pharma to address another simple problem so government and corporate leaders can further expand their portfolios. Obesity, although many times it involves a genetic component or is a manifestation of previous abuse or other adverse life experiences, for many, it's mostly about choice. One's DNA does not generally force one to make that trip to the Taco Bell drive-through or to eat that first, second, or third piece of cake. A healthy diet and exercise are all that are most often needed to maintain a healthy weight. It's a simple equation: Eat less and move more.

Parents must take charge of their own food choices and what their children put into their bodies. We worry so much about drugs and alcohol, but the most dangerous items children consume these days may be the food sitting on their dinner plates. Parents can address and solve this epidemic by simply adjusting their family's lifestyle and the ways in which they consume. Parents can provide their kids with smaller portioned meals and snacks every few hours and choose fresh, whole foods like fruits, nuts, whole grains, and vegetables. Limit treats and processed foods like sugary drinks, chips, cookies, and fast food items. Adjusting and moderating the family diet can be highly beneficial for all parties, including parents. Many healthy food options can be more expensive, and cost factors can be a major contributor to unhealthy diets. However, many of these dietary issues can be managed at home with only minor tweaks and small increases in expenditures, and if parents take the time and effort to improve the food choices in their home, the result will not only be a healthier and more productive child but a healthier and more productive family unit.

Exercise

Like adults, kids need to stay active. A healthy exercise regimen can not only improve physical health but is linked to improvements in mental health, behavior, and attitude. However, according to CDC statistics, only around half of boys and just over a third of girls are adequately fit, and research shows that 80% of overweight children will grow up to become overweight or obese adults. Unfit kids are at significantly higher risk of not only cardiovascular and chronic diseases such as Type 2 diabetes and heart conditions but also increased prevalence of psychological disorders. This situation has gotten so bad that a large percentage of young adults graduating high school are not even physically fit enough to be considered for military service. The current most prevalent disqualifying factor for young adults attempting to join the military is being overweight, and a recent Pentagon study found that up to 77% of young adults would not qualify for military service today due to being overweight, using drugs, or having other mental or physical health issues. I guess it's a good thing drones and robots do most of the killing for the U.S. government these days.

Of course, we've relentlessly emphasized the detrimental effects of excess screen time, which is a significant factor in the decreased activity of our youth, but the simple fact is that kids today are not as active as kids of the past. The days of riding bikes endlessly through the streets, building ramps, and constructing hidden fortresses in the woods have disappeared into a bygone era. Take a stroll outside these days, and kids are nowhere to be found. Moreover, youth participation in organized sports has significantly declined in the last decade as well. In 2008, 45% of kids ages 6–12 participated in some type of organized sport on a regular basis. This percentage had dropped to 38% by 2018 and continues to decline. Additionally, the COVID-19 lockdowns further exacerbated this situation when organized sports were canceled en masse across large regions of the country.

The most infuriating aspect of this troubling trend is that kids don't need to go to the gym, or hire a personal trainer to help them with their CrossFit routine. For kids, exercise simply means getting off the couch or the floor and playing. Kids can meet all the fundamental elements of physical fitness by merely stepping outside and engaging in activities kids have participated in for generations. Running away from "It" in a high-stakes game of tag creates endurance. Crossing the monkey bars and climbing up trees creates physical strength. Bending down to tie their shoes and contorting their bodies as they jump on trampolines, dance, and swim in local pools all build flexibility. If parents and schools would just let kids be kids, an active lifestyle would naturally emerge from the shadows.

Letting kids play and simply be the active little balls of energy they were born to be strengthens their bones and muscles while creating leaner bodies. They will have a significantly lower chance of becoming overweight and contracting debilitating conditions such as Type 2 diabetes and problems with high cholesterol and blood pressure. By becoming more active, children's stress and anxiety will also be reduced, improving their mental health and creating a better outlook on life. They will sleep better and be more apt to handle the physical and emotional challenges of life as a 21st-century youngster, and an active child will perform better in school across all metrics.

The solution to this problem is quite straightforward. Kids have to transition from the sedentary lifestyles they've recently adopted and move more. Kids and teens sit around all day long on TVs, smartphones, laptops, tablets, and video games. Parents must limit the amount of time they allow their kids to use these devices and get them off the couch. Children between the ages of 2–5 should have no more than an hour of screen time a day, and kids younger than 18 months have no business in front of a screen at all. Keep TVs and gaming systems out of kids' bedrooms, shut down all devices during mealtimes, and ensure children view high-quality, age-appropriate programming and movies. School-aged kids from 6–17 need at least an hour of moderate to vigorous exercise every day, and younger children five and under should be highly active throughout the day, engaging in around three hours of daily exercise.

Parents can be the greatest influence when it comes to physical activity, and it starts with being a role model and incorporating good habits. Use exercise as a means of transportation—walk or ride a bike instead of loading everyone into the SUV. Focus on fun and engaging physical activities like hiking, putt-putt, or a trip to the zoo. Invite other friends with children and turn a physical activity into a social gathering. Use competition as a motivating tool and incorporate technology into the game. Include kids in household activities. Many chores can function as great opportunities to be active, from yardwork to doing the dishes and sweeping. Incorporate activities like cycling, kayaking, or snorkeling into family vacations and give gifts like rollerblades, bicycles, and other sports-related items that promote physical activity.

Active kids are smarter, more physically developed, possess more mental clarity, and perform significantly better at school compared to their less active peers. Find physical activities a child enjoys and incorporate those activities into their daily routines. Creating a more active child can be an extremely easy process, and the small price parents pay to make these simple changes produces amazing and long-lasting results that will not only benefit their children now but will also create a template that will carry them into a healthy adult life.

Sleep

One of the most significant but least discussed topics related to children's health today is sleep. Sleep is an extremely vital aspect of a child's development as well as their everyday physical and emotional health. Sleep helps us problem-solve, form memories, react to situations, and learn. Sleep is even more important for children because during sleep their bodies release hormones that build muscles, repair damaged cells, and aid in growth. This would seem to be nothing more than common sense, yet only around half of U.S. children get adequate sleep. Whether due to early school start times, excessive screen time, or other life-related stressors, 52% of U.S. children from age 6–17 sleep for less than nine hours per night, and this lack of sleep has resulted in a wide array of developmental issues.

Furthermore, kids who get the recommended hours of sleep have a 44% higher chance of acquiring and understanding new information and demonstrate higher levels of curiosity. In addition, kids who maintain healthy sleep routines are 33% more likely to complete homework and 28% more likely to have a positive attitude toward and care about their performance in school. Lack of sleep causes troubles with memory, elevated levels of stress, irritability, low motivation, and difficulty learning, and over time, these problems can escalate into bouts of anxiety and depression. Not getting enough sleep has also been linked to weight gain, mood issues, as well as increases in bad judgment, resulting in higher incidents of accidents. Tired athletes twist more ankles, and sleep deprived students may decide to send that inappropriate photo.

Lack of sleep reduces immune response, and kids are nothing more than walking disease vectors. Children without adequate sleep are much more likely to get sick and miss out on valuable moments in their lives. Moreover, a lack of sleep can result in serious developmental issues, and many researchers have compared the brains of sleep-deprived children to those of a drunk person with delayed and impaired decision-making abilities in combination with a shortened attention span and decreases in functional memory. Sleep deprivation in children has consistently been linked to higher incidents of academic, behavioral, and health problems, in addition to higher levels of risk-taking behavior and mood-related disorders. Loss of sleep has also been associated with ADHD and can induce symptoms that appear like ADHD. Too little sleep has even been associated with increased levels of self-harm and suicide. One of the strongest links between mood and self-harm in high school students is lack of sleep, and students sleeping less than six hours per night are more than three times as likely to engage in suicidal behaviors than those students who sleep eight hours or more.

Kids today simply do not get the sleep they need to function and be successful in school. Children need sleep, and they need a lot of it. Babies less than one year old should sleep between 14–18 hours a day, and children between the ages of 1–10 should sleep for around 10–13 hours per night. As children age into adolescence, they do not require as much sleep, but they should still get between 8–10 hours of sleep per night. Of course, every child is different, and sleep routines vary. But kids should get at least eight to nine hours of sleep per night to be able to function in school.

Parents are the primary gatekeepers of sleep, and it is a parent's duty to ensure a child gets adequate sleep. Children need bedtimes, and those bedtimes must be consistently followed. Nighttime electronic use needs to be persistently managed, and all electronic devices should be turned off an hour before bedtime. Electronic devices should be kept out of children's bedrooms at night to reduce the chance of them sneaking in some screen time when they should be sleeping. Parents must talk to their children about the importance of sleep and never use going to bed early as a punishment or staying up late as an incentive. Optimize the child's sleep environment by ensuring their room is dark, quiet, and comfortable. Lastly, cast going to bed in a positive light so kids will not be as resistant to closing down shop for the night.

Sleep is one of the most vital aspects of our lives, and lack of it can result in a plethora of cascading negative consequences. Adequate sleep is even more imperative for young people due to the impact it has on their physical and mental development. Well-rested children consistently perform better in every area of their lives, and it would benefit parents to work harder to ensure their children get the rest they need to mature into productive, happy, and successful adults.

Miscellaneous Perils to Success

Proper diet, exercise, and sleep are the most important foundational facets of creating a successful template for a healthy, productive, and motivated child. However, there are several other critical health concerns parents must consider that may affect the ability of their children to be successful in the school setting and beyond.

Although drug and alcohol abuse among teens and young children has decreased in the last decade, their use in schools and among students still remains a concern. Based on a 2021 survey, 32% of high school seniors reported using at least one illicit drug, and around 10% of eighth graders reported similar drug use. With legalization increasing in many states, kids' access to marijuana has also increased, and its use is popping up more frequently in elementary schools. More and more elementary-age students show up to school with cannabis-filled vape pens and edibles. Thus, parents who engage in the "green life" must do a better job of ensuring their children have zero access to these drugs. It's very easy to buy a lock box or small safe to keep these drugs and other paraphernalia out of reach.

Parents must be honest about drugs with their children, though and refrain from hyperbolizing and using scare tactics. This strategy will do nothing but create more curiosity and instill an image of drugs being the "forbidden fruit"...we all know how that story ended. Explain to children that these drugs can be highly detrimental to their growth and development and teach them how to make responsible decisions by being upfront and honest about the negative consequences drugs can have on them, especially with the fentanyl crisis rampaging across the nation. Today, merely trying a drug one time can, in fact, be the last time.

Teen drinking has also been on the decline, but 30% of teens still claim they have tried alcohol by the eighth grade, and that grows to 75% by the time they graduate high school. In addition, up to 25% of high school students admit to binge drinking. Realistically, high school kids are going to try alcohol. It's simply everywhere and has infused itself into every realm of our culture. I drank in high school, and I'm sure most adults did as well. So, let's also be honest about alcohol with our kids. Let's emphasize how drinking too much alcohol at a young age can stunt brain growth, learning ability, memory, and other developmental issues. Most importantly, emphasize the importance of not drinking and driving and not getting into a vehicle with a driver who has been drinking. A child must trust parents enough to reach out and ask for help when caught in a sticky situation, and honest conversations about difficult topics are the only way to achieve this.

Stress has been cited as one of the most relevant issues related to the increase in behavioral and mental health among children today. Adults are not the only ones stressed out of their minds, and when parents are highly stressed, this stress nearly always becomes felt by those around them, including their children. When kids become overwhelmed by stress, they begin to have physical symptoms such as sleep problems, digestive issues, or headaches, but these symptoms can quickly escalate into withdrawal, anger, and depression. This increased stress level in today's youth has, no doubt, contributed to the nationwide mental health crisis affecting our children. Parents should ensure their kids feel safe and be more cognizant of their own level of stress and how it may affect those around them by spending adequate, quality time with kids and letting them know someone is there for them even in the most stressful of times.

Thus, there are many perils to success for children today, but we have highlighted some of the most detrimental issues facing kids today. By creating a healthier lifestyle for children with proper diet and exercise, adequate sleep, and being honest with them about the dangers lurking out there, parents can greatly improve their progeny's chances of becoming a successful human. However, this is only the first step in the process. These lifestyle adjustments create an excellent template to build on, but teaching children appropriate ways to manage their behavior and emotions may be the most difficult yet most important factor for their future well-being.

Effective Behavior Management in the Home

There is no specified "normal" behavior for a child. Children's behavior patterns vary based on age, level of development, and personality. Many times, social and cultural expectations also vary not only from country to country but also from region to region or even state to state. Experts generally agree that there is no such thing as a "bad child," yet multitudes of decent parents often produce highly unmanageable children. What's more, some kids do chronically misbehave on purpose, and some actually enjoy it. Several traits are also inherent, like empathy, and these traits are not changed by good or bad parenting. People don't become sociopaths or delinquents overnight, and many of the antisocial adults we see every day roaming this planet began their journey as problematic youths.

However, human behavior is an extremely complicated and multi-faceted beast. Many factors work in conjunction to influence behavior, development, and personality. Genetic factors play a huge role in determining the temperament of a child as well as environmental interactions with family members, including not only parents but siblings and other extended family members. Furthermore, with the recent research surrounding the concept of epigenetics, it appears there is somewhat of an inseparable relationship between genes and the environment, with environmental factors being directly linked to changes in the ways one's genes work and function. Thus, a child's learning environment in daycare or school can also have a significant impact on a child's behavioral development and their interactions with teachers and peers in those settings. Even other institutes such as churches, sports teams, and members of the community can have important roles in a child's development. These and many other elements work in unison to contribute to the growth and development of a child, and although any one of them can be a significant contributor to the problem, there is no single factor that can be pinpointed as the sole cause of behavior problems.

However, there are several reasons why kids may choose to misbehave. Often, a child may merely be trying to get a legitimate need met but may lack the language or communication skills to adequately express that need. Many times, kids are tired, hungry, or just bored, and their outlandish behavior is their way of saying that they are not okay. One of the most frequent reasons for bad behavior is attention-seeking. We live in a busy world, and parents find it harder to find quality time to spend with their kids. Sometimes, behavior problems are nothing more than attempts to get the attention these kids may need and deserve. A child may also want more independence, and their behavior may be a way of expressing a desire to take more control over their own life.

Some children may simply be too young to follow the rules, and it takes time and practice for young children to understand what they are being asked to do. Rules can often be inconsistent or confusing for some kids, and parents and schools should be sure not to have too lofty expectations by making rules clear, concise, and easy to follow and enforce. Many kids, especially in today's world, have high levels of stress and/or strong emotional responses to stimuli. If children are overwhelmed with frustration and anger, they may forget certain rules and become much more impulsive. Kids do not always comprehend how to express their emotions, and these emotions are often expressed via bad behavior.

Parents can be a significant factor in a child's behavior, and there are many ways in which parents can encourage bad behaviors. Being inconsistent with rules and giving into tantrums can actually reinforce negative behavior. Not following through by constantly making empty threats with no real consequences will only create a situation in which the child believes they can do whatever they want without repercussions. This attitude, without a doubt, carries over into the school setting, thus shifting this problem from the home to the classroom. Additionally, making excuses for a child's bad behavior like stating they're just tired or hungry, only worsens the situation, and the child learns there is no need to take any responsibility for their actions.

Laughing or smiling at bad behavior is one of the worst ways to respond to it. Outlandish behavior can be quite comical. That's why we love to watch the Three Stooges and any Jim Carey movie. However, bad manners and inappropriate behaviors are not fun or funny for everyone else involved, especially when those behaviors trickle into the classroom. Laughing at bad behavior does nothing but encourage and reinforce inappropriate behavior, and we already have enough damn stooges in classrooms as it is.

Yelling and threatening a child almost never results in positive outcomes. That merely teaches the child that those are appropriate ways to respond to life's setbacks as well as damaging the relationship with that child. Speaking firmly, though, is not the same as yelling just as a warning is not the same as a threat. Constantly threatening children, especially when those threats are mostly empty, only creates more incentive to misbehave and further damages the relationship with the child. Yelling and threatening can also lead to hitting. Despite personal opinions on corporal punishment, research shows that spanking children increases aggression and antisocial behavior while reducing self-esteem and empathy. In addition, the child is being taught that violence is a good way to approach solving problems and dealing with conflict. Kids who get hit are generally kids who hit others. Plus, many kids simply learn how to avoid the pain and not how to actually regulate their behavior and make better choices. What's more, using physical means of discipline can tip-toe and even cross the line into child abuse. These physical means of discipline can have long-lasting psychological and physiological consequences and side effects that could impact certain kids for the rest of their lives.

Parents have to take charge of their homes and stop letting children run the show. The behavior of young children today is worse than it's ever been. They are ill-mannered, rude, disrespectful, aggressive, violent, and lack the most basic skills to function as productive human beings. While we can point the finger at many factors, ultimately, parents are the responsible parties for this troubling trend. Creating a life makes one responsible for the actions of that child, and many of today's parents are clearly not doing their job. Parenting is not an easy task, but this should be even more of a reason to think twice before bringing life into this world. Kids show up to school without the basic skills needed to operate in a school setting. It is not the school's job to teach children how to share, get along with others, not hit people, and follow simple directions. Parents must do their part to prepare their children for the first day of school in order for their child to have any chance of success, and there are several strategies parents can implement to better prepare their child for this monumental moment.

Always give care and respect to children, and be sure to set aside time to spend one-on-one with them. Listen to what kids say. When kids feel respected and heard, they are much less likely to act out. Kids today are screaming for attention. Attention-seeking is behind a large percentage of behavior problems in schools. Most of the time, all I need to do is give a kid a thumbs up and a smile or ask him how his day is going, and it brings immediate sunshine to that kid's face, changing their entire demeanor. Kids want to be seen and heard, and they want to know they are important. This can only be demonstrated by paying attention to their needs and spending quality time with them. In addition to improving behavior, spending quality time with a child can greatly increase their self-esteem, which is extremely important. Kids see themselves through their parents' eyes, so tone of voice, body language, and other expressions significantly influence how a child views themself.

Be sure to catch kids doing good things and compliment them whenever possible. Many times, parents and schools tend to focus on the negative behaviors kids engage in and forget to point to times when they are doing what's right. Make communication a priority and be honest with children. Explain to them what they need to do and why they need to do it. When kids ask questions, simply answer them. They are curious little critters, and that curiosity should be encouraged and supported. Be a good role model for children. Kids learn by watching those around them, and parents are hopefully around their children quite often. Kids who are aggressive at school generally live in aggressive homes. Kids learn behaviors, and they learn from their environments. Model positive traits like honesty, gratitude, and kindness, and teach children proper manners and how to respect others.

Parents must also be flexible, and as a child grows and adapts to his or her environment, discipline tactics will need to be adjusted to fit the child. Very young children ages birth–2, first and foremost, should not spend much, if any, time on screens, because they are not great for development. Time out can be very effective for children in this age range, and it is important to be wary about spanking children, especially at this age. Children this young are usually unable to make the connection between the punishment and their behavior and only feel the physical pain. Kids are also very observant during this phase of development; therefore, an environment rife with aggressive behaviors could be misconstrued as the proper means to address conflict. It's important to begin to create some basic routines and schedules for kids in the latter parts of this stage, like bedtime, bath time, or dinnertime. This practice will help reduce their anxiety, as well as prepare them for the highly routinized schedule they will face in school.

For children ages 3–8, explain what is expected, set ground rules, and consistently enforce them. The earlier a parent establishes the expectation that adults set the rules and children are expected to listen and accept the consequences of their actions, the more successful the child will be in almost any setting. Following rules and accepting consequences is a skill every person must learn because there is no escaping them at any point in life. We are required to follow rules to some extent every day until the day we die, and teaching this concept early and often will result in more success for any child. Empty threats are one of the biggest mistakes parents make during this stage. They undermine a parent's authority and increase the likelihood of creating a child who loves to test limits. Be consistent, and don't forget to reward good behaviors. Incentivize positive behaviors and actions whenever possible.

It's also important to encourage independence in this stage and push kids to learn how to solve their own problems. As a child begins to move into the latter stages of this age group, be sure that punishments are natural, logical, and not too harsh. Over punishing a child can lead to decreases in motivation to change the negative behaviors and can create an unhealthy and resentful relationship over time.

As children get older, discipline strategies will need to change. For those children from ages 9–12, natural and logical consequences are of high importance. During this stage, it is also imperative not to rescue kids from mistakes and let them learn the hard way at times. Of course, parents must keep kids safe, but children must begin to learn how to accept responsibility for their actions and deal with life's consequences. This is also a great stage to remove certain privileges, especially in the realm of electronics. Kids love devices, and using these devices as disciplining tools can be highly effective. Taking away cell phones, tablets, and gaming systems when kids engage in negative behavior is a great way to encourage and motivate better decision-making and self-control. An effective punishment must be something the offender cares about, and today's kids care more about electronics than anything else.

Once a child has made it to the teenage years, a parent has hopefully laid the groundwork. Children should know what to expect and what will happen if they stray too far from those expectations. However, it is highly imperative not to let up on discipline during this stage. These kids may seem like little adults, but they are still developing with highly plastic brains. The landscape has changed during this stage, though, and parents must be even more vigilant in many areas. Rules should be set up regarding homework, time with friends, dating, and curfews, and these items must be discussed to ensure kids understand exactly what is expected. Employ meaningful punishments like taking away the car, electronic devices, or the ability to attend fun activities for a specified period of time, but also be sure to explain why the behavior is unacceptable and/or dangerous. Parents must remember to give kids as much control over their lives as possible during this late stage though, because it will help the child become more self-aware and independent as they move into adulthood.

Disciplining a child as a parent can be a daunting task. Many parents don't want to hurt their child's feelings and fear they may damage the relationship, but by not properly disciplining children, parents not only do more harm but further damage their relationship in the long run. Remember as a parent, a child is not a friend, and children should never see a parent as their peer. There are many ways to discipline a child while still showing them the love and respect they deserve. What's more, many kids want to be disciplined no matter how much they resist, because it shows someone cares enough about them to spend the time ensuring they get it right.

Quite frankly, kids are out of control today, and lack of structure in the home and improper parenting are the major contributors to this trend. However, we can all do a better job. This chapter is not intended to offend, blame, or ostracize any party, and we must all work together. Parents and schools both have high stakes in this game, and they must figure out how to cooperate to create the best learning environment for our children.

Creating a Meaningful Partnership

Parents and schools must work as partners to ensure the success of our nation's youth. The relationship between parents and public schools has become rife with drama, finger-pointing, and contention while kids watch adults act like children. When schools and parents cannot work in unison to create the best learning experience for students, only the students suffer. Parents have to engage in the role they accepted when they made the decision to birth a human, but schools must also do a better job of building relationships with parents and mending those that have long been broken.

For starters, schools should communicate more effectively with parents. Our current technological revolution has given the world endless outlets to connect, and schools can now seek out as many avenues as possible to create more consistent contact with parents. Parental feedback is very important for the success of students, and while schools must seek out better means of reaching parents, parents must also put forth more effort to engage in meaningful conversations with teachers and administrators. Communication should be frequent but concise, and schools should refrain from using school jargon, acronyms, and buzzwords parents may not understand. Schools must share accountability and focus on building relationships with parents through positive and productive rapport.

Schools must also remember to share positive experiences with parents. Parents are often only contacted when their child gets into trouble or is not performing well. Instead, schools should highlight positive behaviors and academic success in communications with parents. If parents are bombarded with negative comments every time they interact with the school, they will, no doubt, decrease that contact as much as possible. No one wants a Negative Nancy knocking at their door every 5 minutes.

Schools must get parents more involved in the educational process. Invite parents into schools to observe and help out in classrooms or in the cafeteria at lunch. Develop workshops, conduct informative meetings, and create parent-led organizations that enrich the learning experiences in schools. Schools can even conduct structured home visits for certain at-risk groups of students. These visits can build trust and provide a safe and comfortable place for meaningful conversation. Research has shown that school districts that have implemented home visits have seen significant reductions in behavior problems as well as improvements in attendance and academic performance.

Many parents simply lack accessibility to schools because they do not have access to Wi-Fi, cell service, or certain technological devices; some parents don't even have transportation to visit the campus. Schools must work harder to ensure these parents are included by creating more unique ways to share valuable information. Language barriers have also become a stumbling block to parent/school communication, but with the litany of translation programs now available, this should not be a major concern. Schools will, however, need to consider the varying cultural and societal norms they encounter among student families today. Parents come from a variety of backgrounds, and schools must be sure to respect the cultural standards that exist among their parent populations.

If schools and parents truly care about the future of our nation's youth, they must work harder to build better relationships with one another. Schools have long been pillars of the community, and it is time they return to their long-lost form. The evidence is unarguable and overwhelming that increased parental involvement in the educational process does nothing but improve student and teacher performance across the board. The future of public education looks quite bleak, and honestly, most signs point to that fact. However, the first step to creating a brighter future is for parents and schools to unite and work together to create the best possible learning experience and most successful outcomes for students across the land.

Part IV: The Road Ahead

Chapter 15: The Great Disaster—Covid-19 and Public schools

"The spring of 2020 will forever be known as the season when tens of millions of American families took a crash course in homeschooling." ~Michael Petrilli

"Technology is not a silver bullet. It's only as good as the teachers...using it as one more tool to help inspire, and teach, and work through problems." ~Barack Obama[1]

Public schools were teetering on the precipice before COVID-19. After COVID-19, or more specifically after the government's complete and utter mishandling of the situation, public schools are nothing more than a pile of rubble at the bottom of the ravine. The result of school closures for well over a year in many parts of the country resulted in massive learning losses for all types of students. These closures also significantly impacted the mental and physical health of students across the nation. Additionally, school lockdowns had a tremendous negative effect on the lives of parents—all parties can agree that the virtual learning experience was a complete and utter disaster.

Researchers even suggest the U.S. economy will suffer greatly over the next 10–20 years because of the cognitive and social deficits that school lockdowns inflicted upon students of all ages. It is estimated the United States could lose between $128–188 billion every year as these students enter the workforce; schools continue to struggle to figure out ways to fill in these gaps and recover the losses inflicted by nothing more than bad government and irresponsible decision making.

The COVID-19 pandemic disrupted schooling in over 150 countries, affecting over 1.5 billion students worldwide. The most infuriating aspect of these massive lockdowns is that government leaders and so-called experts were warned of the impending doom that would result from shutting down schools for indefinite periods of time. The United Nations Educational, Scientific, and Cultural Organization (UNESCO) cautioned that school closures would create drastic social and economic costs for people across all communities, with their impacts being felt more severely by the most vulnerable and marginalized groups.

They warned of interrupted learning and negative effects on growth and development, as well as the poor nutrition that would result from eliminating school lunches. They pointed to the massive teacher confusion and stress that would ensue from the kneejerk shift from traditional to distance learning and the litany of problems unprepared parents who lacked the proper education or resources would face as the classroom relocated to their dining rooms. They alerted us to the learning gaps that would be created as well as the behavioral and social regression that would be inflicted upon widespread populations of our youth. They apprised us of the high economic costs that would result from shutdowns and the challenges that would accompany virtual learning. They even warned us of the further strain school closures would place on health care workers due to medical professionals becoming homeschool teachers.

But no one listened, and here we are...

As some schools began to finally reopen, they faced severe staff shortages and unprecedented rates of student absenteeism. Teacher unions encouraged protestors to storm the streets demanding teachers be protected, often hyperbolizing both their risks and the risks of their students. Rolling school closures and overly strict quarantines continued to pull teachers and students from the classroom. As more and more students began to slowly return to campuses, schools noticed the extent of the learning gaps that had developed. Meanwhile, rates of violence, disruption, and other types of misbehavior soared. These kids lost a year or more of their lives, and the damage that lost time has inflicted upon them significantly impacts their daily existence.

---

1. https://medium.com/giving-every-child-a-fair-shot/connecting-americas-classrooms-d20a2169ac14

Our students have now fully returned to the classroom. There are no more quarantines, and school closures are a past failure the nation is trying hard to forget. Yet, forget we cannot, and now we must pivot and begin the hard and grueling process of recovery. However, like any disaster, we must first assess the damage—and the damage is quite extensive.

Learning Losses

I'm sure many have heard of the *summer slide*—a euphemism for the sometimes significant loss of knowledge that results from being out of school over the summer months. The effects of the *COVID slide* are exponentially worse. Widespread learning losses have occurred in every state, and those losses are greater in math than in reading. The average student lost around 116 days' worth of instruction in reading and up to 232 days of math instruction. Learning losses were, as expected, significantly greater in marginalized groups. Low-income students in many areas suffered as much as twice the level of regression as their higher-income counterparts, and only one-fourth of academically struggling students had a teacher available to help them at least once a day.

Looking at recent student test scores, the landscape is even more grim. Two decades of growth have been completely decimated by a mere 2 years of pandemic disruptions. Combined scores have shown that reading performance has experienced the largest decline in over 30 years, and long-term math performance has declined for the first time ever. These declines are even more pronounced in marginalized and struggling students. Early math and literacy performance are two of the strongest predictors of future academic performance, so these are very troubling results. Furthermore, recovering these losses will be extremely difficult due to the required teaching expertise and the additional materials and resources schools simply do not have. Additionally, the remedies required to address these losses will take years to fully implement.

Quite a bit of data have been collected and analyzed since schools reopened, and although a small percentage of students are beginning to recover some losses, the widespread regression that has impacted learning across the country could be even worse than we have anticipated. Data analyses by the NWEA discovered that average student performance fell by 3–6 percentile points in reading and 8–12 points in math. It does appear that younger students are recovering losses to an extent, with up to a quarter of their losses being recovered since returning to school, but there is still a long road ahead.

For example, a study of second-grade math students found that before the pandemic, 61% of students were considered to be on grade level, but after the pandemic, that level declined to only 49%. This cohort of students has since increased that level to 52%, but they are still a long way from the original baseline of 61%. In another study of reading levels in first graders, researchers found that 58% of students read on level before the pandemic. That number had dropped to 44% by the end of lockdowns. Once again, that percentage has improved to 48%, but it is still a long way from the original baseline.

That, folks, is the good news. When researchers looked at the performance of middle school students, they found that seventh and eighth graders had recovered almost none of their lost learning, and eighth graders have actually fallen further behind in math since returning to campuses. Much of this could be due to the increase in behavior and emotional problems inflicted by the school shutdowns, but I'm getting a bit ahead of myself. This lack of progress in middle school is extremely concerning because these students may not have enough schooling time left to recover these losses.

Of course, lower test scores and wide achievement gaps were highly prevalent for lower-income students and students of color well before COVID-19 arrived, but the losses of these students from lockdowns were far greater than those of their White and higher-income peers. Additionally, the limited research coming in also shows that students who received their learning remotely, not surprisingly, fell much further behind than those who opted to come back to school when the doors first opened.

There is not one simple answer to fixing this problem. To begin with, teachers and other school staff must work to foster stronger relationships with students. Students need to feel safe and trust adults in their school, and by building positive relationships, this goal can be attained much easier. Teachers should also begin to incorporate authentic and relevant experiences into their curricula. Schools must create learning experiences in which kids can see themselves reflected in what they study. This increases engagement and buy-in throughout the recovery process. Schools should continue to regularly assess students to gauge their progress, but these assessments should be presented as creative and informal checks for understanding. Schools should not push more standardized testing into schools—this only produces more anxiety, stress, and confusion. Teachers and schools must also be willing to adapt...frequently. And flexibility will be a crucial asset.

Outside the classroom, schools will need to increase tutoring, whether in person or online, to fill in these achievement gaps. Teachers and other support staff will need to be trained in different research-based strategies to aid in diagnosing and improving the academic deficits inflicted by lockdowns. Schools will have to create new and innovative extended learning programs that offer additional instructional time after or before school, on the weekend, and during the summer months. It will also be imperative for districts to educate families to better understand and fulfill their role in this recovery process. It is definitely going to take the entire village to fix this problem. It will mostly likely take years to mend the broken fences the storm of school closures has inflicted upon the youth of our nation, but with hard work, fiscal responsibility, and a team approach, the nation can eventually pull itself out of this mess.

There is also one positive takeaway from this widespread academic catastrophe. Learning losses are generally fairly easy to pinpoint. The hard part is addressing these losses and creating ways to recover them. Schools generate a lot of academic data through testing, grading, and teacher observations, so discovering what's been lost, where it's been lost, and who has lost it is not an extraordinarily difficult task to accomplish. However, understanding the effects school closures have had on students' behavior, social skills, and overall mental health is a much more daunting endeavor.

Mental Health and Behavior Problems

Before the COVID-19 outbreak, there was a disturbing trend in rising mental health issues surrounding America's youth. Yet, government agencies and teacher unions across the country decided it was a good idea to separate young people from some of the most vital resources available to them during the most crucial developmental phases of their lives, and exponential increases in anxiety, chronic stress, depression, and a wide array of social and behavior problems have been the result.

The number of behavior referrals has soared as upticks in disruptive, disrespectful, and violent behavior have infiltrated hallways and classrooms at unprecedented levels. Students fight in the parking lot, vandalize school bathrooms, skip school, run out of class, and assault teachers. Many of these acts are nothing more than a reflection of the stress and hardships resulting from having their entire social lives, daily routines, and schooling capsized. These lockdowns have inflicted kids with massive amounts of trauma, and the trauma has re-wired their brains, constantly pushing them into survival mode and triggering them to be on high alert. Some are definitely fighting, and others are choosing to flee. Yet, some kids are turtling up like clams, putting their heads down, and refusing to talk or interact with the world. Schools are not the only ones noticing this trend either; 35% of parents claim they are extremely concerned about the mental health of their children.

This is not hyperbole or fear-mongering by any means. The data are undeniable. According to federal statistics, nearly 90% of public schools have stated that the shutdowns have significantly harmed the social and emotional development of students. Further investigation from the U.S. Department of Education shows that 87% of schools have experienced a decline in social development and 83% stated that behavioral development has been stunted. There have been increases in bad behavior across the board: classroom disruptions (54 percent), disruptions outside the classroom (49 percent), disrespect towards teachers (48 percent), inappropriate use of electronics (42 percent), and fighting (21 percent). In addition, many kids are simply opting out of school, with 72% of districts reporting a rise in chronic absenteeism, which refers to students who miss 10% or more of the school year.

School closures and other lockdown-related stressors have also had more of a severe impact on younger students still in the early stages of development. Many pre-K, kindergarten, and first-grade classrooms are out of control. These students were not only unable to attend school, but day cares, parks, camps, and every other outlet for young children to learn and practice how to be a human closed their doors and locked their gates. These kids have turned into little disrespectful, incredibly incompetent, and self-centered monsters who want all of the teacher's attention, and they are willing to attack peers and wreck the classroom to get that attention. They cannot share and interact properly with others. They constantly steal toys, supplies, and objects from their peers. These children throw tantrums, some of which can be extremely violent when they don't get their way. They have zero self-control, hitting, kicking, biting, and spitting at other students and teachers when their outbursts become extreme. In addition, emergency room visits for mental health-related issues for 5 to 11-year-olds have increased by 24%. This large group of kids has simply missed out on the critical social experiences that prepare them for school and life in general, and it has significantly impacted their mental health.

Although school closures most likely had the most significant impact on young students, older students were by no means spared. Furthermore, young children are very resilient, and the social and behavioral losses they've encountered can be recovered in due time. However, time is not on the side of older students, especially for high schoolers, who will be thrust into an unforgiving world very soon. According to the CDC, emergency room visits for adolescent suicide attempts jumped by 31% in 2020. These students missed out on several extremely critical milestones and events in their young lives, such as the prom, homecoming, sporting events, and graduation ceremonies. High schoolers have become more likely to drop out, and many seniors have decided to opt out of college or any postsecondary training at all. One survey suggested that 17% of high school seniors who had post-secondary education plans abandoned those plans, and that number increased to 26% among low-income students. Of course, this could also be due to the ridiculous rise in tuition and the lack of trust these institutes of higher learning have recently experienced, but that's fodder for another discussion.

This preventable disaster will have long-term consequences for our nation's health and our economy. The ripple effect of closures on older students may ultimately result in these young adults losing opportunities for meaningful employment, as well as meaningful relationships. They will lack the skills and resources to start and support a family, and those who try will struggle to be successful. This country definitely does not need any more broken homes. These individuals will have higher incarceration rates, more health problems, and lower rates of political participation. It is even estimated that these students will earn up to $60 thousand less over their lifetime, and the impact on the U.S. economy could be nearly $200 billion annually. These students will earn less money and produce less innovation; thus, economic productivity will decrease. In addition, individuals who do not graduate from high school have been shown to die earlier than those who do.

Well, that's the overwhelmingly bad news. There is a bit of a clearing on the horizon, though. While we may have completely screwed our older high school students, there is time to heal our younger, still-developing youth. First, schools need to hire more staff to address these social and behavioral issues and create new programs to expand their influence. Perhaps broadening extra-curricular activities such as art, theater, athletics, and social clubs to incorporate more students could also help kids sift through their emotions and make better connections.

The American Rescue Plan Act and Elementary and Secondary School Emergency Relief Fund provided U.S. schools with $190 billion in education and health grants, some of which can be earmarked for mental health-related resources. Schools should, for once, incorporate some fiscal responsibility and be sure this money is well spent—invest in partnerships with local mental health agencies and university programs and use this extra money to hire and/or train mental health experts like psychologists, counselors, and social workers. Behavior and psychological referrals are rising to ridiculously high levels, and schools need the staff to address the needs of these students.

Parents must do their part at home too by modeling appropriate social skills and giving their children time to engage in high-quality social interactions with their peers. Go to the park, skating rink, or arcade. Kids need to play and socialize to practice the skills they need to navigate the world. Encourage and develop social skills by praising and rewarding kids when they get it right. Show interest in children and spend quality time with them to better understand them and their needs. Read together, play together, and relax together.

Poor decisions and hyperbolized narratives during the pandemic wrecked the mental well-being of large numbers of children across the entire country. The situation does look quite bleak, but we must not give up. The kids in schools today are the future adults who will be guiding the country a couple of decades from now. That is a very alarming proposition, but it's a fact we must face. We must all work to heal the trauma experienced by our young people, and we must work together to teach them the social skills they need to survive in the real world.

The data on learning losses and mental health declines are extremely worrisome, but there is a path, although fraught with much difficulty, to a better future. However, as hard as it is to believe, the issues do not stop there. School closures and the blockade of a myriad of other resources have created some major concerns in the cognitive development of our most fragile population—our children.

Developmental Issues

In addition to learning losses and decreased mental health and social skills, school closures have had a troubling effect on the cognitive and motor development of young children. I've witnessed first-hand primary-grade students struggling to speak, hold a crayon, and solve basic problems. This does not even consider the loss of social skills and the ability to follow everyday behavior norms we discussed in the previous section. Recent research has found that pandemic-related disturbances have caused losses in cognitive and motor development skills as well as young students' motivation and attitudes toward school, and the youngest children in the most critical developmental stages of their lives have suffered the worst.

The most disconcerting discovery from this recent research is that these developmental issues begin even before a child is born. Lockdowns and other pandemic-related disturbances caused pregnant mothers a great deal of stress for a litany of reasons, and these elevated stress levels have been linked to problems with fetal brain development. This research is still in the early stages, and many more studies must be conducted. However, the limited results coming in are quite concerning. Brown University found that children born during the pandemic had reduced cognitive, verbal, and motor performance. Pandemic-born babies scored nearly 2 standard deviations lower than those born before the pandemic. Columbia University recently discovered that pandemic-born babies scored lower on motor and social aptitude tests as early as six months of age. Researchers in Canada have also reported elevated risks of developmental delays among 1-year-olds born during lockdowns. There has even been research linking heightened emotional stress during breastfeeding to developmental delays in infants and toddlers.

Throughout the pandemic, parents faced illness, job losses, and multiple disruptions to their daily lives and social support systems. Parents and other caregivers were stressed, isolated, depressed, lonely, and anxious, and their children incorporated and mirrored many of these emotions. Kids had limited to no access to green spaces; they were stuffed into cramped living quarters with family members dealing with a wide array of pandemic-induced mental and physical health issues. Stress can have an overwhelming impact on child development, including language and social skills, and the upheaval created by government-induced lockdowns compromised the quality of the parent-child relationship and uprooted family structures across the entire planet. The ability of children to function is highly dependent on their parent's ability to function, and during these troubling times, parents did not function well.

Parents and other caregivers also lacked access to spaces where their young children could interact with other adults and their peers. These personal interactions are vital for young children and states haphazardly pulled access to these interactions from under the feet of families across the nation. Young kids simply lost access to the meaningful interactions that shape their development and teach them how to function as a human. The loss of access to these critical spaces, such as playgrounds, daycares, play dates, and parks, did not only affect the social development of young children; speech and language delays are increasing at unprecedented rates among incoming preschool and kindergarten-aged kids. Many speech-language pathologists are blaming the pandemic for these setbacks. Children were isolated and had limited exposure and time to practice language skills. It's quite difficult to learn how to speak when everyone is wearing a mask. Kids must hear clear speech and be able to see facial expressions and movements of the mouth and lips to learn how to communicate; thus, it should not be surprising that these kids have difficulty with language development. We removed every means available for them to learn these skills.

Children's nutrition and physical health also suffered due to school closures and other disturbances. We already know how important proper nutrition and exercise are to a child's development. States removed access to many of the places where kids play, and play is the kid version of exercise. Parents were justifiably terrified due to the lack of understandable information emanating from government officials and media pundits that seemed to change every 5 minutes, often contradicting the information from the day before. These cautious parents may have opted to keep their kids locked up even when some locations began to ease restrictions. We can't place the entire blame on parents because many were merely trying to make the best choices based on the chaotic and confusing world in which they suddenly found themselves.

Food banks were also overrun with hungry families during lockdowns, with up to 17 million children being considered food insecure, which is an increase of six million compared to pre-pandemic numbers. Much of this food insecurity was a result of limited or no access to school lunches and breakfasts. A huge number of students depend on public schools for a significant portion of their weekly food consumption. Many schools still offered these meals even during closures, but kids and their parents often lacked transportation or other resources to get access to those meals. Schools also provide a litany of services for homeless students and families, and it is estimated that over 400,000 fewer homeless students were provided services by schools during lockdowns.

The combination of all these factors results in one simple conclusion: COVID-19-related lockdowns and school closures significantly impacted the overall development of young children across the entire country. The research is still very limited, but study after study is reaching the same conclusions. Poor decisions by our government leaders and misguided, confusing, and biased fearmongering by mainstream media pushed our children inside, removing nearly all opportunities for them to properly develop the cognitive, motor, social, and language skills they need to not only be prepared for the first day of school but also for life. Fortunately, young children are very plastic and have the ability to bounce back quickly with the right support structures in place. The doomsday predictors who claim we have lost an entire generation may prove to be correct, but if we work together as a community to support the recovery of these lost skills, there may yet be hope for these younger kids.

The Disaster Formally Known as Remote Learning

Whether through hearsay or from actual firsthand experience, most have come to realize what an utter failure the remote learning experience turned out to be. As schools shut down with little to no notice, classrooms were immediately transported into living and dining rooms across the entire country. The only problem was that teachers, students, and parents were not prepared for this breakneck shift in the learning process. It also seems that government leaders forgot one important aspect of this plan—remote learning requires access to technological resources, and between 12 to 15 million students did not have access to these required resources. In fact, most schools had little to no data addressing this issue; many districts simply had no idea how many of their students had access to devices or adequate Wi-Fi service. This should be pretty pertinent information before moving to a fully virtual model.

The sad fact is many students simply lacked the appropriate resources to participate in this remote learning experiment due to the digital divide in this country. In addition, the locations they may have normally accessed to acquire these resources, such as libraries, coffee shops, churches, community centers, or fast-food chains, closed their doors for months on end. Thus, even if schools had the ability to provide every single student with a computer without a Wi-Fi signal, that computer would become nothing more than a high-priced paperweight. Survey after survey showed that internet access issues were the number one challenge for students and parents during school closures, and these challenges were the greatest in low-income and marginalized communities.

Unfortunately, however, those students who had the fanciest devices and the strongest Wi-Fi signals did not fare much better. Surveys indicate that only around 60% of students participated regularly in remote learning sessions. Up to three-fourths of teachers stated their students were less engaged, and engagement declined as the year progressed. A survey of teenage students showed that a majority of them did not maintain daily contact with their teachers, and a quarter of those surveyed claimed they were in contact with their teachers less than once per week.

School districts in every state consistently reported that elementary students attending class via remote learning experienced significant learning and behavioral difficulties compared to their peers receiving in-person instruction. Remote learners showed more signs of hyperactivity and issues with peers, and virtual learners were much less likely to be motivated or socially engaged and showed high levels of work avoidance and defiance. These losses go beyond academics and behavior. Children develop close bonds and friendships at school, and many missed out on these opportunities, further increasing their loneliness, anxiety, and depression, which wrecked their self-esteem. Kids in classrooms tend to build a sense of community—an important part of creating their own personal identity and independence. These opportunities for social and self-discovery were completely unavailable in the virtual world of education.

Many parents reported problems with their child's sleep patterns as a result of remote learning. Parents consistently reported that their kids could not fall asleep, wanted to sleep with them, or woke up throughout the night, many times due to horrible nightmares. In addition, parents of students with disabilities did not receive many of the services they had been promised because many of these services could not be offered online. Around 20% of parents stated their child did not receive their required special education services, and over 80% of school staff reported that it was difficult or sometimes impossible to provide these required services remotely.

Remote learning became an instant detriment to the most marginalized and struggling students, creating massive inequalities. Teachers reported that low-income students and students of color were significantly more likely to be absent or unengaged during remote learning. Only around 50% of teachers in low-income schools reported that most of their students attended virtual lessons daily, but for middle and upper-income schools, that number was a mere 16%. In addition to technology access and connection issues, students from these marginalized groups faced other roadblocks. Many students from low-income families have responsibilities at home, one of which may be caring for younger siblings. It's a bit difficult to attend a virtual lesson when one has to care for two younger brothers and a second cousin because Aunt Sally was evicted from her apartment.

Pandemic-related stress hit these communities the hardest, which even further aggravated the mental health of these students and their ability to learn in the home. Data also show school closures actually increased gun violence because almost all guns are located in students' homes. Furthermore, if these students resided in an abusive household, the move to remote learning did nothing but increase the opportunities for this abuse. For many kids, school is the only safe haven from their disastrous and chaotic home lives, and this safety net was snatched right out from under them in the blink of an eye.

So, what lessons did we learn from this experiment in remote education? For starters, technological availability is key to virtual learning. Without access to a reliable computer and Internet connection for all students, remote learning simply cannot work. Teachers, we discovered, are more critical than we imagined, and this failed experiment is proof that they play a vital role in the learning process. Technology can be a great supplemental support agent for any learning environment, but it is currently not the end all be all many claim. We also soon found out that education is an endeavor that requires intense human interaction, and meaningful two-way communication with teachers and peers is highly imperative. This failed undertaking also showed us the importance of parent involvement—without their hard work throughout the remote learning experience, the results most likely would have been even worse.

There is, however, one positive outcome resulting from this poorly thought-out experiment. For the first time, parents across the entire nation were forced into the classroom, and a large majority of them did not like what they saw. Remote learning exposed firsthand the multitude of weaknesses within the public school system and gave parents an up-close look into the outdated and ineffective curricula being taught to students. It's no coincidence that outraged parents soon began to show up at school board meetings and clamor for change shortly after the virtual schooling experiment commenced. Local congressmen's phones began to ring off the hook, and the quality of our public schools has become one of the hottest political topics today. Parents are demanding change, and they're lining up at the polling stations in an attempt to make that change. Parents seem to be more involved in the educational process now than at any time this century, and they are motivated to push for meaningful change. This new parental revolution may have eventually come to fruition, but the complete and utter failure of the remote learning experiment definitely sped up this movement.

Final Thoughts

All the entities we depend on during a crisis situation did nothing but fail us during the pandemic when we needed them the most. Government agencies rushed to shut down one of the most vital resources for students in this country. They let political ideologies, ambition, greed, and misguided and corrupt science guide their decisions. Furthermore, many teacher unions turned to the dark side during the pandemic, embedding themselves in the political nonsense and making demand after demand with no consideration for the impact those demands would have on the children their members were supposed to support and protect. They took to the streets with picket signs depicting child-size coffins, not only greatly hyperbolizing their own risk but the risk to their students. Mainstream media outlets made matters even worse by further politicizing the crisis and reporting dishonest, invalid, and manipulated information and statistics.

The U.S. statistics on COVID-19 were fraught with inconsistencies, corruption, and outright bad science, but we all know now that children faced almost no risk of dying from COVID-19. Sure, there were some outliers, and those were greatly unfortunate but generally isolated among extremely unhealthy children with one or more comorbidity factors. The real truth is that there was never any real danger of widespread casualties among children, especially younger children. What's more, based on the data we do have, teacher death rates were no higher than the overall rate for U.S. workers and even lower compared to deaths of essential workers. All this uproar and chaos seem like it may have been much ado about nothing.

One of the most infuriating aspects of these lockdowns was the arbitrary ways in which decisions about what should stay open and what should be closed unfolded. It's incomprehensible how Walmart, Target, liquor stores, and marijuana dispensaries remained open throughout lockdowns, yet schools were closed. Even when mandates began to ease with gyms, bars, restaurants, salons, and a litany of other businesses being permitted to open their doors in many states, schools kept their doors shut. Although many may argue for a good cause, thousands of citizens were allowed to roam the streets, protesting and wreaking havoc on cities across the nation, yet schools remained closed. How did these government officials and experts determine school was not essential? How did they not understand the impact and long-term consequences of closing down schools for more than a year in some places?

These are puzzling questions that demand answers because there was overwhelming evidence of exactly what would happen if they made the ill-thought-out decisions they made. In 2005, after the devastating impact of Hurricane Katrina, many schools were shut down for 6 months, and some were closed for the entire school year. These students returned to school with an average loss of two grade levels, and many lost even more. Additionally, these losses were much higher in mathematics. Furthermore, behavioral, social, and cognitive development significantly declined. The learning losses were also very predictable by race, socioeconomic status, and student age. Sound familiar? New Orleans and other districts have mostly recovered since then, but some say the effects are still being felt over 15 years later. Like always, we did not learn our lesson.

It's time for government officials to finally be accountable for their actions during this crisis. The damage they have done to our children is extensive, hard to measure, and could have been prevented. However, we must all work together as one community to mend the devastation caused by incompetent, corrupt, and misguided decision-making by those we are supposed to trust the most. There will be a large number of students who will not recover from this disaster, and we must work hard to provide them with the best resources we can for their survival. However, for a large portion of our student population, there is hope. Kids can be very resilient, even more resilient than many adults at times. If parents, schools, and community leaders work diligently and in unison, there is still hope we can pull our children out of the darkness and into a brighter future.

Chapter 16: Teacher Shortages

"The impending teacher shortage is the most critical education issue

we will face in the next decade." ~David Price

"Winners quit all the time. They just quit the right stuff at the right time." ~Seth Godin

Teacher workloads and responsibilities have continued to increase, while unrealistic expectations and student behavioral issues have done nothing but escalate. Salaries are being left in the dust by inflation, and teachers are finding themselves constantly unsupported by administrators, parents, and even government officials. Furthermore, COVID-19 related issues and uproar over CRT and SEL have infused political chaos into classrooms. Recently, teachers have also lost the trust of communities, and mandates demanding what to teach and what not to teach, as well as how to teach it, have stripped teachers of what little control they still possess. Teachers are tired, they get zero respect, and they are fed up with this situation.

Three fourths of surveyed teachers stated that job conditions have worsened in the past five years, and this same percentage of teachers said they would not recommend prospective teachers enter the profession. Additionally, this same percentage of teachers report frequent stress on the job which is a significantly higher rate than other workers. Teachers are exiting the field of education in droves, yet some still want to minimize this troubling trend that could lead to a nationwide crisis. While some high-ranking officials call increasing teacher shortages a "five-alarm fire", others claim that no shortages exist at all. How can this be possible?

Well for starters, there is no comprehensive set of national data on teacher turnover or vacancy rates. Once again, well done, U.S. government. The Bureau of Labor Statistics does maintain a database of "local government education" employees, but this category includes cafeteria workers, administrators, bus drivers, and other support staff. There simply is no reliable data available on this issue. However, like in most circumstances, the truth remains somewhere in the middle. There are parts of the country where districts have more students than they can support, while some districts don't have enough students to fill classrooms. Thus, there are some districts with little to no serious teacher shortages, yet many other districts are struggling to fill any and all vacancies with some states dealing with shortages of bus drivers, teaching assistants, cafeteria workers, and other support staff who are vital cogs in the public education wheel.

Unfortunately, this debate is nothing more than a game of semantics. There is no actual agreed upon definition of a "shortage", so there is really no way to know when the loss of teachers hits the "shortage" threshold. More so, when does this shortage become a "crisis"? These government officials and media pundits continue to play this game while the rest of us suffer. Truthfully, there is a nationwide teacher shortage. There were on average around 275,000 incoming teachers in 2010, but that number dropped to 200,000 by 2020. What's worse, that number is predicted to decline to 120,000 by 2025. At the start of the 2022-23 school year, the average U.S. school reported 3.4 open teaching positions. That may not seem like a high number, but in most elementary schools, that represents and entire grade worth of teachers. Lower socio-economic schools reported even higher vacancies rates at 4.4 per school. I have seen this unfold first-hand, and it's the kids who are the ones who suffer the most.

While teacher shortages affect teachers and the system as a whole, it is the students who are most often left empty-handed. Lack of qualified or sufficient teachers can threaten any student's ability to learn and be successful in the classroom, and the high teacher turnover states are experiencing can also devour economic resources that could be much needed in other areas. Thus, these shortages continue to further accelerate the bad reputation and outlook the community has on public schools. This troubling trend only further exhibits how broken and incompetent this system has become, while simultaneously solidifying the most commonly negatively held beliefs about public education that have spread throughout the country. This negative reputation does nothing but further perpetuate the problem by legitimizing the negative stereotypes and portraying schools as the unprofessional and incompetent caricatures they have become.

Teachers are fleeing the field, and there is no one waiting on deck to fill the void. The real question the nation must address is the extent of this shortage and how it can be mitigated. With all 50 states reporting shortages in at least one subject area, an estimated 200,000–300,000 openings left unfilled nationwide, and 55% of surveyed teachers stating they're considering leaving the profession, it may be time to take this matter a bit more seriously.

Roots of the Problem

We've discussed teacher turnover previously, but turnover is the baseline driver of teacher shortages. Turnover is simply the rate at which employees who leave a profession are replaced by new incoming employees. Turnover has become a major issue in school districts across the entire nation because there are currently not enough incoming employees to replace outgoing employees. A recent report from the American Association of Colleges for Teacher Education showed that in 1970, education degrees peaked at 200,000, but fewer than 90,000 education degrees were awarded in 2019. In 2010, around 13% of college applicants expressed interest in the field of teaching. By 2020, that number dropped to 7%. Additionally, in the late 1980s, teacher turnover rates sat at around 5.2%, but those rates have risen to around 8% in the last decade. What's even more concerning is that rookie teachers have the highest turnover rate, with nearly 45% of new teachers leaving the profession within the first 5 years.

Education is, undeniably, a profession overwhelmingly dominated by women, and there have been many more opportunities available for women in other professions in the last few decades, which have lured many of them into other fields. In 1970–71, 36% of all bachelor's degrees earned by women were in the field of education, yet by 2018–19, that number had dropped to only 6%. Women are seeking greener pastures, and schools have put zero effort into enticing men to join the teaching profession. In many schools where I have worked, the only males on campus, other than myself, were the custodians.

Education degrees are not the sole route to teaching, and most states have several alternative certification agencies. This is the route I took to get my teaching credentials. In most states, as long as an applicant possesses a bachelor's degree, they can apply to an alternative certification program where, if accepted, they embark on an accelerated path to becoming a teacher. This process can take less than a year, and most of the classwork can be accomplished over a single summer. This is an excellent means of bringing more teachers into the field. However, these agencies have seen a widespread decline in applicants in nearly every state. Since 2010, enrollment in alternative certification programs has decreased by more than a third, with some states experiencing up to a 50% decline. What's worse, nearly 30% of those accepted into these programs drop out before finishing.

The pipeline of incoming teachers has simply been cut down to a trickle, and states are struggling to find ways to entice young prospective teachers to the field. With low wages, raging parents and students, poor working conditions, little autonomy over their day, and mounting safety concerns, should we wonder why teachers are exiting the field en masse and no one can be found to replace them?

This is not a complicated problem to understand. Teachers have pointed to three main areas that have pushed them to leave. First, they lack any authority to make daily decisions about learning and teaching for their students; thus, the administrative bureaucratic beast has devoured almost all of teachers' autonomy in the classroom. Secondly, they want respectable wages that are comparable with their non-teaching peers, and they want to be treated with respect by the community. Teacher pay has continued to stagnate, and teachers have consistently been under extreme scrutiny as of late by parents, government officials, and other community leaders. Lastly, teachers require a safe and conducive work environment, and the resources to effectively teach their students. Many schools fail to maintain safe and productive work environments and provide teachers with the support systems they need to be successful.

Teachers are simply worn out. They continue to take on more responsibilities while their paychecks and the respect they receive continue to dwindle. Teachers are not only falling behind in wages in the midst of raging inflation but they also spend money from their own pockets to support their classrooms. Many teachers have to provide their own supplies, incentives, snacks, and other resources. Additionally, teachers bring much of their work home, which not only takes away from time with family and the ability to decompress, but it requires teachers to use more of their own resources to fulfill their job duties. As teaching positions remain unfilled, the teachers who stick around are forced to take on even more responsibilities to pick up the slack, which results in increased class sizes, more paperwork, increased levels of special education students being thrust into their classrooms, and more overall chaos to their already exhausting day.

The shortage of special education teachers and assessment personnel has been particularly taxing on those teachers left to pick up the pieces. Classes are being filled with highly disruptive and dangerous incoming students with severe disabilities simply because there is nowhere else to put them. These students must wait for months on end before someone becomes available to evaluate them, and even once assessed and diagnosed, they are many times inserted back into the same classroom due to the lack of special education staff and resources. This practice does nothing but infuse more stress, work, and turmoil into the daily lives of teachers who are already hanging on by a thread.

There has also recently been an extreme rise in violence and safety issues in schools, and teachers are now facing extensive verbal as well as physical abuse in their classrooms. Unfortunately, this phenomenon is not uncommon in lower socioeconomic schools, but violence has begun to seep into all schools regardless of student makeup. Teachers should not have to deal with the disrespect and emotional strain they endure daily, and there is no excuse for a teacher to ever be physically harmed by a student. Yet, this happens on campuses every day in every state.

Even if teachers can escape the constant verbal and physical abuse many of their peers experience, they have little hope of breaking free from the cultural and political wars that rage in many schools. Teachers face diversity issues regarding racial theory, slavery, racism, sex education issues involving SEL instruction, and issues around sexual orientation and identity. They don't know what name to call some of their kids or what pronoun to use, as if they don't already have enough to worry about. Teachers have suddenly found themselves jammed into the nation's ideological divide without the experience, expertise, or training to deal with some of these issues. What's more, they don't get paid enough to deal with all this nonsense. So, they leave.

Teachers have been forced to take on more roles and responsibilities than ever before, yet their pay continues to stagnate, and the level of respect they receive continues to decline. Teachers have found themselves morphing into counselors to address the litany of mental health issues affecting hordes of students in their classes. They put on their nurse's hat, dish out Band-Aids, and tend to the wounds of their students. They act as mediators between parents and the school while trying to maintain the highest level of professionalism. They serve the roles of a general education teacher, a special education teacher, and an ESL teacher all at the same time in many classrooms.

If this list of grievances wasn't already long enough...along came COVID-19. The mishandling of the COVID-19 pandemic wreaked massive havoc on school systems around the world, and the United States, as discussed in the previous chapter, did an atrocious job of handling this crisis. Teachers were at their wit's end well before the lockdowns and closures began to unravel an already vulnerable, failing system. Teachers have now lost even more support and respect during these troubling times while their workload has increased and their stress levels have soared. After the closures ended and teachers came back to the classroom, the situation was even worse. School closures and poor crisis management did nothing but further escalate the negative working conditions for teachers, and for many, it was the last straw. Before the pandemic, around one in six teachers (approximately 16%) expressed a desire to leave their jobs. After the pandemic, that number rose to over one in four (about 25%).

These teachers are not bluffing. With the job market much more promising in the private sector post-pandemic, teachers have found many other options available to them. As much hate as teachers get, surprisingly, the private sector loves them. Former teachers generally have few problems finding other employment. Teachers have, at minimum, a bachelor's degree, and many have graduate degrees. They also possess a wide range of skills and knowledge because they have had to become Renaissance men and women to effectively execute the ever-changing roles they have had to take on and to cope with the ever-evolving environments in schools. When many teachers survey the educational landscape, they find few legitimate reasons to remain in the profession.

Teachers clearly have had to take on a more intense workload with greater responsibilities and unrealistic expectations. They have had to dodge pencils and fists while they struggle to pay bills, and throughout the entire process, they get minimal to no support from parents and school leadership. Teachers are not getting the respect they deserve, and they are letting the world know by throwing in the towel and walking away. Public perception of the profession is at an all-time low, and the current increase in scrutiny has become too much to bear. Society can point its ever-blaming finger at teachers, but it is the system that has not only failed teachers—it has failed us all. Schools and communities must reverse course and find new and innovative ways to keep the remaining teachers in the field and entice more young people to join the profession. This impending disaster can be averted, but school leadership, government officials, and the communities they serve must find productive ways to fix this problem.

How Not to Fix the Problem

As districts come to grips with the effects of the teacher shortage, many have continued their trend of bad ideas and poorly thought-out decisions. Although this situation must be addressed, and it must be addressed fairly quickly in some regions, school districts need to take the time to ensure they do not further exacerbate the problem. Educational leaders cannot engage in knee-jerk reactions and implement cringe-worthy policies. This teacher shortage is, no doubt, more severe in certain parts of the country, particularly in the South, but states should pause, take a step back, and reflect on the best ways to move forward. Surely, schools will need some short-term solutions that may not work out in the long run, but states need to focus on the best long-term solutions to this problem, which currently has no end in sight.

One of the most concerning moves many school districts are making is loosening teacher certification requirements. For example, California has begun to permit teacher candidates to skip their subject matter and skills examinations if they have taken certain approved college courses, and New Mexico has moved to replace subject matter tests with portfolios. The list does not stop there. Oklahoma has completely eliminated its General Education Test for teachers, and Alabama has licensed prospective teachers who failed to meet certification testing standards. Missouri has ceased the practice of taking teachers' overall college grades into account, and Arizona now allows non-degreed individuals to begin teaching as long as they are currently enrolled in some type of college or university.

While loosening the certification requirements would obviously bring more teachers into the field, schools don't merely need more bodies in classrooms. They need reliable, well-trained, and effective teachers. Not only will reducing or removing certification expectations create more problems by inserting poorly trained and improperly educated teachers into the classroom, but this solution will bring with it even higher levels of disrespect and mistrust from the communities these schools serve. Public schools are already viewed as incompetent and unprofessional entities, so thrusting unprepared teachers into the current volatile environment will only escalate the problem. Additionally, the least experienced and most unprepared teachers are generally placed in lower-income or high-risk schools where most teachers do not want to teach. Ineffective and inexperienced teachers are the last thing these students need.

Some states have chosen not to lower their certification standards, yet their ways of addressing shortages are not much more promising. Many districts have begun to use long-term substitutes to replace full-time certified teachers. There are many adequately skilled substitute teachers out there, and many of them are former educators or studying to be teachers. However, most of these individuals are nothing more than well-dressed babysitters. Many lack the training and skills required to effectively address the learning needs of students; instead, they function more as crowd control. Although this option could be used as a short-term measure in emergency situations, it should not become the norm.

Several states have even considered using non-degreed veterans to teach classes, and Florida has already begun to implement this practice. Veterans in Florida will soon be allowed to enter classrooms without a bachelor's degree, requiring only a temporary teaching certification. This is a slap in the face to highly qualified teachers who take their jobs seriously. There is a reason why teachers are properly trained and required to prove their skills by fulfilling certification requirements. They need these skills to be effective teachers. If there is a doctor or police officer shortage, would we simply allow any Tom, Dick, or Harry to show up off the street and take hold of the nearest stethoscope or Glock? I think not.

These responses are not good, but sadly, they may be necessary on a temporary basis. It should be stressed again that measures reducing teacher entry requirements are a very bad solution, but in some circumstances, they may be a necessarily evil that should only be considered as an emergency, short-term option. Research has consistently shown that teachers have a more significant impact on student achievement in the classroom than any other factor, and these quick fixes will most likely backfire when this unprepared and untrained new wave of teachers enters classrooms.

While these strategies so far do not look promising, the situation gets even worse, looking at other schemes and mindsets schools have begun to adopt. The worst possible response schools can have to the teacher shortage is downplaying it. When schools downplay shortages, they become nothing but even more unprepared for them. Therefore, in the face of a teacher shortage, their only options are to double up on class sizes, force teachers to cover other classes, or even send administrators and counselors in to supervise classrooms. This is obviously not a great plan for a barrage of reasons. Some districts have even shifted to a punishment model, which is far from a productive measure. Certain districts have begun to fine teachers for quitting mid-year or suspend their licenses, which only further increases overall shortages because these teachers will now struggle to find another teaching job and will most likely be forced into a different profession. This, of course, would be a blessing in disguise for the individual teacher, but it does nothing to address the teacher shortage, which was a factor in causing that teacher to quit in the first place.

Several districts have also begun to offer sign-on bonuses for new teachers or those who opt to teach in high-need areas. While this may sound like a great way to incentivize prospective teachers, it does nothing to reward longevity and expertise, which are the antidote to turnover. Further, this method fails to address the salary gaps between teachers and other professionals, a primary cause of teachers leaving the field. These teachers will remain underpaid once the bonus is spent, and in the current economy, that money will definitely not last long. Additionally, once the lure of the bonus wears off, these new teachers will still find themselves dealing with the same issues that have caused all those before them to toss their lesson plans in the waste bin and walk out the door.

Lastly, districts must stop insulting teachers and support staff by bringing in donuts, having wear-your-jeans-to-work days, and advising everyone to practice self-care. These tactics only prove that schools lack the competence and motivation to make meaningful change. These are nothing more than bribes to make teachers look the other way while they continue to get railroaded. Offering emotional benefits to bump up teacher dopamine levels for a few hours is offensive and condescending, and it must stop. Corporations consistently use this playbook, and it's pathetic to watch employees fall for it every time. They cater tacos, order pizza, and layout pallets of cake in the breakroom. They let you wear hats and crazy socks every other Friday. These are merely tactics to distract workers from heinous work conditions and the disrespect and lack of consideration they endure on a daily basis. Employees stand in the breakroom with a smile on their faces while pizza cheese hangs off their chins, only to return to their unappreciated and underpaid grind anew. No...thank you notes and barbeque will not fix the teacher wage gap, or the chaos unleashed daily in classrooms around the nation.

So, while some of these strategies may be necessary on an emergency, short-term basis, none of them are adequate or appropriate long-term solutions. Additionally, many of these discussed strategies are completely counter-intuitive and will only further exacerbate the problem, creating even more shortages. There are several paths forward that can alleviate some of these teacher shortages, but these paths will be difficult and will require brave and ambitious leaders who are willing to finally step up and push for meaningful change.

Real Potential Solutions

Several long-term solutions can address and even reduce the escalating teacher shortage our country is now facing. The first step districts must take is to improve teacher and other support staff and/or specialist pay. According to teacher surveys, low pay is nearly always at the top of their long list of grievances. This will help improve shortages in every area by enticing more individuals to the teaching profession and by encouraging specialists such as psychologists, counselors, and speech pathologists to seek employment in public schools instead of the private sector. This move will also motivate many current teachers who are considering quitting the field to stick around at least a bit longer.

Of course, raising the base salary of teachers and other support personnel will lead to increases in applicants. It's exactly how our capitalist society works for better or for worse. Graduate degreed specialists have zero incentive to work in public schools today, and there is no legitimate reason to blame them. Who would when the private sector is so much more appealing? Furthermore, why would anyone want to be a lowly paid custodian or bus driver when one can make $20 an hour delivering pizzas or working in an Amazon warehouse? Schools simply need to raise baseline salaries across the board, and although they will surely moan and groan about where to it...the money is there. School districts simply need to stop wasting it. Perhaps a start would be to reduce their administrative bloat by whittling down some of the hundreds of administrative positions, siphoning off millions of wasted tax dollars a year. Additionally, the federal government recently doled out nearly $200 billion in COVID-19 relief funds to public schools. Billions of dollars have rained down into state coffers across the country, and it's about damn time they put it to good use.

Raising base salaries is a great way to lure more individuals into the field of education, but there are also several other ways of creating financial incentives for would-be teachers. For one, districts could implement a loan forgiveness system to pay off a portion of teachers' educational debt. A variety of districts have already experimented with this strategy, and it has produced positive results, especially when used to encourage teachers to accept jobs in high-risk or low-socioeconomic schools. Districts could also create scholarship funds through normal budgetary means or by expanding the areas in which bonds can be used to finance and pay for all or some of the costs associated with getting an education degree. Individuals accepted into this program would then be required to teach in the district for a specified amount of time.

Some states have conjured up even more creative means to incentivize teachers—Connecticut provides mortgage assistance to teachers. Bonus systems could be implemented that go well beyond the limits of a sign-on bonus. Districts could move to pay teachers certain bonuses based on different levels of performance, and milestone bonuses could be incorporated to give teachers a financial reward for every 5 years of service instead of a measly certificate and a pin. Districts possess a wide variety of means and resources to design systems and policies to increase the financial incentives available in the teaching profession. It's time for states to finally show teachers the respect they deserve, and it starts with cold, hard cash...not donuts and jeans days.

In addition to increasing the financial incentives, schools should work harder to ensure safe and productive working conditions for teachers. This may be the most difficult task to accomplish. It's easy to throw money at a problem, but actually addressing the day-to-day perils and roadblocks teachers face in their classrooms will take time, energy, resources, and the courage of school leaders to act. With one in five teachers reporting that they have been threatened by a student and one in eight reporting that they have actually been physically attacked by a student, everyone can agree this situation has to change. Teachers are forced to take on a litany of roles, many of which they are not trained to do. Districts must figure out ways to improve the daily life of teachers and the staff who support them. Discipline policies should be completely revamped; the curricula and the way in which they're taught need to be updated and improved. Low pay paired with chaotic and unsafe working conditions has worked in unison to push teachers right out the front door. By addressing these two issues, school districts can take the first steps to recovery. However, these are not the only means of alleviating teacher shortages.

Schools could work harder to provide meaningful professional development opportunities as well as the support and resources teachers need to successfully reach their students. The opportunities available for professional growth for current teachers and those new teachers joining the profession are abysmal. They are generally a waste of everyone's time. Districts simply need to ask teachers what they need to be successful and actually listen to them for once. Additionally, schools have to do a better job of mentoring new teachers and ensuring they are not lost in the shuffle during their first couple of years. All the data available show that new teachers leave the field at a very high rate, most often because they are unprepared and overwhelmed. Districts should reposition their time and resources to provide these new teachers with the skills and confidence they need to adequately perform their jobs. When new teachers feel lost, confused, overwhelmed, and unsupported, they will not stick around for long.

Districts must also improve the relationships between teachers and administrators and between teachers and parents. Teachers and administrators need to work in unison for a school to have any chance of success. The adversarial interactions that are increasingly common in schools among administrative staff and teachers have to reverse course. Administrators should function as supportive individuals who help teachers and keep them safe. They should not behave as dictatorial gatekeepers who look for any and every reason to bring someone down—they must work *with* teachers instead of *against* them. Teacher surveys have also shown that parents have become a major stressor and are one of the top reasons some leave the field. Schools need to find ways to mend this broken bond. In the past, teachers and parents worked together as a team to ensure students had all the resources they needed to be successful, and it worked much better than the antagonistic relationships that have blossomed between parents and teachers as of late. When parents and teachers work together, students perform at higher levels, and teachers who receive confidence, trust, and support from parents and the community at large will, without a doubt, stick around much longer.

Increasing diversity in the workforce is yet another way to improve situations for teachers and students. Many schools have disproportionally low numbers of non-White teaching and support staff. Districts must work harder to bring in more teachers from a variety of backgrounds and cultures. Diversity will improve student engagement and teacher morale. I cannot overemphasize how badly schools need male teachers, especially at the elementary level. Young boys are out of their damn minds today and providing them the opportunity to be around positive male influences will only improve their behavior. Many of these kids, primarily from low-income and/or marginalized communities, have no father at home and often no male figure in their lives whatsoever. Then, they show up to a schoolhouse full of females. Women are great teachers, and they do an amazing job dealing with the rowdy, incorrigible, and reckless boys in their classrooms, but an overwhelming amount of research shows that young boys need positive male role models. They are not getting them at home, they are not getting them at school, and they are certainly not getting them from social media or YouTube. We need more men in public schools. It's as simple as that.

Of course, there are several other methods schools could use to reduce teacher turnover, such as decreasing class sizes, reducing standardized testing, and ceasing the endless loads of extra work districts continue to pile upon teachers. Not censoring and harassing teachers and controlling every aspect of what they say or do in their classrooms would also be a huge step in the right direction. However, the most obvious and important yet unaddressed problem is data. Until states begin to collect, publish, and analyze data concerning teacher turnover and vacancy rates, the process of recovery will be difficult to commence. Rigorous and transparent data that include school and teacher characteristics relating to demographics, credentials, and levels of experience must be collected. The creation of strong data systems is a critical first step districts should take to address and improve the impending teacher shortage crisis.

Teachers are the most vital cog in the public education machine, and states across the nation must find new and innovative ways to improve the profession. Regardless of whatever game of semantics and data manipulation the experts and pundits want to play, there is overwhelming evidence that a teacher shortage definitely exists in this country. Although it may not yet be the earth-shattering crisis many claim, it is already having devastating effects on certain regions of the country, and the situation is only getting worse. It is urgent and imperative that government and school leaders act expediently but efficiently to address these shortages and create long-term solutions to reverse the crash course we are currently on.

Chapter 17: School Choice

"The idea of school choice is spreading like wildfire around the country, because it's the one education reform that puts real choices and real opportunities in the hands of families who desperately need them." ~Clint Bolick[1]

"If you want a good education, go to private schools. If you can't afford it, tough luck. You can go to the public school.[2]" ~Paul LePage[3]

One of the hottest debated topics surrounding education in the United States today centers around school choice and the voucher programs that support it. Historically, this debate has been the loudest in areas where public schools have not lived up to their promises. But recently, the school choice movement has become mainstream, with many parents in well-performing districts searching for better options. Parents simply want more opportunities and choices, and they want to seize more control over the daily lives and education of their children.

Students have long been forced to attend the school closest to where they live, regardless of its quality. For most parents, the situation has historically been binary since the only viable options were to suffer through the failings of their assigned campus or spend tens of thousands of dollars for private schooling. The costs involved in private schools have continued to soar, and public schools have become wrought with bad curricula, safety concerns, and overall poor outcomes. Fortunately, times have changed, and new and innovative systems and models for educating our youth are beginning to arise. However, these changes are accompanied by some potential negative drawbacks to the overall system that must be considered, so let's first take a look at a bit of the history behind school choice and the options parents have.

Roots of School Choice

The original roots of school choice can be traced as far back as the colonial age. Throughout the entire colonial era and up to nearly a century after the American Revolution, parents remained the primary gatekeepers over how their children were educated. It was not until the latter half of the 19th century that parents began to lose control over their child's learning as the government slowly seized more control over the educational process. By the early part of the 20th century, public schooling had become compulsory in every state; the government had finally established the educational monopoly it had long sought to achieve. Children were assigned to whatever public school was located within the boundaries of their region. This three-headed monster of compulsory schooling, partnered with complete government administration and financing, resulted in weakening the natural market forces and removed nearly all power and control from parents. Of course, private schools were an option, but most could not afford their high costs.

By the mid-1900s, any modicum of educational freedom had nearly ceased to exist, and children were forced to enroll in their assigned school regardless of the quality of that institute. This all began to change when the economist and intellectual Milton Friedman burst onto the scene. In 1955, Friedman released an essay titled, *The Role of Government in Education*, arguing for the incorporation of free market principles in the education sector, going so far as to suggest that tax dollars be allowed to follow students as opposed to schools receiving all the funding. He went on to champion more competition within the schooling system, thus promoting and increasing schools'

1. https://www.azquotes.com/author/50565-Clint_Bolick

2. *https://www.quotemaster.org/qe746ca28f0d34be008f20bddd55c5ab6*

3. https://www.quotemaster.org/author/Paul+LePage

effectiveness, efficiency, and innovation. Friedman proposed vouchers that could be used to pay for alternative means of schooling, which would sever educational financing from its delivery.

Although Friedman's ideas caught the attention of those who listened, it would take several decades before any move to implement them would arise. In 1974, Ray Buddle of the University of Massachusetts proposed the concept of charter schools in his paper, *Education by Charter*, in hopes of granting more power to teachers. However, his ideas did not take off until the release of Reagan's *A Nation at Risk,* which showed how poorly the current model of public education was performing compared to the nation's international peers. The idea of school choice and charter schools finally became a reality in the late 1980s and early 1990s. In 1989, the state of Wisconsin created the first voucher system, enabling families from low socio-economic groups to use vouchers to cover the costs of private schooling, and in 1992, the U.S.'s first charter school was established in Minnesota. By the early onset of the 21st century, 18 states as well as the District of Columbia, had launched voucher programs, and as of today, nearly every state offers the opportunity to enroll in some type of charter school.

However, it is important to understand the different options available in the school choice realm as well as how these various entities operate. For starters, there are two paths to follow along the school choice journey—the private school choice route and the public school choice route. Each of these paths is quite different and accompanied by its own unique pros and cons.

Public vs. Private

Compared to public schools, private schools have long been touted as a much better schooling option. Private schools have historically offered much smaller class sizes, more rigorous curricula, and a better chance to get into that upper-tier university, but this path requires parents to cover nearly all the costs of educating their child. This is where voucher programs come into play. Some states have offered parents vouchers, allowing them to receive funds from the government to use toward private schooling costs. These dollar amounts vary by state, but they most often fall short of the total cost involved in private schooling. Additionally, these funds are reallocated from public school coffers, thus potentially creating a negative impact on the resources available to those public schools.

I must put forward another sort of caveat for this section. I am the product of a private school education; I attended a private Catholic school from fourth to 12th grade. My parents were definitely not wealthy, nor were they eligible to receive any type of financial assistance. I was lucky enough to have grandparents, who, when the state decided I would be bused to an extremely low-performing public school because district boundary lines had been redrawn, agreed to cover the tuition to send me to a private school. My family was not even Catholic, but religious-based private schools seemed to offer the best educational experience where I grew up. After over 20 years of working in public education, I definitely believe I received a much better education in a private school. I feel that experience better prepared me for college and the professional world, and if I had children of my own, I would work as hard as I could to find a way to enroll them in a private school. But that was my experience, and it does not necessarily prove this is the right path for every child. Parents should be diligent in researching local options to determine the best route for their kids and their family.

Three types of voucher systems are available to parents. In the traditional voucher program, states simply give parents a certain amount of public funding to use toward any costs associated with private schooling, whether that school is religious-based or not. Another route is the education savings account (ESA). In this program, states put money aside in an individual account for parents, which acts as a debit card, allowing parents to pay for fees associated with private schooling. This route generally has more lenient guidelines, and some states allow parents to use this money for homeschooling needs, online learning programs, tutoring, and even community college expenses. The third route is a tax credit scholarship. In this program, individuals or businesses can donate money to a scholarship organization in return for tax credits, which can then be accessed by students who qualify.

The idea behind these voucher programs reinforces the ideologies first expressed by Milton Friedman over half a century ago. The vision that parents, rather than the government, should have the ability to control the education of their children was finally becoming a reality. Tax dollars normally being spent for public education were now being given directly to parents, enabling them to educate their children as they saw fit. However, these voucher programs have come at a cost, and their increased use is becoming quite controversial.

The primary advantage of school vouchers fits perfectly with the main goal of school choice—increased control for parents. Vouchers give parents who lack the financial resources for private schooling an opportunity to choose the school that best fits their child, whether based on religion, culture, race, or simply access to better curricula. Some claim vouchers improve performance and increase innovation in public schools by creating a competitive market, and vouchers can offer students from lower socio-economic or marginalized groups more access and opportunities for a better education. Vouchers also prevent parents from paying double for the education of their children since vouchers serve as a form of reimbursement for taxes parents have already paid to fund public schools.

Additionally, many proponents of school choice state that vouchers offer families a much better educational experience. Vouchers allow parents and their children to have more flexibility, access to more varied and up-to-date curricula, and create higher levels of safety. In private schools, behavior is almost never a problem. With near zero tolerance for unruly students, private schools can provide a much safer, engaging, and conducive learning environment. Furthermore, an overwhelming majority of parents involved in voucher programs report high rates of satisfaction with the system.

There are, however, several negative factors associated with voucher programs that should be taken into consideration. These programs do in fact take money away from public schools, and the level of impact can sometimes be significant depending on the district in question. Some school districts have extremely tight budgets, and reducing their funding could, in fact, undermine or destabilize the public education system. Additionally, many private schools are religious-based and provide religious instruction. According to a recent survey, the number one reason parents cited for sending their child to a private school was for a religious-based environment or instruction. For example, in Milwaukee, 85% of students afforded vouchers attended a religious school, which resulted in Catholic schools receiving up to a million dollars in taxpayer money. Thus, the situation arises where government funds are being used to support a religious institute, which could be viewed as an outright violation of the separation of church and state guaranteed in the U.S. Constitution. Voucher programs also have been accused of siphoning the best and highest quality students out of public schools, making it much more difficult for public schools to meet their required standards. Private schools can also potentially discriminate against certain demographics because they have the ability to pick and choose who they accept.

One major problem with private schools is that they are not required to follow IDEA guidelines or the Americans with Disabilities Act; thus, private schools do not have to provide special services to students with disabilities as public schools are legally required to do. Therefore, there is no due process, no individual education plans, and no free and appropriate education requirements placed on private schools. Furthermore, private schools can generally expel students for a variety of reasons without much recourse for parents. Private schools also don't have to follow the same hiring guidelines as public schools, and many teachers in private schools do not hold teaching certifications or possess the same amount of training as their public school counterparts. Likewise, private schools do not have to administer standardized tests, and while many would consider this a positive aspect, there is often a high level of unaccountability for private institutes since they are not required to provide student performance data to the state.

So what's the verdict? Are private schools and voucher programs a move in the right direction to improve the condition of the nation's failing education system? Well, the answer is not quite so simple and may depend more on the region in question and other local factors. Private schools, without a doubt, most often provide a smaller class size, fewer behavior problems, more modern resources, and a much more varied curriculum and learning experience in which teachers possess more control. On the other hand, public schools are more diverse and provide a much more uniform curriculum. Public schools can sometimes offer a larger number of academic programs, support students with disabilities, and students generally have many more opportunities to participate in extracurricular activities such as athletics, organizations, and clubs.

One of the major concerns for parents today is school safety and the increase in behavioral issues affecting schools across the nation. Private schools can most often provide a much safer and more conducive learning environment, and students who attend private schools are generally more engaged in their studies and more prepared for life after graduation. Reviewing teacher surveys comparing public to private schools, the results are quite one-sided. Private school teachers report significantly fewer behavioral problems than their public school peers as shown in the table below:

Percentage of Surveyed Teachers Who Identified Certain Issues as Serious Problems

Issue	Public School Teachers	Private School Teachers
Student disrespect toward teachers	17%	4%
Use of alcohol	7%	3%
Drug abuse	6%	2%
Student tardiness	10%	3%
Student absenteeism	14%	3%
Students unprepared to learn	30%	5%
Lack of parent involvement	24%	3%
Student apathy	21%	4%

But what about performance? The fact is private schools and voucher programs do not always result in improved student performance. While private schools have outperformed public schools on some metrics, they have performed similarly or even worse on other metrics. For example, there are data exhibiting increased scores and performance across all grade levels, socio-economic groups, and ethnicities in private schools, and many also claim that recent data show private schools close achievement gaps at a better rate when underperforming students make the switch from public to private schooling. However, data from various cities throughout Louisiana, as well as Milwaukee and Indianapolis, reveal their voucher systems have had no impact on student performance, and voucher-eligible students in Louisiana had a 50% greater likelihood of failing math with significant negative effects on reading, social studies, and science. Thus, the performance level comparison between private and public schools seems to be much more reliant on regional and local factors than the system itself, but much more research should be conducted in this area.

The most common and serious allegation against private schools and voucher systems is that they take large sums of money away from public schools, and this trend could further hasten their eventual downfall. While this may very well be the case for districts in some regions of the country, this seems to be an overall hyperbolic claim. Analysis of voucher programs in Milwaukee and Washington DC, actually showed an increase in funds available for public schools. Additionally, most states do not transfer the entire per-pupil funding out of the public system for a particular voucher-eligible student. Most states take only a percentage of those per pupil funds; therefore, theoretically, these schools should, in fact, have more money. Some could also argue that if schools lose those students, they do not need the funds earmarked to educate them in the first place. Once again, it appears as though the money issue can most likely be attributed to the ongoing problem of public schools' continued mismanagement and misuse of funds.

Thus, like many issues in education, there is no definite verdict. While private schools may benefit some children, they may simply not be worth the cost for others. Parents must weigh the pros and cons and consider the local and regional variables at play in the landscape in which they reside. Choosing a school can and should be a difficult and time-consuming process, and many parents lack the knowledge, background, and/or time to properly evaluate the best path for their child. Both private and public schools offer a myriad of benefits, as well as detriments, to the long-term goal of educating America's youth and preparing them for the world ahead. At the end of the day, this will remain a hot topic of contentious debate, but regardless of what the politicians, media pundits, and experts claim, it will ultimately be parents who must ensure their children get the proper education they deserve.

The Public Realm of School Choice

The private school option is only one side of the school choice coin. School choice and vouchers relating to private schooling often take center stage when it comes to these hot debates, but there is a litany of other public options available to parents who want a better educational path than the traditional one.

Intra/Inter-District School Choice

One of the most basic publicly funded options is inter- or intra-district school choice. This is often referred to as open enrollment and affords parents the option to choose a publicly funded school other than the one assigned to them based on their zip code. With intra-district choice, parents are given the option to choose any school that is located within their district. Inter-school choice provides even more flexibility by allowing parents to choose any school within the entire state or a defined region. Not all states offer this, and there could be some potential drawbacks. Schools typically give enrollment preference to families who reside within the school or district lines, and these policies can result in student demographic shifts or overcrowding at times. Additionally, students accepted into schools outside their assigned campuses can be removed and sent back to their assigned campuses due to behavioral issues. Nonetheless, this may be one of the easiest and most cost-effective options for parents.

Charter Schools

Another publicly funded school choice option is charter schools. Charter schools were discussed in detail in Chapter Three, so perhaps a mere refresher course will suffice. These independently run public schools are a hybrid public/private model. These schools are completely funded by taxpayer money, but they are exempt from many of the rules and regulations traditional public schools are required to follow in exchange for their promise of better results. These schools receive many more applicants than can be accepted, so students are enrolled in charter schools based on a lottery system.

Charter schools can give parents much more choice in their child's education and provide an atmosphere similar to a private school but generally at no additional cost to parents. Charter schools do not have to follow the same testing standards as public schools, and they offer online learning programs, provide more resources to students, and encourage competition among schools. Charter schools generally have fewer students with smaller class sizes, fewer discipline problems, and more flexible curricular paths to address individual student needs. However, these schools often lack proper oversight, have yielded very mixed student outcomes, and are vulnerable to corruption, which has run rampant in many charters. Teachers are often not held to the same certification standards, student populations are less diverse, and transportation may not be offered. Additionally, these schools have fewer extracurricular activities, do not accept or work with many disabled students, and can be shut down if their contract expires or is revoked. Some charter schools also require more from parents, like additional fees for uniforms, more rigorous attendance requirements, or a required minimum number of volunteer hours. Charter schools also take funds away from traditional public schools, which could further degrade an already struggling system.

Charter schools, without a doubt, provide more educational options for parents, but it is important to remember that more choices do not always translate into better choices. Parents should carefully consider whether a charter school is the best fit for their child. Parents must weigh the advantages and disadvantages and the pros and cons before signing on the dotted line. Charter schools are gaining more and more steam, but whether they will help pull the nation's education system out of its current mire or bury it deeper within is yet to be determined.

Magnet/STEM Schools

Another school choice option in the public realm for parents is what's called a magnet school. Today these schools are more frequently referred to as STEM (science, technology, engineering, and math) or STEAM (science, technology, engineering, arts, and math) programs. These are free and fully publicly funded schools that focus on a particular discipline and offer much more specialized curricula than traditional public schools. These schools focus on a hands-on approach to learning that can capitalize on and cultivate the individual strengths and interests of students. Children in these types of schools are enrolled based on their talents and interests instead of where they live.

Magnet schools can be traced back to the late 1960s and emerged as a means to aid desegregation. By providing a more attractive educational experience, magnet schools were implemented to encourage families to voluntarily desegregate their children by enrolling them in these types of schools. Although these schools still help increase diversity, they have recently taken on more of a competitive role in education, only admitting between 10–20% of students who apply. Magnet schools have moved to promote academic excellence to attract gifted and talented students, with a third of these schools using academic performance as a main selection criterion. Magnet school enrollment has continued to grow. Over 4,000 schools now serve around 3.5 million students nationwide. Yet, these schools come with several advantages and disadvantages compared to their counterparts.

Magnet schools provide an extremely diverse learning experience through a curriculum that focuses on students' strengths and interests and prioritizes academic excellence. These schools provide smaller class sizes and seek out the best and most qualified teachers, as well as family/community partnerships. Magnet schools generally have fewer behavior problems due to a more interesting curriculum that ignites and maintains high student engagement, and like private schools, magnet schools can expel unruly students, sending them back to their campus of origin. Magnet schools offer online learning opportunities and generally provide families with much more flexibility and many more educational choices.

There are, however, several negative aspects surrounding magnet schools. Students in these schools are often separated from neighborhood friends, and many districts require parents to provide their own transportation. If transportation is provided, it may involve an extremely long bus ride, up to an hour each way. Magnet schools can lack the oversight placed on traditional public schools, and if a child has problems regulating his or her behavior, that child will often not last long at most magnet schools. Very few extracurricular activities are available in many magnet schools, and those that are often require extra parental participation or equipment fees that parents must pay. Magnet schools also receive extra funding from the government, so their existence may result in needed funds being removed from traditional public school coffers. The most glaring disadvantage of magnet schools, however, is the high selection criteria used for enrollment. Many of these schools operate on a lottery system or use certain criteria that may disqualify a large percentage of students, and magnet schools have been accused of rejecting applicants with an IEP or those who have certain disabilities.

Thus, even if a magnet school is a great fit for a particular student, being accepted into that school may be quite an uphill battle. With applicants often exceeding the enrollment capacity, many families find themselves stuck in whatever low-performing or unsafe school the government has assigned to them. There are many pros and cons to magnet schools, and parents must simply decide if the pros outweigh the cons, and if so, cross their fingers and hope their child's name gets pulled out of the magic hat.

Homeschooling

Homeschooling is an alternative form of education that gives parents the most control over the education of their children. Homeschooling, like its name signifies, occurs in the home; however, this type of schooling comes with an extremely wide range of rules and regulations depending on state regulations. The number of parents opting for the homeschool route has continued to rise recently, and the racial and ethnic diversity of families choosing this path has also greatly increased. Between 1999 and 2012 the U.S. homeschooling population doubled from 850,000 to 1.8 million, and currently, there are over three million homeschool students.

Homeschooling has quite an interesting and surprising history, and the concept of homeschooling is, in fact, centuries old. Before compulsory attendance laws were put into effect, many children were educated in their homes. As the 20th century unfolded and school attendance was mandated, homeschooling ceased to be a relevant player in the education field. The idea of homeschooling re-emerged in the 1970s from an interesting point of origin: hippies. When the counterculture movement swept across the United States, countless progressives—hippies—removed their children from public schools and educated them at home or in communes.

This homeschooling movement continued to grow throughout the 1970s, but as the country entered the 1980s, the conservative Christian right began to take over the movement, increasing its popularity but shifting the basis of its overarching goals and ideologies. So, while the homeschool revolution was kicked off by long-haired, anti-war, pot-smoking progressives, it was expanded and accelerated by White, religious, straight-laced conservatives. Although it seems these two groups would differ greatly in their motivations, both sides rejected the state-controlled, institutional model of schooling, preferring a more personalized approach to learning that reflected their values, culture, and beliefs.

During the following two decades, the number of homeschooled students skyrocketed, and states began to create varying means of government oversight. Homeschooling oversight now runs the gamut. Some states require strict measures such as curriculum and testing approval while other states have no oversight at all. So, it is important for parents to study and become knowledgeable about all the rules regarding homeschooling in their state. The demographics of the average homeschooling family have also altered quite significantly as of late. Homeschoolers are becoming more urban, nonreligious, and racially or socioeconomically diverse. Many more single or dual-working parents are adopting the homeschooling model as well. Between 2007 and 2012, the number of Black homeschoolers doubled, and the Hispanic homeschool population continues to mirror that of their overall distribution. *Business Insider* recently described homeschooling as "the smartest way to teach kids in the 21st century." But are they correct? Is homeschooling the solution to providing parents with the ultimate level of school choice?

Homeschooling, without a doubt, offers a personalized family-centered approach that no public or private school has the ability to offer. The homeschool movement has expanded for a variety of reasons. Lack of satisfaction with public school performance and safety, as well as the high cost of alternative private school options, appear to be some of the main drivers, but there are several glaring disadvantages to this educational option as well.

Homeschool parents have complete control over scheduling and much of the curriculum and can adapt teaching methods however they see fit. This option provides parents the most control compared to any other school choice option. Parents can provide religious and ethical instruction and discuss controversial topics forbidden in public schools. Homeschooled children can spend time developing skills and talents that interest them and receive more individualized instruction that fits their personality and needs. This option also removes children from the violence, drugs, and disruptive behavior that plague a majority of public schools. Homeschooling also allows parents to spend extra time with their children, many times creating stronger familial bonds, and a homeschool schedule allows families to take vacations or visit loved ones anytime they choose.

Homeschooling, however, can become quite an expensive endeavor because parents are responsible for much of the cost of books and other needed learning materials. Some of the costs could be covered by vouchers such as ESAs, but those funds may not be adequate enough to cover all the required expenses. Additionally, in order to homeschool a child, someone must be in the home. This means the homeschooling option may not be feasible or may be extremely difficult and stressful if both parents work full-time. Furthermore, while spending all day every day with a child could create stronger familial bonds, it could also have the opposite effect. Homeschooling requires much patience and restraint, and quite frankly, kids can be annoying. Thus, being around their children all day long may take quite an unexpected toll on parents. This was apparent during the COVID-19 lockdowns when, after only a few weeks, parents were begging schools to open their doors due to the increased levels of stress associated with forcing the classroom into their homes.

Parents opting for this model must also be highly adaptable and able to motivate their children to ensure they are engaged, especially in the face of normal distractions in the home. What's more, one of the biggest negative impacts on homeschooled students falls in the social realm. Kids learn how to socialize by engaging in activities and conversations with their peers, and this is the only way a child develops the social skills they need. Parents opting for homeschooling must actively seek out situations for their child to spend time with other children, because they usually do not get the social interactions they would encounter in a school setting. This is not a deal breaker, but homeschooled children should be involved in sports, fine arts, clubs, and other activities where they can socialize and interact with peers. This will most likely add costs to the experience, but it is the only way these students will acquire the social skills they need to navigate the real world.

So, homeschooling comes with many benefits and disadvantages. It can be a costly and stressful process but can also be very rewarding, yielding positive educational outcomes and providing more family connections. Homeschooling certainly offers parents the highest level of choice when it comes to their children's education, but parents opting for this route must be willing to make the commitment and be sure to properly research all the rules and guidelines in their state before deciding if this is the right path for them and their family.

Other School Choice Options

There are also several other less popular publicly funded school choice options that some states offer. One popular option that has become more available since the COVID-19 lockdowns is virtual schooling. Remote learning paths are available in the private setting, but there are also several options for parents in the public realm. Some states even allow certain types of vouchers to be used to pay for virtual schooling costs. Many publicly funded charter schools offer full-time and part-time remote learning opportunities, but this mode of learning has proven to be highly questionable. For a refresher, the pros and cons of remote learning were discussed in detail in Chapter 15.

Virtual schooling can offer more flexibility and control for parents and can be a very affordable option compared to in-person private schools. However, virtual learning comes with several pitfalls, like excessive screen time, lack of opportunities for social interactions with peers, and the commitment and discipline required to stay engaged and motivated to maintain the level of work needed to stay on track. In addition, parents opting for the virtual schooling route many times find it difficult to get the support they need from the school, and research shows that students enrolled in remote learning courses generally perform at much lower levels than their peers. A study of standardized testing scores in Philadelphia showed that students enrolled in virtual schools had a 100% failure rate. While this is only one study in one city, parents must ensure they understand all aspects of remote learning before opting for the virtual school route.

There are also several options available for parents that combine the homeschooling model with other types of structures and designs. Some districts offer a hybrid homeschool model that enables students to split their time between the traditional classroom and home. The details vary by state, but this could be a good option for parents wanting to dip their toes in the homeschooling pool without jumping in head first. Some families have taken homeschooling to the next level and created what's referred to as personalized learning pods. With this option, families in local communities form small pods where their children are taught in small groups by parents, tutors, or privately hired teachers using personalized curricula. Certain states also allow the use of various voucher programs to fund these pods, which can be used as a stand-alone educational option or as a supplemental hybrid model. Another emerging option is micro-schooling, which is simply learning pods on steroids. Micro-schooling involves the reincarnation of the one-room schoolhouse of centuries past. In this model, parents form their own one-room school with around 15 students of varying ages with curricula and scheduling that fit the individual needs of the students. Micro-schools can be operated publicly, privately, or through a charter school. However, these schools are a fairly new concept, vary in availability depending on the state, and much more research and data collection must be conducted on their level of effectiveness.

Thus, there are many options available for parents today when it comes to education. Parents must be sure to weigh all available options and be willing to commit time to research and decide what path may be best for their children and the overall well-being of their family. Each path will be accompanied by its own unique set of advantages and disadvantages, but if parents want to seize more control over the education of their children, there are more options available now than at any time before.

Is School Choice the Answer?

The educational options available for parents today continue to grow, and with many states now offering ways to reduce the costs of forgoing traditional public schools, parents are increasingly looking for better educational opportunities for their children. Private schools appear to offer many advantages to students, but the annual costs associated with these schools are more than most families can bear, as illustrated below (Educationdata.org):

School Type	Elementary	Secondary	K–12	All Private
Nonsectarian	$20.9K	$28.9K	$25.7K	$25.1K
Catholic	$4.8K	$11.2K	$10.2K	$6.08K
Other Religious	$9.2K	$18.9K	$9.4K	$10.2K
Average	$8.7K	$14.5K	$15.2K	$12.4K

Rates for private schools vary greatly depending on the region, type of school, and grade level, but parents can expect to pay at least several thousand dollars a year for the majority of private schools. For many who can afford the price, these costs are worth it, but unfortunately, for most families, private school is simply out of reach. School vouchers can help cover these costs, but they most often meet only a portion of the total fees involved in private schooling.

Parents who lack the resources for private school, fortunately, now have multiple publicly funded options. However, these options come with various pros and cons and require varying levels of time and commitment. Homeschooling and its hybrid models offer parents the highest level of control but also require the highest level of sacrifice and commitment. Charter schools and magnet schools can provide a much more specialized learning environment that lacks many of the pitfalls of traditional public schooling, but these types of schools enroll students based on lottery systems or maintain high levels of selection criteria, with most students often having little to no chance of acceptance.

It is imperative that parents spend the time and effort required to research the best possible educational path for their children. Every state is different, and it is important to fully understand what types of educational opportunities and resources are available. Finding the right school for a child can be quite a confusing and somewhat discouraging process, but states across the nation are beginning to hand over more control to parents. It is time for parents to seize this opportunity to provide the best learning experience possible and create the best path to success for their children.

Chapter 18: The Future of Education

"Our rapidly moving, information-based society badly needs people who know how to find facts rather than memorize them and who know how to cope with change in creative ways.You don't learn those things in school." ~Wendy Priesnitz

"There is no future without education." ~Rosa Parks

Unfortunately, the future of education in the United States is not very bright. From increasing staff shortages and safety concerns to outdated curricula and embarrassing performance results, public schools have simply failed the citizens of this nation. However, parents, teachers, and other advocates have finally had enough. It almost feels like a bit of revolution is brewing amongst the masses, with debates about the failures of the education system taking center stage around the country and hordes of parents and teachers demanding change.

Perhaps a full-scale educational revolution is exactly what this country needs. When a house becomes so dilapidated that it is no longer livable, we don't call in contractors with caches of sheetrock, concrete, and paint. Instead, we level the deteriorated, broken-down house and erect a new one in its place. This is exactly how public education in the United States should be viewed. The system is in complete shambles, and reformation may no longer be an option. Public schools may have reached the point at which the bulldozers must line up and demolish the entire apparatus, clearing away a foundation to build a new and better path forward. But how would the process even begin? With the level of incompetence, corruption, and lack of motivation among government officials and educational leaders, is there any hope for a better future?

It starts with students. The primary goal of public education is to prepare the youth of the nation for adulthood and provide them with the skills they need to be successful in the real world. The current system has not come close to reaching this goal and seems to be drifting further away from it daily. Although public schools are wrought with a cornucopia of problems and ineffective policies, the number one culprit for their failures is the one-size-fits-all model that has not evolved much since the pre-Civil War era. Public schools have created the same path for every student regardless of that student's skills, talents, and strengths, with college admission representing the designated finish line. Both public education and the Industrial Revolution ended up at the assembly line. The difference between them is the Industrial Revolution made way for the technological revolution. Our educational system has not. Expecting every high school student to be admitted to college has always been an unrealistic expectation. It is even more out of touch with reality as the nation moves well into the 21st century.

It is time to reassess this one-way road. The only way to improve the current situation is to completely eliminate this one-size-fits-all model that has not worked in decades and continues to be highly ineffective. Educational leaders must work together to create varying paths for students, depending on their individual strengths, talents, and interests. This is the only way to increase engagement and performance while providing students the skills they need to be successful in **THEIR** path, not **THE** path.

The simple fact is that most kids will not go to college, and a large percentage of those who do will not obtain a degree. Currently, only around two-thirds of high school students attend some type of college, with a mere 45% enrolling in 4-year programs. Furthermore, of those students enrolled in college, nearly 20% drop out within the first year—the overall dropout rate for colleges and universities in the United States is 40%. So, to recap, only around two-thirds of all high school students attend any type of college, and nearly half of those drop out. What's worse, many of those who drop out will still be riddled with student debt for the rest of their lives. Additionally, many students who do obtain a degree wind up having extreme difficulty finding that high-paying career they were promised.

These are by no means hidden or mysterious data, yet public schools continue to ram the idea of college down the throats of parents and students in every state across the country when the simple truth is that less than half of our high school students ever reach that goal. Goals should be challenging and stretch individual potential, but when goals are unrealistic and unattainable, they are useless. That is the precise position public schools are in. They have created a system that focuses on developing skills designed to reach a goal that most students will never reach, no matter how much time, energy, and money is thrown at them.

So, is college even worth it today? With ridiculously high tuition, student debt upending countless lives, and social and political ideologies driving university curricula, college may not be the golden goose it was once touted to be. What's more, these institutes have recently morphed into authoritarian behemoths hell-bent on controlling every aspect of campus life, censoring free speech and independent thinking while still masquerading as beacons of free thought and independence. But people are waking up, and many are no longer interested in what these snake oil salesmen hawk. More and more high school students and their parents are second-guessing this system, and many are seeking alternative options. A college degree, without a doubt, still holds immense value in this world for some individuals, but when the data are examined more closely, that value fades. While college may be the answer for some students, there are alternative paths for the millions of students who do not possess either the aptitude or desire to attend college.

Is College Worth It?

This debate can be traced as far back as the colonial founding of New College in 1636, which would later become the prestigious Harvard University. But parents and students find themselves asking this question now more than ever before. Here are a couple of interesting statistics. Today, we have around 20 million college students. And we have nearly 45 million individuals carrying a whopping $1.5 trillion in student debt. College tuition has ascended to ridiculous levels, and student loan debt is crushing people across the country of all ages and backgrounds. Furthermore, young adults graduating with a college degree are finding it harder and harder to find that high-paying job. The situation only worsened when the COVID-19 pandemic hit, and universities across the land locked up students in their dorms and shifted to remote learning. When these institutes of higher education continued to raise tuition or charge students the same rates for basically teaching themselves, the straw finally broke the camel's back.

The fact is many high school students are no longer convinced college is the best path to success. Undergraduate college enrollment has dropped by over 5%, according to the National Student Clearinghouse Research Center, resulting in a loss of nearly one million students. Based on recent surveys, only around half of individuals surveyed stated that college is worth the cost, and around 45% of parents said they'd prefer not to send their child to a 4-year college, citing cost as the main reason. Private colleges now cost an average of $39,723 a year, and public out-of-state colleges cost an average of $22,953. Even public in-state colleges run an average of $10,423. Over the last decade college tuition has increased by more than 25%, while inflation increased by less than 3% (based on 2020 data). That's nearly a tenfold increase comparing tuition to inflation.

So even if a student opts for the cheapest alternative, public and in-state, their annual tuition will be more than $10 thousand, and most college students today take 6–8 years to earn a bachelor's degree. Additionally, these prices only include tuition and fees. Students still need to live somewhere and eat, so when living expenses such as room and board, books and supplies, transportation fees, and other related costs are figured into the equation, the average overall cost for an in-state bachelor's degree can exceed $100 thousand. And those students wanting the private school experience? Well, they better have a very rich daddy, a massive endowment fund, or be willing to rack up a quarter-million-dollar debt.

If this situation doesn't seem bad enough, students who make it to the finish line with a diploma in hand and a pointy hat on their head often find themselves standing behind a counter serving cappuccinos or mai tais. In 2020, only half of all college graduates obtained a full-time job within 6 months of graduating, and over a third of college graduates are considered underemployed or work in a job that does not require a degree. In addition, many emerging markets, such as technology, social media, and transportation no longer require employees to have a college degree. Programming, building, and coding involve hands-on skills and problem-solving techniques that many colleges don't offer. Companies like Google, Apple, IBM, and Tesla are more concerned about prospective employees' current knowledge and skill sets, as opposed to that framed piece of paper on their bedroom wall.

Thus, the debate rages on. While recent evidence indicates the college experience may not be worth the cost of admission, obtaining a degree still comes with many advantages, and overall, those who possess a degree generally earn more money, receive more benefits, and live longer and healthier lives. However, the devil is in the details. Some degrees are certainly more valuable than others. It should be no wonder when someone with a bachelor's degree in Russian literature or transatlantic gender studies finds themself wearing a barista apron every morning. Fortunately, this is not the only option available for young adults looking to advance their knowledge and skills after graduating high school. Community colleges, trade schools, and apprenticeships offer low-cost alternatives for those seeking educational options other than price-gouging 4-year universities. To fully understand whether college is the best option, it is necessary to look more closely at the available data and lay out the pros and cons of university life.

Pros and Cons of College

Despite the recent negative atmosphere and rhetoric surrounding colleges across the nation, many still believe they offer the best path to a successful and fulfilled life. Proponents of college claim graduates have higher employment rates, earn more money, and receive more benefits. Yet, rising student debt has inhibited many college graduates from getting married, buying a house, or saving for retirement. The college path may still lead many to the promised land, but for a large percentage of graduates, this path has led them to nothing but a dead end. So, is college worth it anymore?

It has been estimated that the average college graduate earns more than half a million dollars over a lifetime compared to non-degreed peers. Earnings for college graduates are between 70–135% higher than high-school graduates, and The Federal Reserve Bank has calculated a 14% rate of return on a bachelor's degree. Furthermore, college graduates earn an average salary of $78,000 annually, while employees with a high school diploma earn around $45,000 a year. In addition, among *Forbes'* list of America's 400 Richest People, around 85% were college grads.

However, with around 44 million Americans owing an excess of $1.5 trillion in student debt, the return on investment does not appear to be anywhere near what has been promised. Nearly half of those with student debt state that college was not worth it and around 60% of graduates have outstanding debt balances equal to 60% of their yearly income. In addition, missed or late payments result in added fees and lower credit scores, which further exacerbates the problem. Further, interest rates are so high for many graduates it takes years or even decades to begin paying off the actual principal amount. So, while a college graduate may earn significantly more money than a high school graduate, the outrageous amount of debt that accompanies many college degrees eats away at the net gains from that college degree.

Today, only 20% of millennials own their own home, and most claim student debt has delayed home ownership by at least 7 years. What's more, this stat has been brought up previously, but it's mind-blowing that a shocking 40% of parents currently have at least one adult child still living at home. This is an alarming and somewhat pathetic trend, and many of these adult children are college graduates who have not found meaningful employment or lack the finances and/or independent skills to live alone.

This system has spiraled out of control and has become an embarrassment compared to our international peers. In the United Kingdom, college tuition at public universities is capped at €10,000 per year. Further, loans are paid in installments and only after reaching a specified income level. Public universities in France cost students under €1,000 per year, and in Switzerland, tuition at public universities does not exceed €5,000 annually. Germany and Norway offer free tuition to all international students, and Sweden offers free PhD programs for anyone, regardless of nationality. Something has definitely gone awry in this country, and although the European model may not be appropriate for the United States, government and educational leaders must find a way to mend the broken and corrupt financial situation that is plaguing colleges and universities across the entire country. When mountains of debt are figured into the equation, for many students, a college degree may actually be more of a future detriment than an asset.

But what about all those job opportunities accompanied by the litany of benefits and other touted perks? The number of jobs requiring college degrees has grown tremendously in the 21st century. In the 1970s, 72% of jobs required a high school degree or less, but by 2017, that number had decreased to 34%. According to Georgetown University data, from 2010 to 2016, 99% of job growth fell to workers with some type of college degree, including associate's degrees. Furthermore, unemployment rates have almost always remained lower for college graduates compared to non-degreed workers, and nearly 60% of college-degreed workers state they are extremely satisfied with their jobs compared to 50% of those with a high school diploma and 40% of those without a high school diploma. Many jobs requiring college degrees also come with more benefits. Around 70% of college graduates have access to employer-provided health insurance as well as access to some type of retirement plan compared to only around 50% of high school graduates. However, with debt collectors now seizing portions of borrowers' retirement accounts and social security benefits, the long-term gains may not be realized for those students with mounds of unpaid debt.

The truth is that many college graduates do find jobs. The problem is that many of these jobs do not require the degree these graduates worked so hard to attain and racked up so much debt to afford. According to data from the Department of Labor, up to 17 million college graduates work in jobs that do not require a college degree, and a third of all college graduates are employed in jobs that require a high school diploma or less. These overqualified graduates who work in fields that do not require the degree they worked so hard to earn make 30–40% less than their peers who obtained a job that requires a degree. Additionally, the unemployment rate for recent college graduates was around 4% in 2019, which was actually higher than the overall unemployment rate of 3.6%.

Times are changing, and they're changing at a whirlwind pace. More and more high-quality, high-paying jobs do not require a college degree. Based on 2018 data, 90% of employers stated they would consider candidates without 4-year degrees. This trend escalated even further during the mishandling of the COVID-19 pandemic. As some states shut down businesses and sent millions of workers home, the government continued to dole out thousands of dollars in COVID-aid as well as ridiculously high unemployment payouts. People simply stopped working. When companies and businesses finally began to open their doors as the crazed overreactions died down, they found it extremely difficult to find workers, causing them to expand their scope of potential applicants.

Companies are beginning to put more emphasis on practical skills and hands-on experience, which many colleges and universities don't offer. A college degree no longer equates to talent, and many can learn valuable skills like coding and programming by merely watching YouTube videos. The opportunities to achieve a high rate of success without a college degree continue to grow with big players—Tesla, Google, and Apple no longer require all candidates to possess a degree. The Bureau of Labor Statistics has stated that of the 30 fastest-growing jobs, only six require a bachelor's degree, and another six require a graduate degree. Additionally, there are more ways to tap into one's entrepreneurial spirit today than ever before, allowing savvy go-getters to start their own business in a matter of days or even hours. So, while college graduates have historically been provided many more options for high-quality, lucrative careers, that trend is shifting. Furthermore, a litany of opportunities to control one's own destiny have begun to emerge in a variety of fields and formats.

But what about the claim that degreed individuals live a longer and healthier life with happier and healthier children? Much of the data available do suggest this claim is, in fact, true. In fact, 83% of college graduates report being in excellent health compared to 73% of non-degreed workers. Adults over the age of 65 with a college degree report less cognitive decline, and college graduates smoke significantly less and exercise significantly more than those without a degree. College graduates even report lower blood pressure and lower levels of obesity, and those with college degrees live around six years longer than their non-degreed peers.

Available data also indicate that college graduates have healthier offspring. Children of college graduates have lower mortality rates and significantly lower levels of obesity at only 6% compared to 14% for children of non-degreed parents. Higher levels of letter recognition, as well as much higher participation rates in extra-curricular activities, were also reported for students who had at least one college degreed parent.

Perhaps the data concerning increased positive health outcomes for college graduates are due to a decreased level of safety concerns and injury-related tasks associated with white-collar work. Many non-degreed workers work in fields that expose them to a barrage of unhealthy factors like poor air quality, chemical exposure, or the perils that accompany manual labor. Nonetheless, from the data available, it does appear that a college degree will most likely lead to a healthier life. However, this trend may level off or even reverse itself as the new generation of college grads finds it even more difficult to land that lucrative, meaningful career, struggle to pull themselves out of debt, and likely face increasing mental health issues and other declines in quality of life.

The debate over college is also not only an individualistic issue but a potential powder keg that can affect the entire nation. College students who do not graduate cost taxpayers a buttload of money. Students who drop out within the first year of college cost the federal government around $300 million, and states spend approximately $1.3 billion a year due to wasted grants and other appropriations. Students who do not graduate in at least six years account for nearly $4 billion in lost income and over $700 million in lost state and federal tax revenue. Some financial experts also warn that the continued widespread accumulation of student debt could lead the United States into a financial crisis similar to the recent 2007 housing bubble disaster that sent the world into a tailspin. If institutes of higher education keep operating in the corrupt and dastardly manner in which they conduct business, they may drive our financial markets straight off a cliff yet again.

From a collective stance, however, there are several benefits to graduating from college. College graduates are generally more productive members of society. High school dropouts are over 60% more likely to be incarcerated. Degreed individuals also engage in double the amount of volunteer work and donate blood at much higher levels. Historically, college graduates have had lower levels of unemployment, thus placing less financial strain on society (although this trend seems to be reversing). College graduates most often do not participate in government aid programs, receive private health care, and, overall, cost the country less money than those without a college degree.

There are, of course, many other negative and positive aspects of obtaining a college degree, but the main takeaway is that the college landscape has changed significantly in the last decade. The altering of this landscape was even further catalyzed by the COVID-19 pandemic, and more young people and their parents are asking themselves if college is the right path. Only a couple of decades ago, this was an easy decision, but today, college may, in fact, not be the best option. Tuition has soared while colleges and universities continue to serve up useless curricula that do not prepare students for the real world. What's more, many of these so-called free-thinking institutes of higher education have morphed into authoritarian gatekeepers, infecting their students with various political and social ideologies and mandating that students fall in line with what some might fairly call Orwellian policies. People are simply not interested in what these charlatans offer anymore.

For families who can afford tuition or those students willing to take an alternative route and save money while earning credits through low-priced community colleges and working the system instead of allowing the system to work them, college may be a sensible option. If a student is lucky and talented enough to earn an athletic scholarship or smart and savvy enough to qualify for academic scholarships, college might also be the right path. But keep in mind students on athletic scholarships do pay for college. They just pay with pounds of flesh instead of pounds of greenbacks. Many former college athletes, like myself, face a lifetime of physical health problems due to the wear and tear inflicted upon their bodies through years of intense training and competition. Those ailments are also accompanied by a litany of lifelong mental and physical anguish, as well as the increased medical costs associated with treating those chronic conditions.

It's time for public schools to take notice. Many parents no longer want their children placed on this one-size-fits-all runaway train with a one-way destination that ends at the college admissions office. This can no longer be the one and only goal of our public education system. While a college degree is a great option for some students, those who do not fit the college mold are simply left out in the cold. If the United States really wants to reach the goal of no child left behind, the nation is going to have to make some serious adjustments to the entire foundation of its public education system.

An overwhelming percentage of high school students do not go to college, and many who do never obtain a degree. Schools are doing a horrible disservice to the millions of students who have no desire to go to college or do not possess the skills or resources required for college. The travesty lies in the fact that there is no viable alternative option for these millions of students. States have shut down vocational programs and job training initiatives, and they have shifted away from teaching any type of marketable skills or trades. It is imperative that public schools create alternative paths so every student has a chance to learn and practice the skills that match their strengths and interests. This is the only way the nation can create productive adult citizens who live healthy lives, form nurturing families, meet the needs of their communities, and finally move out of their damn parents' basement.

Turning Back the Clock: The Return of Vocational Training

The future does look quite bleak, but there are several means by which the nation can pull itself out of this disastrous mess. The first step is going back to our roots. Despite the technological takeover that has swept across the globe, the need for vocational training has not been eliminated, and schools must rewind the clock and get back to basics.

Vocational training teaches students valuable skills and trades that prepare them to work in a given field immediately after high school. Vocational programs offer training in such arenas as culinary arts, horticulture, carpentry, electricity, cosmetology, communications, programming, video game and web development, automotive technology and repair, and health care. Public schools can combine meaningful curricula with worthwhile vocational training to better prepare students who may not be college material with an alternative path to success. Vocational education can be offered as a standalone, self-contained school, a separate school that operates within the realm of a traditional school, or as a hybrid model in which students attend a traditional school for part of the day and travel to another location for vocational instruction.

This is not a revolutionary or innovative idea but something public schools have long offered throughout our nation's history. The federal government has provided funding for vocational education since 1917, which has helped millions of students acquire marketable skills that can be used to earn lucrative salaries right out of high school. Vocational training has also been associated with higher future wages. However, vocational education has been on a steep decline for several decades. Starting in the 1980s, states began to increase the number of required courses as well as the number of core subjects needed to graduate. This move led to massive decreases in vocational funding. Combined with the growing notion that a 4-year college degree offers the only metric for success, the result was a drastic decline in the number of students participating in vocational programs. From 1990 to 2009, the number of vocational credits earned by U.S. high schoolers dropped by nearly 15%.

Recently, however, this trend has begun to reverse. In 2015, close to 40 states instituted new policies and regulations related to vocational training, but this recent uptick in vocational interest has not gone far enough. Vocational education has been stigmatized as not good enough, and this elitist, college-bound-or-nothing attitude is what has gotten the nation into this mess. The truth is that many students who leave high school with vocational training can make the same or even more money than their peers who opt for college. Furthermore, vocational training does not necessarily have to substitute for college or other higher education participation after high school. Many vocational students go on to colleges or trade schools to further fine-tune the skills they learned in high school, even further increasing their chances of landing a lucrative job. Computer programmers, electricians, and dental hygienists can earn over $70,000 a year or more—without assuming the burden of student debt. Furthermore, many of the skills acquired in vocational training will be needed in sectors least likely to be taken over by artificial intelligence or will provide skills in areas in which humans will most likely work alongside their future AI counterparts.

Work hard in school so you can earn that scholarship to attend college and obtain that perfect job you need in order to be a happy and productive member of society. That's what kids have been told for the last half-century, but is it true? Students have been overwhelmingly encouraged not to follow their passions, and the nation's obsession with college has created an idealized, utopian world that simply does not, will not, and cannot exist. Public schools make promise after promise to students that they are unable to deliver on, and countless numbers of students are handcuffed from ever reaching their true potential.

There are millions of kids who are excited and motivated to use their hands and minds to engage in solving real-life problems. This is exactly what vocational education provides, and these kids deserve a hell of a lot more than what public schools offer them. There's a pretty obvious reason why dropout rates are lower at vocational schools—kids want to be there. I recently had the opportunity to tour a vocational school, and my mind, as well as the minds of the young students who were with me, were utterly blown. The state-of-the-art resources and facilities this school possessed were like nothing I had ever observed before in a public school. It was the first time I'd actually witnessed students (and myself) become excited about something a public school was offering. Students were building drones and rockets, editing and mixing various forms of media, fixing car and boat engines, working in commercially modeled kitchens, designing video games, and even cultivating plants and raising livestock.

I found myself wondering why this type of instruction was not more widespread and offered to any and all students. It was the first time I've actually seen a school actually using its funds to create the type of learning kids need. But like any aspect of the public education system, cons always accompany the pros. So, is vocational training the key to improving the dire situations affecting schools today, or is it just another bad, overhyped idea?

Overall, the advantages of implementing some type of vocational education in public schools appear to far outweigh the disadvantages. Students in vocational programs learn by doing and spend significantly more time learning, practicing, and applying tangible skills that are required in the workplace. Experience becomes part of the course, and students in these programs graduate with practical experience in a wide variety of fields. Students in vocational programs are exposed to a variety of diverse ideas, cultures, and life experiences, which better prepare them for the highly globalized world of the 21st century. Students can learn how to better communicate and problem-solve with individuals from different backgrounds and gain the insight they need to be successful in the real world.

Students in vocational programs also spend many hours working closely with other students and their instructors, allowing them to build strong, collaborative relationships. These students get the rare chance to actually pursue their passions and work toward goals that interest them instead of the stale and boring one-size-fits-all model they've long been forced to follow. Students in vocational programs generally work harder, are more engaged, and enjoy the school experience at much higher levels. Students perform better and have to deal with a minimal amount of behavior-related issues in vocational classrooms. Many students, especially male students, who struggle to succeed in traditional classrooms that require the ability to stay quiet and remain focused tend to perform much better in vocational settings where they can engage in activities requiring more movement, and these students have opportunities for dozens of daily hands-on activities. Vocational instruction is also highly adaptable, and students can have access to virtual learning as well as opportunities to engage in learning during off-hours, such as evenings, nights, and weekends.

Teachers in vocational programs are most often highly qualified and possess a high degree of program-specific expertise and knowledge about the subjects they teach. Not only can many vocational students finish school faster, graduating ahead of their peers, but they also have a much easier time finding a job. These students graduate from high school with hours and hours of work experience as well as specific training in their chosen field. With increased levels of career guidance, placement, and support, vocational students frequently exit high school with the assets and abilities to immediately move into an apprenticeship, a specialized college or training program, or straight into a professional career. While college-bound students are still fumbling around with admissions paperwork and navigating through the incomprehensible barrage of financial aid brochures, many vocational students are already entering the workforce, collecting paychecks, contributing to society, and creating an independent and successful future for themselves. Vocational students are purchasing cars and signing apartment leases while their college-bound peers are setting up shop in their parent's garage.

There are, however, a few challenges that face vocational programs. Students in these programs do have less of an opportunity to explore a wide range of diverse subjects and topics. Thus, some vocational students may not be as well-rounded as those studying in traditional programs. Vocational education focuses primarily on subjects and curricula centered on the core discipline, providing these students with fewer opportunities to participate in electives and other classes outside their concentration. This could make them a bit less adaptable in the workplace, limiting them to certain types of career paths. Additionally, vocational education is not cheap. Districts will need to become much better at fiscal responsibility, which has not historically been at the top of their list of strengths. Proper equipment and supplies must be purchased for these programs, and highly effective trained instructors must be hired. Schools are going to have to reallocate funds to adequately supply and equip these programs. But remember, the money is there. Schools just have to spend the money more effectively and responsibly.

Thus, it's quite apparent that the pros of vocational training far outweigh the cons. A push for more vocational education will require a total makeover of the ways public schools spend money, but the reconstruction of this ugly duckling (aka school finance) is long overdue. It is time for schools to hit the reset button, and this includes the way in which schools are budgeted as well. Too much money funnels to the wrong places, and the amount of funds that simply get washed down the drain is utterly infuriating.

Vocational education is not the end all be all. It is not the magic bean to sprout a new and innovative system that revives the nation's education system. But it's a damn good start. By moving away from the one-size-fits-all model that continues to fail students and their parents, schools can take the first step to fixing this long-broken system. What's more, the vocational training of today can implement artificial intelligence as well as virtual and augmented worlds into daily curricula, even better-preparing students for the world that lies ahead, giving them the skills and practice they will need to compete against or work in unison with the technological landscape that is usurping the globe. Vocational training is not a new concept; thus, schools will not be required to reinvent the wheel. They merely need to turn back to their roots and resurrect the system that, for over a century, has instilled the skills and provided training for millions of students to achieve high levels of success immediately after high school.

This is the first step to recovery, and it is a fairly easy one. Re-creating thriving vocational programs will act as a sort of litmus test for public schools. If they cannot achieve this goal, any hope for meaningful reform or a re-imaging of a better system may be forever lost. But even if this goal is accomplished, it is merely the first step in a long journey to recovery.

Possible Future Trends in Public Education

Not only have public schools remained unchanged for much of the last century, but they also still function based on an educational model that dates back to the mid-1800s. Times have changed drastically in the last 150 years, while public education has remained mostly stagnant, seemingly unwilling or too inept to adapt to an evolving environment. Of course, new and failed ways of instructing students have surfaced, and technology has slowly begun to infiltrate classrooms. Yet, the methods, values, and ideologies surrounding public education have not shifted to match the realities the world faces today. The ultimate endgame did deviate from the assembly line to the college admission line after WWII, but the framework built around the public education system in the United States still operates via Horace Mann's long outdated Prussian model.

Robots and other artificially intelligent machines (or children in Africa and East Asia) handle most assembly line work these days—the Industrial Revolution has long since passed. Yet, we continue to teach students in factory-model-schools while the factory carries little significance for the overwhelming majority of people across the country. For example, even the bells that signify it's time to go to your next class is an undying remnant of the bells that signified lunch times and shift changes in factories. Today's educational model has shifted to funneling students into institutes of higher learning as opposed to factory life, but as previously discussed, a large percentage of students will never reach that goal. Public schools in the United States have simply lost the ability to adequately prepare young people for any modicum of success in the real world. Students graduating from high school are not prepared for college, and they are not prepared to work in a full-time job. Many don't even possess the skills to function socially. If public schools were a corporation, they would have gone out of business decades ago. They continue to fail to provide the services promised, and they create mediocre products at best.

This situation must change, and more and more parents and other advocates are taking the reins and demanding something be done to fix this mess. Changes are slowly starting to surface in different regions across the country, but these changes have been only moderately effective. However, there are several new trends already beginning to emerge, and researchers have begun to look ahead in hopes of predicting the next wave of reforms that may spark an educational revolution. But are these predictions wishful thinking, a sign of better things to come, or omens of a system-wide collapse? Many of these claims seem near-apocalyptic in nature, while others paint a much more promising utopian-like future. Let's take a look at some of these future predictions.

Today's classrooms have, no doubt, changed since the dawn of the 21st century. Students use tablets and Chromebooks instead of heavy backpacks filled with 40 pounds of textbooks and a plethora of notebooks and binders. Chalkboards and overhead projectors now lie in landfills while teachers and students use high-tech, interactive smartboards. But these are merely cosmetic, material additions that have slightly enhanced the learning experience. The system itself remains largely unchanged.

It has been predicted that new forms of education will emerge for a variety of reasons. For one, the recent surge of technology has provided new and innovative means to deliver instruction and increase student engagement at relatively low costs. These new technologies do come with many downsides. However, the current technological revolution has made its way into public education, and it will continue to lead the charge as schools move to improve how they operate. Many schools in certain regions of the country have also faced significant revenue declines, and decades of fiscal mismanagement are finally catching up to their bottom lines. Schools will be forced to make the best use of the resources they have at their disposal, and many districts will have to significantly alter the ways in which they provide instruction. When these trends are combined with the recent surge in public sector innovations, new systems could naturally emerge to fill in the gaps to meet the needs of parents and students.

Experts and researchers have predicted several new models of schooling that may surface over the next decade. With teacher shortages showing no signs of improvement, it is predicted virtual schools could begin to sprout up around the nation. Teachers could eventually function more as facilitators, spending most of their time monitoring students' self-paced learning, assessing, grading, and assisting with problems as they arise. Hybrid schools could also likely become the norm in which full-time instructors manage the online learning experience by monitoring progress and assigning work, but students would also have access to virtual as well as face-to-face support from certified teachers, tutors, or paraprofessionals. Schools that function as brokers of instruction by contracting out hourly-rate teachers may also crop up to provide specific instruction in areas such as music, science, or math taught by individuals working in the industry or by grad students. Schools may also partner with local colleges or universities to provide instruction under a pay-per-course model.

Public schools have so far not demonstrated much confidence in their ability to solve teacher shortages; therefore, options like these may be the only path forward. However, these models may prove to be a step in the wrong direction and an excuse for the problem rather than an actual fix to the system. So, while the actual physical model of future schooling is almost impossible to accurately predict, the methods by which students receive instruction will definitely change, and researchers predict that the current one-size-fits-all system will have no choice but to deteriorate. Hopefully, they are correct.

The future of education could and should provide a way for each child to have a customized learning experience tailored specifically to augment and encourage their strengths while also improving their weaknesses. Flexible classroom arrangements, schedules, and assignments could be the future norm, with teachers ceasing the practice of one assignment and one assessment for all. By creating more flexible classroom environments, students could be provided with multiple mediums to demonstrate their comprehension of a variety of subject matters by using dioramas, recorded videos, creative PowerPoint presentations, research papers, or the old-school fill-in-the-blank or multiple-choice assessments.

The regurgitative model public schools currently implement does not address many of the needs that are becoming increasingly important in the new world; thus, learning will have to become more personalized, self-paced, and self-directed. Schools will need to evolve to teach children the skills they will need to survive in the changing world in which we live. Schools will be forced to focus more on how global awareness and how the world at large affects the everyday lives of citizens in the United States. If nothing else, the COVID-19 pandemic surely taught the world that. Students will need to learn analytical and problem-solving skills to increase innovation and creativity. They will need to understand advanced technological topics such as programming and data science. Knowing how to stream your favorite Netflix show or create the next viral TikTok video simply won't cut it anymore. Students will also need to acquire a much higher level of interpersonal skills related to cooperation, emotional intelligence, and social aptitude. It can be blamed on social media, the pandemic, poor parenting, or the weather, but the result remains the same: children today have completely lost social competence.

Many predict this needed shift to a more personalized and flexible learning experience will alter the role teachers play, reallocating them to more of a facilitator role than content deliverers. With more self-paced and project-based learning emerging through increased digitized content and online models, teachers may soon take a back seat in the learning process. This may not seem like an ideal situation, but with teachers leaving the field en masse, schools may not be left with many other options. Teachers may find themselves in a situation where they spend most of their time creating individualized lesson plans for students and then allow those students to move ahead at their own pace, with the teacher functioning more as a guide on the side than an instructor.

Some of these predicted trends, however, could result in cascading effects that upend the entire education system. One trend that many predict will continue is the decline in public school enrollment. Historically, around 90% of students in the United States attend public schools, but that number has fluctuated, dipping down to 85% in recent years, and it continues to decline. Many families who can afford the costs are switching to private schools, and the number of homeschooled students continues to rise, especially with privately formed learning pods popping up across various communities. What's more, with kindergarten attendance being non-compulsory in many states, some parents are opting out of the experience altogether, instead sending their kids to daycare or keeping them at home.

This decrease in enrollment could, in turn, lead to a significant decrease in funding for public schools since many receive money based on per-student attendance. Of course, with fewer students, schools would naturally need less money; however, they would no doubt be faced with an even further strain on dwindling resources. Hopefully, this trend would force public school administrators and leaders to adopt more fiscally responsible practices, but this is probably a utopian pipe dream. What will happen if the day comes when states can no longer provide enough funding or hire enough teachers for public schools to function? Parents and students across the nation may, unfortunately, find out.

As public school budgets continue to wither and teachers proceed with their mass exodus from the field, the landscape surrounding schools may be compelled to adapt. Parents could increasingly begin to opt for the homeschool route as more and more public schools deteriorate into wastelands unable to meet the needs of their students. Virtual schooling and e-learning could become the norm as students are forced out of classrooms due to a lack of teachers and the resources needed to create positive and productive learning environments. Physical campuses could cease to exist in many regions, with students forced to huddle up in libraries, recreational centers, and other public spaces that hopefully offer a strong Wi-Fi connection.

The worst-case scenarios could play out for millions of families who cannot afford private schooling, do not have the time or energy to homeschool, or lack the resources required for virtual schooling options. These unfortunate families may find their children literally being factory educated with dozens or even hundreds of students housed in large warehouse-like structures sitting in front of computers while a contracted instructor roams the aisles facilitating and assisting students as they work through self-paced lessons run by artificially intelligent systems. Schools may be forced to simply plug students into the matrix and hope for the best.

But this worst-case scenario does not have to be a reality. Schools can create a better path forward, and many experts and researchers point to technology as the holy grail. Augmented and virtual reality is predicted to greatly enhance the learning experience for all students. Augmented reality (AR) would allow students to visualize additional information layered over what they see in the real world, and this technology can be accessed simply via smartphone apps. By incorporating AR-enabled wearable devices, students would be able to explore whole new worlds without having to hold up a device. Virtual reality systems would also allow students to transport themselves to any place in the world at any time throughout history, creating completely immersive educational opportunities. Students would be able to take virtual field trips and create simulations to practice a wide array of skills, whether academic, behavioral, or social.

As 3D printing becomes more affordable, schools will possess the ability to print realistic models to better educate students on a variety of subjects and concepts that are difficult to mentally visualize and grasp. Dogs would no longer be able to eat homework as cloud computing could become the norm for receiving and turning in assignments. Students would be able to use their electronic devices to access all their notes, homework, and other learning resources, giving countless students the freedom to work on projects and assignments anywhere, anytime. Students could also tap into digital libraries, allowing them unfettered access to the district's wide selection of reading material. Social networking would allow students to create virtual worlds while sharing ideas freely while teachers moderate.

Humans have now become like goldfish with attention spans now sitting at an estimated paltry span of 8 seconds. Bite-sized learning could become the norm, and game-based learning will need to be implemented at high levels to keep students engaged. Students would even be able to build and design their own games, helping them develop a variety of skills such as problem-solving, language, and storytelling. Super, high-tech devices may find their way into classrooms with paper-thin note-taking pads and flexible, lightweight OLED-based displays that can be folded up like a newspaper. Biometric eye tracking could even find its way into many schools, providing educators with valuable feedback relating to whether a student is engaged and understands the concepts being taught. Eye movement patterns could be integrated with interactive artificial intelligent systems that adjust content to individual student learning styles. Public schools may, in fact, begin to resemble scenes and settings only previously imagined in Isaac Asimov's novels.

This is the best-case scenario, but is this possible future a reality? As Moore's law continues to take over, the costs of these technologies will continue to decline, allowing schools more access to them. But to create the utopian, futuristic landscape described above, schools will have to become much more fiscally responsible, and they will need to find a way to hire and maintain the workforce needed to implement this new educational wonderland.

This section has touched on some of the ways in which public schooling could evolve throughout the 21st century. Many of these predictions are quite promising while others paint a very dim picture. The worst-case scenarios seem unimaginable, but quite a few unimaginable events have transpired as of late. The best-case scenarios would be ideal, but thus far, public schools have not proven they are capable of shifting course in a positive direction. The true future of education, like most topics discussed in this book, will most likely land somewhere in the middle of the swinging pendulum.

A Realistic Future

So far, we've looked at various future outcomes in public education that seem to cover the entire spectrum of possibilities. But based on the current landscape, what is the most likely scenario that will play out over the next couple of decades? Fully embracing emerging technology and properly incorporating it into the classroom will no doubt be the only realistic path forward; however, the world is most likely a decade or more away from technology advancing to the stage where it can be seamlessly infused into the curricula and daily operations of public schools. Artificial intelligence and other innovations like virtual and augmented reality are simply not ready to be fully incorporated into the learning process. Therefore, the more pertinent question may be how schools need to adapt in the meantime. The world of public schooling seems to be entering a sort of purgatory-like era in which an optimistic future can be seen on the horizon, yet the system may not be able to hold itself together until it reaches the end of the rainbow.

Teachers, some campus administrators, and other support staff are exiting the field at an alarming rate, and there do not seem to be any answers on how to slow down this mass exodus. What's worse, no one is waiting on deck to fill these openings, leaving schools desperately searching for anyone even remotely qualified to fill them. It appears that the best way forward may be creating a new system where artificially intelligent systems form a quasi-marriage with teachers, working together simultaneously and seamlessly to create individualized, self-paced learning that can connect with a wide range of students. From my observations, many schools are already in the very early stages of transitioning to this type of model because students already work for large portions of the day individually on their Chromebooks or laptops while teachers facilitate the process. Furthermore, although this may not seem like an ideal path forward, and I personally don't believe it is most optimal, there do not seem to be any other promising options available. Schools will simply be checkmated into adapting the best they can based on the resources available.

However, this technological vision is still quite far out of reach, and it is undetermined whether the public education system can sustain itself until this new world materializes. If these battered schools can manage to limp ahead, dragging themselves across the finish line, the distant future of public education could, in fact, be very bright. But, the entire institute will have to completely revamp its mindset and the ways in which it operates throughout the next decade and beyond.

Future teacher training would need to be fully reinvented, with up-and-coming educators being coached on how to successfully operate all the required technological devices as well as how to work in unison with the artificial intelligence systems that would guide the learning process. Teacher shortages would be less impactful as artificial intelligence systems pick up the slack. These new-age teachers would be molded into a hybrid being unrecognizable by today's teachers. This new breed of educators would need to be highly tech-savvy and fully understand how to incorporate this bold system into meaningful learning opportunities for any type of student. Students would be guided throughout their learning by artificial intelligence-led learning systems where the teacher would act as a facilitator, ushering students through the learning process. These new teachers would need to be able to address both technical and educational issues that arise; thus, they would need to be trained as educators and technicians. Additionally, this new type of educational model would have different variations and means of implementation, allowing it to be used in traditional, vocational, or special education classrooms with teachers who would be trained to address the specific needs of students in those programs.

This may seem like a scenario from the latest sci-fi movie streaming on Netflix, but a system like this may be the only reasonable means of survival for public schools in the future. Revamping the teacher's role paired with incorporating artificial intelligence systems looks to be the most optimistic and realistic path forward. I'm by no means suggesting this is a perfect model, or even a very good one, for that matter. I am only postulating that this may be the best model moving forward based on the resources and staff public schools have at their disposal. This is the road every other industry is embarking on—why should public education be any different? Technology has become enmeshed in nearly every aspect of our lives, and artificial intelligence is advancing at a mind-blowing pace. Most workers of the future will work hand-in-hand with these new technologies, and public schools will have to hop aboard this train if they do not want to find themselves twiddling their thumbs at the station.

Of course, some kinks would need to be worked out of this new system. Sports and other extra-curricular activities would be greatly affected by this new world of public education. Whether the staff and funds would still be available to support these programs remains a mystery for now. A time may come when these programs need to be shifted to a privatized sector where a hybrid model could be created with schools working in unison with private organizations to ensure students get equal opportunities to participate in sports, the arts, or music-related activities and programs. This type of system would definitely come with some potential negative outcomes, but it could be the only way to sustain these programs in the future.

This new system would also be plagued with creating means for students to interact in social situations to build their social and emotional intelligence. Naturally, students would interact with each other online in a wide variety of ways, from chatting and conferencing to creating virtual and augmented spaces in which to interact. However, these students would still need to spend time interacting in the physical world. Therefore, recess and physical education classes would have to remain in place, as well as other means for real social interaction in order to ensure students have ample opportunities to be physically active and practice interacting in physical spaces with their peers.

Despite the obvious drawbacks and many unforeseen problems associated with implementing a completely new way of educating our youth, this way forward appears to be the most realistic and conducive way for public education to proceed. The bottom line is that the current outdated model is failing everyone...students, parents, teachers, administrators, and the nation as a whole. It is time for a reckoning, an educational awakening if you will, somewhat like a new Age of Enlightenment in which the country shifts its entire mindset on how public schools should operate. There will, however, be a barrage of impending roadblocks. It's going to be quite a bumpy ride for the foreseeable future.

Even if this new innovative future becomes a reality, schools must still discover some means of propping up and underpinning this collapsing institute while they wait for this innovative future to arrive. It's extremely difficult to predict the rate of technological advancement, but based on current trends, it could be a decade or more before this new type of hybrid system or something similar can be fully implemented in the public school realm. These next 10 years could prove to be the hardest decade schools have ever faced, and it will take time and effort to keep this ship afloat until the lifeboats appear on the horizon.

I walk through schools every day, and I witness the chaos unfolding in classroom after classroom. I can't help but notice the distraught looks of abdication smeared across the faces of most teachers and administrators. I see unengaged students, who have zero interest in what is being taught to them, haphazardly attempt to navigate the social perils of today's public school environment with little to no social aptitude, resulting in nothing but insults, bullying, threats, and downright assaults. I encounter confused and frustrated parents struggling to raise their children while their faith and trust in their communities and the schools that serve them wanes more every day. And most troubling of all, I see those around me relinquishing all hope, throwing in the towel, and walking away.

Unfortunately, most interested parties have not yet figured out the best way for this system to hang on until this seemingly promising future comes into view. And, after over 2 decades working in public schools, other than the ideas that have been suggested in this book, I have also yet to discover the magical elixir to rehabilitate this shattered institute. My guess is that it's going to take quite a bit of luck. However, if educational and government leaders finally stand up, do the work they're being paid copious amounts of money to do, and push for meaningful change, there is hope the nation's public education system can sustain itself long enough for the cavalry to arrive.

Thus, the situation in public schools today does, in fact, seem to be as dire as many claim, but it is not hopeless. However, there is one promise I can make: The situation will definitely get much worse before it gets better. Teachers and support staff are leaving in droves, violence is running rampant in schools across the nation, curricula are outdated and unengaging, and kids are, quite frankly, not doing well in today's world by any meaningful metrics. Yet, throughout history, the United States has managed to pull itself out of one horrendous mess after another, so perhaps, as usual, we will figure it all out in the end. The question that remains is how much damage will be done to our nation's youth during this impending educational reformation.

Chapter 19: Epilogue

The strength of the United States has begun to waiver more than at any time since the Civil War wrecked the nation a century and a half ago. A highly educated population is the foundation of a strong society, and a focus on increasing the literacy rate and overall education of the citizens of this country is exactly what accelerated its rise to the top. Unfortunately, the country has shifted away from creating and maintaining properly functioning, competent, and effective educational institutions. The nation's relationship with public education has become akin to a broken marriage in which everyone keeps showing up, but no one really seems to give a hot damn anymore. Educational leaders must cease this going-through-the-motions mindset and start actually earning their paychecks.

The future of public education could unfold in a variety of ways, and no one really knows for certain how that future will play out. The forthcoming utopia predicted by some is most likely far from a reality, but the apocalyptic-like scenarios anticipated by others do not have to manifest themselves either. A multitude of strategies and policies can be adopted and put into practice by states and districts across the country, which could create a better path forward for the nation's public education system.

The number one issue that public education must address is the widespread fiscal irresponsibility that plagues school districts in every state in the union. States and local districts must stop crying about not having enough money and instead spend the hordes of cash they receive from tax-paying citizens in a more competent and responsible manner. Before any other issue is to be addressed, these financial problems must first be remedied. As I type these words, neighborhoods are scattered with giant placards urging voters to approve a multi-million-dollar bond package that will infuse hundreds of millions of dollars into a nearby school district. Great, right? Well, maybe not.

The problem with this spending package is that it is earmarked for costs only associated with infrastructure, security, and technology. Additionally, recipients must ensure they spend every single dollar, regardless of whether they actually need that much money; otherwise, they risk not getting as much the next time the bond wagon comes rolling through town. What about higher-priority needs that must be addressed, such as the staff shortages that are crushing schools throughout the district? What about the lack of special education resources that have dwindled to the point where the district does not even have the competence required to meet state laws and expectations? What about resources to address the cornucopia of behavioral and mental health issues more and more students deal with today? Instead, if passed, they will spend this $300 million-plus bond package to buy more computers for kids to play Minecraft in lieu of listening to teachers. They'll drop countless millions on door locks, security cameras, and bulletproof glass in the astronomically low chance a school shooter happens to show up in the front office. They will deplete tens of millions more to upgrade football stadiums and build new but shoddily constructed, portable buildings to house the kids they can't find teachers to teach.

It's time for a little math. At a salary of around $60,000 a year, this district in question could use that $300 million to hire 5,000 teachers. There are currently only around 1,500 teachers employed in the entire school district. This is simply one example of hundreds, if not thousands, of cases across the nation in which government and educational leaders have grossly mismanaged funds. When schools spend money haphazardly, everyone suffers, and the damage trickles down, infecting every aspect of the system. By merely creating methods to ensure the billions of dollars injected into public education are spent where that money is actually needed, schools can begin to address the real problems they face daily. What's more, the only way to address these problems before they bring down the entire system is to manage money more responsibly and effectively. If there are no teachers left to teach, it won't matter how nice the new stadium looks or how many upgraded Chromebooks are plugged into the nearest charging port. By adopting fiscally responsible practices, schools can, instead, create a system that focuses on spending money where it is needed most.

Teacher shortages are one of the top issues affecting countless regions across the country. Allocating more money to raise teacher salaries and create more financial incentives is the only way to address this issue. There is simply not enough incentive for young people to take the time and spend the money required to become certified teachers. The yearning to change young lives and create future generations of productive innovators has withered away. Even those who are still able to find this intrinsic motivation to teach most often become highly disillusioned after only the first couple of years. Young people are opting for other professional fields that offer more money and come with more perks and prestige. Public schools must find ways to lure workers, and financial incentives are by far the best allurement. Pay has to be increased for teachers across the board, and salaries must also be raised for paraprofessionals, substitute teachers, and other support personnel.

These funds can be quite easily reallocated. A great example was just discussed—bond packages are simply not a great way to fund schools. They lock schools into a very narrow window of options on what can be purchased and if the money is needed or would be better spent elsewhere...well, that's just too bad. Unless a means can be created to allow bond spending to be less restrictive, it has to go. Additionally, public schools have way too many district administrators. Take a brief tour of any district website and scroll through the myriad of contact lists for all the bigwigs resting on their laurels down at the administrative castle. Dozens or, most likely, hundreds of these administrators will be found, and most of them have minimum annual salaries starting in the mid to upper $70,000 range, with many earning six figures. The number of administrators in public education has risen more than six-fold compared to teachers over the last 2 decades. Cutting administrative positions will not only save money but it will also naturally reduce the bureaucratic burden placed on countless schools throughout the land. It's not that complicated. By merely cutting a significant percentage of these positions, districts will suddenly find themselves with a budget surplus and significantly fewer bureaucratic hurdles over which to leap.

This extra surge of capital can also be used to mend the incredibly broken special education system that is collapsing at an even faster rate than the overall school system and may very well become the final nail in the coffin. These high-need students can be found wrecking general education classrooms across the nation, but this landscape has evolved only because there is not enough staff available to support them. The teacher shortage crisis has become even more detrimental to special education programs. These are not easy jobs. These students are extremely difficult to work with, and it is nearly impossible to find quality teachers to take on these positions. Furthermore, many districts cannot even hire an adequate number of specialists and evaluation personnel, which are an essential foundation for the entire system. But why is this trend continuing to worsen?

Well, other than the chaotic and poorly run bureaucratic mess in which these individuals would find themselves stuck, it's mostly about the money. When one can earn significantly more money with significantly fewer headaches in the private sector, there's not much incentive to work in public education. Special education teachers must be paid more than their general education counterparts, whether by means of a simple salary increase or through added annual stipends. Additionally, evaluators and other specialists should be paid at rates similar to those in the private sector. This is the best and most likely the only way to entice these individuals to view public education as a realistic career path.

Better fiscal management is also the first step in addressing the outdated and unengaging learning models public schools have adopted. It is also a way to create more real-world-centered curricula that will actually prepare students for the life ahead of them. Schools must create more student-centered models of instruction that are highly personalized and flexible. A student's strengths, weaknesses, and interests should be detected early on, and each student's learning should proceed based on this valuable information. Some students excel at sitting at a desk all day listening to the teacher and remaining highly engaged in all required activities and tasks. Unfortunately, most kids don't operate like this anymore. Many are highly visual learners, and a large percentage, especially boys, are tactile learners who must move and be actively engaged, not only mentally but physically. The one-size-fits-all model public schools continue to use does not work, and by persistently sticking with this method, more and more students are falling through the cracks.

There is also an ongoing crisis in this country with young males. Throughout the last half-century, the United States has consistently leveled the playing field in education between girls and boys, and girls have begun to take over. When female students were finally allowed the same opportunities as boys, they shined. More girls now graduate high school than boys, and 60% of college students today are female, while significantly more boys have behavioral problems than girls, with a 25% higher suspension rate. In 10 out of 50 states, girls are a full grade level ahead of boys, and in all 50 states, girls are, on average, half a grade ahead of their male counterparts. Seventy percent of high school valedictorians are girls. Additionally, men have accounted for over 70% of the overall drop in college enrollment over the past 5 years, and it is estimated that within a few years, there will be twice as many female college graduates as males. Girls are simply better at school, and more specifically, they function better in the current model. Overall, girls have a much easier time sitting at a desk all day, following instructions, and remaining engaged in the mind-numbing tasks students are required to complete daily.

This trend cannot continue. We need both males and females to have the same opportunities for success in public schools. It's great that females have now moved beyond their male counterparts who dominated them throughout...well...all of history. However, as a nation, we need both boys and girls to graduate from high school with skills to function in the real world, and there are two main ways to achieve this.

First, schools must figure out a way to hire more male teachers. Only around 25% of all public school teachers are male, and less than 20% of elementary teachers are male. That is a disgrace to the system. Public schools consistently talk about hiring more diverse sets of teachers, yet over 80% of elementary teachers are female. It's no wonder why young boys struggle so much when the only male they see on campus is the custodian. It would be illegal and highly unethical to pay men more than women in education, but schools must find a way to de-feminize the teaching profession. There is no easy answer to this problem, but it starts with finding ways to encourage young college-aged males to join the field. A good start would be for districts to infuse massive recruiting efforts into job fairs, high schools, and colleges in hopes of convincing more males to view teaching as a legitimate career path. In addition, increasing salaries across the board will naturally pique more interest among all potential applicants, including males.

The second way schools can improve the situation for males has already been discussed in detail: vocational training. The techniques and philosophies embedded in vocational education match the personalities and strengths of males more than any other educational model. Males often learn best kinesthetically, and this type of learning is best found in vocational training. Boys who cannot sit still, who are highly unengaged, and who consistently act out nearly always improve on every metric when moved into a vocational program. Once again, by becoming more fiscally responsible, public schools can find new and innovative ways to increase the population of male teachers and create more hands-on learning opportunities that can be most easily addressed via vocational education.

Public schools spend close to $2 billion a year on standardized testing, which is enough money to hire over 33,000 teachers at a $60,000 annual salary. Standardized testing is no longer a very accurate measure of student performance. Of course, schools will need to have some means of assessing student growth and overall progress, but there are many other ways to accomplish this task. Portfolios, GPA scores, work samples, game-based assessments, performance-based assessments, multiple measures, or low-stake testing are all great alternative ways to gauge student progress. With the increased infusion of new technology into classrooms and a continued shift away from the one-size-fits-all model of learning, standardized testing should become as extinct as dinosaurs. There is no longer a standard student; ergo, there is no longer a need for standardized testing.

More money also means more access to emerging technology, but this can become a tricky situation for schools. Schools must be careful not to simply embark on the technological spending sprees that often accompany the previously discussed massive bond packages. Instead, they must responsibly budget for meaningful and effective technology that will be used frequently by students and teachers to enrich the learning experience and environment. Technology will have to remain an integral part of public education, but it must be the correct technology. Principals do not need upgraded 50-inch computer monitors, and closets should not be filled with unused robots, drones, and stacks of iPads and Chromebooks. Many schools act like they've just received a million-dollar voucher to embark on a spending frenzy at the local Best Buy. Schools have to do a much better job at actually looking at the data and doing the research required to understand exactly what technology they need and how it can be used to improve student performance and outcomes.

Every student should have access to some type of computing device in school, whether it's a laptop, desktop, or tablet. Virtual and augmented reality will also, no doubt, become the future, and public schools will have to find meaningful ways to incorporate this technology into classrooms. When the time is right, technology has reached a reasonable cost point, and a plan has been formulated to address exactly how the technology will be used to improve the learning experience, then...and only then...should schools go all in on the technology. However, timing is everything, and schools must be sure the technology they spend millions of tax-payer dollars on is going to have long-term benefits for students. Schools will also have to do a much better job of monitoring new technology and ensuring that students do not abuse it or use it inappropriately or maliciously. Technology will be a major player in the future of public education, but schools must improve upon the methods used to purchase and implement this equipment.

COVID-19 recovery ia one of the biggest obstacles schools will face in the coming decade. Students from all ages, all regions, and all walks of life were completely wrecked academically and emotionally during the COVID-19 pandemic. Recovery will be an extremely difficult process as the academic performance of a majority of students in all grades fell drastically due to school closures and other COVID-related lockdowns. Behavior problems have escalated to unprecedented levels, and mental health issues have begun to spread throughout student populations like wildfire. However, there is some good news. The federal government has allocated nearly $200 billion for public schools to address the litany of deficits inflicted upon students by these school closures.

Yet again, though, schools must use this money in a responsible manner. The rules regarding spending this money are quite loose, so schools have a high level of autonomy over its use. If these funds are directed to the high-need areas discussed above, like staff issues, better curricula and learning models, increased hands-on learning opportunities, and meaningful and effective technology, schools will naturally address and improve many of the deficits inflicted by the poor management of the COVID-19 pandemic. This money could also be used to hire quality teachers or tutors and the proper resources needed to bring these struggling students back to where they need to be academically and socially. This will not, however, be an easy process, especially in the social development realm.

Students today simply lack adequate social and behavior management skills to function productively in the real world. Whether due to poor parenting, excess technology use, something in the water, or the overall collapse of society, kids today struggle significantly to control their emotions, build positive relationships, and interact socially with their peers and adults. This deteriorating landscape has been a key catalyst to the wave of violence, disruption, and chaos infecting schools across the land. Districts will need to allocate more resources to hire qualified staff and increase curricula related to social and emotional learning. Remember, real and honest SEL is not about sexual identity or orientation, it is not about critical race theory, and it is not about any other socioeconomic issues. Topics like these are nothing more than social engineering. Any attempt to indoctrinate a child with questionable ideologies is not SEL but some lunatic educator gone rogue. SEL is simply about teaching kids how to be better humans.

There are several reasons why young adults today cannot live independently, cannot find and maintain meaningful employment, and cannot form and sustain quality relationships, but one glaring cause is a lack of adequate social and emotional intelligence. If schools hope to prepare young people for the world ahead of them, they are going to have to address these social deficits, and they are going to have to find a way to convince parents to get on board. The hyperbolic scare tactics surrounding SEL have seriously clouded the issue. Yes, there are, without a doubt, some slimy little weasels out there attempting to indoctrinate and harm children, but it is certainly not the norm. Fear-mongering zealots have instilled terror in parents across the country, causing them to shriek in horror at the mere sound of the phrase social and emotional learning. But fear not, this curriculum is **PROPERLY** designed to create better behaved, more productive, more socially apt, and overall happier children. Schools will have to learn to work in unison with parents as a team to better equip today's youth with the social aptitude and behavior management skills they need to achieve and maintain a productive and meaningful life.

The rise in behavior issues is one of the most important concerns in public education today, but schools will naturally see decreases in violence, aggression, and overall disruptions in the classroom and in the home if parents and school personnel simply work together to improve the social and emotional well-being of these students. However, increased SEL instruction cannot be the only means to solve this issue; schools also need to discover new and unique ways to address the barrage of discipline problems facing them daily. A recent push for more restorative justice practices could be a good start. With restorative justice, students would seek to mend the harm they have inflicted and rebuild the damage done to relationships affected by their actions, giving students a better chance to move past their transgressions with a clean slate. This practice can teach students conflict resolution skills, forgiveness, and empathy.

Consequences must also become more logical, consistent, and reasonable. Suspensions, detentions, and alternative placements simply do not have a real impact on today's students. If a student vandalizes a restroom, then that student should have to clean the restroom every day for a specified number of days. If a student wastes class time or disrupts the learning environment, then that student should have to come in on Saturday to make up that time. If a student bullies or threatens peers or staff, they must write a detailed apology that lists all the positive attributes and characteristics of the person whom they offended. Students who decide to fight each other must come together in a face-to-face meeting, work out their differences, and then be required to complete some type of school-based project together. Schools of the future will need to focus on turning punitive consequences into valuable social learning opportunities.

But schools will, of course, have to convince parents to hop aboard their train to a brighter future. Parent involvement is the number one predictor of student success. Schools will need to find new ways to encourage parents to take an active role in the education of their children, and parents are going to have to step up and commit to dedicating the time and energy necessary to create a partnership with local schools in their community. Only by building positive and productive relationships can schools and parents form the alliances needed to guide today's students through the labyrinth of life they are facing.

Parents want their children to be educated, not indoctrinated. School leaders must push back relentlessly against the constant salvo of political, cultural, and social contagions that have begun to infiltrate and infect schools. The classroom is no place for these viral ideologies—they do nothing but create tension and distract students from achieving their ultimate goals. Politics and cultural nonsense have weaseled their way into every domain of our lives. Dinner parties are overwhelmed with contentious debates, family members turn on each other, never speaking again, political ads and signs litter every landscape in site, and it's impossible to get through 5 minutes of a sporting event without someone trying to make you aware of some impending social disaster. It's high time we all strive to turn schools into a safe space immune from all this absurdity. Kids today are distracted and confused enough as it is.

Thus, the future of education does not have to follow the projected path of self-destruction. There is a better path forward. Rebuilding this collapsing system will not be easy, but it is not impossible. If government leaders and school officials stand up and demand more fiscal responsibility to actually address the critical needs impacting public education, the road to recovery can begin, but that will merely be the catalyst that gets the engine started. Educational leaders must, in turn, move away from their one-size-fits-all model and implement alternative approaches to learning in which **ALL** students have the opportunity to reach their full potential. Technology will be an integral player in this future landscape, but schools must ensure this new technology is used effectively and appropriately. Parents and schools will need to form partnerships and commit to working together to provide the best environments in the classroom and in the home, with all parties working in unison to ensure students get the academic, emotional, and social support they need to prepare them for the real world. This partnership can establish a foundation that will function as the key to the future success of not only our children but also the strength and stability of our nation.

"Do or do not. There is no try." ~Yoda

Notes

Notes for the Introduction

Gatto, John Taylor. *Weapons of Mass Instruction*. Gabriola Island, British Columbia. New Society Publishers. 2009.

K12 Academics. (2022). "The History of Education in the United States."

Wikipedia. (2022). "History of Education in the United States."

Anderson, James D. (1988.) The education of Blacks in the South, 1860–1935. University of North Carolina Press.

Center on Education Policy. (2007). Why we still need public schools: Public education for the common good.

Center on Education Policy. (2011). Public schools and the original land grant program.

Kaestle, C. (1983). Pillars of the republic: Common schools and American society, 1780-1860. Hill and Wang.

Katznelson, I., & Weir, M. (1985). Schooling for all: Class, race, and the decline of the democratic ideal. Basic Books.

Neem, J. N. (2017). Democracy's schools: The rise of public education in America. Johns Hopkins University Press.

Pangle, T. L., & Pangle, L. S. (1993). The Learning of liberty: The educational ideas of the American founders. University Press of Kansas.

Tyack, D., & Lowe, R. (1986, February). The Constitutional moment: Reconstruction and Black education in the South. American Journal of Education, 94(2), 236-256.

Wikipedia. (2022). "Prussian Education System."

Notes for Chapter 1

Startz, Dick. "Do teachers work long hours?". *Brookings Institute: Brown Center Chalkboard*. June 12, 2019.

Krantz-Kent, Rachel. "Teachers' work patterns: when, where, and how much do U.S. teachers work?". *Monthly Labor Review*. March 2008.

Rode, David. (2022). Teachers Work a Shocking Amount of Overtime Hours and It's All Unpaid. BoredTeachers.

McLoud, Shannon. (June 10, 2019). I Get Paid for 180 Days of Work Each Year, but I Actually Work More than 250. WeAreTeachers.

Murray, Corey. "How Many Hours Do Educators Actually Work?" *EdTech Magazine.* August 5, 2013.

Williams, Taryn. "Teachers like me face stigma and guilt when we take a day off- and it's a big reason why behind the mass exodus from my field". *Business Insider.* March 22, 2022.

Riggs, Liz. "The Myth of a Teacher's 'Summer Vacation'". *The Atlantic.* July 2, 2015.

Will, Madeline. "With No Paid Parental Leave, Many Teachers Return to Class Before They're Ready". *Education Week.* April 1, 2019.

Herman, Keith C., Jal'et Hickman-Rosa, and Wendy M. Reinke. "Empirically Derived Profiles of Teacher Stress, Burnout, Self-Efficacy, and Coping and Associated Student Outcomes". Journal *of Positive Behavior Interventions.* 2018. Volume: 20(2). Pages 90-100.

Walker, Tim. "Getting Serious About Teacher Burnout". *NEA News.* November 12, 2021.

Gosner, Sarah. "Schools, Not Teachers, Must Reduce Stress and Burnout - Here's How". *Edutopia.* February 11, 2021.

Gershenson, Seth, and Stephen Holt. "How much do teachers struggle with stress and burnout?". *Brookings Institute: Brown Center Chalkboard.* February 8, 2022.

Notes for Chapter 2

Seril, Lindsey. (December 8, 2021). Teacher Salary by State. Study.

McCarthy, Niall. "The Evolution of U.S. Teacher Salaries In The 21st Century". *Forbes.* April 2, 2019.

Walker, Tim. "Teacher Pay Rises Modestly: 'Now Isn't the Time to Rest'". *NEA News.* April 26, 2021.

Ed 100. (September 2022). Teacher Pay: How Much Do Teachers Get Paid? Ed100.

Reilly, Katie. "'I Work 3 Jobs And Donate Blood Plasma to Pay the Bills.' This Is What It's Like to Be a Teacher in America". *Time.* September 13, 2018.

Huetteman, Emmarie. "Unwieldy Health Costs Often Stand Between Teachers and Fatter Paychecks". *Kaiser Health News.* June 18, 2018.

Value Penguin. (July 30, 2020). Nearly Half a Million Teachers Do Not Have Health Insurance, Leaving Some Financially Exposed to Potential Covid-19 Healthcare Costs. ValuePenguin.

Chang, Alvin. "Teacher pay is falling. Their health insurance costs are rising.". *Vox.* March 16, 2018.

Carrig, David. "How generous are teacher benefits and do they make up for lower pay?". *USA Today.* May 16, 2016.

Milburn, Forrest. "For Many Texas Teachers, Health Insurance Premiums Are Huge – But So Are The Hospital Bills". *Kera News.* April 14, 2019.

Costrell, Robert M. "The Rising Cost of Teachers' Health Care". *Education Next.* January 20, 2013.

Aldeman, Chad. "Teacher pension plans are getting riskier – and it could backfire on American schools". *Brookings Institute.* February 25, 2020.

Aldeman, Chad. (October 25, 2018). Do All Teachers Get Pensions? TeacherPensions.

Kan, Leslie. (April 13, 2016). What Is the Average Teacher Pension in My State? TeacherPensions.

Equable. (September 10, 2020). Understanding the State of Teacher Pension Funding in 2020.

Phipps, Melissa. "The History of Pension Plans in the U.S." *The Balance.* October 14, 2021.

Wikipedia. (May 11, 2022). Pensions in the United States. Wikipedia.

Ed 100. (October 2022). Pension: How Good is a Teacher's Pension? Ed100.

Winters, Marcus A. and Josh B. McGee. "Modernizing Teacher Pensions". *National Affairs.* Winter 2015.

Indeed Editorial Team. (September 30, 2021). What Are Advancement Opportunities for Teachers? And 6 To Consider.

The University of Texas at Austin: College of Education. "Career Paths for Teachers". *Texas Education.* Updated as of 2023.

Tow, David. "Increasing Career Paths for Teachers". *Edutopia.* September 13, 2018.

White, Ron. "Advancement Opportunities in a Teaching Career". *Hearst Newspapers.* June 29, 2018.

Teaching Project. (2015). Teacher Advancement Opportunities.

Learn.org. (Updated 2023). What Are Some Career Advancement Options for Teachers?

Notes for Chapter 3

Eden, Max. "Issues 2020: Public School Spending Is at an All-Time High". *Manhattan Institute.* July 25, 2019.

Peter G. Peterson Foundation. (July 14, 2021). How Is K-12 Education Funded?

Raise Your Hand Texas. (2021). Here is Where We Stand on Public School Funding.

Allovue. (2022). How State & Local Dollars Fund Public Schools. Allovue Blog.

American University. (September 10, 2020). Inequality in Public School Funding: Key Issues & Solutions for Closing the Gap.

Allovue. (2022). How Are Public Schools Funded? Allovue Blog.

Wikipedia. (2022). Public school funding in the United States.

Robinson, Rick. "How Do School Bonds Work?" *Biz Fluent*. November 8, 2018.

Semuels, Alana. "Good School, Rich School; Bad School, Poor School". *The Atlantic*. August 25, 2016.

Bachemin, Micah. February 20, 2020. "Experiences in Title I vs. Non-Title I Schools".

We Go Public. (2022). How Do School Bonds Work?

Camera, Lauren. "How the Title I Money Is Distributed". *US News*. June 1, 2016.

Office of State Support. (October 24, 2018). Improving Basic Programs Operated by Local Educational Agencies. www2.ed.gov/programs/titleiparta/index.html.

National Center for Educational Statistics. (2021). Title I (Fast Facts).

International Center for Settlement of Investment Disputes. (2022). How much money do schools spent on sports?

Smith, Morgan. "Athletics: Where Budget Balancers Fear to Tread?" *Texas Tribune*. February 11, 2011.

Busted Coverage. (April 7, 2021). How Much Do High Schools Spend on Sports Vs. Education?

Koba, Mark. "High School Sports Have Turned Into Big Business". *CNBC News*. December 9, 2012.

Silvy, Tyler. "Sports spending per athlete outpaces per-pupil spending on math, science, English". *The Coloradoan*. December 27, 2013.

Wolf, Calvin. "Should We Keep Funding Public Schools Sports?" *Soapboxie*. December 9, 2020.

Chen, Grace. "Hello Budget Cuts, Goodbye Sports: The Threat to Athletics". *Public School Review*. October 8, 2020.

Ed Choice. (2022). How does school choice affect public schools' funding and resources?

Reschovsky, Andrew. "The Future of U.S. Public School Revenue From The Property Tax". *Lincoln Institute of Land Policy*. July 2017.

Public School Revenue Sources. "Since 2000-01, public school revenues have increased by 27 percent in constant dollars, and public school enrollment increased by 7 percent". *The Condition of Education 2020*. Chapter: 1/Preprimary, Elementary, and Secondary Education. Section: Finances. (2020).

Valant, Jon. "What are charter schools and do they deliver?" *Brookings Institute: Policy 2020*. October 15, 2019.

Robison, Clay. "New study documents high rate of charter school failures". *TSTA/NEA*. August 14, 2020.

Jason, Zachary. Summer 2017. "The Battle Over Charter Schools". *Harvard University*.

Greene, Peter. "Report: The Department of Education Has Spent $1 Billion on Charter School Waste and Fraud". *Forbes*. March 19, 2019.

Environmental Conscience. (2022). Advantages and Disadvantages of Charter Schools.

Fischler, Jacob. "Understanding Charter Schools vs. Public Schools". *US News*. October 19, 2021.

Nelson, Libby. "Everything you need to know about charter schools". *Vox*. April 30, 2014.

Spring, David and Elizabeth Hanson. (2022). Weapons of Mass Deception.

Auletto, Amy. (March 30, 2016). "Grand Pianos, Subway Sandwiches, and Bounce Houses: Are Public Schools Spending Tax Dollars Efficiently?" *Green & White*.

Estes, Skip and Jay Park. (August 4, 2020). Education Spending is Increasing, but Where is the Money Going?

Lanier, Ryan. "School districts are wasting COVID relief funds". *The Hill*. November 7, 2021.

USDA. (2022). National School Lunch Program.

P3 Cost Analysis. (December 8, 2021). Average School Electricity Bill: How Much Energy Do Schools Use?

Martha. (November 13, 2021). "How much money is the food waste in schools worth?" *International Centre for Settlement of Investment Disputes*.

Wenders, John T. "How Much Do the Public Schools Waste?" *Foundation for Economic Education*. January 1, 2003.

McDonald, Kerry. "School Security Is Now $3 Billion Dollar Annual Industry. Is There a Better Way to Protect Kids?" *Foundation for Economic Education*. January 8, 2019.

U.S. Department of Energy. (February 2002). Myths about energy in schools.

Newberry, Laura. "Kids are losing interest in organized sports. Why it matters". *Los Angeles Times*. December 6, 2021.

Notes for Chapter 4

Gatto, John Taylor. *Weapons of Mass Instruction*. Gabriola Island, British Columbia. New Society Publishers. 2009.

Labaree, David F. "Two cheers for school bureaucracy". *Phi Delta Kappan*. January 6, 2020.

Ewers, Henry. (July 19, 2020). The 20 biggest mistakes school communicators make and how to avoid them. BadgeMessenger Blog.

Henderson, Dr. S Brook. (July 10, 2015). Is it time to abandon the Prussian Model of education? LinkedIn.

Davis, Stephen. "Eye on Education: Prussia model influences American public school system". *Daily Republic*. October 14, 2019.

Wikipedia. (2022). "Prussian Education System".

Forced Government Schooling. (2022). The Prussian Model.

Hyde, Bryan. "Our Prussian Model of Public Schooling: Controlling the Masses". *St. George News*. March 14, 2012.

K12 Academics. (2022). Origin of Prussian Education System.

Margeson, Mike and Justin Spears. "The History and Results of America's Disastrous Public School System, Part I". *Foundation for Economic Education*. May 13, 2019.

Stoll, Ira. "Growth in Administrative Staff, Assistant Principals Far Outpaces Teacher Hiring". *Education Next*. October 1, 2020.

Smith, Aaron Garth. "Public Education Spending: More Money, More Administration". *Reason Foundation*. October 19, 2015.

Mitchell, Daniel J. "Government Schools: More Bureaucracy, Lower Performance, and Higher Costs". *American Institute for Economic Research*. February 18, 2021.

Collum, Tera. "Teachers Have a Lack of Confidence in Administration". *Texas Scorecard*. January 29, 2021.

Perry, Mark J. "Chart of the Day: Administrative Bloat in US Public Schools". *American Enterprise Institute*. March 9, 2013.

Pulda, Arnold. "Three Differences Between Teaching and Administration". *Education World*. February 23, 2004.

Watkins, John. "School and District Bureaucracy Has Failed Us All. What Are Some Alternatives?" *Next Generation Learning Challenges*. July 19, 2021.

Schwartz, Mark. "The Good And The Bad Of Bureaucracy". *IT Revolution*. October 26, 2020.

World Press. (May 5, 2011). Bureaucracy in Schools: The Good, the Bad, and the Ugly.

Notes for Chapter 5

The Editorial Team. (2022). K-12 Teacher Tenure: Understanding the Debate. *Resilient Educator.*

Gershom, Livia. "The Rise of Teacher Unions". *JSTOR Daily.* May 9, 2016.

AFT: Share My Lesson. (March 11, 2020). The Vital Role of Teacher Unions in Women's History.

The Labor and Working Class History Association. (2022). A Century of Teacher Organizing.

Maker, Jackie. "The rise of teacher unions: A look at union impact over the years". *The Hechinger Report.* September 19, 2012.

Nomadic Child Theme on Genesis Framework. (2022). Do All Public Schools Have Teacher Unions?

ProCon.org. (January 13, 2011). Should Teachers Get Tenure? *Britannica.*

Chen, Grace. "Are Teacher Unions a Help or a Hindrance to Public Education?" *Public School Review.* May 18, 2022.

Gaille, Louise. (August 1, 2017). 13 Pros and Cons of Teacher Unions. Vi*ttana.org Personal Finance Blog.*

Miller, Keith. (2022). 15 Teacher Unions Pros and Cons. *Future of Working.*

Pok, Brian. "The Origin of Unions and Their Application to Teachers". *Yale Education Studies.* April 29, 2017.

Hroncich, Colleen. "Unions and their impact on teachers". *Commonwealth Foundation.* October 5, 2018.

Eberts, Randall W. "Teacher Unions and Student Performance: Help or Hindrance?" The Future of Children: Brookings Institution Press. Volume 17: Number 1. Spring 2007.

Notes for Chapters 6 and 7

Kleinberg, Rabbi Darren. "Schools need to ask: What's the end goal of education?" *The Jewish News of Northern California.* September 13, 2018.

Texas Association of School Boards. (2022). School Boards: What Is the Purpose of Public Education.

Pinnacle Xplore. (March 19, 2021). What Should Be The Ultimate Goal of Education?

Horn, Michael B. "Begin With The End: What's The Purpose Of Schooling?" *Forbes.* April, 15, 2021.

McAllister, Peter. "A Teacher's Perspective on What's Wrong with Our Schools". *Cato Institute: Cato Journal.* Winter 2018.

Aydin, Hasan, Burhan Ozfidan and Douglas Carothers. "Meeting the Challenges of Curriculum and Instruction in School Settings in the United States". *Journal of Social Studies Education Research.* 2017: 8 (3), 76-92.

Barrington, Kate. "The 15 Biggest Failures of the American Public Education System". *Public School Review.* May 27, 2022.

Continually Learning: Kyle and Sarah. (2022). The Problems with Curriculum.

Doman, Ellen. "A Thousand Different Things: What's Wrong with the Current Curriculum". *The NACD Foundation.* Volume 33 No. 10, 2020.

Professor's House. (2020). The Problem with School Curriculum.

Wolpert-Gawron, Heather. "What Is the Purpose of Public Education?" *Huffington Post.* May 25, 2011.

Nelson, Libby. "Everything you need to know about the Common Core". *Vox.* May 13, 2015.

Loveless, Tom. "Why Common Core Failed". *Brooking Center Chalkboard.* March 18, 2021.

CCSSO. (2022). Common Core Standards.

George Lucas Education Foundation. "Social Emotional Learning: A Short History". *Edutopia.* October 6, 2011.

Field, Kelly. "Social and emotional learning is the latest flashpoint in the education wars". *The Hechinger Report.* February 21, 2022.

Zhao, Yong. "Another education war? The coming debates over social and emotional learning". *Phi Delta Kappan.* April 27, 2020.

Ray, Rashawn and Alexandra Gibbons. "Why are states banning critical race theory?" *Brookings Institute.* November 2021.

McPheeters, Riley. "What is Critical Race Theory?" *VOA News.* August 12, 2021.

Anderson, Bryan. "Critical race theory is a flashpoint for conservatives, but what does it mean?" *PBS News Hour.* November 4, 2021.

McCausland, Phil. "Teaching critical race theory isn't happening in classrooms, teacher say in survey". *NBC News.* July 1, 2021.

Wikipedia. (2022). Critical Race Theory.

George, Janel. "A Lesson on Critical Race Theory". *American Bar Association.* January 11, 2021.

Moschella, Melissa. "Critical Race Theory, Public Schools, and Parental Rights". *The Heritage Foundation.* March 24, 2022.

ProCon.org. (December 7, 2020). History of Standardized Tests. *Britannica.*

Pigeon, Sean-Michael. "Don't blame the tests: Getting rid of standardized testing means punishing poor students". *USA Today.* March 23, 2021.

National Education Association. (June 25, 2020). History of Standardized Testing in the United States.

Choi, Young Whan. (March 31,2020). How to Address Racial Bias in Standardized Testing. NextGenLearning.

American University: School of Education. (July 2, 2020). Effects of Standardized Testing on Students & Teachers: Key Benefits & Challenges.

Bhattacharya, Shriya. "Education advocates say the best way to address racial bias in standardized testing is to eliminate the tests completely". *Prism Reports.* January 31, 2022.

Berwick, Carly. "What Does the Research Say About Testing?" *Edutopia.* October 25, 2019.

Nixon, Bryan. (2022). The Pros and Cons of Standardized Testing. *Whitby.*

ProCon.org. (December 7, 2020). Do Standardized Tests Improve Education in America? *Britannica.*

Kantrowitz, Mark. "How Admissions Tests Discriminate Against Low-Income And Minority Student Admissions At Selective Colleges". *Forbes.* May 21, 2021.

INcompassing Education. (February 11, 2022). Why Does the US Use Standardized Testing?

Notes for Chapter 8

Esteves, Kelli J. and Shaila Rao. (November/December 2008). The Evolution of Special Education. *National Association of Elementary Principals.*

Lewisville Independent School District. (2022). What Is Special Education?

Rosenthal, Brian M. "Special education is widely misunderstood. Here's what parents need to know". *Houston Chronicle.* 2016.

Wright, Peter W.D. and Pamela Darr Wright. (August 8, 2020). *Wrightslaw.*

IDEA. (2022). A History of the Individuals With Disabilities Education Act.

Purdue Online. (2022). What Is Special Education?

Rosenkrantz, Holly. "What is Special Education?" *US News.* December 9, 2021.

Understanding Special Education. (2022). Special Education Terms and Definitions.

Riser-Kositsky, Maya. "Special Education: Definition, Statistics, and Trends". *EdWeek.* December 17, 2019.

Mock, Devery R., Jennifer J. Jakubecy, and James M. Kauffman. (2022). Special Education: Current Trends, Preparation of Teachers, International Context History Of.

American University: School of Education. (January 12, 2021). Why is There a Special Education Teacher Shortage?

Cal State LA. (2022). IDEA provides definitions of the 13 disability categories.

Shaikh, Massrat. "Special Education Needs- 4 things we can do differently in 2022". *GESS Education.*

Griffith, Michael. "A Look at Funding for Students with Disabilities". *Education Commission of the States.* Vol. 16: No. 1. March 2015.

K12 Academics. (2022). Federal Funding for Special Education.

Edmentum: Educator Network. (February 4, 2021). 5 Current Issues in Special Education.

Blouin, Lou. (February 7, 2022). Confronting special education's race problem.

Unknown Author. (2022). Special Education: Current Trends.

King, India. "What is Response to Intervention (RTI) & Why it's Important". *Kickboard.* December 5, 2017.

RTI Action Network. (2022). What is RTI?

Bachrach, Steven. "504 Education Plans". *Kids Health.* (2022).

Mauro, Terri. (May 23, 2022). 504 Plans for Students with Disabilities.

Mississippi College. (December 27, 2021). 5 Expected Trends in the Future of Special Education Systems.

Presence Learning. (July 20, 2021). Three Predictions for Special Education.

Soumakian, Gabe. (March 10, 2022). The Future of Special Ed and How to Redesign Services. LinkedIn.

Jones, Carolyn. "Less siloed, more inclusive: Changes to special education teacher preparation expected to have big impact on schools". *Ed Source.* November 30, 2020.

Levenson, Nathan. (2022). 10 Best Practices for Improving Special Education.

Notes for Chapter 9

Christensen, Debi. (July 2, 2019). The history of the emergence of technology in education. *Classcraft.*

Huls, Alexander. "The Evolution of Technology in K-12 Classrooms: 1659 to Today". *EdTech Magazine.* January 31, 2022.

PowerGistics. (March 2, 2022). Education Technology Trends.

Gray, Lucinda and Laurie Lewis. "Use of Educational Technology for Instruction in Public Schools: 2019-20". US Department of Education: Institute of Education Sciences- NCES 2021-017. November 2021.

Bui, Sean. (November 19, 2020). Top Educational Technology Trends in 2020-2021. *eLearning Industry.*

Unknown Author. (2022). Technology in Education.

American University: School of Education. (June 25, 2020). How Important is Technology in Education? Benefits, Challenges, and Impact of Students.

Purdure Online. (2022). How Has Technology Changed Education?

Best, Jackson. (August 17, 2020). 13 Pros and Cons of Technology in the Classroom Teachers Need to Know.

Celebree Administration. (2022). The Pros and Cons of Technology in Education.

Rosen, Andrew. (2022). Technology, Screen Time, And Children's Mental Health. *The Children's Center for Psychiatry, Psychology, & Related Services.*

Ganimian, Alejandro J., Emiliana Vegas and Frederick M. Hess. "Realizing The Promise: How can education technology improve learning for all?" *Brookings Institute.* 2022.

Johnson, Jon. "Negative effects of technology: What to Know". *Medical News Today.* February 25, 2020.

Bruce, Alyvia. "Bridging the Technological Divide in Education". *Harvard Political Review.* November 23, 2020.

Brown, Casey. (May 16, 2019). 12 Pros and Cons of technology in the classroom. *Classcraft.*

Limone, Pierpaolo and Giusi Antonia Toto. "Psychological and Emotional Effects of Digital Technology on Children in Covid-19 Pandemic". *Multidisciplinary Digital Publishing Institute.* Volume 11 (9): 1126. August 25, 2021.

Clark, Maria. (June 3, 2021). 19 Negative Effects of Technology on Mental Health. *Etactics.*

Children's' Bureau. (September 30, 2019). Effects of Technology on Mental Health. All4Kids.

Staff Writer. (November 4, 2022). Cyberbullying in School. Accredited Schools Online.

Notes for Chapter 10

Find Law Team. (June 20, 2016). School Discipline History. *Find Law.*

Murray, Morgan. (2022). History of Discipline in Education.

Mustafa, Mr. (August 10, 2022). Why Do Students Not Pay Attention in Classs? (And What You Can Do About It).

Hanson, Erika. (2022). Screen Time Might Be To Blame For Poor Demeaner In Schools. Go2Tutors.

Hogan, Sean. (March 21, 2022). Yes, Student Behavior Is Worse Than Ever-But We Can't Blame the Kids. WeAreTeachers.

Jones, Carolyn. "How school discipline – student misbehavior – has changed during the pandemic". *Ed Source.* November 17, 2020.

National Center for Educational Statistics. (July 6, 2022). More than 80 Percent of US Public Schools Report Pandemic Has Negatively Impacted Student Behavior and Socio-Emotional Development.

Carnegie Mellon University: Eberly Center. (2022). Address Problematic Student Behavior.

Hauck, Stephanie. (January 6, 2020). OPINION: What Schools Are Getting Wrong on Discipline. WeAreTeachers.

Cascio, Christopher. (2022). "Typical Causes of Poor Behavior in the Classroom". *Seattle Post-Intelligencer.*

Barton, Angela. (October 14, 2021). Students are Out of Control This Year, and Teachers Aren't Having It! BoredTeachers.

Chen, Grace. "Dealing with Behavioral Issues in Middle and High School". *Public School Review.* August 2, 2022.

Hymowitz, Kay S. "Who Killed School Discipline?" *City Journal.* Spring 2000.

Novak, Dan. "US Schools Struggle with Behavior, But See Opportunity". *VOA News.* April 12, 2022.

Higgins, John. "Bad behavior in school can sometimes predict future success, new research shows". *The Seattle Times.* September 24, 2015.

Desautels, Lori. "Aiming for Discipline Instead of Punishment". *Edutopia.* March 1, 2018.

American Federation of Teachers. (2022). Reclaiming the Promise: A new path forward on school discipline practices.

Walker, Hill M., Elizabeth Ramsey and Frank M. Gresham. (2022). How Early Intervention Can Reduce Defiant Behavior- and Win Back Teaching. *American Federation of Teachers.*

Illinois Department of Human Services. (2022). What Is Childhood Trauma? Look Through Their Eyes Organization.

Brueningsen, Christopher. "Boys in Crisis: Schools are failing young males. Here's what needs to change in classroom". *USA Today.* October 9, 2021.

Reeves, Richard. *Of Boys and Men.* Washington, D.C., United States. The Brookings Institute. 2022.

Haidt, Jonathon and Greg Lukianoff. *The Coddling of the American Mind.* New York, New York. Penguin Press. 2018.

Hari, Johann. *Stolen Focus.* London, England. Bloomsbury Publishing. 2022.

Van Der Kolk, Bessell. *The Body Keeps the Score.* New York, New York. Viking Publishing. 2014.

Notes for Chapter 11

George Lucas Education Foundation. "Social Emotional Learning: A Short History". *Edutopia.* October 6, 2011.

Field, Kelly. "Social and emotional learning is the latest flashpoint in the education wars". *The Hechinger Report.* February 21, 2022.

Zhao, Yong. "Another education war? The coming debates over social and emotional learning". *Phi Delta Kappan.* April 27, 2020.

Novelly, Thomas. "Even more young Americans are unfit to serve, a new study finds. Here's why". *Military News.* September 28, 2022.

Mathis, Joel. "Why U.S. teens aren't getting their driver's license". *The Week.* February 16, 2023.

Penn State Extension: Better Kid Care. (October 2004). Why Do Children Misbehave.

Lloyd, William C. (September 1, 2020). Top 10 Children's Health Concerns.

Peterson, Tanya J. (January 17, 2022). Is There Such a Thing as a Bad Child?

Notes for Chapter 12

Ray, Rashawn and Alexandra Gibbons. "Why are states banning critical race theory?" *Brookings Institute.* November 2021.

McPheeters, Riley. "What is Critical Race Theory?" *VOA News.* August 12, 2021.

Anderson, Bryan. "Critical race theory is a flashpoint for conservatives, but what does it mean?" *PBS News Hour.* November 4, 2021.

McCausland, Phil. "Teaching critical race theory isn't happening in classrooms, teacher say in survey". *NBC News*. July 1, 2021.

Wikipedia. (2022). Critical Race Theory.

George, Janel. "A Lesson on Critical Race Theory". *American Bar Association*. January 11, 2021.

Moschella, Melissa. "Critical Race Theory, Public Schools, and Parental Rights". *The Heritage Foundation*. March 24, 2022.

Stannard, David E. *American Holocaust*. Oxford, England. Oxford University Press. 1992.

Notes for Chapter 13

K12 Academics. (2022). History of School Shootings in the United States.

Kowalski, Robin M. "School Shooting: What we know about them, and what we can do to prevent them". *Brookings Institute*. January 26, 2022.

O'Donnell, Dan. (May 27, 2022). Debunking Every Major Mass Shooting Myth. *MacIver Institute*.

Safer Watch. (2022). Can School Shootings Be Prevented?

Fox, James Alan. "School shootings are not the new normal, despite statistics that stretch the truth". *USA Today*. February 20, 2018.

Campus Safety Staff. "51 Years of Data: k-12 School Shooting Statistics Everyone Should Know". *Campus Safety Magazine*. January 28, 2022.

Sandy Hook Promise. (2022). 17 Facts About Gun Violence and School Shootings.

Vigderman, Aliza and Gabe Turner. (August 25, 2022). A Timeline of School Shootings Since Columbine.

Center for Homeland Defense and Security. (2022). Shooting Incidents at K-12 Schools: January 1970-June 2022.

Harper, Kristen, Renee Ryberg and Deborah Temkin. "Data sources make it difficult to know how many school shootings happen each year". *Child Trends*. August 27, 2018.

Notes for Chapter 14

The Center for Comprehensive School Reform and Improvement. (2022). Getting Parents Involved in Schools. *Reading Rockets*.

PBS Kids. (August 16, 2016). The Role of Parents. *PBS Kids for Parents*.

Pellissier, Hank. (July 15, 2022). 15 Rights parents have in public schools. GreatSchools.

Hanson, Rachel, Chris Pugliese and Sarah Grady. Institute of Educational Sciences. "Parent and Family Involvement in Education: 2019". *National Household Education Surveys Program.* NCES 2020-076: July 2020.

Chen, Grace. "How Diet and Nutrition Impact a Child's Learning Ability". *Public School Review.* May 20, 2022.

The Royal Children's Hospital Melbourne. (2022). Nutrition—school-age to adolescence.

Mayo Clinic Staff. (2022). Childhood Obesity.

Murphey, David and Samuel Beckwith. "A parent's health is one of the strongest predictors of a child's health". *Child Trends.* January 9, 2019.

Ben-Joseph, Elana Pearl. (August 2022). Kids and Exercise. KidsHealth.

Cordeiro, Brittany. (August 2014). 10 tips to get kids to exercise. *MD Anderson Cancer Center.*

Griffin, R. Morgan. (May 1, 2013). This Is Your Kid's Brain Without Sleep. WebMD.

SickKids staff. (April 13, 2020). Sleep: Benefits and recommended amounts.

Desrosiers, Florence MD. "Lack of Sleep Can Harm a Child's Health". *Nationwide Children's.* April, 2, 2010.

Curley, Christopher. "Only Half of U.S. Children Get Enough Sleep: Why that's a serious problem". *Healthline.* October 24, 2019.

Lloyd, William C. (September 1, 2020). Top 10 Children's Health Concerns.

Peterson, Tanya J. (January 17, 2022). Is There Such a Thing as a Bad Child?

Lee, Katherine. "7 Ways Parents Encourage Bad Behavior in Kids". *Verywell Family.* April 16, 2020.

Patel, Deepak S. (April 2022). What You Can Do to Change Your Child's Behavior.

KidsHealth Medical Experts. (2022). 9 Steps to More Effective Parenting.

Peterson, Tanya J. (January 16, 2016). Parenting 101: What You Must Know about Raising Kids.

O'Donnell, Lauren M. (June 2018). Discipling Your Child. KidsHealth.

Penn State Extension: Better Kid Care. (October 2004). Why Do Children Misbehave.

Hiatt-Michael, Diana. "Parent Involvement in American Public Schools: A Historical Perspective 1642-2000". *School Community Journal.* Vol. 4, No. 2: Fall/Winter 1994.

Chen, Grace. "Parental Involvement is Key to Student Success". *Public School Review.* May 20, 2022.

Brooks, Ashley. (November 18, 2019). Experts Discuss the Importance of Positive Parental Involvement in Education.

NAESP. (2022). Five Barriers to Parental Involvement.

Larson, Jennifer. (October 5, 2019). 10 Strategies for Schools to Improve Parent Engagement. GettingSmart.

Novelly, Thomas. "Even more young Americans are unfit to serve, a new study finds. Here's why". *Military News.* September 28, 2022.

Mathis, Joel. "Why U.S. teens aren't getting their driver's license". *The Week.* February 16, 2023.

Van Der Kolk, Bessell. *The Body Keeps the Score.* New York, New York. Viking Publishing. 2014.

Notes for Chapter 15

Barnum, Matt. "The state of learning loss: 7 takeaways from the latest data". *Chalkbeat.* July 18, 2022.

UNESCO. (2022). Adverse Consequences of School Closures.

Camp, Emma. "New Data Show COVID School Closures Contributed to Largest Learning Loss in Decades". *Reason Magazine.* September 6, 2022.

Winthrop, Rebecca. "Top 10 risks and opportunities for education in the face of COVID-19". *Brookings Institute.* April 10, 2020.

Bloomberg, Michael. "Pandemic Learning Loss Is a National Crisis". *The Washington Post.* September 14, 2022.

UNICEF Press Release. (January 23, 2022). COVID-19 Scale of education loss 'nearly insurmountable' warns UNICEF.

Dorn, Emma, Bryan Hancock, Jimmy Sarakatsannis and Ellen Viruleg. "COVID-19 and education: The lingering effects of unfinished learning". *McKinsey & Company.* July 27, 2021.

Lanschool. (June 3, 2021). 5 ways schools can address learning loss.

Kuhfeld, Megan, Jim Soland, Karyn Lewis and Emily Morton. "The pandemic has had devastating impacts on learning. What will it take to help students catch up?" *Brookings Institute.* March 3, 2022.

Kerr, Wendy. (April 21, 2021). How to Address Learning Loss Due to Covid-19.

Mahnken, Kevin. 'Nation's Report Card': Two Decades of Growth Wiped Out by Two Years of Pandemic". *The 74.* September 1, 2022.

Simon, Clea. "Snapshot of pandemic's mental health impact on children". *The Harvard Gazette.* April 21, 2022.

UNICEF Press Release. (October 4, 2021). Impact of COVID-19 on poor mental health in children and young people 'tip of iceberg'.

Chatelain, Ryan. "In survey, public schools blame pandemic for rise in behavioral problems". *NY 1*. July 9, 2022.

Belsha, Kalyn. "Stress and short tempers: Schools struggle with behavior as students return". *Chalkbeat*. September 27, 2021.

Vestal, Christine. (November 9, 2021). COVID Harmed Kids' Mental Health—And Schools Are Feeling It. *Pew*.

Campbell, Leah. "Impact Of Covid-19 On Children's Social Skills". *Forbes*. October 31, 2021.

Bergman, Rebekah and Sara Romero-Heaps. (April 12, 2022). 4 strategies for combatting learning loss and supporting social-emotional learning with Nearpod. *Nearpod*.

Einhorn, Erin. "Covid is having a devastating impact on children – and the vaccine won't fix everything". *NBC News*. December 15, 2020.

Moyer, Melinda Wenner. "The COVID generation: how is the pandemic affecting kids' brains?" *Nature*. January 12, 2022.

Adams, Richard. "Younger children most affected by Covid lockdowns, new research finds". *The Guardian*. May 17, 2022.

Gonzalez, Meliza, Tianna Loose[1], Maite Liz[2], Mónica Pérez[3], Juan I. Rodríguez-Vinçon[4], Clementina Tomás-Llerena [5]and Alejandro Vásquez-Echeverría[6]. "School readiness losses during the COVID-19 outbreak. A comparison of two cohorts of young children". *Child Development*. Vol. 93, Issue 4: pages 910-924. February 23, 2022.

Herman, Christine. "You Asked: Will the Pandemic Have Lasting Effects on Child Development?" *WFYI News*. July 14, 2021.

Adams, Caralee. "How the pandemic is affecting babies' brains". *The Hechinger Report*. February 24, 2022.

Morin, Amanda. (September 9, 2021). 5 Reasons Students Aren't Engaging in Distance Learning.

Plitnichenko, Lisa. (June 2020). 10 Challenges of E-Learning during COVID-19. Jellyfish Tech Blog.

---

1. https://srcd.onlinelibrary.wiley.com/authored-by/ContribAuthorRaw/Loose/Tianna

2. https://srcd.onlinelibrary.wiley.com/authored-by/ContribAuthorRaw/Liz/Maite

3. https://srcd.onlinelibrary.wiley.com/authored-by/ContribAuthorRaw/P%C3%A9rez/M%C3%B3nica

4. https://srcd.onlinelibrary.wiley.com/authored-by/ContribAuthorRaw/Rodr%C3%ADguez%E2%80%90Vin%C3%A7on/Juan+I.

5. https://srcd.onlinelibrary.wiley.com/authored-by/ContribAuthorRaw/Tom%C3%A1s%E2%80%90Llerena%C2%A0/Clementina

6. https://srcd.onlinelibrary.wiley.com/authored-by/ContribAuthorRaw/V%C3%A1squez%E2%80%90Echeverr%C3%ADa/Alejandro

NPR: Morning Edition. (July 13, 2020). Coronavirus Pandemic Spotlights Problems With Online Learning. *NPR*.

Mostafavi, Beata. (June 13, 2022). Children in remote school faced more sleep, behavior and social challenges. *University of Michigan: Michigan Medicine*.

Barnum, Matt and Claire Bryan. "America's great remote-learning experiment: What surveys of teachers and parents tell us about how it went". *Chalkbeat*. June 26, 2020.

B., Krista. (May 3, 2022). Teacher Shares Eye-Opening Effect of School Changes and COVID-19 on America's Youth. *Boys and Girls Club of America*.

UNESCO. (2022). Education: From School Closure Recover.

Hill, Paul. (April 2020). What Post-Katrina New Orleans Can Teach Schools About Addressing COVID learning losses.

Notes for Chapter 16

Garcia, Emma, Matthew A. Kraft and Heather L. Schwartz. "Are we at a crisis point with the public teacher workforce? Education scholars share their perspectives". *Brookings Institute*. August 26, 2022.

Malatras, Jim, Thomas Gais and Alan Wagner. "A Background on Potential Teacher Shortages in the US". *Rockefeller Institute*. July 2017.

Cineas, Fabiola. "Are teachers leaving the classroom en masse?" *Vox*. August 18, 2022.

Barnes, Adam. "Here's what's driving the nationwide teacher shortage". *The Hill*. April 21, 2022.

ABC News. (August 11, 2022). US has 300,000 teacher, school staff vacancies, NEA President Rebecca Pringle says. *ABC News*.

Thompson, Derek. "There Is No National Teacher Shortage". *The Atlantic*. August 24, 2022.

Barnum, Matt. "Is there a national teacher shortage? Here's what we know and don't know". *Chalkbeat*. August 11, 2022.

Roth, Samantha-Jo and Eden Harris. "Education Secretary Cardona addresses nationwide teacher shortage: 'At the end of the day... it's about respect'". *NY 1*. August 15, 2022.

Garcia, Emma and Elaine Weiss. "The teacher shortage is real, large and growing, and worse than we thought". *Economic Policy Institute*. March 26, 2019.

Camera, Lauren. "Cardona: Americans Shouldn't be Surprised by Teacher Shortage". *US News*. June 9, 2022.

Pearce, Katie. (August 15, 2022). A Broken Pipeline: The Issues Contributing to the U.S. Teacher Shortage.

Lurye, Sharon and Rebecca Griesbach. "Teacher shortages are real, but not for the reason you heard". *Associated Press News.* September 12, 2022.

Wolf, Zachary B. "Is There a Teacher Shortage? It's Complicated". *CNN News.* August 13, 2022.

Tran, Henry and Douglas A. Smith. "The most recent efforts to combat teacher shortages don't address real problems". *The Conversation.* August 8, 2022.

Fernandez, Anne Lutz. "OPINION: There are lots of bad ideas for solving the teacher shortage, but not enough for improving the profession". *The Hechinger Report.* August 16, 2022.

Flannery, Mary Ellen. "The Teacher Shortage Can Be Addressed – With Key Changes". *NEA Today: NEA News.* October 10, 2020.

Duncan, Eric. (April 28, 2022). Addressing Teacher Shortages In the Short and Long Term. *The Education Trust.*

Camera, Lauren. "Sharp Nationwide Enrollment Drop in Teacher Prep Programs Cause Alarm". *US News.* December 3, 2019.

Notes for Chapter 17

Rosenwinkel, Jack, Lindsey Burke and Jude Schwalbach. "Free to Succeed: A Brief History of School Choice". *The Daily Signal.* January 31, 2020.

Panchal, Rahul. (2022). 24+ Main Pros and Cons of School Choice.

Howard, Carlon. (December 4, 2017). A Brief History of School Choice: 1955 to now. *New Leaders Council Rhode Island.*

Kelly, Kate. (2022). School Vouchers: What You Need to Know.

Kasparian, Ana. (2022). 27 Main Pros & Cons of School Vouchers & School Choice. Environmental-Conscience.

Gaille, Louise. (March 28, 2019). Private School vs Public School Pros and Cons. *Vittana.*

Chen, Grace. "The Ongoing Debate Over School Choice". *Public School Review.* February 10, 2020.

Chen, Grace. "Public or Private? Which School is Best for Your Child?" *Public School Review.* April 30, 2021.

Gaille, Louise. (June 26, 2017). 12 Pros and Cons of Charter Schools. *Vittana.*

Ed Choice. (2022). How does school choice affect public schools' funding and resources?

Reschovsky, Andrew. "The Future of U.S. Public School Revenue From The Property Tax". *Lincoln Institute of Land Policy.* July 2017.

Public School Revenue Sources. "Since 2000-01, public school revenues have increased by 27 percent in constant dollars, and public school enrollment increased by 7 percent". *The Condition of Education 2020.* Chapter: 1/Preprimary, Elementary, and Secondary Education. Section: Finances. (2020).

Valant, Jon. "What are charter schools and do they deliver?" *Brookings Institute: Policy 2020.* October 15, 2019.

Robison, Clay. "New study documents high rate of charter school failures". *TSTA/NEA.* August 14, 2020.

Jason, Zachary. Summer 2017. "The Battle Over Charter Schools". *Harvard University.*

Greene, Peter. "Report: The Department of Education Has Spent $1 Billion on Charter School Waste and Fraud". *Forbes.* March 19, 2019.

Environmental Conscience. (2022). Advantages and Disadvantages of Charter Schools. Environmental-Conscience.

Fischler, Jacob. "Understanding Charter Schools vs. Public Schools". *US News.* October 19, 2021.

Nelson, Libby. "Everything you need to know about charter schools". *Vox.* April 30, 2014.

Spring, David and Elizabeth Hanson. (2022). Weapons of Mass Deception.

Walden University. (2022). What Is a Magnet School, and Does it Offer a Better Education?

Chen, Grace. "What Is A Magnet School?" *Public School Review.* August 17, 2022.

Gaille, Louise. (April 8, 2019). 21 Magnet Schools Pros and Cons. *Vittana.*

National Center for Educational Statistics. (2022). Homeschooling.

McDonald, Kerry. "Homeschooling and Educational Freedom: Why School Choice Is Good for Homeschoolers". *Cato Institute.* September 4, 2019.

Coalition for Responsible Home Education. (2022). A Brief History of Homeschooling.

Loveless, Becton. (2022). Benefits and Disadvantages of Homeschooling. EducationCorner.

Gaille, Louise. (June 9, 2019). 17 Central Pros and Cons of Virtual Schools. *Vittana.*

Ed Choice. (2022). Types of School Choice.

Gatto, John Taylor. *Weapons of Mass Instruction.* Gabriola Island, British Columbia. New Society Publishers. 2009.

Notes for Chapter 18

Marr, Bernard. "The 2 Biggest Future Trends in Education". *Forbes*. January 21, 2022.

Daren, Sarah. (March 5, 2018). 5 Ideas On What Classrooms Of The Future May Be Like. TeacherCast.

Freitag, Emily. "Let's fight about the future of public education". *Chalkbeat*. October 30, 2020.

Hill, Paul. (January 2021). In the future, diverse approaches to schooling. *Center on Reinventing Public Education*.

Chen, Grace. "Should Public Schools Provide Students with Vocational Opportunities?" *Public School Review*. May 20, 2022.

Lambert, Keith. (2022). What Happened to Vocational Education (and Why We Need It Back)? *Education World*.

Bedi, Sidhant. (2022). The Pros and Cons of Vocational Educational Training. *EHL Insights*.

Jacob, Brian A. "What we know about Career and Technical Education in high school". *Brookings Institute*. October 5, 2017.

Kelly, Kate. (2022). Vocational education in high school: What you need to know.

Balan, Robert S. (November 17, 2022). Is College Worth It in 2022?

Uvaro. (August 22, 2022). Is College Still Worth It in 2022? Half of America Is Saying No! Uvaro Blog.

Lieber, Ron. "Some Colleges Don't Produce Big Earners. Are They Worth It?" *The New York Times*. August 20, 2022.

Pophal, Linda. (March 3, 2022). The Value of a College Degree in 2022. *Accurate News*.

Dickler, Jessica. "Is college really worth it? Here's why it's so hard to figure out the return on investment". *CNBC News*. February 15, 2022.

Kerr, Emma and Sarah Wood. "See the Average College Tuition in 2022-2023". *US News*. September 12, 2022.

Hill, Rachel R. (August 25, 2022). Glimpse at How Education Will Possibly Look Like in 2050. StudyCrumb.

TypeKids. (2022). The school of the future.

Poh, Michael. September 15, 2020). 8 Technologies That Will Shape Future Classrooms.

Paviova, Iveta. (August 18, 2022). 6 Trends for the Classrooms of the Future: What Will Change? GraphicMama.

Gatto, John Taylor. *Weapons of Mass Instruction*. Gabriola Island, British Columbia. New Society Publishers. 2009.

Reeves, Richard. *Of Boys and Men*. Washington, D.C., United States. The Brookings Institute. 2022.

Hari, Johann. *Stolen Focus*. London, England. Bloomsbury Publishing. 2022.

About the Author

Jared Hiple is a behavior specialist for a North Texas school district. He has been involved in public education for over 20 years. Hiple has worked as a substitute teacher, a special education teacher in a behavior management program, taught multiple grade levels in a long-term disciplinary center, and has worked as a behavioral specialist in multiple school districts in both special and generation education arenas. He earned a bachelor's degree in criminal justice and obtained a master's degree in biology from the University of Texas at Arlington. Hiple also possesses teaching certifications in special education (PK–12), English as a second language (PK–12), and generalist (4–8). He has also ventured into multiple fields outside of the public education realm, including stints as an insurance agent, a financial services representative, as well as manager of a small business. He currently resides in the Dallas/ Fort Worth area.

www.ingramcontent.com/pod-product-compliance
Lightning Source LLC
Chambersburg PA
CBHW081142130726
47996CB00009B/2942

* 9 7 9 8 2 2 4 9 9 2 6 4 5 *